Domestic Wastewater Treatment in Developing Countries

Domestic Wastewater Treatment in Developing Countries

Duncan Mara

London • Sterling, VA

First published by Earthscan in the UK and USA in 2004

ISBN: 1-84407-019-0 paperback
       1-84407-020-4 hardback

Typesetting by MapSet Ltd, Gateshead, UK
Printed and bound in the UK by Cromwell Press, Trowbridge
Cover design by Danny Gillespie

For a full list of publications please contact:
Earthscan
8–12 Camden High Street, London, NW1 0JH, UK
Tel: +44 (0)20 7387 8558
Fax: +44 (0)20 7387 8998
Email: earthinfo@earthscan.co.uk
Web: **www.earthscan.co.uk**

22883 Quicksilver Drive, Sterling, VA 20166-2012, USA

Earthscan publishes in association with WWF-UK and the International Institute for
Environment and Development

A catalogue record for this book is available from the British Library

Library of Congress Cataloging-in-Publication Data

  Mara, D. Duncan (David Duncan), 1944-
   Domestic wastewater treatment in developing countries / Duncan Mara.
      p. cm.
  Includes bibliographical references and index.
   ISBN 1-84407-020-4 (alk. paper) – ISBN 1-84407-019-0 (pbk. : alk. paper)
   1. Sewage disposal–Developing countries. 2. Sewage--Purification–Developing
  countries. I. Title.
   TD627.M37 2004
   628.3'09172'4–dc

                                                                    2003023959

This book is printed on elemental chlorine free paper

Contents

List of Figures and Tables   ix
Preface   xiii
Principal Notation   xv
List of Acronyms and Abbreviations   xvii

1 What is Domestic Wastewater and Why Treat It?   1
Origin and composition of domestic wastewater   1
Characterization of domestic wastewater   2
Wastewater collection   5
Why treat wastewater?   5
Investment in wastewater treatment   6

2 Excreta-related Diseases   8
Environmental classification of excreta-related diseases   8
Global burden of excreta-related diseases   18

3 Essential Microbiology and Biology   20
Introduction   20
Viruses   22
Bacteria and Archaea   24
Protozoa   35
Algae   37
Helminths   37
Freshwater micro-invertebrates   38

4 Effluent Quality   41
Wastewater treatment objectives   41
Wastewater re-use   42
Discharge to inland waters   43
Discharge to coastal waters   52
BATNEEC or CATNAP?   54

5 BOD Removal Kinetics   56
First-order kinetics   56
Hydraulic flow regimes   60
Limitations of simple first-order kinetics   64
Worked examples   67

6	**Domestic Wastewater Treatment Options**	**69**
	Sustainability issues	69
	Appropriate wastewater treatment options	71
	Sustainable wastewater treatment options	72
7	**Domestic Wastewater Flows and Loads**	**74**
	Domestic wastewater flows	74
	Domestic wastewater loads	77
	Future projections	77
8	**Preliminary Treatment**	**78**
	Purpose	78
	Screening	78
	Grit removal	81
	Flow measurement	84
9	**Waste Stabilization Ponds**	**85**
	Types and functions of WSP	85
	Advantages of WSP	89
	Perceived disadvantages of WSP	93
	WSP usage	94
	High altitude WSP	100
	WSP or other treatment processes?	100
	Macrophyte ponds	101
	Advanced pond systems	102
10	**Anaerobic Ponds**	**105**
	Function	105
	Design	108
	High-rate anaerobic ponds	110
	Anaerobic ponds in series	110
	Design example	112
11	**Facultative Ponds**	**114**
	Function	114
	Design	118
	Algal biomass	125
	Purple ponds	130
	Wind-powered pond mixers	132
	Design examples	132
12	**Maturation Ponds**	**136**
	Function	136
	Pathogen removal mechanisms	137
	Design for *E coli* removal	141
	Design for helminth egg removal	148

	BOD removal	148
	Nutrient removal	149
	Pond effluent polishing	151
	Design example	152
13	**Physical Design of WSP**	**158**
	Pond location	158
	Geotechnical considerations	158
	Pond lining	162
	Pond geometry	163
	Inlet and outlet structures	166
	By-pass pipework	169
	Anaerobic pond covers	169
	Treebelt	171
	Security	172
	Operator facilities	173
	Upgrading and extending existing WSP	173
14	**Operation and Maintenance of WSP**	**175**
	Start-up procedures	175
	Routine maintenance	175
	Desludging and sludge disposal	176
	Staffing levels	179
	Pond rehabilitation	180
15	**Monitoring and Evaluation of WSP**	**182**
	Effluent quality monitoring	182
	Evaluation of pond performance	183
	Data storage and analysis	186
16	**Wastewater Storage and Treatment Reservoirs**	**188**
	Single reservoirs	188
	Sequential batch-fed reservoirs	189
	Hybrid WSP–WSTR system	190
	Design examples	190
17	**Constructed Wetlands**	**194**
	Subsurface-flow wetlands	194
	Wetlands or waste stabilization ponds?	198
18	**Upflow Anaerobic Sludge Blanket Reactors**	**200**
	Treatment principles	200
	Design	202
	UASBs or anaerobic ponds?	206

19   Biofiltration   **207**
Function   207
Design   207
Fly control   211
Design example   212

20   Simple Activated Sludge Variants   **213**
Aerated lagoons   213
Oxidation ditches   225

21   Wastewater Re-use in Agriculture   **230**
Why re-use wastewater?   230
Public health protection   232
Crop health   242
Treatment options for re-use   245
Quantitative microbial risk analysis   246
Irrigation with untreated wastewater   251

22   Wastewater Re-use in Aquaculture   **253**
What is aquaculture?   253
Wastewater-fed aquaculture   256
Wastewater-fed fishpond design   257
Integrated agricultural–aquacultural re-use   259
Design example   260

References   262
Index   289

List of Figures and Tables

FIGURES

1.1	Composition of Domestic Wastewater	3
2.1	Four-year old African girl with a Distended Abdomen	15
3.1	The Tree of Life	23
3.2	Common Bacterial Shapes	25
3.3	The Bacterial Batch-culture Growth Curve	27
3.4	The Catabolic, Anabolic and Autolytic Reactions of Aerobic Microbiological Oxidation	29
3.5	Five of the Commonest Ciliated Protozoa in Wastewater Treatment Works	36
3.6	Micro-invertebrates Used to Assess the Biological Quality of Tropical Waters	39
4.1	The Dissolved Oxygen Sag Curve	44
4.2	Discharge of an Effluent into a River	50
5.1	Generalized BOD Curves	57
5.2	Thirumurthi Chart for the Wehner–Wilhelm Equation	62
5.3	Typical Tracer Study Results	63
7.1	Diurnal Variation of Wastewater Flow and Load at Nakuru, Kenya	76
8.1	Simple Manually Raked Screen	79
8.2	Mechanically Raked Screen	80
8.3	Flow Elements in a Parabolic Channel	82
8.4	Trapezoidal Approximation to a Parabolic Section	83
9.1	One of the Phase II 21-ha Primary Facultative Ponds at Dandora, Nairobi, Kenya	85
9.2	Algal–bacterial Mutualism in Facultative and Maturation Ponds	86
9.3	Typical WSP Layout	87
9.4	Variation of Discount Rate and Land Price below which WSP are the Cheapest Treatment Option	91
9.5	The Phase I WSP at Dandora, Nairobi, Kenya	95
9.6	The '55 East' WSP Series at Werribee, Melbourne, Australia	97
9.7	The Mangere WSP, Auckland, New Zealand, in 1996	99
10.1	Anaerobic Pond, with Partial Scum Coverage, at Ginebra, Valle del Cauca, Southwest Colombia	106
10.2	Variation of the Proportions of Hydrogen Sulphide, Bisulphide and Sulphide with pH in Aqueous Solutions	107

10.3   High-rate Anaerobic Pond with a Mixing Pit   111
11.1   Diurnal Variation of Dissolved Oxygen in a Facultative Pond   115
11.2   Variation of Surface BOD Loading on Facultative Ponds with
       Temperature According to Equations 11.2 and 11.3   119
11.3   Diurnal Variation in Facultative Pond Effluent Quality   122
11.4   Variation of Chlorophyll a with Surface BOD Loading on
       Primary Facultative Ponds in Northeast Brazil   129
11.5   Photosynthetic Purple Sulphur Bacteria   131
12.1   Variation of k_B with Surface BOD Loading on Primary
       Facultative Ponds in Northeast Brazil   144
12.2   Variation of k_B with In-pond Chlorophyll a Concentration in
       Primary Facultative Ponds in Northeast Brazil   145
13.1   Embankment Protection by Concrete Cast *in situ*   160
13.2   Embankment Protection by Precast Concrete Slabs   161
13.3   Embankment Protection by Stone Rip-rap   162
13.4   Anaerobic Pond Lined with an Impermeable Plastic Membrane   163
13.5   Anchoring the Pond Liner at the Top of the Embankment   164
13.6   Calculation of Top and Bottom Pond Dimensions   165
13.7   Inlet Structure for Anaerobic and Primary Facultative Ponds   166
13.8   Inlet Structure on a Facultative Pond with Integral Scum Box   167
13.9   Inlet Structure for Secondary Facultative and Maturation Ponds   168
13.10 Outlet Weir Structure   169
13.11 By-pass Pipework for Anaerobic Ponds   170
13.12 Covered Anaerobic Pond at the Western Treatment Plant,
       Melbourne, Australia   170
13.13 Partial View of the Al Samra WSP, Amman, Jordan   171
13.14 Fence and Warning Notice in English and Kiswahili at a Pond
       Site in Nairobi, Kenya   172
13.15 Upgrading a WSP Series to Treat Twice the Original Flow   174
14.1   Sludge Depth Measurement by the 'White Towel' Test   177
14.2   Pond Desludging in Northern France   178
14.3   A Very Badly Neglected Facultative Pond in Eastern Africa   181
15.1   Details of Pond Column Sampler   186
16.1   Single WSTR in Israel   189
16.2   Wastewater Storage and Treatment Reservoir Systems   190
16.3   Sequential Batch-fed WSTR at Arad, Israel   192
17.1   A 100-m Long Subsurface-flow Constructed Wetland in Egypt   195
17.2   A Horizontal-flow Constructed Wetland at a Hotel in Kandy,
       Sri Lanka   197
18.1   A UASB at Ginebra, Valle del Cauca, Southwest Colombia   201
18.2   Schematic Diagram of a UASB   202
18.3   Influent Distribution Channel and Distribution Boxes   203
18.4   Details of a Submerged Phase Separator   205
19.1   Sectional Perspective View of a Circular Biofilter   208
19.2   Distribution of Settled Wastewater on to a Rectangular Biofilter 209

19.3   Rectangular Biofilters with High-density Polyethylene Netting to
        Control Fly Nuisance   211
20.1   An Aerated Lagoon   214
20.2   Floating 'Aire-O$_2$ Triton' Aerator–mixer   215
20.3   Typical Oxidation Ditch Installation   226
21.1   Excess Prevalence of *Ascaris* and Hookworm Infections in
        Sewage Farm Workers in India   233
21.2   Excess Intensity of *Ascaris* and Hookworm Infections in Sewage
        Farm Workers in India   234
21.3   *Ascaris* Prevalence among Residents of Western Jerusalem,
        1935–1982   235
21.4   *Ascaris* Prevalence among Residents of Selected German Cities
        Immediately After the Second World War   236
21.5   Generalized Model Showing the Levels of Relative Risk to
        Human Health Associated with Different Combinations of
        Control Methods for the Use of Wastewater in Agriculture and
        Aquaculture   240
21.6   Drip Irrigation of Cotton with Maturation Pond Effluent at
        Nicosia, Cyprus   242
21.7   Classification of Irrigation Waters Based on Conductivity and
        Sodium Absorption Ratio   244
22.1   Some of the Kolkata East Wastewater-fed Fishponds   253
22.2   Harvesting Indian Major Carp from the Kolkata East
        Wastewater-fed Fishponds   254

TABLES

1.1   Composition of Human Faeces and Urine   2
1.2   Wastewater Strength in Terms of BOD$_5$ and COD   4
1.3   Average BOD$_5$ Contributions per Person per Day   5
2.1   Environmental Classification of Excreta-related Diseases   9
2.2   Major Excreta-related Pathogens Identified Since 1973   17
2.3   Global Diarrhoeal Disease and Geohelminthiases Statistics for
        1990   18
3.1   Micro-invertebrate Groups Used to Assess the Biological Quality
        of Tropical Waters   40
3.2   Simplified Biotic Index for Tropical Waters   40
4.1   Normalized Unit Values for Dissolved Oxygen, Total Dissolved
        Salt and Turbidity Used to Calculate WQI$_{min}$ 49
4.2   The UK Royal Commission's Classification of River Water
        Quality   50
4.3   The UK Royal Commission's Standards for Wastewater Effluents
        Discharged into Rivers   51
4.4   Effluent Quality Requirements for Domestic Wastewaters
        Discharged into the Marine Environment of the Wider Caribbean
        Region   54

5.1 BOD Removal Results in Primary Facultative Ponds in Northeast Brazil   66

6.1 Comparison of Factors of Importance in Wastewater Treatment in Industrialized and Developing Countries   70

9.1 Costs and Land Area Requirements for WSP and Other Treatment Processes   90

9.2 Excreted Pathogen Removals in WSP and Conventional Treatment Processes   92

10.1 Design Values of Volumetric BOD Loadings on and Percentage BOD Removals in Anaerobic Ponds at Various Temperatures   109

10.2 Variation of BOD Removal with BOD Loading and Retention Time in Anaerobic Ponds in Northeast Brazil at 25°C   109

11.1 Examples of Algal Genera Found in Facultative and Maturation Ponds   116

12.1 Performance of a Series of Five WSP in Northeast Brazil   137

12.2 Bacterial and Viral Removals in a Series of Five WSP in Northeast Brazil   139

12.3 Settling Velocities for Parasite Eggs and Cysts   140

12.4 Helminth Egg Removal in Waste Stabilization Ponds in Northeast Brazil   141

12.5 Reported Values of $k_{B(20)}$ and ϕ for Use in Equation 12.2   146

12.6 Performance Data for WSP with Different Depths and Length-to-Breadth Ratios in Northeast Brazil at 25°C   147

14.1 Recommended Staffing Levels for WSP Systems   179

15.1 Parameters to be Determined for Level 2 Pond Effluent Quality Monitoring   184

15.2 Parameters to be Determined for the Minimum Evaluation of WSP Performance   185

16.1 Operational Strategy for Three Sequential Batch-fed WSTR for an Irrigation Season of Six Months   191

20.1 Solubility of Oxygen in Distilled Water at Sea Level at Various Temperatures   219

20.2 Design Criteria for Oxidation Ditches in India and Europe   227

21.1 Crop Yields for Wastewater and Freshwater Irrigation in India   230

21.2 Recommended Maximum Concentrations of Boron in Irrigation Waters According to Crop Tolerance   245

21.3 Recommended Maximum Metal Concentrations in Irrigation Waters   246

21.4 Physicochemical Quality of Three Waste Stabilization Pond Effluents in Israel   247

21.5 Values of N_{50} and α for Excreted Viral and Bacterial Pathogens   249

22.1 Percentage of Free Ammonia (NH_3) in Aqueous Ammonia ($NH_3 + NH_4$) Solutions at 1–25 °C and pH 7.0–8.5   259

Preface

This book is primarily written for final year undergraduate civil engineering students in developing country universities, for post-graduate masters students in environmental, public health and sanitary engineering, and for practising engineers working in developing countries or working on wastewater treatment projects in these countries. The primary emphasis of the book is on low-cost, high-performance, sustainable domestic wastewater treatment systems. Most of the systems described are 'natural' systems – so called because they do not require any electromechanical power input. The secondary emphasis is on wastewater re-use in agriculture and aquaculture – after all, it is better to use the treated wastewater productively and therefore profitably, rather than simply discharge it into a river and thus waste its water and its nutrients. The human health aspects of wastewater use are obviously important and these are covered in detail, including an introduction to quantitative microbial risk analysis.

Over the last 30 or so years that I have been working on wastewater engineering in developing countries, I have been helped by many colleagues and friends. I particularly wish to express my gratitude to all of the following: Professor Richard Feachem (University of California San Francisco and Berkeley), Dr Mike McGarry (Cowater International, Ottawa), Emeritus Professor Gerrit Marais (University of Cape Town), Professor Howard Pearson (Universidade Federal do Rio Grande do Norte), Emeritus Professor Hillel Shuval (Hebrew University of Jerusalem), Professor Sandy Cairncross and Dr Ursula Blumenthal (London School of Hygiene and Tropical Medicine), Emeritus Professor Takashi Asano (University of California Davis), Professor Marcos von Sperling (Universidade Federal de Minas Gerais), Professor Peter Edwards (Asian Institute of Technology) and Dr Andy Shilton (Massey University); and at the University of Leeds: Emeritus Professor Tony Cusens, Emeritus Professor Donald Lee, Professor Ed Stentiford, Dr Nigel Horan and Dr Andy Sleigh. Advice on the content of Figure 3.1 was generously provided by Dr Ian Head (University of Newcastle).

Docendo dedici. Many of my former doctoral students have made major contributions, including Dr Rachel Ayres, Dr Harin Corea, Dr Tom Curtis, Dr Martin Gambrill, Dr Steve Mills, Dr John Oragui, Dr Miguel Peña Varón, Professor Salomão Silva, Dr David Smallman, Dr Rebecca Stott and Dr Huw Taylor.

Finally, but most importantly, I wish to express a lifelong gratitude to Kevin Newman, Emeritus Professor of Classics at the University of Illinois, who taught me as a teenager how to think – the greatest gift a teacher can bestow.

Principal Notation

SYMBOLS

A	area
B	breadth
C	concentration
D	depth; dissolved oxygen deficit
E	number of helminth eggs
e	net evaporation
F	soluble BOD
k_1	first-order rate constant for BOD removal
k_2	first-order rate constant for surface reaeration
k_B	first-order rate for *E coli* removal
L	BOD; length
M	mass
Q,q	flow
r	infectivity constant
S	solids
T	temperature
t	time
V	volume; velocity
X	cell concentration
Y	yield coefficient
y	oxygen consumed
α	coefficient of retardation; infectivity constant; ratio of oxygen transfer in wastewater and tap water
β	ratio of oxygen solubility in wastewater and distilled water
γ	sludge loading factor
δ	dispersion number
ε	porosity
θ	retention time
κ	first-order rate constant for soluble BOD removal
λ	loading rate
μ	specific growth rate
ϕ	Arrhenius constant

SUBSCRIPTS

a	anaerobic
c	critical
e	effluent
f	facultative
i	influent
m	maturation, mean, mixture
r	river
s	surface
v	volumetric

List of Acronyms and Abbreviations

AIPS	advanced integrated pond system
AIWPS®	advanced integrated wastewater ponding system
BATNEEC	best available technology not entailing excessive cost
BOD	biochemical oxygen demand
CATNAP	cheapest available technology narrowly avoiding prosecution
CBOD	carbonaceous BOD
COD	chemical oxygen demand
DO	dissolved oxygen
EU	European Union
FAO	Food and Agriculture Organization
FC	faecal coliforms
GAOP	gross algal oxygen production
GDOP	gross dissolved oxygen production
HRAP	high-rate algal ponds
NRCD	National River Conservation Directorate
O&M	operation and maintenance
PAR	photosynthetically active radiation
PPFD	photosynthetic photon flux density
QMRA	quantitative microbial risk analysis
SRT	solids retention time
SS	suspended solids
ThOD	theoretical oxygen demand
UASB	upflow anaerobic sludge blanket reactor(s)
USAID	United States Agency for International Development
USEPA	United States Environmental Protection Agency
WHO	World Health Organization
WSP	waste stabilization pond(s)
WSTR	wastewater storage and treatment reservoir(s)

1

What is Domestic Wastewater and Why Treat It?

ORIGIN AND COMPOSITION OF DOMESTIC WASTEWATER

Domestic wastewater is the water that has been used by a community and which contains all the materials added to the water during its use. It is thus composed of *human body wastes* (faeces and urine) together with the water used for flushing toilets, and *sullage*, which is the wastewater resulting from personal washing, laundry, food preparation and the cleaning of kitchen utensils.

Fresh wastewater is a grey turbid liquid that has an earthy but inoffensive odour. It contains large floating and suspended solids (such as faeces, rags, plastic containers, maize cobs), smaller suspended solids (such as partially disintegrated faeces, paper, vegetable peel) and very small solids in colloidal (ie non-settleable) suspension, as well as pollutants in true solution. It is objectionable in appearance and hazardous in content, mainly because of the number of disease-causing ('pathogenic') organisms it contains (Chapter 2). In warm climates wastewater can soon lose its content of dissolved oxygen and so become 'stale' or 'septic'. Septic wastewater has an offensive odour, usually of hydrogen sulphide.

The composition of human faeces and urine is given in Table 1.1, and for wastewater, in simpler form, in Figure 1.1. The organic fraction of both is composed principally of proteins, carbohydrates and fats. These compounds, particularly the first two, form an excellent diet for bacteria, the microscopic organisms whose voracious appetite for food is exploited by public health engineers in the microbiological treatment of wastewater. In addition to these chemical compounds, faeces and, to a lesser extent, urine contain many millions of intestinal bacteria and smaller numbers of other organisms. The majority of these are harmless – indeed some are beneficial – but an important minority is able to cause human disease (Chapter 2).

Sullage contributes a wide variety of chemicals: detergents, soaps, fats and greases of various kinds, pesticides, anything in fact that goes down the kitchen sink, and this may include such diverse items as sour milk, vegetable peelings, tea leaves, soil particles (arising from the preparation of vegetables) and sand

Table 1.1 *Composition of Human Faeces and Urine*

	Faeces	Urine
Quantities		
Quantity (wet) per person per day	135–270 g	1.0–1.3 kg
Quantity (dry solids) per person per day	35–70 g	50–70 g
Approximate composition (%)		
Moisture	66–80	93–96
Organic matter	88–97	65–85
Nitrogen	5.0–7.0	15–19
Phosphorus (as P_2O_5)	3.0–5.4	2.5–5.0
Potassium (as K_2O)	1.0–2.5	3.0–4.5
Carbon	44–55	11–17
Calcium (as CaO)	4.5	4.5–6.0

Source: Gotaas (1956)

(used to clean cooking utensils). The number of different chemicals that are found in domestic wastewater is so vast that, even if it were possible, it would be meaningless to list them all. For this reason wastewater treatment engineers use special parameters to characterize wastewaters.

CHARACTERIZATION OF DOMESTIC WASTEWATER

As is explained more fully in Chapter 5, wastewaters are usually treated by supplying them with oxygen so that bacteria can utilize the wastewater contents as food. The general equation is:

$$\text{wastewater} + \text{oxygen} \xrightarrow{\text{bacteria}} \text{treated wastewater} + \text{new bacteria}$$

The nature of domestic wastewater is so complex that it precludes its complete analysis. However, since it is comparatively easy to measure the amount of oxygen used by the bacteria as they oxidize the wastewater, the concentration of organic matter in the wastewater can easily be expressed in terms of the amount of oxygen required for its oxidation. Thus, if, for example, half a gram of oxygen is consumed in the oxidation of each litre of a particular wastewater, then we say that this wastewater has an 'oxygen demand' of 500 mg/l, by which we mean that the concentration of organic matter in a litre of the wastewater is such that its oxidation requires 500 mg of oxygen. There are basically three ways of expressing the oxygen demand of a waste:

1   **Theoretical oxygen demand** (ThOD) – this is the theoretical amount of oxygen required to oxidize the organic fraction of the wastewater completely to carbon dioxide and water. The equation for the total oxidation of, say, glucose is:

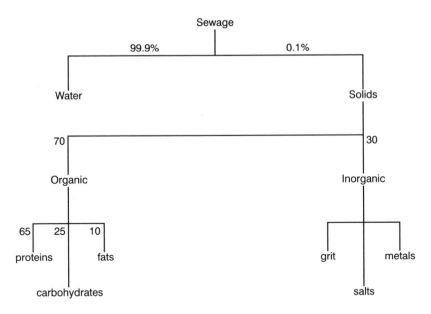

Source: Tebbutt (1998)

Figure 1.1 *Composition of Domestic Wastewater*

$$C_6H_{12}O_6 + 6O_2 \longrightarrow 6CO_2 + 6H_2O$$

With C = 12, H = 1 and O = 16, $C_6H_{12}O_6$ is 180 and $6O_2$ is 192; we can thus calculate that the ThOD of, for example, a 300 mg/l solution of glucose is (192/180) x 300 = 321 mg/l. Because wastewater is so complex in nature its ThOD cannot be calculated, but in practice it is approximated by the chemical oxygen demand.

2 **Chemical oxygen demand** (COD) – this is obtained by oxidizing the wastewater with a boiling acid dichromate solution. This process oxidizes almost all organic compounds to carbon dioxide and water, the reaction usually proceeding to more than 95 per cent completion. The advantage of COD measurements is that they are obtained very quickly (within 3 hours), but they have the disadvantages that they do not give any information on the proportion of the wastewater that can be oxidized by bacteria, nor on the rate at which bio-oxidation occurs.

3 **Biochemical oxygen demand** (BOD) – this is the amount of oxygen required for the oxidation of a wastewater by bacteria. It is therefore a measure of the concentration of organic matter in a waste that can be oxidized by bacteria ('bio-oxidized' or 'biodegraded'). BOD is usually expressed on a 5-day, 20°C basis – that is as the amount of oxygen consumed during oxidation of the wastewater for 5 days at 20°C. This is because the 5-day BOD (usually written 'BOD$_5$') is more easily measured

than is the ultimate BOD (BOD_u), which is the oxygen required for the complete bio-oxidation of the waste. (The reason for the seemingly arbitrary choice of 20°C and 5 days for the measurement of BOD is given in Chapter 4; see also Baird and Smith, 2002.) The correct concept of BOD is fundamental to wastewater treatment, and a rigorous treatment of BOD removal kinetics is given in Chapter 5.

From the foregoing it is apparent that:

$$ThOD > COD > BOD_u > BOD_5$$

There is no general relationship between these various oxygen demands. However, for untreated domestic wastewater a large number of measurements have indicated the following approximate ratios:

$$BOD_5/COD = 0.5$$

$$BOD_u/BOD_5 = 1.5$$

The presence of industrial or agricultural wastewaters alters these ratios considerably.

Wastewater strength

The higher the concentration of organic matter in a wastewater, the 'stronger' it is said to be. Wastewater strength is often judged by its BOD_5 or COD (Table 1.2). The strength of the wastewater from a community is governed to a very large degree by its water consumption. Thus, in the US where water consumption is high (350–400 l/person day) the wastewater is weak (BOD_5 = 200–250 mg/l), whereas in tropical countries the wastewater is strong (BOD_5 = 300–700 mg/l) as the water consumption is typically much lower (40–100 l/person day).

The other factor determining the strength of domestic wastewater is the BOD (= amount of organic waste) produced per person per day. This varies from country to country and the differences are largely due to differences in the quantity and quality of sullage rather than of body wastes, although variations in diet are important. A good value to use in developing countries is 40 g BOD_5 per person per day (Table 1.3). In Brazil the BOD contribution per person per day was found to vary with income – poor people produce less

Table 1.2 *Wastewater Strength in Terms of BOD_5 and COD*

Strength	BOD_5 (mg/l)	COD (mg/l)
Weak	<200	<400
Medium	350	700
Strong	500	1000
Very strong	>750	>1500

Table 1.3 *Average BOD$_5$ Contributions per Person per Day*

	USA	Developing countries
Personal washing	9	5
Dishwashing	6	8[b]
Garbage disposal[a]	31	
Laundry	9	5
Toilet – faeces	11	11
urine	10	10
paper	2	1[c]
Total (average adult contribution)	78	40

Sources: Ligman et al (1974), Mara (1976)
Notes
[a] Sink-installed garbage grinder
[b] Includes allowance for food scraps
[c] Cleansing material may not be paper – water, maize cobs and leaves are common alternatives

BOD than richer people (Campos and von Sperling, 1996*)[1] (further details are given in Chapter 7). This is undoubtedly true in all developing countries, but currently data only exist from Brazil.

WASTEWATER COLLECTION

Domestic wastewaters are collected in underground pipes which are called 'sewers'. The flow in sewers is normally by gravity, with pumped mains only being used when unavoidable.

The design of conventional sewerage (the sewer system used in industrialized countries and in the central areas of many cities in developing countries) is described in several texts (eg Metcalf and Eddy, Inc, 1986) and is detailed in national sewerage codes (eg for India, Ministry of Urban Development, 1993). However, it is extremely expensive. A much lower cost alternative, which is suitable for use in both poor and rich areas alike, is 'simplified' sewerage, sometimes called 'condominial' sewerage. The design of simplified sewerage is fully detailed by Mara et al (2001a*).

WHY TREAT WASTEWATER?

Untreated wastewater causes major damage to the environment and to human health. Almost always, therefore, wastewater should be treated in order to:

- reduce the transmission of excreta-related diseases (Chapter 2)
- reduce water pollution and the consequent damage to aquatic biota (Chapter 4).

Only if there is a very large available dilution (>500) in the receiving watercourse can consideration be given to discharging untreated wastewater (see Table 4.2). For example, the city of Manaus (population in 2000: 1.4 million) in the Amazon region of Brazil discharges its wastewater untreated via a river outfall into the Rio Negro, a tributary of the River Amazon, which has a flow of ~30,000 m^3 per second. The available dilution is >>500 and therefore the pollution induced is negligible.

In developing countries only a small proportion of the wastewater produced by sewered communities is treated. In Latin America, for example, less than 15 per cent of the wastewaters collected in sewered cities and towns is treated prior to discharge (Pan American Health Organization, 2000). Often the reason for the lack of wastewater treatment is financial, but it is also due to an ignorance of low-cost wastewater treatment processes and of the economic benefits of treated wastewater reuse (Chapters 21 and 22); and also because too many decision-makers appear happy to accept the status quo: the continued discharge of untreated wastewater with its resultant damage to the environment and human health. Currently the global burden of excreta-related disease is extremely high (Chapter 2). Over half the world's rivers, lakes and coastal waters are seriously polluted by untreated domestic, industrial and agricultural wastewaters (United Nations Environment Programme, 2002*; Beach, 2001*), and they contain high numbers of faecal bacteria (Ceballos et al, 2003*). Effective wastewater treatment needs to be recognized, therefore, as an environmental and human health imperative.

INVESTMENT IN WASTEWATER TREATMENT

Developing country governments and their regulatory agencies, as well as local authorities (which may be city or town councils, or specific wastewater treatment authorities, or more generally water and sewerage authorities), need to understand that domestic and other wastewaters require treatment before discharge or, preferably, re-use in agriculture and/or aquaculture. They also need to act, but first they need to decide where, when and how much to invest in wastewater treatment (Mariño and Boland, 1999*). Advice on the economic analysis of investment projects is given by the World Bank (1996*; see also Kalbermatten et al, 1982*).

Wastewater treatment for re-use in agriculture and aquaculture can be subjected to classical benefit–cost analysis using discounted cash-flow techniques to show if the present value of future additional crop yields is more than the present value of wastewater treatment. However, wastewater treatment prior to discharge to inland or coastal waters is less easy to analyse. Central government, with its national perspective, must set national environmental and environmental health priorities. It can enforce these by lending money only for wastewater treatment projects that lie within these priorities. Local authorities can then apply for a loan for a 'priority' wastewater treatment project. Generally, and ideally, priority projects should be dealt with on the basis of river basin catchment areas, as this is the best method of integrated water resources management, with central government deciding which river basin is (or which river basins are) to be protected first, what level of protection is needed now and how this can be developed to progressively higher levels of protection in the future.

Wastewater treatment is needed on a truly enormous scale in developing countries, and the purpose of this book is to show how it can be done at low cost, and how treated wastewaters can be profitably and safely used in agriculture and aquaculture – for wastewaters are simply too valuable to waste.

NOTE

1   An asterix after the year in a reference indicates that the publication referred to is available on the Internet – see *References*.

2

Excreta-related Diseases

As noted in Chapter 1, one of the principal aims of domestic wastewater treatment in developing countries is to reduce the numbers of excreted pathogens to levels where the risks of further environmental transmission of the diseases they cause are substantially reduced. Wastewater treatment processes that are especially suitable for use in developing countries, such as waste stabilization ponds (Chapters 9–13), are often designed specifically for excreted pathogen removal. Wastewater treatment plant designers need, therefore, to have a good understanding of excreta-related diseases, the pathogens that cause them and how the plants they design can remove them.

ENVIRONMENTAL CLASSIFICATION OF EXCRETA-RELATED DISEASES

A simple list of the 50 or so excreta-related diseases is not helpful to engineers, nor is one which divides the list into viral, bacterial, protozoan and helminthic diseases. What engineers (and other non-medical professionals) need is a list that organizes the excreta-related diseases into categories according to their environmental transmission route. This type of classification is called an 'environmental' classification, and this chapter presents the environmental classification of excreta-related diseases developed in the early 1980s by Professor Richard Feachem and his co-workers, mostly at the London School of Hygiene and Tropical Medicine (Feachem et al, 1983*). In this chapter Feachem's classification has been annotated for use by wastewater treatment and re-use engineers.

Table 2.1 gives an overview of Feachem's environmental classification of excreta-related diseases. There are seven categories (originally Feachem et al had six; Mara and Alabaster, 1995, added the seventh). The first five comprise the excreted infections – those in which pathogens in the excreta of one person infect another person or persons. The last two categories are the vector-borne excreta-related diseases – those excreta-related diseases spread by insects and rodents.

Table 2.1 *Environmental Classification of Excreta-related Diseases*

Category	Environmental transmission features	Major examples of infection	Environmental transmission focus
I *Non-bacterial faeco-oral diseases*	Non-latent Low to medium persistence Unable to multiply High infectivity No intermediate host	*Viral:* Hepatitis A and E Rotavirus diarrhoea Norovirus diarrhoea *Protozoan:* Amoebiasis Cryptosporidiosis Giardiasis *Helminthic:* Enterobiasis Hymenolepiasis	Personal Domestic Wastewater
II *Bacterial faeco-oral diseases*	Non-latent Medium to high persistence Able to multiply Medium to low infectivity No intermediate host	Campylobacteriosis Cholera Pathogenic *Escherichia coli* infection Salmonellosis Shigellosis Typhoid Yersiniosis	Personal Domestic Wastewater Crops
III *Geohelminthiases*	Latent Very persistent Unable to multiply No intermediate host Very high infectivity	Ascariasis Hookworm infection Strongyloidiasis Trichurasis	Peri-domestic Wastewater Crops
IV *Taeniases*	Latent Persistent Able to multiply Very high infectivity Cow or pig intermediate host	Taeniasis	Peri-domestic Wastewater Fodder crops
V *Water-based helminthiases*	Latent Persistent Able to multiply High infectivity Intermediate aquatic host(s)	Schistosomiasis Clonorchiasis Fasciolopsiasis	Wastewater Fish Aquatic species or aquatic vegetables
VI *Excreta-related insect-vector disease*		Bancroftian filariasis transmitted by *Culex quinquefasciatus*	Wastewater
VII *Excreta-related rodent-vector disease*		Leptospirosis	Wastewater

Note: For medical details of all the diseases mentioned see, for example, Chin (2000) and Cook and Zumla (2002)

Excreted infections

The successful transmission of an excreted infection depends on the following factors:

- excreted load
- latency
- persistence
- multiplication
- infectivity
- susceptibility.

The first five of these are properties of the pathogen, and the last is a property of a potential host (ie the next person in the transmission chain).

Excreted load

Excreted load is the number of pathogens excreted by an infected person, and it varies widely. For example, a person with cholera (a Category II disease) may excrete ~10^{13} cholera vibrios per day. Someone with a light infection of *Ascaris lumbricoides*, the human roundworm (Category III), may excrete a few hundred thousand eggs per day (each female worm can produce up to ~200,000 eggs per day).

The excreted load depends on the state of infection: as the cholera victim, for example, becomes better, the number of vibrios excreted falls – eventually, of course, to zero. Another good example is schistosomiasis (Category V): infected children generally show few clinical signs of the disease but excrete large numbers of schistosome eggs, whereas adults in the terminal stage of the disease excrete very few or no eggs.

The number of excreted pathogens in a wastewater depends on the number of pathogens excreted by infected individuals in the community producing the wastewater. Generally, numbers of endemic excreted pathogens in wastewater are a few hundreds or thousands, occasionally tens of thousands, per unit volume of wastewater considered (generally 100 ml for excreted bacteria, 1 l for excreted worm eggs and protozoan cysts, and 10 l for excreted viruses – see Chapters 11 and 12).

Latency

This is the interval between the excretion of a pathogen and it becoming infective to another person or persons. Many excreted pathogens, including all viruses, bacteria and protozoa (except *Cyclospora*), are non-latent: that is, they are infective immediately upon excretion. Latency is an important property, therefore, only of the helminths, and all the excreted helminths of importance in wastewater treatment and re-use are latent. Their latency varies from a few days to a few weeks, and during this time the worm changes from a non-infective form to its infective form. This development may occur wholly in the environment outside the body, as with the geohelminths (Category III), or it may take place partly in the environment and partly in an intermediate host – a cow or pig in the case of the tapeworms (Category IV), or a water snail and possibly also a fish or an aquatic vegetable in the case of the water-based trematode worms (Category V).

Persistence
How long an excreted pathogen can survive in the environment outside the body is the property most indicative of the health hazard it poses. A pathogen that is very persistent – for example, *Ascaris* eggs, which can survive for many months, even years – are a risk in wastewater treatment and re-use. Even excreted bacteria, which generally survive for only a few weeks, also constitute a risk in this way.

Multiplication
Some excreted pathogens can, given the right environmental conditions, multiply in the environment several thousand-fold or several million-fold: for example, excreted bacteria in food and milk, and the water-based trematodes in aquatic snails. Thus, a low excreted load can rapidly multiply to increase the risk of infection. Excreted viruses and excreted protozoa cannot multiply and, therefore, for them to be able to be transmitted successfully their infectivity has to be very high.

Infectivity
Knowledge about infectivity – the probability of infection from one organism – is far from perfect. What information there is has usually come from volunteer studies: known pathogen doses are given to groups of volunteers who are then monitored to see if they become infected (and, if they do, they are then quickly treated). Generally, the volunteers have been healthy adults from non-endemic areas, and their response is very different from that of malnourished children in developing countries. Nevertheless, we cannot ignore infectivity, however imperfect our knowledge. In general terms, we use the following descriptive categories for the probability of infection from one organism:

- High infectivity $>10^{-2}$
- Medium infectivity $10^{-2}–10^{-6}$
- Low infectivity $<10^{-6}$.

Quantitative microbial risk assessment (Chapter 21) is used to calculate the risks of infection and disease that may be associated with wastewater re-use. Provided the wastewater has been well treated – specifically for pathogen removal, especially in maturation ponds (Chapter 12) – these risks are very low indeed.

Susceptibility

The excreta of one person will cause disease in an infected person, but only if that person is susceptible. Host susceptibility governs the severity of the disease: a person may be susceptible or, due to immunization or previous exposure, be immune or have a varying degree of resistance.

Definition of terms

The terms 'infection' and 'disease' are often used interchangeably, but strictly they have distinct meanings – an infected person may, or may not, become diseased, depending on his or her susceptibility to the disease in question.

Incidence and prevalence are two important terms. **Incidence** is the number of new cases of a particular disease in a community that occurs in a specified time period (a week, a month or a year, but there is no relationship between, say, weekly and annual incidences as all cases in a given year may have only occurred in a given week). Incidence is generally used for acute diseases (eg those in Categories I and II below). **Prevalence** is the number (or proportion) of people in a community with a particular disease at a specified point in time. It is used for chronic infections or diseases such as the various excreta-related helminthiases (Categories III–V below). It is possible to refer to the incidence of one of these chronic diseases, but this has the meaning given above (and is useful, for example, when determining reinfection following community-wide antihelminthic chemotherapy).

Category I: Non-bacterial faeco-oral diseases

The term **faeco-oral** is used to describe the beginning and end of the excreted pathogen's transmission route: it leaves one person in his or her faeces and enters another person through his or her mouth. This category includes all the excreted viral and protozoan diseases, and these excreted pathogens are non-latent, have a low-to-medium persistence, are unable to multiply, have a high infectivity and do not have an intermediate host. These infections are mainly spread in a very direct person-to-person way wherever personal and domestic hygiene is poor. However, those that can survive for several days (the protozoa, for example) are also important in wastewater treatment and re-use.

The most important viruses in this category are rotaviruses and noroviruses (until recently the latter were called Norwalk and Norwalk-like viruses), which are the principal causes of viral diarrhoea in both developing and industrialized countries. Rotaviruses cause 350,000–600,000 deaths per year in children under five years old, 82 per cent of which are in developing countries (Parashar et al, 2003*). Other important diarrhoeagenic viruses are adenoviruses, astroviruses and other caliciviruses.

There are four main protozoa that cause diarrhoea: *Entamoeba histolytica*, *Giardia intestinalis* (also called *G lamblia*), *Cryptosporidium parvum* and *Cyclospora cayentanensis*. The first three are non-latent, whereas *Cyclospora* is latent and requires a period of seven to ten days to sporulate into its infectious form (Relman, 1998). Outbreaks of cyclosporiasis in the US and Canada during 1996–2000, associated with the consumption of Guatemalan raspberries (see Ho et al, 2002*), resulted in a ban on their import into the US and consequent huge economic losses and unemployment in Guatemala. The prevalence of cyclosporiasis amongst Guatemalan raspberry farm workers, especially children under the age of ten, was higher than in non-farm workers (Bern et al, 2000*). There was an outbreak of cyclosporiasis in south-west Germany in 2000–2001 associated with the consumption in a restaurant of salad side dishes prepared with lettuce imported from southern France and herbs and spring onions from southern Italy (Döller et al, 2002*).

Category II: Bacterial faeco-oral diseases

The transmission features of the bacterial excreted pathogens are that they are non-latent, have a medium-to-high persistence, are able to multiply, have a medium-to-low infectivity and do not have an intermediate host. These infections can be transmitted in the same direct person-to-person way as Category I infections, but their greater persistence means that they are even more important in wastewater treatment and re-use.

The major excreted bacterial pathogens are *Campylobacter* spp, diarrhoeagenic *E coli*, *Salmonella* spp, *Shigella* spp and *Vibrio cholerae*. Most of the global incidence of bacterial diarrhoea is associated with *Campylobacter* and diarrhoeagenic *E coli*. The two species of *Campylobacter* pathogenic to humans are *Campylobacter jejuni* and *Campylobacter coli*, and they are often present in waters and wastewaters (Jones, 2001*). Children are most at risk, especially those under the age of two years, in whom polymicrobial infection is common (ie infection with both *Campylobacter* and one or more other gastrointestinal pathogens) (Coker et al, 2002*). Guillain–Barré syndrome (the most common form of acute neuromuscular paralysis) is a potential severe outcome of *C jejuni* infection (which is the most usual cause, although it can be induced, but generally at lower severity, by other non-excreted bacteria and viruses) (Hadden and Gregson, 2001*).

Most *E coli* strains are non-pathogenic commensal inhabitants of the gastro-intestinal tract of humans and most animals. However, diarrhoeagenic *E coli* strains are extremely pathogenic; they comprise several types termed (mainly after their pathogenesis) enterotoxigenic *E coli* (or ETEC), enteropathogenic *E coli* (EPEC), enterohaemorrhagic *E coli* (EHEC), enteroaggregative *E coli* (EAEC), enteroinvasive *E coli* (EIEC) and diffusively adhesive *E coli* (DAEC) (Nataro and Kaper, 1998*; Hunter, 2003*). ETEC is a very common pathogen (see Chart, 1998*) and is the second most important bacterial cause of diarrhoea after *Campylobacter*. EHEC includes *E coli* O157, a virulent serotype causing high mortality in the most vulnerable groups (the very old and the very young).

Categories I and II are very similar, the only difference being the greater persistence of the excreted bacteria. Categories III–IV are very different: they comprise the excreted helminthic infections, the pathogens are all latent and very persistent, and some have one or more intermediate hosts. An excellent introduction to helminthic diseases is given by Muller (2001*).

Category III: Geohelminthiases

This category contains the geohelminths – the soil-transmitted nematode worms. The main ones of importance in wastewater treatment and re-use are:

- *Ascaris lumbricoides* – the human roundworm
- *Trichuris trichiura* – the human whipworm
- *Ancylostoma duodenale* and *Necator americanus* – the human hookworms.

Their transmission features are that they are latent, very persistent, unable to multiply, have a very high infectivity and do not have an intermediate host.

They are extremely common pathogens, especially *Ascaris* and the hookworms. In low-income areas of developing countries prevalences are often over 50 per cent (ie over half the population is infected), and prevalences greater than 90 per cent occur frequently. The number of worms per person (the 'worm burden', a measure of the intensity of infection) can also be high (Figure 2.1).

Adult female *Ascaris* worms each produce up to ~200,000 eggs/day, which leave the body in the faeces, and adult female hookworms each produce 5000–20,000 eggs/day, which also leave in the faeces. Egg numbers in wastewater can thus be quite high in endemic areas, up to ~3000/l. Fortunately they are easily removed in several of the wastewater treatment processes described in this book (Chapters 9–19), and thus compliance with the World Health Organization's guideline value of ≤1 egg/l treated wastewater used for crop irrigation, or ≤0.1 egg/l when children under 15 are exposed usually is not a problem (World Health Organization, 1989*, 2004*; see also Blumenthal et al, 2000*); further details are given in Chapters 12 and 21.

Category IV: Taeniases

This category contains the two main human cestode worms: *Taenia saginata*, the beef tapeworm, and *Taenia solium*, the pork tapeworm. Their transmission features are that they are latent, persistent, able to multiply, have a very high infectivity and have a cow or pig intermediate host. Around 10^5–10^6 eggs are produced per day by each worm, and these leave the body in the faeces inside gravid segments of the worm, from which the eggs are released into wastewater. *Taenia* eggs are also easily removed in wastewater treatment processes.

The embryonic form of *T solium* (the 'cysticercus') can enter the brain where it may induce neurocysticercosis. This is the leading cause of epilepsy in developing countries (except Muslim and other countries or communities where pork is not eaten) (Sotelo, 2003*).

Category V: Water-based helminthiases

This category contains all the water-based human trematode worms. There are several of these, but only three genera are of major importance:

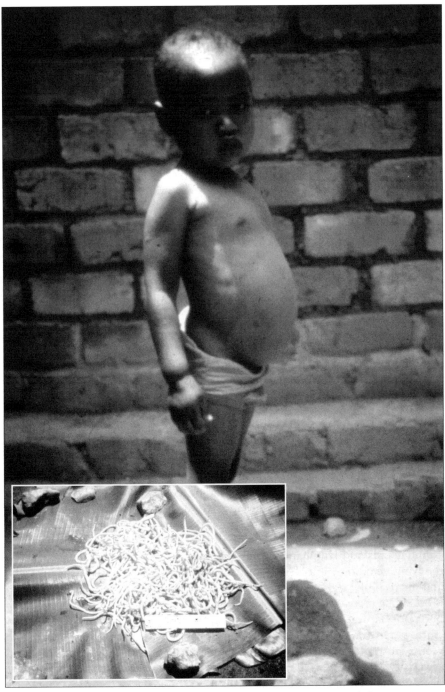

Figure 2.1 *This 4-year old African Girl with a Distended Abdomen was Given an Appropriate Dose of the Vermifuge Levamisol; Shortly Afterwards she Excreted the Large Number of Adult* Ascaris lumbricoides *Worms Shown*

- *Schistosoma mansoni, S japonicum* and *S haematobium,* the main human schistosomes or blood flukes
- *Clonorchis sinensis,* the oriental liver fluke (found mainly in China, Japan, Korea and Vietnam)
- *Fasciolopsis buski,* the giant human intestinal fluke (found mainly in India, Bangladesh, Thailand, Cambodia, China, Malaysia, Indonesia, Vietnam, Laos and the Philippines).

Their transmission features are that they are latent, reasonably persistent, able to multiply, have a high infectivity, and have one or two intermediate aquatic hosts – a snail (all three) and then either fish (*C sinensis*) or aquatic vegetables (*F buski*).

Adult female schistosomes produce up to ~1000 eggs/day, adult female *Clonorchis* worms up to ~4000 eggs/day, and adult female *Fasciolopsis* worms ~25,000 eggs/day. The eggs are voided in faeces (or, in the case of *S haematobium,* in urine), and they hatch in wastewater to form miracidia, which then have to enter a specific species of water snail in order to continue their life cycle. These trematode infections are potentially important in the aquacultural re-use of treated wastewaters (Chapter 22), but they are easily removed during wastewater treatment.

Category VI: Excreta-related insect-vector diseases
The only disease in this category important in wastewater treatment and re-use is Bancroftian filariasis when it is transmitted by the mosquito *Culex quinquefasciatus,* which can breed in poorly maintained wastewater treatment plants (Chapter 14). It is a serious disease caused by the nematode worm *Wuchereria bancrofti.* Adult worms live in the lymphatic ducts of humans, and embryo worms (called 'microfilariae') are shed in large numbers into the bloodstream at night. If a culicine mosquito ingests microfilariae during its blood meal, they develop inside the mosquito over a period of 10–15 days to become infective larvae. When the mosquito feeds again, they are introduced into another person where they develop over 3–12 months into adult male and female worms that establish themselves in the lymphatic system, and the cycle of microfilarial production recommences. After a few years of infection the lymph glands and lymphatic vessels become partially blocked and swollen as the lymph cannot drain. This leads to swelling of the genitalia, legs or arms, and the resulting gross deformity is called 'elephantiasis'. Bancroftian filariasis is becoming increasingly common in urban areas that have good water supplies but poor sanitation – the resulting wastewaters pond in garbage-blocked stormwater drains and natural drainage channels, so permitting the culicine vector mosquitoes to proliferate. The solution is to install low-cost simplified sewerage (Mara et al, 2001a*) and a properly designed wastewater treatment plant that is well-operated and maintained.

Category VII: Excreta-related rodent-vector diseases

The only disease in this category of relevance in wastewater treatment and re-use is leptospirosis, which is caused by the bacterium *Leptospira interrogans*. Leptospirosis is primarily a disease of brown rats, and humans become infected when they come into contact with infected rat urine. The leptospires then enter the body through damaged skin (a cut or abrasion). In humans the infection can be asymptomatic with mild (influenza-like) symptoms, or severe – the severest form is Weil's disease, and this can be rapidly fatal if not treated; symptoms include jaundice – skin and eye haemorrhages, and liver and kidney failure. Sewer maintenance workers are especially at risk, but the disease is also a potential risk in wastewater treatment and re-use. It is a becoming a more common infection in India, for example (Chaudhry et al, 2002*).

Emerging infectious diseases

Many excreta-related diseases are 'new' diseases – in the sense that their causative agent is a newly discovered pathogen. These diseases are termed 'emerging' infections, and several very important excreta-related pathogens have only been discovered in the last 30 years (Table 2.2). Some diseases are 're-emerging' as, due to changing circumstances (eg a high HIV/AIDS prevalence), the pathogens are now able to infect more people more frequently. Unquestionably, more emerging excreta-related pathogens will be found, but it should be relatively easy to assign them to the appropriate category in the environmental classification of excreta-related diseases given above.

Excreta-related cancers

Long-term infection with some excreted pathogens can induce cancer – for example, the water-related helminths (Category V): bladder cancer is induced by *Schistosoma haematobium*, colorectal cancer by *S mansoni* and *S japonicum*, and bile duct cancer by *Clonorchis sinensis* (Mara and Clapham, 1997*). *Helicobacter pylori*, a faeco-oral (and also oro-oral) bacterial pathogen that causes stomach ulcers, can induce stomach cancer. It is

Table 2.2 *Major Excreta-related Pathogens Identified Since 1973*

Year	Pathogen
1973	Hepatitis A virus
1973	Rotavirus
1976	*Cryptosporidium parvum*
1977	*Campylobacter* spp
1979	*Cyclospora cayetanensis*
1982	*Escherichia coli* O157
1983	*Helicobacter pylori*
1990	Hepatitis E virus
1992	*Vibrio cholerae* O139

Source: Satcher (1995*); Favorov and Margolis (1999)

extremely common, with infection prevalences of 50–80 per cent in developing countries, and it is the only bacterium to be designated as a known human carcinogen (International Agency for Research on Cancer, 1994; see also Engstrand, 2001*; Frenck and Clemens, 2003*).

GLOBAL BURDEN OF EXCRETA-RELATED DISEASES

A 'snapshot' of the global burden of all diseases in 1990 is given by the World Bank–World Health Organization study conducted by the Harvard School of Public Health (Murray and Lopez, 1996a, 1996b). Table 2.3 lists the global incidence of diarrhoeal diseases and the global prevalence of geohelminthic infections in 1990, essentially all of those which occurred in developing countries. Indeed, diseases due to deficient water supplies, deficient sanitation and deficient hygiene were together responsible for 7 per cent of all deaths in the world in 1990, second only to malnutrition, which caused 15 per cent of all deaths (Murray and Lopez, 1996a). However, by 2000 the proportion of deaths due to these diseases had fallen to 4 per cent (Prüss et al, 2002*). (Deaths from HIV/AIDS are increasing rapidly, especially in Africa – see *The Lancet*, 2002*, and are likely to overtake deaths due to deficient water sanitation and hygiene soon.)

The incidence of excreta-related diseases shows little sign of decline, especially in developing countries, but also in industrialized countries – for example, in England the annual incidence of infectious intestinal disease from all causes (but mainly food-borne diarrhoea) is 0.2 per person (Wheeler et al, 1999*), much lower than the incidence of diarrhoea in developing countries (1.3/person/year, Table 2.3), but even so is very high. In developing countries diarrhoea is still a major killer: some 1.3 million children under the age of five

Table 2.3 *Global Diarrhoeal Disease and Geohelminthiases Statistics for 1990*

Disease	Number	Remarks
Diarrhoea	4,073,920,000 episodes	56% in children aged 0–4 94% in developing countries
Ascariasis	61,847,000 persons with high-intensity infection	73% in children aged 5–14 All in developing countries
Trichuriasis	45,421,000 persons with high-intensity infection	79% in children aged 5–14 All in developing countries
Human hookworm infection	152,492,000 persons with high-intensity infection 36,014,000 persons with anaemia	84% in adults aged 15–59 All in developing countries 72% in adults aged 15–44 All in developing countries

Note: The world population in 1990 was 5.3 billions, of which 3.9 billions (74%) were in developing countries
Source: Murray and Lopez (1996b)

die from it each year (ie one diarrhoeal-disease child death every 25 seconds). More insidiously, diarrhoea in infancy is associated with 'stunting' (a medical term for low height-for-age, ie impaired growth) and also with poor cognitive function (ie impaired mental development) in later childhood (Berkman et al, 2002*). Children under the age of five years form only 10 per cent of the world's population, yet they bear at least 40 per cent of the total global burden of environmental – including excreta-related – disease (World Health Organization, 2002*).

Geohelminthic infections are extremely common: approximately one-third of the world population – some 2 billion people – has intestinal worms (Chan, 1997*). These worms eat their food before they do, so contributing to malnutrition and hence retarded growth and impaired cognition. In the case of the human hookworms, which hook into their hosts' stomach wall and drink their blood, anaemia is common, and women of child-bearing age can lose more blood in this way than through menstruation.

Wastewater treatment engineers, and more generally tropical public health engineers, have an extremely important role in reducing the environmental transmission of excreta-related diseases and, by so doing, in greatly contributing to socio-economic development in developing countries. This contribution is potentially enormous: Pearce and Warford (1993) quote data for 1979 (with the implication that more recent data did not exist): in that year some 360–400 billion working days in developing countries were lost from water- and excreta-related diseases that kept people from work. Valuing a working day lost at only US$0.50, these countries therefore lost US$180–200 billion in that year and, as the GNP of all developing countries was then US$370 billion, output was below potential production by as much as 33–35 per cent. Of course, good wastewater treatment is only one of the means tropical public health engineers have to combat excreta-related diseases, but it is an important one. Treatment combined with productive re-use (Chapters 21 and 22) contributes even more directly to socio-economic development.

3

Essential Microbiology and Biology

INTRODUCTION

Wastewater treatment and re-use engineers need a good understanding of wastewater microbiology for two reasons: first because wastewaters contain micro-organisms that cause human disease (Chapter 2), and secondly because most wastewater treatment processes are microbiological (we generally use the term 'biological wastewater treatment' to reflect this, but we should say 'microbiological wastewater treatment'). Wastewater treatment engineers also need to understand the effect of untreated, partially treated and fully treated wastewaters on the biology – really, the aquatic ecology – of the receiving watercourse.

This chapter provides an introduction to the important groups of micro-organisms in wastewater treatment and reuse: viruses, bacteria, algae, protozoa and helminths (more detailed information is given in, for example, Mara and Horan, 2003). It concludes with a brief description of a simplified technique for the biological assessment of tropical freshwater quality using aquatic micro-invertebrates.

What are micro-organisms?

Micro-organisms (often simply called 'microbes') are small single-celled organisms: viruses, bacteria, micro-algae and protozoa. To see them we need to use a microscope. (Helminths are multicellular animals and therefore not microbes, but we include them in the general topic of tropical sanitary microbiology, although this should be more properly described as tropical sanitary microbiology and parasitology.)

Micro-organisms are the ancestors of all organisms that exist (or have existed) on Earth, and they are the most numerous of all organisms: a handful of soil contains many hundreds of billions of microbes, mostly bacteria – more than the world's stock of plants and animals ('macro-organisms'). Micro-organisms are relatively simple life forms, but it is a mistake to think of them as 'primitive' – they are complex biochemical 'machines' which serve us well (they are the prime movers in the biogeochemical cycles of oxygen, carbon and nitrogen, for example, without which no life would exist), but which can also serve us badly (the Spanish influenza pandemic of 1918–1919, for example, killed ~40 million people; Brainerd and Siegler, 2003*). Fortunately only a few micro-organisms serve us badly.

Nomenclature

The naming of organisms follows strict international rules. Each organism is given two Latin names (both of which are written in italics): the first (which always commences with a capital letter) denotes the organism's genus, and the second (which does not) its species. Thus the common mammalian gut bacterium *Escherichia coli* belongs to the genus *Escherichia* and its specific epithet (ie species name) is coli. The organism is often referred to as *E coli* (ie the generic name is abbreviated to its initial letter, sometimes to its initial two or occasionally three letters to avoid confusion). Similar genera are grouped into families. *Escherichia coli* belongs to a family of gut bacteria called the Enterobacteriaceae (bacterial family names have the distinctive ending 'aceae', and are not italicized).

We can refer only to the genus – for example, *Escherichia*. We can also refer to an unnamed species of this genus as *Escherichia* sp, or to more than one unnamed species as *Escherichia* spp. More informally, we can refer to some important (usually medically important) genera as, for example, salmonellae (for *Salmonella* spp), shigellae (*Shigella* spp) and vibrios (*Vibrio* spp).

Singulars, plurals and adjectival forms

The singular, plural and adjectival form of types of microbes are mainly Latin or Greek, as follows:

- Bacterium, bacteria; bacterial
- Virus, viruses; viral
- Protozoon, protozoa; protozoan
- Alga, algae; algal.

It may seem pedantic to introduce these points of grammar, but few engineers use these terms correctly (and there is no real excuse for this – not even 'microbiological ignorance').

Domains of life

Modern evolutionary biologists now consider a 'Tree of Life' with three 'Domains': the Bacteria, the Archaea and the Eukarya (Woese et al, 1990; see also Gupta, 2000*). This three-domain paradigm (Figure 3.1) shows how all living organisms derived from a single common ancestor (long since extinct or at least as yet undiscovered). Both the Archaea and the Bacteria are prokaryotes – that is, they are single-celled organisms which do not have a clearly defined cell nucleus. The first cell (or cell-like entity) emerged more than 4 billion years ago, and the Bacteria developed from the 'last universal ancestor' (ie a descendent of the first cell) roughly 3 billion years ago. The evolutionary development that set the Bacteria apart from these earlier cells was that of an essentially rigid, completely enclosing, external cell wall (termed a 'sacculus', basically the microbial equivalent of an exoskeleton) which enabled them to withstand a high internal osmotic pressure (ie it prevented the cells from rupturing) (Koch, 2003). The Archaea evolved from the last common ancestor (or one of its non-Bacterial descendents) later; they are a very important group for wastewater engineers as they include the methane producers. The Archaea and the Bacteria thus comprise the micro-organisms that we have for the past 120 years or so called 'bacteria'.

All other life forms (ie all fungi, plants and animals – including ourselves) are eukaryotes (ie their cells have a clearly defined nucleus) and they form the third domain: the Eukarya, which also evolved from the last common ancestor, probably after the Archaea. The domain Eukarya includes the familiar kingdoms of Animalia, Plantae and Fungi (with the helminths within the Animalia), and also the green algae and the protozoa.

This modern view of the Tree of Life emphasizes the huge importance of the microbial world, not only in sheer numbers but also in the ecology of Earth and in the evolution of Life.

The microbes of importance to wastewater treatment engineers come mainly from the Bacteria, some from the Archaea, and some from the Eukarya (eg the pathogenic protozoa – Chapter 2; and the green algae that are the 'workhorses' of facultative and maturation waste stabilization ponds – Chapters 9, 11 and 12). Some higher Eukarya are also important – for example the pathogenic helminths (Chapters 2 and 21) and the plants used in constructed wetlands (Chapter 17).

Good introductory texts on microbiology are Heritage et al (1996, 1999). Suitable reference texts on environmental microbiology are Hurst et al (2001) and Bitton (2002), and on water and wastewater microbiology Water Environment Federation (2001) and Mara and Horan (2003).

VIRUSES

Viruses are extremely small (~20–200 nm) parasitic microbes which can reproduce only by invading a host cell whose reproductive processes they redirect to manufacture more viruses. The structure of viruses is extremely simple: they comprise a core of either DNA or RNA surrounded by a protein 'coat' (or 'envelope').

Once an infectious virus enters a host cell, the virus replicates itself hundreds or thousands of times; these new viruses leave the host cell and in so doing destroy it – and it is the death of these cells that causes disease in the host. Viruses are mostly very specific in their choice of host – plant viruses cannot invade animal cells, for example. Domestic wastewater contains many human viruses, including the rotaviruses and noroviruses that are the major viral causes of diarrhoea (Chapter 2).

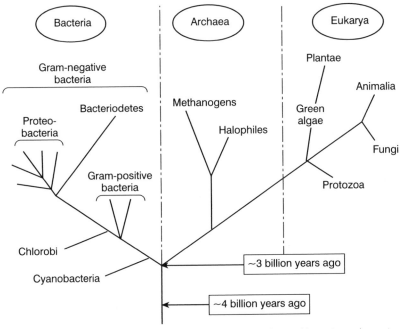

Note: This is a very simplified version which highlights the organisms of importance in wastewater treatment. The branch locations in the bacterial and archaeal domains are not chronological or even indicative as the relative time at which the different groups evolved is not known with any certainty. For simplicity the bacterial domain, in particular, is presented in only the barest outline. The Gram-negative phylum Proteobacteria has five classes (alpha to epsilon) and contains a very large number of the micro-organisms of importance to wastewater treatment engineers – for example, the enteric bacteria (coliforms, *E coli*, salmonellae, shigellae, vibrios, etc), most of the important chemoheterotrophs (eg the 'BOD (biochemical oxygen demand) removers') and chemo-autotrophs (including most of the nitrifiers), and some phototrophs (the purple bacteria, the Chromatiaceae). Other important bacterial phototrophs are the Cyanobacteria and the Chlorobi (containing the Chlorobiaceae). The phylum Bacteroidetes, also Gram-negative, contains the Bacteroides-like anaerobes and the Cytophaga–Flavobacterium complex of aerobic heterotrophs. There are two main phyla of Gram-positive bacteria: the Firmicutes (including *Bacillus* spp and *Clostridium* spp) and the Actinobacteria (eg *Nocardia* spp, implicated in foaming).

Figure 3.1 *The Tree of Life with its three Domains*

Bacterial viruses are called 'bacteriophages' and these can be used to model viral die-off in waste stabilization ponds (Chapter 12).

Viruses do not fit into the three-domain Tree of Life shown in Figure 3.1 – their evolutionary position is not yet fully understood. They may possibly be prokaryotes that have evolved from intracellular parasitic forms (ie prokaryotes that could only reproduce inside the cells of a eukaryotic or prokaryotic host) to become the 'simple' packets of RNA or DNA that they are today. (There is one other group whose evolutionary position is also not understood: the prions, which are protinaceous infectious particles that cause diseases such as the spongiform encephalopathies – scrapie in sheep, 'mad cow disease' and human Creutzfeldt-Jacob diseases, including 'kuru' and new variant CJD.)

BACTERIA AND ARCHAEA

Although the Bacteria and Archaea are as different, in evolutionary terms, from each other as they both are from the Eukarya (Figure 3.1), they are considered together in this section since they are both prokaryotic and their growth follows the same rules. In general (and unless otherwise indicated) the terms 'bacterium', 'bacteria' and 'bacterial' are used in this book to refer to both the Bacteria and the Archaea – strictly speaking, of course, it would be better to refer to them as prokaryotes (but sometimes scientific exactitude can be too confusing, or at least too obfuscatory).

Shape, size and structure

Bacteria and Archaea are small, just a few micrometres (μm) in size, and their mass is around a picogram (pg – ie 10^{-12} g), although some 'giant' bacteria do exist (for example, *Thiomargarita namibiensis* is 100–300 μm in diameter; Schulz, 2002), and they come in several different shapes (Figure 3.2). To see them we need to use a microscope; for our engineering purposes a light microscope is sufficient, with an oil-immersion x100 objective lens and a x10 eye-piece to give a magnification of x1000. Unless we use a phase-contrast microscope, we need to stain the bacteria before looking at them under the microscope. The staining procedure most commonly used is the Gram stain (devised in 1884 by Hans Christian Gram, a Danish bacteriologist); illustrated details of the procedure are given by the University of Leicester (2002*). Gram-positive bacteria appear purple and Gram-negative bacteria red when stained according to this procedure. This difference is very important, not just as a staining technique, but because Gram-positive and Gram-negative bacteria are different in a much more fundamental way: Gram-positive bacteria have a cell wall structure comprising a single membrane (so they are called 'monoderms'), whereas Gram-negative bacteria have a double-membrane cell wall structure ('diderms'). All Archaea are Gram-positive and so, in evolutionary terms, Gram-positive Bacteria are closer to the Archaea than Gram-negative Bacteria are (Gupta, 2000*).

Environmental requirements

Bacteria vary widely in their environmental requirements and preferences. For example, some bacteria can only grow in the presence of oxygen – the 'obligate aerobes'; some can only grow in its absence – the 'obligate anaerobes'; and some can grow in both its presence and in its absence, although growth is better in its presence – the 'facultative anaerobes' (or simply 'facultative bacteria'). Most bacteria cannot use carbon dioxide as a source of cell carbon, but some can (and prefer to do so); those that cannot are termed 'heterotrophs'

cocci   streptococci   staphylococci

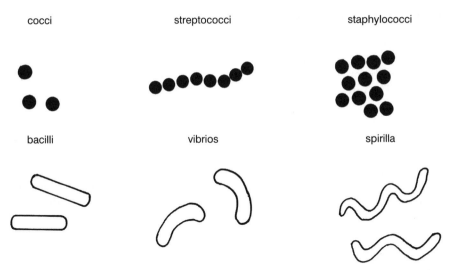

bacilli   vibrios   spirilla

Figure 3.2 *Common Bacterial Shapes (cocci are ~1 μm in diameter, and bacilli are typically 1 x 3–6 μm)*

and those that can are 'autotrophs'. Some bacteria can photosynthesize, and these are either 'photoheterotrophs' or 'photo-autotrophs'; however, most bacteria cannot photosynthesize and they are therefore either 'chemoheterotrophs' or 'chemo-autotrophs'.

Temperature is a very important environmental parameter. Most bacteria grow well in the temperature range 15–40 degC and are termed 'mesophils'; some grow best at lower temperatures – the 'psychrophils'; and some require much higher temperatures (some even close to the boiling point of water) – the 'thermophils'. In wastewaters in tropical and subtropical regions most bacteria are, as would be expected, mesophilic.

The pH of the environment in which bacteria grow is another important environmental parameter. Most bacteria prefer near neutral or slightly alkaline conditions, around pH 6.5–8.5; some can tolerate pH >9 (eg *Vibrio cholerae*, the causative agent of cholera); and some generate very acid conditions (eg *Thiobacillus thioparus* which produces sulphuric acid at pH <2 and so causes rapid sewer crown corrosion in warm climates).

Salt is an environmental parameter of importance, for wastewater treatment engineers, only in that freshwater and faecal bacteria cannot grow in very saline waters (the sea, for example; this is relevant when treated wastewaters are discharged into coastal waters – Chapter 4). Marine bacteria, in contrast, are 'halophils'.

Domestic wastewater fortunately contains roughly the right balance of nutrients for bacterial growth – a BOD:N:P ratio of ~100:5:1. The presence of industrial effluents can alter this ratio and the wastewater may need nitrogen and/or phosphorus supplements.

Bacterial growth kinetics

Bacteria grow by binary fission: a cell divides into two daughter cells. These grow and each divides into two more cells; so the sequence of cell numbers originating from one cell is 1, 2, 4, 8, 16 and so on, reaching 2^n after n divisions. The rate of growth (ie the number of divisions per unit time) depends on many factors in the immediate environment of the dividing cells, as described above. Often one factor is growth-limiting; this could be oxygen (for aerobes), temperature (which is why we store food in a refrigerator), a suitable source of carbon (or nitrogen or phosphorus, or an essential micronutrient such as a vitamin), or too low or too high a pH.

If a bacterium takes T minutes to divide into two, then it takes nT minutes to multiply to 2^n cells. This type of growth is *logarithmic* (or *exponential*) and it is described by the equation:

$$N_t = N_0 \exp(\mu t)$$

(3.1)

where N_t and N_0 are the number of cells present at time t (minutes) and initially, respectively; and μ is the specific growth rate, which has units of reciprocal time (usually day^{-1}, but here $minute^{-1}$). The term 'exp' means 'e to the power of what follows in brackets, where e is the base of Naperian logarithms (denoted 'ln') and equals ~2.7183.

If $t = T$ (which is the doubling, or mean generation, time), then from equation 3.1 with $N_t = 2N_0$:

$$\mu = (\ln 2)/T = 0.69/T$$

(3.2)

The bacterial growth curve

If we introduce a few bacteria into, say, a litre of soluble waste, and if no further additions of waste are made, the bacteria will typically exhibit four distinct phases of growth (Figure 3.3). The first is the *lag phase*, during which time cell numbers do not increase; the bacteria are, however, internally active, manufacturing if necessary any intracellular catalysts ('enzymes') that they may require in order to be able to oxidize the waste. Next comes the *exponential phase* in which logarithmic growth occurs; during this phase the bacteria lay down food reserves within their cells which they may use when there is little or no food left in their environment. The bacteria are now growing as fast as they are able to in the waste; equation 3.1 is therefore rewritten as:

$$N = N_0 \exp(\mu_{max} t)$$

(3.3)

where μ_{max} is the maximum specific growth rate.

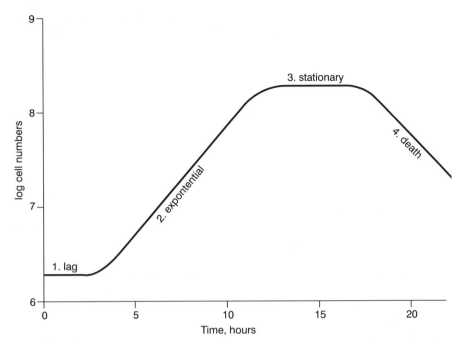

Figure 3.3 *The Bacterial Batch-culture Growth Curve (axis numbers are illustrative only)*

The exponential phase ceases, often abruptly, either because the supply of an essential nutrient has been exhausted or because there has been an accumulation of toxic end-products of bio-oxidation (an example of the latter is the accumulation of acid that is an end-product of the bio-oxidation of sugars; the pH falls to a growth-inhibiting level). In the ensuing *stationary phase* the number of new cells is approximately balanced by those that die, so that the cell population does not change. When the death rate exceeds the growth rate, the culture enters the *death phase* and the population steadily declines. During both the stationary and death phases there is a substantial proportion of cells which neither die nor subdivide; they exist by utilizing the intracellular food reserves laid down during exponential growth, a process known as 'endogenous respiration'. When a cell has depleted its food reserves, it starts to oxidize itself; this process, known as 'autolysis' (ie self-destruction), leads of course to death.

Continuous culture
The microbiological processes used for wastewater treatment operate continuously, 24 hours a day for 7 days a week and 52 weeks a year, rather than as a batch process. Bacterial growth in a continuous reactor occurs at a rate less than the maximum growth in batch culture – that is $\mu < \mu_{max}$. The value of μ depends on the value of the growth-limiting substrate; this may

often be the wastewater strength, expressed in terms of BOD (Chapter 1), but it could be another parameter (such as ammonia, if nitrification is being considered – see later in this chapter). The Monod equation is used to determine the value of μ:

$$\mu = \mu_{max} \left(\frac{L}{L + K_L} \right) - b$$

(3.4)

where L is the BOD in the reactor, mg/l; K_L is the Monod 'half saturation' constant (= the value of L when $\mu = \mu_{max}/2$), mg/l; and b is the endogenous decay rate, which has the same units as μ, usually day^{-1}.

First-order BOD removal kinetics (Chapter 5) are generally used for microbiological reactor design, rather than equation 3.4, although the latter is used in activated sludge design and also for nitrification in aerated lagoons (Chapter 20). Monod kinetics have recently been applied to facultative waste stabilization ponds (Kayombo et al, 2003*).

Equations 3.2 and 3.4 combined are important in reactor design, as they give the minimum cell retention time in a continuous-flow microbiological reactor at which cell growth is balanced by the number of cells leaving the reactor. If the cell retention time is less than this, then the cells will be exponentially 'washed out' of the reactor and reactor failure quickly ensues. Wastewater treatment engineers have to ensure that the cell retention time in the treatment units they design is longer than this minimum value.

Anabolism and catabolism

Bacteria oxidize wastes to provide themselves with sufficient energy to enable them to synthesize the complex molecules such as proteins and polysaccharides which are needed to build new cells. Thus bacterial metabolism has two component parts: catabolism ('breaking down') for energy and anabolism ('building up') for synthesis. The verbal 'equation'

wastes + oxygen $\xrightarrow{\text{bacteria}}$ oxidized waste + new bacteria

is instructive but oversimplified in that the anabolic and catabolic reactions are not distinguished; nor is there mention of autolysis, which is an important form of catabolism. The following three equations describe these processes separately:

- *Catabolism*

$$C_xH_yO_zN + O_2 \xrightarrow{\text{bacteria}} CO_2 + H_2O + NH_3 + energy$$

- *Anabolism*

$$C_xH_yO_zN + energy \xrightarrow{bacteria} C_5H_7NO_2 \text{ (ie bacterial cells)}$$

- *Autolysis*

$$C_5H_7NO_2 + 5O_2 \xrightarrow{bacteria} 5CO_2 + NH_3 + 2H_2O + energy$$

As a general guide ~1/3 of the available BOD is used in catabolic reactions and ~2/3 in anabolic reactions (Figure 3.4). The equation for autolysis does not proceed to completion since approximately 20–25 per cent of the cell mass is resistant to bacterial degradation.

Bacteria in wastewater treatment

Wastewater contains many billions of bacteria, and most of these are faecal bacteria. However, these bacteria, once outside their normal habitat (ie when they are in the 'extra-intestinal' environment), are unable to survive for very long. This is because they are outcompeted by the large numbers of *saprophytic* bacteria which grow naturally and profusely in the nutrient-rich aquatic environment of a microbiological wastewater treatment reactor. These 'saprophytes' obtain their energy, cell carbon and other essential nutrients from the organic and inorganic compounds in the wastewater. They are very well adapted to this environment, whereas the faecal bacteria are not – and so they

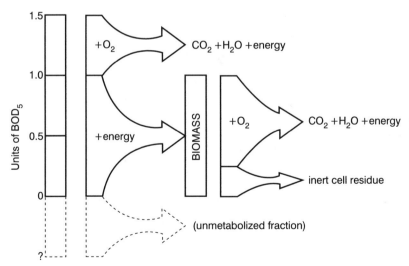

Note: In a real (finite time) continuous microbiological reactor some of the organic matter (ie BOD) in the influent escapes oxidation; in batch culture at infinite time the unmetabolized fraction is zero.

Figure 3.4 *The Catabolic, Anabolic and Autolytic Reactions of Aerobic Microbiological Oxidation*

die, some quickly and some more slowly (the kinetics of faecal bacterial die-off is important in the design of maturation ponds – Chapter 12).

The most commonly isolated saprophytic bacteria in aerobic microbiological treatment systems are Gram-negative, facultative, heterotrophic rods. They mostly belong to the genera *Achromobacter, Bacillus, Flavobacterium, Pseudomonas* and *Zooglea*, together with the non-faecal coliforms (see below); all these bacteria are Proteobacteria (Figure 3.1).

Nitrification

Nitrification is the oxidation of ammonium to nitrate, which is done by two groups of obligately aerobic autotrophic proteobacteria. First ammonium is oxidized to nitrite by the ammonium oxidizers – for example, *Nitrosomonas* spp and *Nitrospira* spp:

$$NH_4^+ + 1.5O_2 \rightarrow NO_2^- + H_2O + 2H^+$$

The nitrite so produced is then oxidized to nitrate by the nitrate oxidizers, typically Nitrobacter spp, with the oxygen atom added to the nitrite ion coming from water (rather than from molecular oxygen):

$$NO_2^- + H_2O \rightarrow NO_3^- (= NOO_2) + 2H^+$$

A more descriptive equation for overall nitrification, which shows the formation of nitrifying bacterial cells ($C_5H_7NO_2$), is the following (Horan, 1990):

$$NH_4^+ + 1.83O_2 + 1.98HCO_3^- \rightarrow 0.021C_5H_7NO_2 + 0.98NO_3^- + 1.04H_2O + 1.88H_2CO_3$$

This shows that 1 mole of ammonium-N (ie 14 g N) requires 1.83 moles of oxygen (58.6 g O_2) for nitrification – that is the nitrification oxygen demand is 4.2 g O_2 per g ammonium-N. However, this equation does not take into account the fact that the oxygen used in the oxidation of nitrite to nitrate comes from water, not molecular oxygen. To allow for this, $0.98H_2O$ must be added to each side of the equation:

$$NH_4^+ + 1.34O_2 + 1.98HCO_3^- + 0.98H_2O \rightarrow 0.021C_5H_7NO_2 + 0.98NO_3^- + 2.02H_2O + 1.88H_2CO_3$$

This equation shows that the nitrification oxygen demand is 3.1 g O_2 per g N. Most process engineers use 4.2 g O_2 per g N, but this overestimates the actual nitrification oxygen demand by around 35 per cent.

The above equations show that only 0.021 mole of nitrifying bacterial cells are produced per mole of ammonium-N nitrified, or 0.17 g of cells per g N nitrified. This very low yield reflects the fact that nitrifying bacteria grow very slowly (see Chapter 20). The equations also show that the nitrification of 1 mole of ammonium-N consumes 1.98 moles of bicarbonate alkalinity, or 8.6 g of HCO_3^- per g N nitrified. Expressing alkalinity in its usual unit of $CaCO_3$ is equivalent to 7.1 g $CaCO_3$ alkalinity per g N nitrified (1 g of alkalinity as $CaCO_3 = 1.22$ g HCO_3^-). If the wastewater to be nitrified does not contain this amount of alkalinity, then alkalinity must be added (usually as sodium bicarbonate); otherwise the reaction will stop (and not restart until sufficient alkalinity is added).

Denitrification

Denitrification is the reduction of nitrate to nitrogen gas. It is an anaerobic (or at least an anoxic) reaction achieved by many species of anaerobic and facultative heterotrophic proteobacteria, including those in the genera *Achromobacter*, *Alcaligenes*, *Micrococcus*, *Pseudomonas* and *Thiobacillus*. Nitrate may not always be reduced to N_2 – a variety of nitrogen-based gases may be produced.

The equation for denitrification with, for example, methanol as the carbon source is (Horan, 1990):

$$NO_3^- + 1.08CH_3OH + 0.24H_2CO_3 \rightarrow 0.06C_5H_7NO_2 + 0.47N_2 + 1.68H_2O + HCO_3^-$$

This equation shows not only that oxygen is *not* required for denitrification, but also (and more importantly) that bicarbonate alkalinity is generated as a result of denitrification – nearly half the alkalinity consumed by nitrification is regenerated by denitrification; this is important in combined nitrification–denitrification systems (as now practised, for example, in the 'enhanced pond systems' in Melbourne, Australia – Chapter 9).

Photosynthetic bacteria

Purple and green anaerobic phototrophs are found in facultative ponds (see 'Purple ponds' in Chapter 11). In this habitat they are important as they oxidize sulphides entering the facultative pond from the preceding anaerobic pond (or sewer), and they thus protect us from odour and the pond algae from the toxic effects of sulphides. They do not produce oxygen during photosynthesis (as do algae – see below and Chapter 11) as they oxidize sulphides to sulphur, rather than water to oxygen.

Anaerobic digestion

Anaerobic digestion is a very important process in wastewater treatment in warm climates. It occurs in anaerobic ponds (Chapter 10) and UASBs (Chapter 18) as the major process in conjunction with sedimentation, and it also occurs in primary facultative ponds (Chapter 11) and constructed wetlands (Chapter 17). Anaerobic digestion is achieved by obligately anaerobic bacteria and it is essentially the conversion, under anaerobic conditions, of settled wastewater solids to 'biogas' – that is methane and carbon dioxide. Biogas is a valuable fuel which, at large plants (eg the modern waste stabilization ponds at Melbourne, Australia – Chapter 9), can be profitably recovered to generate electricity.

Anaerobic digestion proceeds in four stages:

1   *Hydrolysis*: The hydrolysis of complex wastewater organics (such as proteins, polysaccharides and fats);
2   *Acidogenesis*: the anaerobic oxidation of fatty acids and alcohols and the fermentation of amino acids and carbohydrates to volatile fatty acids (eg butyrates and propionates) and hydrogen gas;
3   *Acetogenesis*: the conversion of butyrate and propionates to acetates; and
4   *Methanogenesis*: the conversions of acetates, and hydrogen and carbon dioxide, to methane.

Many anaerobic and facultative bacterial species are responsible for Stage 1, such as *Bacillus*, *Clostridium*, *Proteus*, *Micrococcus*, *Staphylococcus* and *Vibrio*.

The acidogens, responsible for Stage 2, include *Butyrovibrio*, *Clostridium* and *Eubacterium*; they convert sugars to volatile fatty acids:

$$C_6H_{12}O_6 \text{ (glucose)} + 2H_2O \rightarrow 2CH_3OOH \text{ (acetic acid)} + 4H_2$$

When the concentration of H_2 becomes high glucose is converted into propionic and butyric acids:

$$C_6H_{12}O_6 + 2H_2O \rightarrow 2CH_3CH_2COOH \text{ (propionic acid)} + 2CO_2 + 2H_2$$

$$C_6H_{12}O_6 \rightarrow CH_3(CH_2)_2COOH \text{ (butyric acid)} + 2CO_2 + 4H_2$$

These acids are converted in Stage 3 to acetic acid by, for example, *Synthobacter* and *Synthrophomonas*:

$$CH_3CH_2COOH + 2H_2O \rightarrow CH_3COOH + CO_2 + 3H_2$$

$$CH_3(CH_2)_2COOH + 2H_2O \rightarrow 2CH_3COOH + 2H_2$$

Stage 4 is the conversion of acetates to methane and carbon dioxide, and of hydrogen and carbon dioxide to methane:

$$CH_3COOH \rightarrow CH_4 + CO_2$$

$$CO_2 + 4H_2 \rightarrow CH_4 + 2H_2O$$

The methanogens are all Archaea of, for example, the genera *Methanothrix*, *Methanosarcina* and *Methanococcus*. They are very slow growing, with generation times of ~24 hours – much longer than the bacterial groups involved in Stages 1–3 – and methanogenesis is thus the rate-limiting stage in anaerobic digestion. The methanogens are also more sensitive than the other groups to environmental stress (eg too low a pH) and, in high-sulphate wastewaters, they are outcompeted by sulphate-reducing bacteria, such as *Desulfovibrio* spp, for hydrogen and acetate (which the sulphate-reducers use in their reduction of sulphate to sulphides – Chapter 10).

Overall the anaerobic treatment of domestic wastewater in warm climates is extremely advantageous, and high removals of BOD (70–80 per cent) at short retention times (8–24 hours) are achieved in anaerobic ponds and UASBs.

Faecal indicator bacteria

The concept of faecal indicator bacteria was developed in the late 19th century to assess the efficacy of *water* treatment: if bacteria of exclusively faecal origin are found in a water, then we *know* that the water has been polluted by faeces and that it *may*, therefore, contain pathogenic faecal bacteria (ie those in Category II, Chapter 2). Conversely, if treated drinking water is shown *not* to contain any faecal indicator bacteria, then it is *unlikely* to contain any pathogenic micro-organisms. Of course, with wastewaters the situation is different: we *know* that wastewaters are faecally polluted – they contain faeces and faecal micro-organisms, including faecal pathogens of most, if not all, of Categories I–V. We use the numbers of faecal indicator bacteria in wastewaters, therefore, not to indicate faecal pollution, but to indicate faecal pathogen removals in wastewater treatment processes, and to estimate the health risks in wastewater re-use (Chapters 21 and 22). This works very well for faecal bacterial pathogens, quite well for faecal viral pathogens, but not at all well for faecal protozoan and helminthic pathogens.

The requirements for an 'ideal' faecal indicator bacterium, as applied to wastewater (rather than drinking water), are that:

• it should be exclusively faecal in origin,
• its numbers in wastewater should be greater than those of faecal viral and bacterial pathogens,
• its removal in wastewater treatment processes should be close to that of faecal viral and bacterial pathogens, and
• it should be simple and inexpensive to count its numbers reliably and accurately.

As might be expected, no bacterium always meets all these requirements, but one comes very close: one (and only one) of the coliform bacteria, namely *Escherichia coli*.

Coliform bacteria

The early *water* bacteriologists identified the coliform group of bacteria as faecal indicator organisms. This group was considered in two parts: 'total coliforms' and 'faecal coliforms', with the former comprising both non-faecal and faecal coliforms. It was originally considered in this way because counting faecal coliforms was initially a two-stage process: first the number of total coliforms in a drinking water sample was determined and then, if any of these were present, the number of faecal coliforms was determined (many water bacteriologists still use the same basic procedure today). However, with wastewater, it is only the faecal coliforms that are relevant (it is basically meaningless to report total coliform numbers in wastewaters, especially tropical and subtropical wastewaters).

Almost all coliforms, faecal and non-faecal alike, oxidize the disaccharide lactose with the production of acid and gas at 37°C (human body temperature) in the presence of bile salts (which are used to inhibit non-intestinal bacteria, although it is now more common to use a surface-active agent, such as Triton X100, with similar growth-inhibiting properties). Lactose comprises equal proportions of the two monosaccharides glucose and galactose, and only coliform bacteria possess the enzyme β-galactosidase which enables it to break down galactose. Thus the modern definition of a coliform bacterium is one that possesses β-galactosidase (or, strictly speaking, the gene that codes for this enzyme). Only faecal coliforms can break down lactose to acid and gas at the higher temperature of 44°C. However, this is true only in temperate regions (and even there not always true); in tropical and subtropical regions some non-faecal coliforms can produce acid and gas from lactose at 44°C, and some true faecal coliforms may not produce any gas from lactose (ie they are 'anaerogenic'). Thus the concept of faecal coliforms is not strictly applicable in warm climates, although the majority of acid and gas producers at 44°C are indeed faecal in origin. Even so, it is now considered much better to count non-faecal coliforms (due to the small proportions of false positives and false negatives – that is non-faecal coliforms growing at 44°C, and some faecal coliforms either not able to grow at this elevated temperature or unable to produce gas from lactose, respectively), but rather to count the single coliform bacterium that really is exclusively faecal in origin. This bacterium is *Escherichia coli*.

Escherichia coli

The early water bacteriologists counted (or, more correctly, tried to count) the bacterium then known as *Bacterium coli communis* (Smith, 1895 – this is the earliest reference to a faecal indicator bacterium). In fact, it was the difficulty of counting only this bacterium that led, in the early 20th century, to the use of total and faecal coliforms to assess the quality of drinking waters, as these could be counted with at least reasonable reliability. *Bacterium coli communis* is now called *Escherichia coli*. Like all coliforms, *E coli* has the enzyme β-galactosidase but, uniquely amongst the coliforms, it also has the enzyme β-glucuronidase (which it uses to break down glucuronate to glucose and uronic acid). Modern media to detect or count *E coli* contain a chromogenic substrate to detect this enzyme and thus give the resulting colonies of *E coli* a distinct colour (usually blue or purple); several such media are commercially available (eg 'Chromagar E coli', on or in which *E coli* forms blue colonies when incubated at 37°C for 24 h; Chromagar, 2002*). Given the ease with which specifically *E coli* counts can be obtained, it is now time (especially in warm climates, but also in temperate climates) to cease counting faecal coliforms and to determine only the numbers of *E coli*. This removes the problem of faecal coliform counts including some non-faecal coliforms since *E coli* is an exclusively faecal micro-organism (and the only faecal coliform currently so recognized – see Edberg et al, 2000*; Leclerc et al, 2001*).

In this book references to faecal coliforms in standards and guidelines (eg those of the Council of the European Communities and the World Health Organization) have been replaced by references to *E coli*. This permits a better interpretation of the intent of these standards and guidelines (and it is to be hoped that future revisions of them will use *E coli* rather than faecal coliforms). However, when reported results of faecal coliform numbers (obtained experimentally or from monitoring programmes) are referred to, this change is not made and the reported designations of faecal coliforms and 'FC numbers' are retained.

PROTOZOA

Protozoa are single-celled eukaryotes. A few are important human pathogens – *Giardia*, *Cryptosporidium*, *Cyclospora* and *Entamoeba*, for example, are major excreta-related pathogens which are consequently present in domestic wastewaters (Category I, Chapter 2). (The genus *Plasmodium* contains the malaria parasites, but malaria is a water-related, rather than an excreta-related, disease.) However, most protozoa are non-pathogenic and very widely distributed in nature.

The protozoa can be conveniently classified into three groups: amoebae, ciliates and flagellates. The last two groups are important in wastewater treatment: flagellates in the class Zoomastigophora are present in very large numbers in wastewater treatment processes, as are many species of ciliates. Flagellate biomass is generally higher than that of the ciliates, although there is a greater species diversity of the latter.

Flagellates generally grow heterotrophically; in wastewater treatment reactors they are thus in competition with the more efficient bacterial heterotrophs. The ciliates display a wider range of morphology and nutrition: some are 'free-swimming', others are 'crawling' organisms, and yet others have a stalk which attaches to particulate material (such as an activated sludge floc) (Figure 3.5). Ciliate nutrition is mainly by 'phagocytosis' – that is they engulf other microbes (bacteria, algae and other protozoa) and digest them enzymatically (an early form of 'eating' as we know it).

Protozoa have been extensively studied in conventional wastewater treatment processes such as activated sludge and biofilters (Chapters 19 and 20). A healthy protozoan population in activated sludge aeration tanks

(a)   (b)   (c)

(d)   (e)

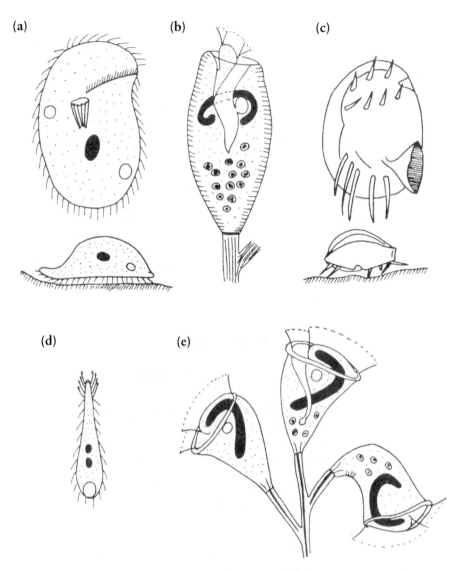

Source: Water Pollution Control Laboratory (1968)

Figure 3.5 *Five of the Commonest Ciliated Protozoa Found in Wastewater Treatment Works: (a)* Chilodonella uncinata, *(b)* Opercula microdiscum, *(c)* Aspidisca costata, *(d)* Trachlophyllum pusillum *and (e)* Carchesium polypinum; *(a) and (c) are crawling ciliates, (b) and (e) stalked ciliates and (d) a free-swimming ciliate*

significantly improves the treatment efficiency – effluent suspended solids concentrations are ~70 per cent less with ciliated protozoa than without them.

Ciliated protozoa have recently been shown to be responsible for some of the removal of *Cryptosporidium* oocysts in constructed wetlands (Chapter 17)

(Stott et al, 2001*, 2003*). Laboratory tests showed ingestion rates of >50 oocysts per hour by *Paramecium*, although isolates from constructed wetlands ingested 4–10 oocysts per hour. The role of ciliated protozoa in waste stabilization ponds (Chapters 9–12) has yet to be determined.

ALGAE

The micro-algae in facultative and maturation waste stabilization ponds (Chapters 11 and 12) are single-celled Eukarya. The cells are green as, like the leaves of higher plants, they contain large amounts of chlorophyll, the pigment that captures light energy in photosynthesis. The algae use this energy to fix carbon dioxide which is their main source of carbon (so algae are photo-autotrophs), although they can grow photoheterotrophically on simple organic compounds (such as acetate). During photosynthesis oxygen is produced from water, and in facultative and maturation ponds this is the main source of oxygen used by the bacterial heterotrophs in the ponds for the removal of BOD. The algae, when they are photosynthesizing rapidly, induce a high pH in the ponds (especially in maturation ponds); the pH can rise to >9.4, which is critical for faecal bacterial die-off in ponds. Further details are given in Chapters 11 and 12.

HELMINTHS

Helminths (worms) are important because a few of them cause disease (Categories III–V, Chapter 2) and because a group of them are highly tolerant of pollution and oxygen depletion in freshwaters (see below). All worms fall into one of three types: nematodes (roundworms), cestodes (flatworms) and trematodes (flukes). Many, especially those that are pathogenic, have quite complicated life cycles, often both in and outwith the human body, but despite this they are extremely successful human parasites: around one-third of the world's population (ie ~2 billion people) is infected with one or more worms. As a result, worm egg numbers in wastewaters in developing countries (in which almost all the worm infections occur) are generally high – up to a few thousand/l in newly sewered communities, although over time (as the opportunities for reinfection decrease as a result of more and more communities being sewered) the numbers decline to <1000 and eventually to <100 or even <10/l.

Egg numbers in treated wastewaters must be reduced to very low levels when the treated wastewaters are used for crop irrigation and/or fish culture (Chapters 4, 21 and 22). For crop irrigation the number of human intestinal nematode eggs (ie those of the geohelminths – Category III, Chapter 2) should be ≤1/l or, if children under the age of 15 are exposed, ≤0.1/l. For fish culture trematode eggs (ie those of the water-based helminths – Category V) must be absent as these worms multiply tens of thousands of times in their first intermediate aquatic host (an aquatic snail), and thus the eggs from one person can potentially infect many hundreds of people.

Well illustrated on-line reference texts include Muller (2001*) for human worm diseases and Ayres and Mara (1996*) for counting the numbers of human intestinal nematode eggs in wastewaters.

FRESHWATER MICRO-INVERTEBRATES

Invertebrates are animals without backbones and in clean unpolluted streams, rivers and lakes there are many different types of small invertebrates. These may be present as adult and juvenile forms, or only the latter (such as larvae and nymphs). Some of these 'micro-invertebrates' are very sensitive to aquatic pollutants, and some are very tolerant of pollution. We can therefore use the micro-invertebrate fauna of a freshwater to assess its 'health' – that is to determine biologically the extent of pollution. The number of different micro-invertebrates present can be used to develop a 'biotic index' of freshwater quality (and this is used to complement physicochemical water quality – Chapter 4).

A large amount of work has been done on assessing freshwater quality in this way, mainly in industrialized countries (eg Welch, 1992; Wright et al, 2000; Adams, 2002; Greenwood-Smith, 2002), with much less application in developing countries (Madhou, 2000; see also Girgin et al, 2003*). In many cases there is very little or no information on micro-invertebrates in unpolluted waters in developing countries; and, even though many waterbodies are seriously polluted, there is not much information on the biological quality of polluted waters. Dudgeon (2002*) details the adverse impacts of human activities on aquatic biodiversity in monsoonal Asia: pollution, excessive exploitation (ie overharvesting), and conversion of riverine wetlands to agriculture have led to dramatic decreases in biodiversity – fewer riverine birds, endangered turtle populations, declining fish populations, and so on.

Biotic index for tropical freshwaters

A simplified biotic index for tropical and subtropical freshwaters is presented by Van Damme (2001*). Ten groups of micro-invertebrates are used, and these are placed into three categories based on their sensitivity to, or tolerance of, pollution (Figure 3.6 and Table 3.1). The presence and relative abundance of members of these groups in a water sample define an approximate biotic index (on a scale of 0–10, with 0 indicating gross pollution and 10 indicating excellent water quality) (Table 3.2).

Procedures for sampling and analysis (ie micro-invertebrate identification using a stereoscopic microscope) are given by Van Damme (2001*) and also in *Standard Methods* (American Public Health Association, 1998). The procedures are very simple and require only minimal equipment – indeed obtaining biotic indices as described by Van Damme is a very good biology class project for secondary school students and university engineering students (see De Pauw et al, 1999).

Indicator Group I: Macroinvertebrate groups highly sensitive to oxygen depletion/pollution

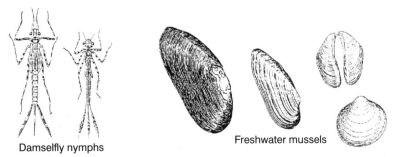

Damselfly nymphs   Freshwater mussels

Indicator Group II: Macroinvertebrate groups moderately sensitive to oxygen depletion/pollut

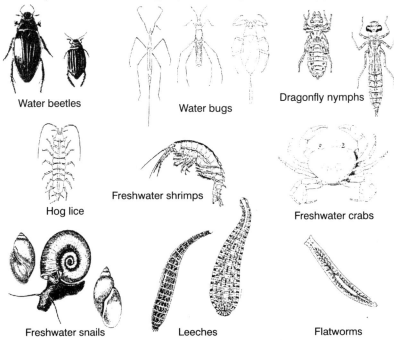

Water beetles   Water bugs   Dragonfly nymphs

Hog lice   Freshwater shrimps   Freshwater crabs

Freshwater snails   Leeches   Flatworms

Indicator Group III: Macroinvertebrate groups little sensitive to oxygen depletion/pollution

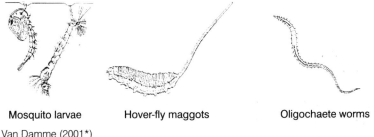

Mosquito larvae   Hover-fly maggots   Oligochaete worms

Source: Van Damme (2001*)

Figure 3.6 *Micro-invertebrates Used to Assess the Biological Quality of Tropical Waters*

Table 3.1 *Micro-invertebrate Groups Used to Assess the Biological Quality of Tropical Waters*

Indicator group	Sensitivity to oxygen depletion	Micro-invertebrates
I	High	Damselfly nymphs
		Freshwater mussels
II	Moderate	Water beetles, water bugs, hog lice
		Dragonfly nymphs
		Freshwater snails
		Shrimps and crabs
		Leeches, flatworms
III	Low	Mosquito larvae
		Hoverfly maggots
		Oligochaete worms

Source: Van Damme (2001*)

Table 3.2 *Simplified Biotic Index for Tropical Waters*

Biotic index	Water quality	Micro-invertebrate groups present[a]
9–10	Excellent	Many Group I
7–8	Good	Some Group I
5–6	Marginal	No Group I, many Group II
3–4	Bad	Some Group II, some Group III
0–2	Very bad	Only Group III

Note: [a] See Table 3.1
Source: Van Damme (2001*)

4

Effluent Quality

WASTEWATER TREATMENT OBJECTIVES

Wastewater treatment must be done for a specified purpose – for example, to produce an effluent suitable for agricultural or aquacultural reuse (or both), or to produce an effluent that can be safely discharged into inland or coastal waters. Wastewater treatment plant designers have to know what is going to happen to the effluent – re-use or discharge – before they design the plant, as the effluent quality requirements will vary accordingly.

Effluent quality requirements, often termed effluent quality standards, are set by regulatory agencies that are empowered by legislation to make such regulations – environmental protection agencies, for example. The regulations that these agencies make are legally binding on the authority responsible for wastewater treatment. Regulatory agencies have a duty, either explicitly defined in the governing legislation or at any rate implicitly, to set sensible regulations. Unfortunately, in many developing countries not all such regulations are as sensible as they should be (Johnstone and Horan, 1994, 1996*), and this also occurs in industrialized countries (Dolan, 1995; Mara, 1996*). Wastewater treatment engineers need to understand how effluent quality standards should be set properly so that, if necessary, they can have a rational dialogue with the regulatory agency to ensure that it does not impose standards that are too high. This is extremely important since compliance with standards that are too high requires an unnecessary expenditure of money (generally on inappropriate high-tech wastewater treatment systems – see von Sperling and Chernicharo, 2002*), and the people who ultimately pay this unnecessarily large amount of money are the local people who generate the wastewater that is treated to too high a standard. Incomes fall, and falling incomes mean poorer health, even deaths. In the US, for example, Miller and Conko (2001*) report that one death is estimated to result from every US$7.25 million spent on regulatory costs through this income effect. As these authors note, 'the expression "regulatory overkill" is not merely a figure of speech'.

If a regulator insists on a very strict national standard for one or more parameters prior to river discharge, wastewater treatment may be so expensive that no city can afford to treat its wastewater. From the regulator's perspective this is a self-defeating situation: treatment plants are not built and the regulator has no effluents to regulate. As regulators are meant to protect the environment, this is a truly nonsensical situation: no treatment plants means continued discharges of untreated wastewater, and hence unabated freshwater pollution, continued risks to human health, and no environmental protection whatsoever.

WASTEWATER RE-USE

Using treated wastewaters for crop irrigation or for fishpond fertilization is a very sensible thing to do, especially in water-short areas. However, it must not cause any excess transmission of excreta-related disease, and therefore the wastewaters must be treated to an appropriate microbiological quality. A detailed discussion on what constitutes an appropriate microbiological quality is given in Chapter 21 for agricultural re-use and in Chapter 22 for aquacultural re-use. Here only the basic principles are addressed.

The re-use of untreated wastewaters in agriculture or aquaculture is known to cause an excess transmission of certain excreta-related diseases, especially those in Categories II, III and IV – the bacterial and geohelminthic diseases, and the water-based trematode diseases (Chapter 2). Thus treatment to remove faecal bacterial pathogens and human intestinal nematode and trematode eggs from the wastewater is essential – but removal to what degree? The answer to this question is that they must be removed to a level which does not cause excess disease in the people working in the wastewater-irrigated fields or wastewater-fertilized aquaculture ponds, or in those who consume the wastewater-irrigated crops or wastewater-fertilized aquacultural produce (fish, for example). The next question is obvious: what is the level that does not cause excess infection? Expressed another way, this question means: what are the safe minimum microbiological requirements for wastewater treatment? The answer to this question is certainly *not* the United States Environmental Protection Agency (USEPA)/United States Agency for International Development (USAID) requirement that, for wastewater-irrigated salad crops and vegetables eaten uncooked, treated wastewaters should contain zero *E coli* per 100 ml (Environmental Protection Agency, 1992), since this is the bacteriological requirement for drinking water and therefore a good example of regulatory overkill.

The World Health Organization has produced guidelines for the microbiological quality of treated wastewaters used in agriculture and aquaculture (WHO, 1989*, 2004*; see also Blumenthal et al, 2000*). These are:

1   for 'restricted' irrigation – that is the irrigation of all crops except salad crops and vegetables eaten uncooked:
    ≤ 1 human intestinal nematode eggs/l (reduced to ≤ 0.1 eggs/l when children under 15 years are exposed), and
    $\leq 10^5$ *E coli*/100 ml.

The nematodes are *Ascaris, Trichuris* and the human hookworms (Chapter 2).

2 for 'unrestricted' irrigation – that is including salad crops and vegetables eaten raw:
≤ 1 human intestinal nematode eggs/l (also reduced to ≤ 0.1 eggs/l when children under 15 years are exposed through their fieldworker-parents bringing home 'unrestricted' produce directly from the fields), and
≤ 1000 *E coli*/100 ml.

The epidemiological and experimental evidence for these guidelines is reviewed in Chapter 21, which also gives risk calculations, based on quantitative microbial risk analysis procedures, to support the *E coli* guideline of $\leq 1000/100$ ml for unrestricted irrigation.

3 for aquacultural re-use:
zero viable trematode eggs/l of treated wastewater, and
≤ 1000 *E coli*/100 ml of aquaculture pond water.

The trematodes of importance are *Schistosoma* spp, *Clonorchis sinensis* and *Fasciolopsis buski*. The rationale for these guidelines is given in Chapter 22.
The risks to public health when these guidelines are applied are extremely small, and certainly less than the World Health Organization's (2003*) tolerable risk of infection of 10^{-3} per person per year – that is it is considered acceptable if one person in every 1000 becomes infected in a 12-month period from consuming salad crops and vegetables irrigated, or fish from fishponds fertilized, with wastewater treated to these guideline levels (see Chapter 21).
In addition to not harming human health, treated wastewaters should not harm the crops, and thus they should meet the physicochemical quality requirements for all waters used for irrigation given by the Food and Agriculture Organization (Ayers and Westcot, 1989*). For treated domestic wastewaters, the most important of these are: electrical conductivity, sodium absorption ratio, boron concentration, total nitrogen concentration and pH. The precise values of these parameters depend on the types of crops being grown as different crops have different sensitivities to them. Details are given in Chapter 21.

DISCHARGE TO INLAND WATERS

If a treated wastewater is discharged into a river it exerts a demand on the oxygen resources of the river. This removal of dissolved oxygen (DO) for wastewater oxidation must be balanced by an addition of oxygen. The most important source of oxygen for reoxygenation of the river is the atmosphere: there is a mass transfer of oxygen from the atmosphere across the water surface to the river water below. The rate of this transfer is proportional to the oxygen deficit in the water (ie the difference between the oxygen saturation

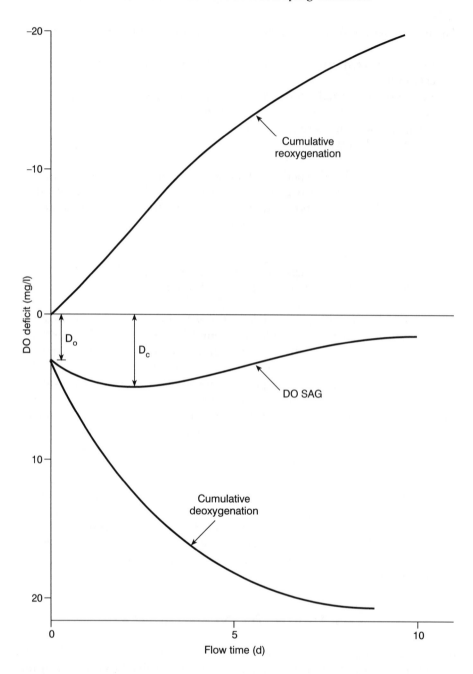

Note: The oxygen sag curve is the sum of the deoxygenation and reoxygenation processes in the river (bacterial oxidation and surface reaeration, respectively). The wastewater is added to the river flow at zero time; the initial deficit D_0 decreases to a maximum or critical deficit D_c at a distance downstream often equivalent to several days flow time.

Figure 4.1 *The Dissolved Oxygen Sag Curve*

concentration and the actual DO concentration). Thus the DO removal that occurs below the point of discharge actually stimulates an increased rate of supply of oxygen from the atmosphere. This competition between deoxygenation and reoxygenation results in a DO profile which typically shows a distinct 'sag' some distance below the point of discharge (Figure 4.1). In order to prevent the river becoming anaerobic, there must be an adequate DO reserve at all points along the river. Analysis of the oxygen sag curve provides a convenient method of determining the degree of treatment that should be given to the effluent before it is discharged, so as to ensure that the lowest DO concentration that occurs is not less than the minimum required to maintain the river water quality at the desired level.

DO sag curve analysis

The first analysis of the DO sag curve was made by Streeter and Phelps (1925) for the Ohio River in the US; full details are given in Phelps (1944). For a single wastewater effluent discharged into a long river with a reasonably constant flow regime, the DO sag curve results from the competition between DO demand and DO supply. The former is due to the *ultimate* BOD (biochemical oxygen demand) of the wastewater effluent, and the latter comes primarily from reoxygenation through surface reaeration by the oxygen in the atmosphere.

The DO deficit (D, mg/l) is defined as the difference between the oxygen saturation concentration (ie its solubility) in the river water at the river water temperature and the actual DO concentration in the river water. The DO demand due to the ultimate BOD of the effluent increases the deficit, and the DO supply by reaeration decreases it. Thus, using the general format of equation 5.1, the Streeter–Phelps equation is:

$$dD/dt = k_1 L - k_2 D$$

(4.1)

where D is the DO deficit at time of flow t (ie assuming a constant velocity of flow in the river, at a given distance downstream of the effluent discharge point), mg/l; k_1 is the first-order rate constant (base e) for BOD removal in the river, day^{-1}; L is the ultimate BOD of the effluent–river-water mixture at time t, mg/l; and k_2 is the first-order rate constant (base e) for surface reaeration, day^{-1}.

Equation 4.1 can be integrated to yield:

$$D = \frac{k_1 L_0}{k_2 k_1} \left(e^{-k_1 t} - e^{-k_2 t} \right) + D_0 e^{-k_2 t}$$

(4.2)

where D_0 and L_0 are the values of D and L at $t = 0$ (ie at the point of discharge).

The most important point in the sag curve is the maximum DO deficit, called the 'critical' deficit, D_c (Figure 4.1). At this point in the curve dD/dt is zero, so from equation 4.1:

$$D_c = k_1 L/k_2$$

(4.3)

The time (or distance) at which D_c occurs is t_c, given by substituting equation 4.3 into equation 4.2:

$$t_c = \frac{1}{k_2 - k_1} \ln \frac{k_2}{k_1} \left[1 - \frac{D_0 (k_2 - k_1)}{L_0} \right]$$

(4.4)

The value of k_2 can be estimated from the following equations (Melching and Flores, 1999*):

- 'Pool and riffle' streams with a flow $Q < 0.556$ m^3/*second*:

$$k_2 = 517(vS)^{0.574}Q^{-0.242}$$

(4.5)

- Pool and riffle streams with $Q > 0.556$ m^3/s:

$$k_2 = 596(vS)^{0.528}Q^{-0.136}$$

(4.6)

- 'Channel-control' streams with $Q < 0.556$ m^3/s:

$$k_2 = 88(vS)^{0.313}H^{-0.353}$$

(4.7)

- Channel-control streams with $Q > 0.556$ m^3/s:

$$k_2 = 142(vS)^{0.333}H^{-0.66}W^{-0.243}$$

(4.8)

where v is the average streamflow velocity in the length of stream considered, m/s (range used for the derivation of equations 4.5–4.8: 0.003–1.83 m^3/s); S is the slope of the water surface, m/m (range: 0.00001–0.06 m/m); Q is the stream flow, m^3/s (range: 0.0028–210 m^3/s); H is the average stream depth calculated from the continuity equation $H = Q/(vW)$, m (range: 0.0457–3.05 m); and W is the average stream top width, m (range: 0.78–162 m). Equations 4.5–4.8 were derived from observations on 500 reaches in 166 streams and rivers throughout the US.

A 'pool and riffle' stream alternates between pools (deep areas, with a nearly horizontal water surface at low flows) and riffles (shallow, high-velocity areas); bed material is sand and gravel in the size range 2–246 mm. 'Channel-control' streams are characterized by reasonably uniform, steady flow with width-to-depth ratios often >40 and water-surface slopes of <0.04; the 'control' can be achieved by hydraulic structures (eg weirs or dams).

In the case of treated wastewater discharges to lakes, k_2 values depend on wind speed (but not on fetch, which is the horizontal wind–water-surface contact distance), as follows (Gelda et al, 1996*):

$$k_2 = \alpha(U_{10})^\beta/H$$

(4.9)

where α is a constant determined by model calibration; U_{10} is the wind speed at a height of 10 m above the lake surface, m/s; β is a constant (taken as 1 for $U_{10} \le 3.5$ m/s and 2 for $U_{10} > 3.5$ m/s); and H is the mean lake depth, m.

Limitations of the Streeter–Phelps equation

The simple Streeter-Phelps equation given above considers only a single point discharge, one oxygen sink (the BOD of the river–effluent mixture), and one oxygen source (surface reaeration). In practice there may be more than one discharge, or the river may receive diffuse pollution from, for example, agricultural run-off. Additionally, plants in the river or growing on its banks may supply oxygen by photosynthesis. However, the most important additional factor to consider, especially in rivers in developing countries, is the so-called 'benthic' oxygen demand. This is the amount of oxygen used by the bacteria in the bottom mud of the river which, due to earlier discharges of untreated wastewater, can often be very high. Dobbins (1964) took this into account, and his version of the Streeter–Phelps equation modified for benthic demand is:

$$dD/dt = (k_1 + k_3)L - k_2D$$

(4.10)

where k_3 is the first-order rate constant for oxygen consumption (ie BOD removal) in the bottom mud, d^{-1}.

Dobbins also developed an equation for D which took into account the other factors mentioned above, but it is really too complicated to use – it is now much better to use one of the commercially available computer models for river water quality, for example, MIKE 11 (DHI Software, 2002*) or River Water Quality Model 1 (Shanahan et al, 2001*, IWA Task Group, 2001).

The above, essentially introductory, discussion on dissolved oxygen supply and demand in a river subject to effluent discharges assumes first order kinetics. In practice this assumption is satisfactory for the in-river processes of DO supply and demand, but much less satisfactory for the determination of the ultimate BOD of the effluent (ie as determined by equation 5.4). This point is considered in more detail in Chapter 5, but it should be noted that an error of underestimation of the ultimate BOD of an effluent results in a corresponding underestimation in the oxygen demand of the river–effluent mixture, and thus introduces error into estimates of the dissolved oxygen balance in the river downstream of the effluent discharge point.

Index of physicochemical river water quality

Regulators generally classify rivers to assess their water use for various purposes (eg potable supply or irrigation) on the basis of their physicochemical quality. An early attempt at this, based on a single parameter, is given in Table 4.2 below. A more comprehensive river water quality index is used by the Environment Agency (for England and Wales): it is based on eight parameters (dissolved oxygen, nitrification-suppressed BOD, total and unionized ammonia, pH, hardness, dissolved copper and total zinc), with maximum values specified for each parameter for each of five classes of river water quality, which range from RE1 (highest quality) to RE5 (lowest). The maximum values are specified on a percentile basis (eg a 95-percentile requirement means that only 5 per cent of samples are allowed to be above the specified maximum). Full details are given in Martin (2002*) and UK Legislation (1994*).

Of course, river water quality indices and classifications developed in industrialized countries are not directly applicable to rivers in developing countries, but they may serve as a general guide. Madhou (2002), for example, has proposed a river water quality index for Mauritius by adapting industrialized country indices for local conditions.

'Minimal' water quality index

Working on the Suquía River in central Argentina, Pesce and Wunderlin (2000*) proposed a very simple river water quality index, which they designated WQImin. It is based on only three parameters: dissolved oxygen, mg/l; total dissolved solids (ie salts in solution), mg/l; and turbidity, NTU (ie turbidity units, dimensionless). WQImin, which has a score range of 0–100 (grossly polluted to extremely high quality), is defined as:

$$\text{WQI}_{\min} = \frac{C_{DO} + C_{TDS} + C_{Turb}}{3}$$

(4.11)

where CDO, CTDS and CTurb are the 'normalized unit values' for dissolved oxygen, total dissolved salts and turbidity, respectively, as given in Table 4.1 for ranges of individual measured parameter concentrations. $\text{WQI}_{\min}$ was found to correlate well with more comprehensive indices which included 20 parameters, although it was recommended that one of the more complete indices be evaluated a few times each year, with $\text{WQI}_{\min}$ being used for routine analysis (once or twice per month).

Table 4.1 *Normalized Unit Values for Dissolved Oxygen, Total Dissolved Salts and Turbidity Used to Calculate* WQI_{min}

DO Concentration (mgl)	Total dissolved salts concentration (mg/l)	Turbidity (NTU)	Normalized unit value (C)
≥ 7.5	<100	<5	100
>7.0	<500	<10	90
>6.5	<750	<15	80
>6.0	<1000	<20	70
>5.0	<1500	<25	60
>4.0	<2000	<30	50
>3.5	<3000	<40	40
>3.0	<5000	<60	30
>2.0	<10,000	<80	20
≥ 1.0	≤ 20,000	≤ 100	10
<1.0	>20,000	>100	0

Example: Suppose the DO concentration was measured as 6.8 mg/l, the Total dissolved salts concentration as 790 mg/l and the turbidity as 16 NTU. Thus $C_{DO} = 80$, $C_{TDS} = 70$ and $C_{Turb} = 70$; and $WQI_{min} = (80 + 70 + 70)/3 = 73$.
Source: Pesce and Wunderlin (2000*)

Effluent standards

It is administratively more convenient to enforce an effluent standard rather than a stream or river standard. The local regulatory agency should select quality standards for wastewater effluents which ensure that rivers do not become unsuitable for their present use or intended purpose. The best known and most widely (and usually inappropriately) applied effluent standard is the so-called '20/30 Royal Commission standard' (ie ≤20 mg BOD5/l and ≤30 mg SS/l). The United Kingdom Royal Commission on Sewage Disposal of 1898–1915 was appointed to consider appropriate methods of sewage treatment and disposal in the *United Kingdom* (it is necessary to stress 'the United Kingdom' because the Commissioners' recommendations were meant to apply only to this country, although they are often indiscriminately applied to other countries in different climatic zones – see Johnstone and Norton, 2000). The Commissioners classified British rivers on the basis of their 65 °F (ie 18.3°C) BOD_5, as shown in Table 4.2. The Commissioners chose a 65 °F BOD because the long-term average summer temperature in the UK is 65 °F, and they chose 5 days as this gave the most reliable and consistent BOD test results. (The standard BOD_5 test is now conducted at 20°C rather than 18.3°C.)

If an effluent is discharged into a river, a mass balance of BOD at the point of discharge (Figure 4.2) yields:

$$L_r Q_r + L_e Q_e = L_m(Q_r + Q_e)$$

$$(4.12)$$

Table 4.2 *The UK Royal Commission's Classification of River Water Quality*

River classification	BOD_5 (mg/l)
Very clean	≤ 1
Clean	2
Fairly clean	3
Doubtful	5
Bad	> 10

where L is BOD_5, mg/l (= g/m^3); Q is flow, m^3/day; the subscript r refers to the river just upstream of the point of discharge; e refers to the effluent; and m refers to the river–effluent mixture just downstream of the point of discharge.

Now if the effluent is diluted with eight volumes of clean river water (ie if Q_r/Q_e = 8 and Lr = 2 mg/l), the maximum BOD_5 of the effluent to avoid nuisance in the river (ie for L_m = 4 mg/l) is given by equation 4.12 as:

$$L_e = [L_m(Q_r + Q_e) - L_r Q_r]/Q_e$$

$$= L_m[Q_r/Q_e) + 1] - L_r(Q_r/Q_e)$$

$$= 4(8 + 1) - (2 - 8)$$

$$= 20 \text{ mg/l}$$

To this standard for BOD_5 the Commissioners added their standard of ≤30 mg/l for suspended solids (SS). Although the 20/30 standard is usually referred to as the Royal Commission standard, the Commissioners in fact recommended standards for each of five ranges of available dilution

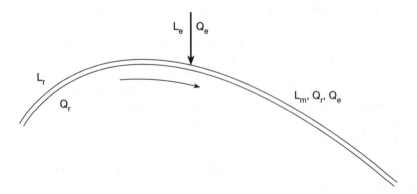

Figure 4.2 *Discharge of an Effluent into a River – definition of terms used in the BOD mass balance*

Table 4.3 *The UK Royal Commission's Standards for Wastewater Effluents Discharged into Rivers*

Available dilution (volumes of clean river water per unit volume of effluent)	Maximum permissible concentration (mg/l)	
	BOD_5	SS
>500	_[a]	_[a]
300–500	_[a]	150
150–300	_[a]	60
8–150	20	30
<8	<20[b]	<30[b]

Notes
[a] No standard recommended; theoretically infinite
[b] Exact values to be decided on the basis of local circumstances

(Table 4.3). There is no evidence to suggest that these Royal Commission standards are directly applicable to climates other than those similar to that in the UK. In many developing countries the 'natural' BOD of a river can be high – for example, the unpolluted River Turkwell in the remote area of northern Kenya has a BOD_5 of 20–45 mg/l (Meadows, 1973).

In many developing countries effluent standards do not exist. Even so design engineers need to ensure that the effluent produced in their treatment works will not pollute the receiving watercourse. A standard is certainly required for BOD (or COD – chemical oxygen demand) and possibly for suspended solids in the case of discharge to inland and coastal waters, for *E coli* in the case of coastal discharges, and for *E coli* and nematode or trematode worm eggs in the case of wastewater re-use in agriculture or aquaculture.

BOD standard
Often a national 'blanket' BOD standard is specified, for example, ≤30 mg/l in India (Central Pollution Control Board, 1996) and ≤25 mg/l in the European Union (Council of the European Communities, 1991a*). This appears to follow the assumed logic of the UK Royal Commission's BOD 'standard' of ≤20 mg/l, but ignores the reasoning behind this value (dilution with eight volumes of clean river water), the available dilution in the receiving river (Table 4.3), and any river water quality objective (eg a required minimum DO level). A useful document for regulators is the report by the former National Rivers Authority (for England and Wales, now the Environment Agency) which sets out its rationale for establishing effluent quality requirements (National Rivers Authority, 1994; see also Martin, 2002*).

Waste stabilization ponds (WSP) in the European Union are required to comply with the above 25 mg/l standard for BOD, but on a *filtered* basis – that is samples are to be filtered before analysis to remove the BOD due to the algae present. This is discussed in more detail in Chapter 11.

In general, a BOD standard should be interpreted as a carbonaceous BOD standard (CBOD) excluding, therefore, the BOD due to the oxygen demand of nitrification (Chapter 3). The addition of 2-chloro-6-(trichoromethyl)pyridine to a final concentration of 10 mg/l in the BOD test bottles inhibits nitrification (American Public Health Association, 1998). However, CBOD should not be used for raw or settled (eg anaerobic pond effluent – Chapter 10) wastewater as it underestimates their strength by as much as 20–40 per cent, and can therefore result in an underdesign of the same amount (Albertson, 1995).

Suspended solids

In India the suspended solids standard is ≤100 mg/l; and in the European Union ≤35 mg/l, although this is only an 'optional' requirement, but WSP effluents have to contain ≤150 mg/l. Many rivers in developing countries have a much higher 'natural' suspended solids concentration, and there is little point in setting a standard more stringent than the background SS concentration in the receiving water.

Ammonia

Ammonia in wastewater is a mixture of dissolved ammonia gas (NH3) and the ammonium ion (NH_4^+), often referred to as 'free' and 'saline' ammonia, respectively. Free ammonia at concentrations >0.5 mg N/l is toxic to fish (Chapter 22). In India, the standard for total (ie free and saline) ammonia is ≤50 mg N/l and for free ammonia ≤5 mg N/l. There is also a standard for total Kjeldahl nitrogen (organic N and ammonia) of ≤100 mg/l. In the European Union there is a total nitrogen requirement of ≤15 mg N/l for populations up to 100,000 and ≤10 mg N/l for larger populations, but this is required only for discharge to 'sensitive' areas (defined as areas which are 'subject to eutrophication'). Total nitrogen is the sum of organic N, ammonia, nitrite and nitrate.

E coli

As discussed earlier in this chapter and also in Chapters 21 and 22, there are specific requirements for *E coli* (also for nematode and trematode eggs) when treated wastewaters are used in agriculture and aquaculture. The question to be answered here is: should there be an *E coli* standard for discharges to inland waters?

In developing countries inland surface waters are often used by rural and periurban communities as their domestic water supply, commonly without treatment. Studies in the Philippines have shown that young children are at a high risk of diarrhoeal disease when their drinking water contains >1000 *E coli*/100 ml, but not when it contains less (Moe et al, 1991). Ideally, therefore, river waters should contain ≤1000 *E coli*/100 ml. Knowing the minimum available dilution in the receiving water and its *E coli* count upstream of the discharge point, an *E coli* requirement can be set for the treated wastewater. This is best attained by waste stabilization ponds, or other treatment processes supplemented by maturation ponds (Chapter 12).

DISCHARGE TO COASTAL WATERS

Forty per cent of the world's population lives within 60 km of the sea, and thus the potential for adverse human impacts on the marine environment is very high (Jasuja, 2002*). These occur because wastewaters from coastal cities and towns are discharged, often with no treatment at all, into the sea or an estuary via an outfall pipe. To minimize these impacts, the outfall pipe should be correctly positioned. Its actual position in any one location depends largely on the pattern of the local tidal currents (see Grace, 1978; Gunnerson, 1988*; Institution of Civil Engineers, 1989; Water Research Centre, 1990, 1995; National Research Council, 1993*; Neville-Jones and Chitty, 1996), but it should be chosen so as to:

- always discharge the wastewater below mean low water level,
- ensure that there is no increased health risk to swimmers,
- prevent the fouling of beaches with wastewater solids of recognizable origin, and
- minimize damage to the marine ecosystem (particularly coral reefs).

The first three of these four criteria are especially important if there is a large tourist industry; bathing waters should contain ≤ 2000 *E coli*/100 ml, preferably ≤ 100/100 ml (Council of the European Communities, 1976*). The fourth criterion is of long-term importance, particularly if the wastewater contains an appreciable proportion of toxic industrial wastes. If there are commercial shellfisheries near the outfall, then the sea water in these areas should contain ≤ 10 *E coli*/100 ml (Council of the European Communities, 1979*).

The fourth criterion is especially important as coral reefs are fragile ecosystems with very high biodiversities. Recently the lethal 'white pox' disease of Caribbean elkhorn coral, *Acropora palmata*, has been shown to be caused by the common faecal bacterium *Serratia marescens* (Patterson et al, 2002*) – this finding, that a human faecal bacterium is a pathogen of a marine invertebrate, is extremely disturbing and indicates the need for effective domestic wastewater treatment. Although discharge to sea is an easy option for wastewater disposal for coastal towns and cities, wastewater treatment and re-use should always be considered as an alternative solution, especially since many coastal areas in developing countries are short of water. Moreover, we should try not to add to, but rather reduce, the pollution of the sea, which is a global resource of considerable economic value and ecological importance.

The Aruba Protocol

In 1983 the Cartagena Convention was drawn up 'for the protection and development of the marine environment of the Wider Caribbean Region' and in 1999 the Aruba Protocol to the Convention was developed to control marine pollution in the Caribbean from 'land-based sources and activities',

Table 4.4 *Effluent Quality Requirements for Domestic Wastewaters Discharged into the Marine Environment of the Wider Caribbean Region*

Parameter	Discharge into Class I waters	Discharge into Class II waters
BOD	≤ 30 mg/l	≤ 150 mg/l
Suspended solids[a]	≤ 30 mg/l	≤ 150 mg/l
Faecal coliforms[b]	≤ 200 per 100 ml	Not applicable

Notes:
[a] Excludes algae in waste stabilization pond effluents
[b] Assumes discharge is into surf zone of bathing beaches
Source: Caribbean Environment Programme (2002*)

including the discharge of domestic wastewaters (Caribbean Environment Programme, 2002*). Effluent qualities are specified for discharge into 'Class I' and 'Class II' coastal waters (Table 4.4). Class I waters are defined as those containing coral reefs, seagrass beds or mangroves; those which are critical breeding, nursery or forage areas for aquatic and terrestrial life; those which provide habitat for protected marine species; and recreational waters (ie those used for swimming and water sports). Class II waters are all other marine areas which are less sensitive to the impacts of domestic wastewaters.

The United Nations Environment Programme has 14 Regional Seas Programmes, one of which is the Caribbean Environment Programme. Details of the other programmes and their discharge requirements are given by the United Nations Environment Programme (2003*).

BATNEEC – or CATNAP?

BATNEEC stands for the 'best available technology not entailing excessive cost' and is often the technology preferred by regulators. From their point of view this is perhaps understandable, but actually what wastewater treatment plant operating authorities want is CATNAP – the 'cheapest available technology narrowly avoiding prosecution' (the acronym CATNAP started as a joke, but actually it is a very apposite descriptor). In practice this means there is no point at all in having a wastewater treatment technology that produces an effluent quality of 5 or even 20 mg BOD/l when the standard is ≤30 mg/l – technology overkill is as bad as regulatory overkill (and both really are bad: if too much money is spent unnecessarily on wastewater treatment to produce an effluent quality much better than is actually needed, then there is less money available for other basic services, such as better health care, better education, better public transport, and so on. Regulatory and technology overkill are in fact worse than economically wanton: they are, to put it bluntly, stupid – but, regrettably, not so uncommon).

Regulators have to remember that most wastewaters in most developing countries are not treated at all. If a city installs a wastewater treatment plant, but for some reason (often financial, sometimes operational or managerial) the plant produces an effluent of, say, 40 (even 60) mg BOD/l, rather that the required ≤30 mg/l, then should it be prosecuted? If other cities in the country (or state, or province) discharge their wastewater untreated into local rivers and are not prosecuted for so doing, then the answer has to be *No* – otherwise there would be no incentive at all to even consider wastewater treatment.

On the basis that 'half a loaf is better than no bread', governments and their regulators (and indeed bilateral and multilateral donors and lending agencies) have to realize that partial treatment is better than no treatment. Phasing in full treatment over several years to achieve a desired river water quality objective is more sensible than doing nothing – 'Rome was not built in a day.' Of course, there will be situations where full treatment may be required now (perhaps in re-use schemes, for example), but this is not the general case in developing countries.

5

Biochemical Oxygen Demand Removal Kinetics

FIRST-ORDER KINETICS

The rate at which organic matter is oxidized by bacteria is a fundamental parameter in the rational design of biological waste treatment processes. It has been found that BOD (biochemical oxygen demand) removal often approximates first-order kinetics; that is, the rate of BOD removal (= the rate of oxidation of organic matter) at any time is proportional to the amount of BOD present in the system at that time. Mathematically this type of reaction is written as:

$$\frac{dL}{dt} = -k_1 L$$

$$(5.1)$$

where L is the amount of BOD remaining (= organic matter still to be oxidized) at time t; and k_1 is the first-order rate constant for BOD removal, which has the units of reciprocal time, usually day^{-1}.

The differential coefficient dL/dt is the rate at which the organic matter is oxidized, and the minus sign indicates a decrease in the value of L with time. Equation 5.1 is the differential form of the first-order equation for BOD removal; it can be integrated to:

$$L = L_0 e^{-k_1 t}$$

$$(5.2)$$

where L_0 is the value of L at $t = 0$.

L_0 is the amount of BOD in the system before oxidation occurs; it is therefore the ultimate BOD (Chapter 1). The amount of BOD removed or 'satisfied' (= organic matter oxidized) plus the amount of BOD remaining (= organic matter yet to be oxidized) at any time must obviously equal the ultimate BOD (= initial amount of organic matter):

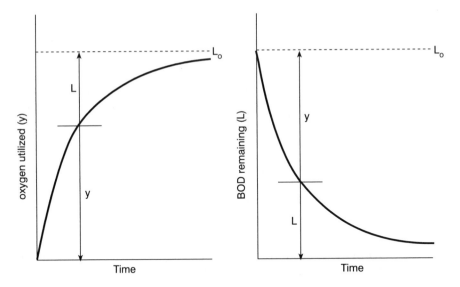

Figure 5.1 *Generalized BOD Curves*

$$y = L_0 - L$$

(5.3)

where y is the BOD removed at time t.

Substitution of equation 5.3 into equation 5.2 yields:

$$y = L_0 (1 - e^{-k_1 t})$$

(5.4)

Generalized BOD curves (plots of equations 5.2 and 5.4) are shown in Figure 5.1, from which the relationship between y, L and L_0 is readily seen.

Equation 5.2 can also be written as:

$$L = L_0 10^{-K_1 t}$$

where $K_1 = k_1/2.3$. Because of the confusion that generally arises between K_1 and k_1, it is best to give the base when quoting k_1 values – for example 0.23 day^{-1} (base e) or 0.10 day^{-1} (base 10). In this book all first-order rate constants are to base e.

Ratio of BOD$_5$ to BOD$_u$

The ratio of BOD_5/BOD_u ($= y_5/L_0$) is given by equation 5.4 as $(1 - e^{-5k_1})$. As the value of k_1 for raw domestic wastewater is typically 0.23 day^{-1} (base e) at 20°C, the ratio BOD_5/BOD_u in raw domestic wastewaters is ~2/3.

ΔCOD

In a wholly microbiological wastewater treatment reactor (ie one in which no non-microbiological BOD removal takes place) the difference between the influent COD (chemical oxygen demand)and the effluent COD (ΔCOD) can be used to determine the BOD_u removal in the reactor. This is because COD equals BOD_u (which is by definition the biodegradable COD) plus the non-biodegradable COD (which by definition cannot change in a wholly microbiological reactor):

$$COD_i = (BOD_u)_i + \text{(non-biodegradable COD)}$$

$$COD_e = (BOD_u)_e + \text{(non-biodegradable COD)}$$

$$\overline{\Delta COD = (BOD_u)_i - (BOD_u)_e}$$

Once the COD/BOD_5 ratios have been determined for both the influent and the effluent, ΔCOD can be used to estimate BOD_5 removal.

Continuous flow processes

Equations 5.2 and 5.4 describe the bio-oxidation of a given quantity of organic matter to which no further addition of organic matter is made. They represent conditions in a 'batch' oxidation process. However, wastewater treatment plants operate with a continuous inflow of raw wastewater and a continuous outflow of treated effluent. Consider, therefore, a mass balance of BOD across a continuously operated microbiological reactor: the quantity of organic matter entering the reactor per day must equal the quantity leaving the reactor per day plus that removed by bio-oxidation. If Q is the flow in m^3/day and L_i and L_e are the influent and effluent BOD, respectively, in mg/l (= g/m^3), then:

$$\left(\begin{array}{c} \text{quantity of BOD entering} \\ \text{the reactor, g/day} \end{array} \right) = L_i Q$$

$$\left(\begin{array}{c} \text{quantity of BOD leaving} \\ \text{the reactor, g/day} \end{array} \right) = L_e Q$$

The quantity of BOD removed in bacterial oxidation is given by equation 5.1 as $k_1 L$ g/m^3 day where L is the BOD of the reactor contents. We will assume that the reactor is completely mixed so that the reactor contents are identical in every respect to the reactor effluent. Under this condition the BOD of the reactor contents is L_e. If V is the working volume of the reactor in m^3, then:

$$\left(\begin{array}{c} \text{quantity of BOD removed} \\ \text{by bacterial oxidation, g/day} \end{array} \right) = k_1 L_e V$$

Thus:

$$L_iQ = L_eQ + k_1LV_e$$

(5.5)

Rearranging:

$$\frac{L_e}{L_i} = \frac{1}{1 + k_1(V/Q)}$$

(5.6)

The ratio V/Q is the mean hydraulic retention time (θ, days), the average length of time a typical 'packet' of wastewater may be expected to remain in the reactor before being discharged in the effluent flow. Equation 5.6 can therefore be written as:

$$\frac{L_e}{L_i} = \frac{1}{1 + k_1\theta}$$

(5.7)

This equation has found direct application in the design of waste stabilization ponds and aerated lagoons (Chapters 11, 12 and 20).

Temperature

The rate constant k_1 is a gross measure of bacterial activity and, in common with almost all parameters describing microbiological growth processes, its value is strongly temperature dependent. Its variation with temperature is usually described by an Arrhenius equation of the form:

$$k_{1(T)} = k_{1(20)}\, \phi^{T-20}$$

(5.8)

where $k_{1(T)}$ and $k_{1(20)}$ are the values of k_1 at $T°C$ and $20°C$, respectively, and ϕ is an Arrhenius constant whose value is usually between 1.01 and 1.09. Typical values are:

Waste stabilization ponds 1.05–1.09
Aerated lagoons 1.035

ϕ values are themselves a function of temperature, decreasing with increasing temperature, but they are normally sensibly constant over a 10–15 degC interval. Thus a ϕ value for the temperature range 5–15 degC will not be the same as that for the range 15–30 degC. Caution must therefore be exercised in using, in developing countries, ϕ values derived from wastewater treatment processes operating in temperate climates.

As a way of avoiding the problem of ϕ values being only valid for a fairly narrow range of temperature, Mara (1987) used a value of ϕ that varies linearly with temperature in the range 8–35°C (see equation 11.3):

$$\phi = (1.107 - 0.002T)^{T-25}$$

(5.9)

HYDRAULIC FLOW REGIMES

The flow of wastewater through a microbiological reactor can approximate either complete mixing or plug flow. These two flow patterns represent two extreme or ideal conditions. In practice the hydraulic regime lies between these two extremes and is described as 'dispersed flow'.

Complete mixing

The influent to this ideal reactor is completely and instantaneously mixed with the reactor contents, which are, as a result of the intense mixing, uniform in composition throughout. The effluent is identical, therefore, in every respect to the reactor contents. The removal of BOD is described by equation 5.7.

Plug flow

The contents of this ideal reactor flow through the reactor in an orderly fashion characterized by the complete absence of longitudinal mixing. The concept of plug flow may be readily grasped by imagining the wastewater, on arrival at the reactor, to be placed in watertight 'packets' which then travel along the length of the reactor – as if on a conveyor belt – with no transfer of material from one packet to another, but with complete mixing within each packet. Since each packet receives no additional BOD and loses none to a neighbouring packet, the removal of BOD within each packet is essentially a batch process, so that BOD removal in a plug flow reactor follows equation 5.2. It is, however, convenient to adopt the notation used in equation 5.7 and rewrite equation 5.2 as:

$$L_e = L_i e^{-k_1 \theta}$$

(5.10)

Equation 5.10 has found direct application in the design of constructed wetlands (Chapter 17) and biofilters (Chapter 19).

Dispersed flow

It is, of course, impossible to build a plug flow reactor in which there is no mixing between packets; in practice some degree of longitudinal mixing always occurs. The degree of inter-packet mixing that takes place is usually expressed in terms of a dimensionless 'dispersion number' (δ), defined as:

$$\delta = D/vl$$

(5.11)

where D is the coefficient of longitudinal dispersion, m^2/h; v is the mean velocity of travel of a typical 'particle' in the reactor, m/h; and l is its mean path length, m. When there is no longitudinal dispersion (ie in the case of ideal plug flow) $\delta = 0$ and when there is infinite dispersion (ie complete mixing) $\delta = \infty$.

In a dispersed flow reactor ($0 < \delta < \infty$) in which bio-oxidation occurs as a first-order reaction, the removal of BOD is described by the equation given by Wehner and Wilhelm (1956*):

$$\frac{L_e}{L_i} = \frac{4a \exp (1/2\delta)}{(1 + a)^2 \exp (a/2\delta) - (1 - a)2 \exp (-a/2\delta)}$$

(5.12)

where $a = \sqrt{(1 + 4k_1\theta\delta)}$. Equation 5.12 reverts to equation 5.10 when $\delta = 0$ and to equation 5.7 when $\delta = \infty$.

Figure 5.2 is a graphical display of equation 5.12 (Thirumurthi, 1969), which shows that, for any given combination of k_1 and θ, maximal BOD removal is achieved in an ideal plug flow reactor, and minimal removal in a completely mixed reactor of the same size. Expressed in another way this means that, for any given value of k_1 and any desired degree of BOD removal, the required retention time is a minimum in a plug flow reactor and a maximum in a completely mixed reactor. A plug flow reactor is therefore always smaller than a completely mixed reactor designed to achieve the same removal of BOD.

For δ values less than 2 (and, as shown in Figure 5.2, a δ value of 2 is quite close to infinity), the second term in the denominator of equation 5.12 is small and can be ignored. The equation becomes:

$$L_e/L_i = [4a/(1 + a)^2]\exp[(1 - a)/2\delta]$$

(5.13)

A least-squares analysis for the solution of equation 5.13 for k_1 and δ is given by Esen and Al-Shayji (1999*).

Dispersion numbers can be determined directly by chemical tracer studies with either an inorganic salt (eg lithium chloride) or a fluorescent dye (eg rhodamine WT) (Levenspiel, 1998; see also Agunwamba, 2002*). Some typical results are shown in Figure 5.3. As an alternative to performing tracer studies, a reasonably good estimate of δ values for facultative and maturation waste stabilization ponds (Chapters 11 and 12) can be obtained from the pond

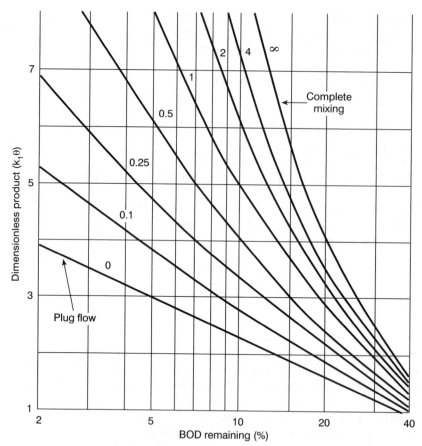

Note: The numbers adjacent to each curve are the corresponding dispersion numbers.

Figure 5.2 *Thirumurthi Chart for the Wehner–Wilhelm equation*

geometry, using the simple equation developed by von Sperling (1999*, 2002*, and 2003*):

$$\delta = (L/B)^{-1}$$

(5.14)

where L and B are the pond length and breadth, respectively, m – that is δ is the reciprocal of the pond's length-to-breadth ratio (Chapter 13).

BOD$_u$ or BOD$_5$?

In equations 5.7, 5.9 and 5.12 which describe BOD removal in continuous flow reactors, the terms L_i and L_e may refer to either the ultimate BOD or the 5-day BOD of the influent and effluent. In practice BOD$_5$ is most commonly

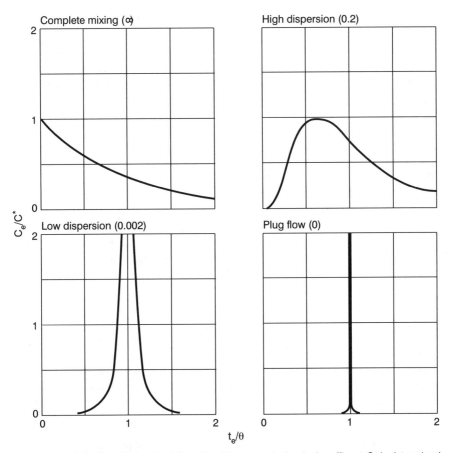

Note: A slug of dye is added to the influent and its concentration in the effluent C_e is determined at various corresponding times t_e. The results are plotted as the dimensionless numbers C_e/C^* and t_e/θ, where C^* is the weight of dye added divided by the reactor volume and θ is the mean hydraulic retention time (= reactor volume/flow rate). In the completely mixed reactor the dye is instantaneously and uniformly distributed so that at zero time $C_e = C^*$; exponential wash out of the dye then follows. In the plug flow reactor all the dye appears in the effluent when $t_e = \theta$. Dispersed flow reactors behave in an intermediate fashion depending on the magnitude of their dispersion number; two examples are shown here, for $\delta = 0.2$ and $\delta = 0.002$.

Figure 5.3 *Typical Tracer Study Results*

used because it is more easily measured; k_1 is thus strictly interpreted as the first-order rate constant for BOD_5 removal.

Which model to use?

The three models – complete mixing, plug flow and dispersed flow – can cause some confusion: which is the most appropriate to use? Sometimes the answer is obvious: in the case of rivers (Chapter 4) and long narrow constructed wetlands (Chapter 17), the plug flow model (equation 5.10) is clearly the most appropriate, and in the case of aerated lagoons (Chapter 20) the complete mix model (equation 5.7) is obviously appropriate. However, for waste stabilization ponds (Chapters 10–12) the choice is less obvious. Theoretically, of course, the dispersed flow model (equation 5.12 or 5.13) is the best, but in practice it is only rarely used. Most commonly the complete mix equation is used to derive a k_1 value from field data; provided that this k_1 value is only used in equation 5.7, then the results will be acceptable (it is wholly wrong to use a k_1 value derived from equation 5.7 in either equation 5.10 or equations 5.12 and 5.13). The assumption that is being made is not that the pond (or other reactor) is completely mixed, but rather that the kinetics are reasonably well represented by the complete mix model (Marais and Shaw, 1961).

A more rational approach has been adopted by von Sperling (1999*, 2003*), who correctly advocates the use of only the dispersed flow model. Using data from waste stabilization ponds in Brazil, he developed the following empirical equation for k_B (the first-order rate constant for *E coli*, rather than BOD, removal) as a function of pond depth and retention time:

$$k_B = 0.92D^{-0.88}\theta^{-0.33}$$

$$(5.15)$$

where k_B is the first-order rate constant for *E coli* removal in a dispersed flow reactor, d^{-1}; and D is the pond depth, m. This equation, corrected for temperature by an equation similar to equation 5.8, and equation 5.14 are then used in equation 5.12 or 5.13. This important approach is discussed in more detail in Chapter 12.

LIMITATIONS OF SIMPLE FIRST-ORDER KINETICS

Equation 5.1 assumes that all the organic components in the wastewater are oxidized at the same rate and that the rate of oxidation remains constant with time. However, it is unlikely that all components of a waste so heterogeneous in nature as domestic wastewater will be oxidized at the same rate, and it has been frequently observed in waste stabilization ponds, for example, that as the retention time increases the rate constant decreases.

Composite exponential

If it is assumed that different fractions of the waste are oxidized at different rates, but that each rate constant does not decrease with time, the simple exponential term $\exp(-k_1 t)$ in equation 5.4 can be replaced by a composite exponential, so that the equation becomes (Gameson and Wheatland, 1958):

$$y = L_0 [1 - f_1 \exp(-k_{f_1} t) - f_2 \exp(-k_{f_2} t) - \dots - f_n \exp(-k_{f_n} t)]$$

$$(5.16)$$

where $f_1, ..., f_n$ are the fractions of the waste oxidized at the rates $k_{f_1}, ..., k_{f_n}$. For example, a domestic wastewater in England was found to be oxidized as if it were a mixture of components of which 40 per cent were oxidized at a rate of 0.8 day^{-1}, 40 per cent at 0.08 day^{-1} and 20 per cent at 0.008 day^{-1}:

$$y = L_0 (1 - 0.4e^{-0.8t} - 0.4e^{-0.08t} - 0.2e^{-0.008t})$$

(5.17)

The effluent from the wastewater treatment works at which this particular wastewater was treated, was oxidized as if it were composed of a 40 per cent fraction oxidizable at a rate of 0.08 d^{-1} and a 60 per cent fraction oxidizable at 0.008 day^{-1}:

$$y = L_0 (1 - 0.4e^{-0.08t} - 0.6e^{-0.008t})$$

(5.18)

These typical results show that the most rapidly oxidizable fraction was totally eliminated during treatment and, as a result, the effluent had a higher proportion of material that could be oxidized, only more slowly. This explains the variation of the BOD_5/COD ratio during wastewater treatment: in raw domestic wastewater it is ~0.5, but in the effluent it is lower, often ~0.2.

Retarded exponential

If, on the other hand, it is assumed that all the components in the wastewater are oxidized at the same rate but that the rate of oxidation decreases with time, then equation 5.1 becomes (Gameson and Wheatland, 1958):

$$\frac{dL}{dt} = \frac{k_1}{1 + \alpha t} L$$

(5.19)

where α is a coefficient of retardation, day^{-1}; and k_1 is now defined as the first-order rate constant at zero time.

The retarded exponential equation for a completely mixed reactor is:

$$\frac{L_e}{L_i} = \frac{1}{1 + [k_1/(1 + \alpha\theta)]\theta}$$

(5.20)

In his research on waste stabilization ponds in northeast Brazil, Silva (1982) obtained the data from primary facultative ponds (see Chapter 11) given in Table 5.1. These results indicate that, as the retention time increases, the values of k_1 from equation 5.7 decrease. Using equation 5.20 Silva found an α value

Table 5.1 *BOD Removal Results from Primary Facultative Ponds in Northeast Brazil*

	BOD loading (kg/ha d)[a]	Retention time (d)	BOD (mg/l)
Raw wastewater	–	–	245
Effluent from:			
Pond F2	258	11.8	54
Pond F3	255	12.0	51
Pond F4	322	9.5	57
Pond F5	162	18.9	40

Note: [a] see equation 11.1
Source: Silva (1982)

of 0.052 for these facultative ponds, so that k_1 was given, for a mean in-pond temperature range of 21–28°C, by:

$$k_1 = 0.527/(1 + 0.052\theta)$$

(5.21)

Estimation of ultimate BOD

In streamflow analysis (Chapter 4) use of equation 5.4 to estimate the ultimate BOD of a wastewater effluent results in a significant underestimation of L_0 and hence in a corresponding underestimation of the oxygen demand in the river downstream of the effluent discharge point (Borsuk and Stow, 2000*). Equation 5.1 can be rewritten as a 'mixed' order equation, as follows:

$$\frac{dL}{dt} = - k_n L^n$$

(5.22)

where k_n is the mixed-order rate constant for BOD removal, $(mg/l)^{1-n}$ day^{-1}; and n is the order of the reaction. Integrating equation 5.22 and using equation 5.3 yields:

$$y = L_0 - [L_0^{1-n} - k_n t(1 - n)]^{1/(1-n)}$$

(5.23)

Borsuk and Stow (2000*) used Bayesian statistics to establish L_0 from long-term data sets of y and t (up to 180 days) for $n \neq 1$. They found the mixed-order model much better at estimating L_0 than the first-order model or indeed the second-order model (ie $n = 2$); n was determined for each of four long-term data sets and found to be in the range 1.30–4.04 (but n values are unique to each data set, so this range in no way constrains possible values of n), and L_0 was underestimated by the first-order model in these four cases by as much as 6–45 per cent. Borsuk and Stow's approach should be adopted for effluent analysis prior to streamflow calculations when there is (or it is possible to obtain) a reasonably long-term data set (say, up to at least 60 days) and when it is important to determine in-river dissolved oxygen concentrations with a high level of confidence.

WORKED EXAMPLES

1 The BOD_5 of a wastewater has been measured as 300 mg/l. If $k_1 = 0.23$ day^{-1} (base e) what is the BOD_u of the waste? What proportion of the BOD_u would remain unoxidized after 20 days?

From equation 5.4:

$$[y_5 = L_0 \left(1 - e^{-k_1 5} \right)$$

$$L_0 = y_5 \left(1 - e^{-k_1 5} \right)^{-1}$$

$$= 300 \left(1 - e^{-(0.23 \times 5)} \right)^{-1}$$

$$= 400 \text{ mg/l}$$

From equation 5.2:

$$\frac{L_t}{L_0} = e^{-k_1 20}$$

$$= e^{-(0.23 \times 20)}$$

$$= 0.01$$

Thus 99 per cent of the waste has been oxidized in 20 days. BOD_{20} is therefore often taken as an approximation for BOD_u.

2 Show that the ratio of the $2\frac{1}{2}$-day, 35°C BOD to the 5-day, 20°C BOD is approximately 1. Take ϕ as 1.05.

From equation 5.4:

$$y_{2.5} = L_0[1 - \exp(-2.5k_{35})]$$

and

$$y_5 = L_0[1 - \exp(-5k_{20})]$$

But from equation 5.8:

$$k_{35} = k_{20} (1.05)^{35-20}$$

$$= 2.08k_{20}$$

Substituting k_{35} in the expression for $y_{2.5}$:

$$y_{2.5} = L_0[1 - \exp(-2.5 \times 2.08k_{20})]$$

$$= L_0[1 - \exp(-5.2k_{20})]$$

$$\approx y_5$$

Thus the BOD$_5$ of a wastewater can be obtained in 2.5 days if the incubation temperature is 35°C rather than 20°C – see Tool (1967). It would actually be more convenient to measure the 3-day BOD at 30°C which can be shown in the way described above to be essentially equal to the 5-day 20°C BOD (in warm climates this obviates the need for a cooled incubator).

6

Domestic Wastewater Treatment Options

SUSTAINABILITY ISSUES

The most commonly quoted definition of sustainable development is that 'which meets the needs of the present without compromising the ability of future generations to meet their own needs' (World Commission on Environment and Development, 1987 – the 'Bruntland Report'). For water resources, Feitelson and Chenoweth (2002*) interpret this as 'water resources left for future generations should be of similar quantity and quality as those available to current generations'.

In almost all parts of the world, but especially in developing countries, there is a huge need for water, and the water to meet these needs is becoming scarcer and scarcer: it is predicted that over half the world's peoples will face water shortages during the next 30 years (Postel, 1997; United Nations Environment Programme, 2002*; Hunt, 2003). Agriculture consumes vast quantities of water (~70 per cent of global water abstraction), as do many industries, and there is an enormous, currently unfulfilled, domestic demand for water. The development and exploitation of water resources to meet these needs must be sustainable (as defined above), and part of this drive towards sustainability concerns domestic wastewater treatment. This includes the direct re-use of treated wastewater in agriculture and aquaculture (Chapters 21 and 22), as well as its indirect re-use, which is discharge into inland surface waters and used by downstream communities for agricultural and industrial use, as well as for domestic supply.

When sustainability is considered in relation to domestic wastewater treatment in developing countries, the following issues are relevant:

- low cost – both in terms of capital and of operation and maintenance,
- simplicity of operation and maintenance,
- low, preferably zero, energy usage – essential for low operational costs,
- low, preferably zero, use of chemicals, especially chlorine or other environmentally damaging disinfectants,
- low land take, although this is only occasionally really relevant,

Table 6.1 *Comparison of Factors of Importance in Wastewater Treatment in Industrialized and Developing Countries*

Factor	Industrialized countries	Developing countries
Efficiency	C•••••	••••
Reliability	C•••••	C•••••
Sludge production	•••	C•••••
Land requirements	C•••••	••
Environmental impact	••••	••
Operational costs	•••	C•••••
Construction costs	••	C•••••
Sustainability	•••	C•••••
Simplicity	•	C•••••

Notes: C, critical; •••••, extremely important → •, no impact
Source: adapted from von Sperling (1996a*)

- high performance – the ability to produce an effluent of the required quality (Chapter 4), and
- low sludge production.

These considerations should be self-evident, yet they are often not taken into account – unfortunately there are too many uninformed professionals in developing countries (and this includes their often expatriate advisers and lenders) who, automatically and thus without due thinking, wish to adopt the wastewater treatment technologies of industrialized countries in the generally mistaken belief that these are the most appropriate technologies to implement. This belief is generally mistaken because, as shown in Table 6.1, industrialized and developing countries have (or should have) different perceptions of what is important in wastewater treatment. Of course, there are certain circumstances when such technologies may be appropriate – in 'megacities', for example, but even here other technologies, such as waste stabilization ponds and effluent re-use, are not always irrelevant (see Chapter 9 for examples of large-scale waste stabilization pond systems).

Decentralized wastewater treatment

In most cities in industrialized countries there is a single central wastewater treatment plant. Such a plant requires an extensive (and expensive) network of trunk sewers to convey all the city's wastewater to it, and this often involves pumping the wastewater from one drainage basin to another. A cheaper alternative for developing countries (which is also applicable to industrialized countries) is to have decentralized wastewater treatment plants, rather than a single central plant (Lens et al, 2001*). This minimizes the costs of trunk sewerage and avoids much, if not all, of the expenditure on pumping. Each decentralized plant serves a single drainage basin or a small number of drainage sub-basins. A good example of this is in Lusaka, Zambia: the city is divided into six catchment areas, each of which has its own treatment plant (Wamukwamba and Share, 2001*). Another example is the city of Curitiba (population ~2 million) in south Brazil, where having decentralized wastewater treatment achieved cost savings of ~40 per cent compared with having a single treatment plant (Catunda and van Haandel, 1996*). When sewering cities for the first time, or when an existing sewerage system has to be extended to deal with new housing areas, consideration should always be given to decentralized wastewater treatment and re-use as they can be more cost-effective.

APPROPRIATE WASTEWATER TREATMENT OPTIONS

In this book the following processes for the treatment of domestic wastewater are discussed:

- waste stabilization ponds (WSP) (Chapters 9–15),
- wastewater storage and treatment reservoirs (WSTR) (Chapter 16),
- constructed wetlands (CW), often simply called 'reedbeds' (Chapter 17),
- upflow anaerobic sludge blanket reactors (UASBs) (Chapter 18),
- biofilters (Chapter 19),
- aerated lagoons (Chapter 20), and
- oxidation ditches (also Chapter 20).

Not all of these technologies are necessarily sustainable or always sensible. Some may not be sensible at all, but are included here because they are often advocated as being a good (sometimes even 'the best') solution. Professionals (and would-be professionals) need to understand these technologies so that they are able to make informed decisions about which is really the best technology, or combination of technologies, to implement in any given situation, and also which technologies to avoid.

Conventional activated sludge systems are not considered in this book, although two of its variants are – aerated lagoons and oxidation ditches (Chapter 20). Conventional systems are described in, for example, Horan (1990), Metcalf and Eddy, Inc (1991) and Water Environment Federation (2001). They should only be used for very large populations ('megacities'), and then only with extreme caution as they consume considerable quantities of electrical energy, are very complicated to operate and maintain (so highly skilled operators are needed), and generally require very large amounts of foreign exchange, both to equip initially and then to maintain. The Latin tag *caveat emptor* ('let the buyer beware') is highly relevant as sales engineers selling conventional wastewater treatment equipment are highly skilled in selling.

Lime-assisted primary sedimentation is a good method of chemically enhanced primary treatment of domestic wastewater, although quite high doses of lime are required (up to 1 g/l) and large amounts of sludge are produced (around 0.14 m^3/m^3 wastewater treated) (Gambrill, 1990; Taylor et al,

1994a*, b*; see also Jiménez-Cisneros et al, 2001*; Harleman and Murcott, 1999*; Environmental Protection Agency, 2000a*). At retention times of 9–12 h and pH 11, Gambrill (1990) found that helminth eggs were removed by 4 log units and faecal coliforms by 4.5 log units, so producing an effluent safe for unrestricted irrigation (Chapter 21). In regions with acid soils the lime sludge can be profitably used to reduce soil acidity (and, although the lime sludge will contain many *Ascaris* eggs, almost all will be damaged by the lime and consequently will be inviable, so not posing a health risk). Lime sludge disposal to even alkaline soils does not raise the soil pH significantly, and yields of cotton, for example, from lime sludge-amended plots were found to be higher than those from control plots (Akrivos et al, 2000*; see also Jiminez et al, 2002).

Membrane bioreactors are a relatively recent wastewater treatment technology. They can produce extremely high quality effluents (see Ben Aim and Semmens, 2003*) – but usually of too high a quality for, and therefore generally inappropriate in, most situations in almost all developing countries at present. Details are given in Stephenson et al (2000) and van der Roest et al (2002); see also Chang et al (2002*) on membrane fouling in these systems.

SUSTAINABLE WASTEWATER TREATMENT OPTIONS

Many developing countries have a warm or hot climate, and often they have sufficient land for land-intensive wastewater treatment technologies (WSP, for example). They should take maximal advantage of their climate and their land availablilty for wastewater treatment. Money spent on land is *not* money wasted (Chapter 9), but money spent on electricity is money gone for ever.

Thus the most sustainable options for domestic wastewater treatment in developing countries are likely to be:

- anaerobic technologies, such as anaerobic ponds (especially high-rate anaerobic ponds) and maybe UASBs, and
- photosynthetic technologies, such as facultative and maturation ponds and maybe constructed wetlands.

Generally these two 'natural' processes are used in series, treating the wastewater first anaerobically and then photosynthetically (see also Gijzen, 2002*). Given modern design the land take for these natural systems need not be as large as their 'opponents' commonly suppose or might suggest. One example will suffice here (the point is considered in more detail in Chapter 9): WSP have been described as suitable 'only if land is relatively cheap (<US\$ 15/m^2)' (Yu et al, 1997). This translates to WSP being suitable at land prices up to US\$150,000/ha, which is in fact a very *high* price for land near almost all towns and cities in developing countries – the best agricultural land in industrialized countries is worth much less than this (in England, for example, the very best 'general purpose arable' land costs up to 'only' US\$20,000/ha).

If a move is made away from these natural treatment processes (or forced away, due to inappropriately high effluent quality requirements – Chapter 4), then there is in effect a trade-off: more money needs to be spent on both capital and operation and maintenance (O&M) costs (especially electrical energy costs), and less on land. In simple financial terms, such as a discounted cash-flow analysis (ie in average incremental cost terms), it is basically almost a straight comparison between land costs and the costs of electromechanical equipment (including their concrete housing structures) and the electricity used. As will be shown in subsequent chapters (especially Chapter 9), natural systems are almost always the most appropriate option. Higher-tech systems are only appropriate when the land for natural systems really is not there. Then one should move up the higher-tech 'ladder' very cautiously, always considering the least higher-tech options first and the most high-tech systems last. It will often be instructive, especially for large wastewater treatment projects, and particularly when high-tech solutions are being considered, to undertake a Bayesian benefit–risk analysis to determine the most sustainable option (Englehardt, 1997*).

7

Domestic Wastewater Flows and Loads

DOMESTIC WASTEWATER FLOWS

Domestic wastewater flows are commonly determined from domestic water consumption:

$$Q_{ww} = 10^{-3}kqP$$

$$(7.1)$$

where Q_{ww} is the wastewater flow, m^3/day; q is the water consumption, l/person day; P is the population connected to the sewerage system; and k is the 'return factor', the fraction of the water consumed that becomes wastewater. The value of k is usually 0.8–0.9. It is lower in rich areas where water is used for car washing and garden watering. Equation 7.1 gives the domestic wastewater 'dry weather flow' (DWF) – a term used principally from the time when 'combined' sewers (ie sewers receiving both sanitary and stormwater flows) were common. (Combined sewers do exist in developing countries, especially in city centres, but the current preference is to separate sanitary and stormwater flows.) Dry weather flow is the average wastewater flow per day over seven consecutive days without any rain which follow seven days with no more than 0.25 mm of rain on any one day. The mean daily flow is often taken as 1.3 x DWF.

Butler and Graham (1995*) describe a computer model called 'Flush' to determine actual DWF values (and also peak flow values – see below) based on detailed surveys of in-house water usage, and also to assess the spatial and temporal variations in DWF.

Campos and von Sperling (1996*) give the following regression equation for the mean domestic wastewater flow (q_{ww}, l/person day) based on household income in Brazil:

$$q_{ww} = 58 + 8N_{ms}$$

$$(7.2)$$

where N_{ms} is the household income expressed as the number of minimum salaries per month (one minimum salary was US$100/month in Brazil in 1996). Equation 7.2 is valid only for Brazil and perhaps other Latin American countries that are socio-economically broadly similar to Brazil. The derivation of similar equations for African and Asian developing countries would be very useful.

Infiltration

Sewer joints are often imperfect; over time they allow groundwater to enter the sewer. This increases the wastewater flow (and decreases the wastewater BOD). For concrete pipes, infiltration is ~20 m³/ha day; and for PVC pipes (which are easier to joint well) ~10 m³/ha day. Thus taking infiltration into account, equation 7.1 becomes:

$$Q_{ww} = 10^{-3}kqP + I$$

(7.3)

where I is the infiltration flow, m³/day.

Industrial wastewaters

In a municipal wastewater treatment project the flow of industrial wastewater must also be taken into account. Equation 7.3 becomes:

$$Q_{ww} = 10^{-3}kqP + I + E$$

(7.4)

where E is the industrial wastewater flow, m³/day.

Many industrial wastewaters are toxic to microbiological wastewater treatment processes, and therefore they should be pretreated prior to discharge to sewer (see Water Environment Federation, 1994a). Failure to pretreat can be extremely serious, and regulators need to work closely with industries to ensure, first by persuasion and later by the imposition of 'pollution charges', that they do pretreat their wastewaters (see Afsah et al, 1996*; D'Arcy et al, 1999*; Wheeler, 2000*; Tilche and Orhon, 2002*; World Bank, 2002*).

In many developing countries, industrial wastewaters are discharged untreated into inland or coastal waters – with huge adverse impacts on the local aquatic ecology. The 2002 Stockholm Statement on global water security strongly recommends that 'the link between economic growth and water degradation be urgently broken' (Stockholm International Water Institute, 2002*). To break this link governments and their regulators must require, either through new legislation or the enforcement of existing legislation, that industrial wastewaters are pretreated before discharge to sewer or properly treated before discharge to inland or coastal waters – and this also applies, of course, to domestic wastewaters since economic growth generally leads to increased urban populations and hence to increased domestic wastewater flows.

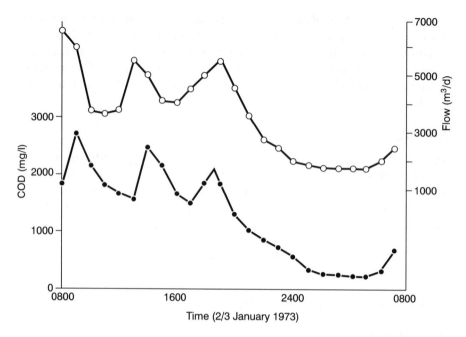

Figure 7.1 *Diurnal Variation of Wastewater Flow (○) and Load (●) at Nakuru, Kenya*

Peak wastewater flows

Equations 7.1–7.4 give the mean daily wastewater flow. However, wastewater flows (and loads) vary throughout the day (Figure 7.1), also through the week and the year. Flows are low at night when people are asleep; they rise sharply around breakfast time; there may be a similar 'peak' at lunchtime and then one again in the evening. Certain household activities may be more common on weekdays, rather than at weekends (eg clothes washing). Finally, during the hot season, people may use more water (eg through showering more frequently).

It is necessary to determine the peak daily flow as this is the maximum flow that arrives at the treatment works and parts of the works must be designed to receive this flow (eg the preliminary treatment units detailed in Chapter 8). The peak daily wastewater flow is the mean daily flow multiplied by a 'peak factor'; this depends on the population served, since the higher the population, the lower the peak factor as flow fluctuations are reduced during the time of flow in the sewer. The peak factor (PF) can be estimated from:

$$PF = 14P^{-1/6}$$

$$(7.5)$$

where P is the population served. Equation 7.5 gives values of ~3 for a population of 10,000, ~2 for 100,000 and ~1.4 for 1,000,000.

DOMESTIC WASTEWATER LOADS

The BOD concentration of domestic wastewater is the BOD contribution in mg/person/day divided by the wastewater flow in l/person day. As noted in Chapter 1, the BOD contribution increases with income. Campos and von Sperling (1996*) give the following regression equation for BOD concentration (L_i, mg/l) based on household income in Brazil:

$$L_i = 247 + \exp(5.9 - 0.26N_{ms})$$

$$(7.6)$$

As with equation 7.2, this equation is valid only for Brazil and perhaps other Latin American countries. Again similar equations for African and Asian developing countries would be very useful.

FUTURE PROJECTIONS

Urban populations will certainly increase, and thus wastewater flows and loads will also increase with time. The following equation is used to predict population growth:

$$P_n = P_0(1 + r)^n$$

$$(7.7)$$

where P_n and P_0 are the sewered populations in n years time and now, respectively; and r is the annual population growth rate expressed as a decimal fraction (rather than as a percentage).

The value of P_0 and the anticipated value of r should be obtained from the local municipal planning department. They should be consistent with values from the recent past, but they also need to take into account any major developments expected to occur in the planning period of n years. Often n is taken as 20 years, but it is best to determine P in steps of 5 years (ie for $n = 5$, 10, 15 and 20 years) in order to decide how best to phase the development of the proposed wastewater treatment facilities. Phasing is important since, rather than building a waste stabilization pond complex to serve the population expected in 20 years time, it is financially more sensible to build it for the population expected in, say, 5 years time and then expand it in 4 years time to serve the population anticipated in 10 years time, and so on. However, there are two things that must be done now: one is to buy all the land required to serve the population expected in 20 years time; and the other is to arrange with the lending agency that the total loan is to be disbursed over time – some now and some more in 4, 9 and 14 years time.

As sewered populations become richer, their per caput water consumption, and hence their per caput wastewater generation, and their per caput BOD contribution will increase (as shown by equations 7.2 and 7.6). This must also be taken into account.

8

Preliminary Treatment

PURPOSE

The first stage of wastewater treatment is the removal of large floating objects (such as rags, maize cobs, pieces of wood) and heavy mineral particles (sand and grit). This is done in order to prevent, for example, floating material accumulating on the surface of waste stabilization ponds and heavy solids entering the pond sludge layer, and to protect from damage the equipment used in the subsequent stages of treatment (for example the floating aerators in aerated lagoons or any pumps which may be used). This preliminary treatment comprises *screening* and *grit removal*.

Manuals of Practice on preliminary wastewater treatment have been prepared by the Institution of Water and Environmental Management (1992) and the Water Environment Federation (1994b).

SCREENING

Coarse solids are removed by a series of closely spaced mild steel bars placed across the flow. The velocity through the screen should be <1 m/s so that the solids already trapped on the screen (the 'screenings') are not dislodged. The spacing between the bars is usually 15–25 mm and the bars are commonly of rectangular cross-section, typically 10 x 50 mm. At small works screens are raked by hand and, in order to facilitate this, the screens are inclined, commonly at 60° to the horizontal (Figure 8.1). The submerged area of the hand-raked screens is calculated on the empirical basis of 0.15–0.20 m² per 1000 population; this assumes that the screens are raked at least twice each day.

For flows >1000 m³/day mechanically raked screens (Figure 8.2) are preferred since they can be cleaned more frequently (every 10–30 minutes) and they are therefore considerably smaller than hand-raked screens. The channel dimensions required for a mechanically raked screen are calculated as follows:

$$\text{flow area} = \frac{\text{flow}}{\text{velocity}}$$

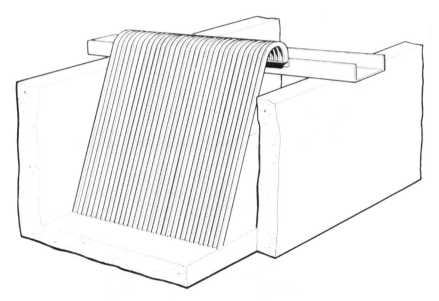

Figure 8.1 *Simple Manually Raked Screen (flow is from left to right)*

The flow area is the channel area corrected for the area of the bars. The flow is the daily maximum (ie 'peak') flow (Chapter 7). The velocity is generally restricted to 0.6 m/s in order to prevent grit deposition and dislodgement of screenings. The equation is therefore:

$$WD_{max}[s/(b + s)] = Q_{max}/0.6$$

$$(8.1)$$

that is

$$W = Q_{max}/\{0.6D_{max}[s/(b + s)]\}$$

$$(8.2)$$

where W and D_{max} are the channel width and depth at maximum flow, respectively, m; Q_{max} is the maximum (ie peak) flow, m^3/s; b and s are the bar thickness and spacing, respectively, in millimetres.

A standby hand-raked screen should be provided for use when the mechanical screen is out of action. This emergency screen is normally the same size as the mechanical screen and it therefore requires raking at frequent intervals when in use.

Disposal of screenings

Screenings are generally obnoxious in both appearance and content and should be disposed of as soon as possible. At small works this is readily achieved by burial, a small area of land being set aside for this purpose. At larger works

Figure 8.2 *Mechanically Raked Screen*

screenings are commonly dewatered in a hydraulic press and then either buried (or sometimes incinerated) on-site or taken away to the nearest landfill. Advice on handling screenings in given by Clay et al (1996*).

The quantity of screenings that is removed varies considerably but, for 10 mm bars at 20 mm spacings, an approximate figure is 0.01–0.03 m³/day per 1000 population.

Fine screening

Fine screens have apertures of 3–15 mm, with 6 mm being the most common, and very fine screens ('milli-screens') are those with apertures of 0.25–3 mm. They produce very large quantities of screenings which are normally washed and dewatered before disposal; these processes are generally an integral part of the fine screen unit – for example, Filtech or Wash-flow screens (Jones and Attwood, 2002*).

Fine screens are now common in many industrialized countries, but in developing countries their applicability is much more limited: their high efficiency is generally too high ('technology overkill' – Chapter 4), they are expensive imported items, and their maintenance is likely to be problematic.

GRIT REMOVAL

Grit (also called 'detritus') is the heavy inorganic fraction of the wastewater solids. It includes road grit, sand, eggshells, ashes, charcoal, glass and pieces of metal; it may also contain some heavy organic matter such as seeds and coffee grounds. Grit has an average relative density of ~2.5 and thus it has a much higher settling velocity than organic solids (~30 mm/s, compared with ~3 mm/s). This difference in sedimentation rates is exploited in grit removal plants where, for ease of handling and disposal, the organic fraction must be kept to a minimum (<15 per cent). There are two basic types of grit removal plant: constant velocity grit channels and the various proprietary grit tanks or traps available commercially.

Constant velocity grit channels

If the velocity of flow of the wastewater is ~0.3 m/s, grit particles settle out but organic solids do not. The problem is to maintain the velocity constant at this value *for all rates of flow*. The best solution is to locate a standing wave (ie Venturi or Parshall) flume immediately downstream of a grit channel of parabolic cross-section (Townsend, 1937; Marais and van Haandel, 1996*). This solution depends on the following two points:

1   provided that it is free-flowing (ie not 'drowned'), a Venturi or Parshall flume produces an upstream depth which is independent of conditions downstream and controlled only by the magnitude of the flow; and
2   if the geometry of the grit channel is such that its cross-sectional area is proportional to the flow, then the velocity of flow through the channel will be constant at all flows – if v = velocity, q = flow and a = cross-sectional area, then $v = q/a$; but if a is proportional to q (ie $a = kq$) , then v is constant.

In order to comply with (2) the channel should have a parabolic cross-section. The explanation for this is as follows:

(a) the flow q through a Venturi flume is given by:

$$q = kbh^{3/2}$$

(8.3)

where k is a constant; b is the flume throat width; and h is the upstream channel depth.

(b) differentiating equation 8.3:

$$dq = \frac{3}{2} kbh^{1/2}dh$$

(8.4)

(c) the flow dq through a cross-sectional element of the channel (Figure 8.3) is given by:

$$dq = Vxdh$$

(8.5)

where V is the velocity of flow and xdh is the area of the element.

(d) equating equations 8.4 and 8.5 and rearranging gives:

$$x = \left(\frac{3kb}{2V}\right) h^{1/2}$$

(8.6)

Equation 8.6 is the equation of a parabola. In practice, for ease of construction, a trapezoidal cross-section is used (Figure 8.4).

If V = 0.3 m/s and X and H are the channel dimensions (m) at maximum flow (Q_{max}, m^3/s), equations 8.3 and 8.6 can be rewritten as:

$$Q_{max} = kbH^{3/2}$$

(8.7)

$$X = 5kbH^{1/2}$$

(8.8)

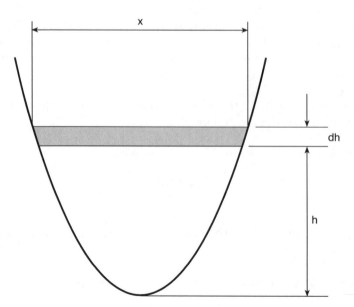

Figure 8.3 *Flow Elements in a Parabolic Channel*

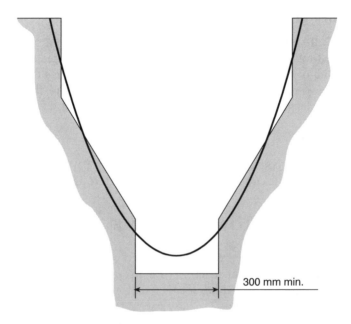

300 mm min.

Figure 8.4 *Trapezoidal Approximation to a Parabolic Section*

Dividing equation 8.8 by equation 8.7 and rearranging gives:

$$X = 5Q_{max}/H$$

(8.9)

Thus the top width of the channel is simply determined from the maximum flow and the corresponding depth. In practice at least two channels are provided so that one may be closed for grit removal. The channel length is determined by the settling velocity of the grit particles.

$$\text{Length of channel} = \frac{\text{channel depth} \times \text{velocity of flow}}{\text{settling velocity of grit particles}}$$

Grit particles typically settle at about 0.03 m/s, so that when the velocity of flow is controlled to 0.3 m/s thus:

$$\text{Length of channel} = 10 \times \text{maximum depth of flow}$$

In practice, to allow for inlet turbulence and variations in settling velocity, the channel length is taken as 20 x maximum depth of flow.

Proprietary grit separators

For flows >5000 m^3/day proprietary grit separators are often more economical than several long constant-velocity grit channels. There are several models available. One of the simplest is the 'Jeta' grit trap which has the advantages that no moving parts come into contact with the grit and that the grit is automatically cleaned before discharge (Jones and Attwood, 2002*).

Grit disposal

The quantity of grit collected is usually in the range 0.05–0.10 m^3/1000 m^3 of wastewater. The grit is either buried on site or taken to landfill.

FLOW MEASUREMENT

The wastewater flow should always be measured in a Venturi or Parshall flume before it enters the treatment reactors (if constant velocity grit channels are used, such a flume is required anyway – see above; if not, then one must be installed). Flow measurements are very useful for determining diurnal flow variations (Chapter 7) and detecting any abnormal flow rates; they are also essential for evaluating the performance of the treatment system (Chapter 15). Digital flow recorders are useful as the data can be downloaded to a computer.

9

Waste Stabilization Ponds

Types and functions of WSP

Waste stabilization ponds (WSP) (Figure 9.1) are large shallow basins enclosed by earth embankments in which raw wastewater is treated by entirely natural processes involving both algae and bacteria. Since these processes are unaided by wastewater treatment engineers (who merely allocate a properly dimensioned place for their occurrence) the rate of oxidation is slower, and as a result hydraulic retention times are longer than in conventional wastewater treatment (eg electromechanical treatment processes such as activated sludge) _ retention times in WSP are measured in days rather than in hours. They are without doubt the most important method of wastewater treatment in developing countries where sufficient land is normally available and where the temperature is most favourable for their operation. Indeed they are so advantageous (see below) that a very good case has to be made for *not* using them.

There are three principal types of WSP: anaerobic, facultative and maturation ponds. Anaerobic ponds (Chapter 10) and facultative ponds (Chapter 11) are designed for BOD (biochemical oxygen demand) removal, and maturation ponds (Chapter 12) are designed for faecal bacterial removal. Some removal of faecal bacteria (especially of *Vibrio cholerae*) occurs in anaerobic and facultative ponds, which are also responsible for most of the removal of helminth eggs; and some removal of BOD occurs in maturation

Figure 9.1 *One of Phase II 21-ha Primary Facultative Ponds at Dandora, Nairobi, Kenya*

ponds, which also remove some of the nutrients (N and P). There are two other types of WSP: macrophyte ponds and 'advanced pond systems' which are described later in this chapter (but they are not generally applicable in developing countries).

Facultative and maturation ponds are *photosynthetic* ponds – that is the oxygen needed by the pond bacteria to oxidize the wastewater BOD is mainly supplied by micro-algae that grow naturally and profusely in these ponds (and thus give them their characteristic green colour); and the carbon dioxide needed by the algae is mainly provided by the pond bacteria as an end-product of their metabolism. Thus there is a 'mutualistic' relationship between the pond algae and the pond bacteria (Figure 9.2). The algae are also extremely important in creating conditions within the ponds for faecal bacterial die-off (Chapter 12).

Arrangement of WSP

The different WSP types are arranged in a series – first an anaerobic pond, then a facultative pond, and finally (and if needed to achieve the required effluent quality – Chapter 4) one or more maturation ponds (Figure 9.3). At any one site there may be more than one series of WSP, each usually receiving an equal proportion of the wastewater flow.

It is commonly observed that the effluent from a series of ponds is of better quality than that from a single pond of the same size. This is because, even if the hydraulic flow regime in individual ponds is closer to complete mixing than it is to plug flow, the overall performance of a series of ponds

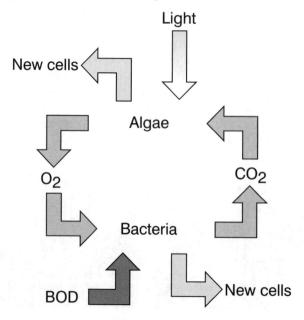

Figure 9.2 *Algal–bacterial Mutualism in Facultative and Maturation Ponds*

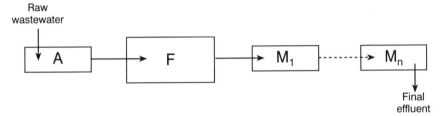

Figure 9.3 *Typical WSP Layout: A, anaerobic pond; F, facultative pond;*
M₁–Mₙ, maturation ponds

approximates that of a plug flow reactor. To illustrate this point, consider a
series of *n* identical ponds and assume that each is a completely mixed reactor
in which BOD removal follows first-order kinetics (Chapter 5). For the whole
series of *n* ponds, equation 5.7 is rewritten as:

$$\frac{L_e}{L_i} = \frac{1}{(1 + k_1\theta)^n}$$

(9.1)

where Le and Li are the BOD of the final effluent and raw wastewater,
respectively, mg/l.

If σ is the total retention time in the series of *n* ponds, then σ = *n*θ and:

$$\frac{L_e}{L_i} = \frac{1}{(1 + k_1\theta)^{\sigma/\theta}}$$

(9.2)

In the limit as θ → 0 (and if σ is to remain the same as *n* → ∞):

$$\frac{L_e}{L_i} = \lim_{\theta \to 0} \left[\frac{1}{(1 + k_1\theta)^{\sigma/\theta}} \right]$$

that is:

$$\frac{L_e}{L_i} = \exp(-k_1\sigma)$$

(9.3)

Equation 9.3 is the equation for a plug flow reactor of retention time σ
(compare equation 5.10). This shows that a plug flow reactor is equivalent to
a series of an infinitely large number of infinitely small completely-mixed
reactors. Since plug flow is the most efficient hydraulic regime (Chapter 5),
equation 9.3 demonstrates that a series of small ponds is more efficient than a
single large pond.

Marais' theorem

This theorem, propounded by Marais (1974), states that '*maximum efficiency in a series of ponds is achieved when the retention time in each pond is the same*'. The theorem is proved here for a series of two ponds, but the proof is applicable in principle for any number of ponds.

Let the retention time in the first pond be θ_1 and in the second pond θ_2, and let $\sigma = \theta_1 + \theta_2$. The effluent BOD from the second pond is given by:

$$L_e = \frac{L_i}{(1 + k_1\theta_1)(1 + k_1\theta_2)}$$

(9.4)

L_e is a minimum when $[(1 + k_1\theta_1)(1 + k_1\theta_2)]$ is a maximum:

$$\text{Let } y = (1 + k_1\theta_1)(1 + k_1\theta_2)$$

$$\therefore y = [1 + k_1\theta_1][1 + k_1(\sigma - \theta_1)]$$

$$= 1 + k_1\sigma + k_1^2\sigma\theta_1 - (k_1\theta_1)^2$$

(9.5)

$$\frac{dy}{d\theta_1} = k_1^2\sigma - 2k_1^2\theta_1$$

(9.6)

$$= 0, \text{ for a maximum}$$

$$\therefore \theta_1 = \sigma/2 = \theta_2$$

(9.7)

Thus, for maximum y and hence minimum L_e, the retention time in the two ponds must be the same. That y is a maximum (and not a minimum) is verified by considering the second differential coefficient:

$$\frac{d^2y}{d(\theta_1)^2} = -2k_1^2$$

(9.8)

Since this is negative, y is a maximum.

However, in practice it is not possible for all ponds in a series to have the same retention time. Anaerobic ponds are sized on the basis of volumetric BOD loading (Chapter 10) and facultative ponds on the basis of surface BOD loading (Chapter 11), and these design procedures result in different retention times which, if they were altered to be the same, would result in an underloaded anaerobic pond and an overloaded facultative pond – clearly undesirable. But maturation ponds (Chapter 12) should be equally sized wherever (as is usually the case) the site geometry permits this.

ADVANTAGES OF WSP

The advantages of WSP are that they are *simple, low-cost, highly efficient* and *robust*.

Simplicity

WSP are simple to construct: earthmoving is the principal activity; other civil works are essentially minimal – preliminary treatment, inlets and outlets, pond embankment construction and protection and, if necessary, pond lining (details are given in Chapter 13). They are also very simple to operate and maintain: routine tasks comprise cutting the embankment grass, removing any scum and floating vegetation from the pond surfaces, keeping the inlets and outlets clear, and repairing any damage to the embankments (details are given in Chapter 14). Less skilled labour is needed for pond operation and maintenance (O&M) than other wastewater treatment technologies. The simplicity of WSP construction also means that flexibility in construction phasing is possible (Chapter 7).

Low cost

If an honest cost comparison is made between WSP and other wastewater treatment options, WSP almost always cost the least, for both capital and O&M costs. The only sensible methodology for such a cost comparison is that described in a World Bank report by Arthur (1983*), which gives a detailed economic comparison of WSP, aerated lagoons, oxidation ditches and biofilters. The data for this cost comparison were taken from the city of Sana'a in the Yemen Arab Republic, but are equally applicable in principle to other countries. Certain assumptions were made: for example, the use of maturation ponds to follow the aerated lagoon, and chlorination of the oxidation ditch and biological filter effluents, in order that the four processes would have an effluent of similar bacteriological quality so that fish farming and effluent re-use for irrigation were feasible. The design was based on a population of 250,000; wastewater flow and BOD contributions of 120 l and 40 g/person day, respectively; influent and required effluent *E coli* numbers of 2×10^7 and $\leq 1 \times 10^4$ per 100 ml, respectively (but we would now design for ≤ 1000 *E coli* per 100 ml of effluent); and a required effluent BOD of ≤ 25 mg/l. The calculated land area requirements and total net present cost of each system (assuming an opportunity cost of capital of 12 per cent and a land cost of US$5/m^2) are shown in Table 9.1. WSP were clearly the cheapest option. The preferred solution is, of course, very sensitive to the price of land, and the above cost of US$5/m^2 was chosen as it represented a reasonable value for land in low-cost housing estates in developing countries.

Table 9.1 *Costs and Land Area Requirements for WSP and other Treatment Processes*

	Waste stabilization pond system	Aerated lagoon system	Oxidation ditch system	Conventional treatment (biofilters)
Costs (million US$)				
Capital	5.68	6.98	4.80	7.77
Operational	0.21	1.28	1.49	0.86
Benefits (million US$)				
Irrigation income	0.43	0.43	0.43	0.43
Pisciculture income	0.30	0.30	–	–
Net present cost (million US$)	5.16	7.53	5.86	8.20
Land area (ha)	46	50	20	25

Source: Arthur (1983*)

The price of land and the opportunity cost of capital (OCC) are the two main variables which decide whether WSP are the cheapest option. Figure 9.4, based on Arthur's (1983*) data, shows how the OCC (or discount rate) influences the land price below which WSP are the cheapest option. In Arthur's study this was US$5–15/m^2 (ie US$50,000–150,000/ha), depending on the OCC within a range of 5–15 per cent. Tsagarakis et al (2003*) found that WSP were the cheapest treatment option in Greece up to a land cost of US$300,000/ha.

WSP do not need electrical energy for their operation, and this saves a considerable amount of recurrent costs. This is well illustrated by the following data for energy consumption by four wastewater treatment processes in the USA for a domestic wastewater flow of 1 million US gallons/day (ie 3780 m^3/d) (Middlebrooks et al, 1982):

- Activated sludge   1 000 000 kWh/year
- Aerated lagoons   800 000 kWh/year
- Biodiscs   120 000 kWh/year
- **WSP**   nil

As noted in Chapter 6, money spent on electricity is money gone for ever, but money spent on land is an investment, for example, the city of Concord, California purchased land for ponds in 1955 at a cost of US$50,000/ha, and by 1975 it was worth US$375,000/ha (Oswald, 1976). Inflation during this 20-year period was more or less 100 per cent, so the land value increased in real terms by 375 per cent (or 6.8 per cent/year).

Colombia

A good example of WSP investment costs is from Colombia, where the Ministry of Economic Development uses the following budget costs:

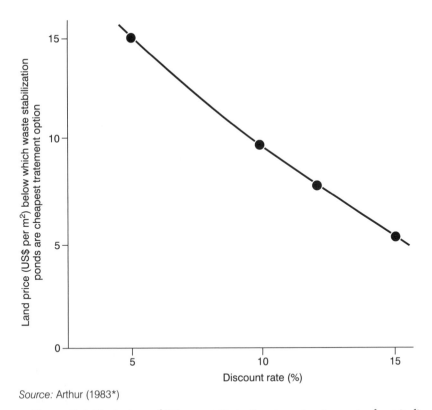

Source: Arthur (1983*)

Figure 9.4 *Variation of Discount Rate (ie opportunity cost of capital) and Land Price below which WSP are the Cheapest Treatment Option*

- WSP   US$30/person
- Activated sludge   US$130/person

Colombian cities of <250,000 population are required by the Ministry to undertake a 'serious' evaluation of WSP as a wastewater treatment option (otherwise they are not considered for a government loan).

High efficiency

WSP are extremely efficient: they can be easily designed to achieve BOD and suspended solids removals >90 per cent, and ammonia removals also >90 per cent (Table 12.1). They are particularly efficient in removing excreted pathogens, whereas, in contrast, all other treatment processes are very inefficient in this respect and require a tertiary treatment process such as chlorination (with all its inherent operational and environmental problems) to achieve the destruction of faecal bacteria. Activated sludge plants may, if operating very well, achieve a 99 per cent removal of *E coli* – this might, at first inspection, appear very impressive, but in fact it only represents a reduction from ~10^7 per 100 ml to ~10^5 per 100 ml (ie in terms of bacterial

Table 9.2 *Excreted Pathogen Removals in WSP and Conventional Treatment Processes*

Excreted Pathogen	Removal in WSP	Removal in conventional treatment
Bacteria	up to 6 log units	1–2 log units
Viruses	up to 4 log units	1–2 log units
Protozoan cysts	99–100%	90–99%
Helminth eggs	100%	90–99%

Note: 1 log unit = 90 per cent removal; 2 = 99 per cent; 3 = 99.9 per cent, and so on

numbers, almost nothing). A properly designed series of WSP, on the other hand, can easily reduce *E coli* numbers from ~10^7 per 100 ml to <10^3 per 100 ml (the WHO guideline for unrestricted irrigation; see Chapters 4 and 21), which is a removal of 99.99 per cent (or 4 log units). A general comparison between WSP and conventional treatment processes for the removal of excreted pathogens is shown in Table 9.2; detailed information is given in Feachem et al (1983*).

Robustness

WSP are very robust: due to their long hydraulic retention time, they are more resilient to both organic and hydraulic shock loads than other wastewater treatment processes. They can also cope with high levels of heavy metals, up to 60 mg/l (Moshe et al, 1972; see also Toumi et al, 2000*), so they can treat a wide variety of industrial wastewaters that would be too toxic for other treatment processes. Strong wastewaters from agro-industrial processes (eg abattoirs, food canneries, dairies) are easily treated in WSP. Moreover, WSP are the only secondary/tertiary treatment process which can readily and reliably produce effluents that are microbiologically safe for re-use in agriculture and aquaculture (Chapters 21 and 22).

India

The National River Conservation Directorate (2003*), which is part of the Ministry of Environment and Forests, Government of India, clearly recognizes the advantages of WSP, as it states that 'only waste stabilization ponds, which are eco-friendly and simple to operate, will be mainly supported to treat wastewater hereafter'. The principal reason for this major shift in policy away from capital- and energy-intensive treatment technologies was the realization that WSP are not only low-cost but are also the most appropriate treatment system to reduce pathogens to levels suitable for safe re-use in agriculture and aquaculture and for safe bathing in the receiving rivers. NRCD considers WSP to be 'people-friendly and relevant for health'.

Perceived disadvantages of WSP

To the unthinking, WSP seem to have the 'disadvantage' of simplicity, which is interpreted wholly erroneously as a lack of sophistication – 'activated sludge *must* be better'! Engineers at least should know better, but unfortunately there are too many who do not. This lack of intellectual critical ability sometimes appears in those who really should be more aware, for example, it was suggested at the Fifth IWA Pond Conference held in 2002 that in one southern Pacific country, because the WSP designed according to the 1974 national WSP design guidelines were not working well, 'advanced pond systems' (see later in this chapter) should be used instead. The logical (and certainly cheaper) option would be to upgrade the existing WSP using the modern design methods given in Chapters 10–12.

Of course, cities and towns can be 'turned off' WSP by a bad experience with them – sometimes resulting from poor operation and maintenance, or allowing them to become seriously overloaded; but this could also be due to poor design by an inexperienced designer or, not uncommonly, a designer experienced with WSP in Europe or North America but who has little idea how to design WSP in warmer climates (one of the purposes of this book is to minimize such occurrences).

There are, however, more serious perceived disadvantages of WSP: a fear of odour release, high land requirements and costs, and 'poor' effluent quality.

Odour release

All overloaded microbiological wastewater treatment plants have odour problems, and WSP are no exception to this. However, WSP that are properly designed and then properly operated and maintained do not have odour problems, and they will not have odour problems until they become overloaded. A WSP system (and this refers especially to anaerobic and primary facultative ponds – Chapters 10 and 11) designed appropriately for a population of N will probably be satisfactory for a population of $~1.2N$ (as there is a factor of safety in the design), but it would be unrealistic not to expect at least some odour from the ponds when they are more heavily overloaded than this. In such cases the WSP should be upgraded (Chapter 13).

Land

WSP do require much more land than conventional treatment processes such as oxidation ditches (Chapter 20) or activated sludge. The choice is between buying land (which is an investment – see earlier in this chapter) or spending a large amount of money each year on electricity. It is quite straightforward to determine where inexpensive land is available and how much it costs to (a) convey the wastewater there and (b) construct WSP – is this cheaper than an activated sludge plant nearer the city? If these cost calculations are done correctly and honestly, the answer to this question is almost always *Yes*.

Strange decisions are, of course, made. For example, the capital city of a large oil-producing country between the Middle East and South Asia chose, after a 40-year deliberation period, activated sludge over WSP – despite the fact that it is surrounded by desert where land is cheap and the treated wastewater is needed for crop irrigation. This example is not, unfortunately, unique.

There will, of course, be some situations where the land for WSP is really not available, or is prohibitively expensive, even at some distance from the town or city. In such cases WSP are obviously inappropriate, and an alternative treatment process has to be selected. The work of Arthur (1983*) suggests that oxidation ditches (Chapter 20) are likely to be the next preferred solution.

Effluent quality

WSP effluents can be high in BOD and suspended solids (SS), but most of this effluent BOD and SS is due to the algae in the pond effluent. In the BOD test algae consume oxygen as the BOD bottles are incubated in the dark, but in a receiving watercourse the algae produce more oxygen than they need for respiration and they are consumed by higher life forms. Algal BOD and SS are thus very different from non-algal BOD and SS, and sensible regulators recognize this, for example, in the European Union the required WSP effluent quality is ≤25 mg *filtered* (ie non-algal) BOD per litre and ≤150 mg SS (ie mainly algal SS) per litre (Council of the European Communities, 1991a*). If this is acceptable in Europe, why not in developing countries? Local regulators in developing countries should at least be aware of these EU requirements for WSP effluents.

If WSP effluents are used for crop irrigation (Chapter 21), the algae are very useful: they act as slow-release fertilizers and over time increase the organic content of the soil and thus its water-holding capacity.

WSP USAGE

WSP are used in all parts of the world – from Alaska to New Zealand. The US has more than 7000 WSP systems (one-third of all wastewater treatment plants), mostly serving populations of less than 5000 (Environmental Protection Agency, 1983). France has over 2500 for populations of usually less than 1000 (Cemagref and Agences de l'Eau, 1997), and Germany (mainly in what was West Germany) has more than 1100, again typically for populations below 1000 (Bucksteeg, 1987). In New Zealand WSP are the most common form of wastewater treatment, with 100 of the 160 plants serving populations under 1000 being WSP (Archer and Mara, 2003*); this included the former Mangere WSP in Auckland (see below). There are many WSP systems in Australia, including those at the Western Treatment Plant in Melbourne. They are common in all parts of the developing world, where they can serve large populations, for example, the Dandora WSP near Nairobi, Kenya serve a

Figure 9.5 *The Phase I WSP at Dandora, Nairobi, Kenya*

sewered population of ~1 million, and the Al Samra WSP near Amman, Jordan serve a population of ~2.6 million.

Examples of large WSP systems

Dandora, Nairobi

Phase I of the Dandora WSP, which was commissioned in 1980, comprises two series of ponds, each of which has a 21-ha primary facultative pond and three 9-ha maturation ponds (Figure 9.5); the design flow was 30,000 m³/day. Phase II, commissioned in 1992, added a further six series, each comprising a 21-ha facultative pond and three 4.5-ha maturation ponds; the design flow was 80,000 m³/day, and the total (Phase I and II) pond area is ~300 ha. Phase II also included three pilot-scale anaerobic ponds ahead of one of the new series (Chapter 10; see Pearson et al, 1996a*). Phase III will be the provision of anaerobic ponds as the first stage in all eight series, so taking the design flow to 160,000 m³/day – equivalent to a population of ~2 million.

Al Samra, Amman

This WSP system (see Figure 13.13) was commissioned in 1985 and currently treats a wastewater flow of ~150,000 m³/day in three series, each comprising two 3.2-ha anaerobic ponds, four 7.25-ha facultative ponds and four 6.25-ha maturation ponds – a total pond area of 181 ha. Full details are given by Al-Salem and Lumbers (1987). The design flow was 68,000 m³/day, so the ponds are overloaded hydraulically by a factor of 2.2; even so, BOD removal is 73–85 per cent (and no electromechanical treatment plant as overloaded as this could do so well) (Mara and Pearson, 1998*).

The arrangement of ponds in each series is not the best – all 10 ponds are in series, and all but the last two maturation ponds are overloaded organically, as well as hydraulically (however, the 10 ponds in each series could be reconfigured relatively easily to provide, for example, 5 series of 6 ponds or even 10 series of 3 ponds). The WSP discharge into the King Talal reservoir, which has a capacity of 78 million m³. This reservoir also receives some freshwater input, as well as some other treated wastewaters; it effectively acts as a wastewater storage and treatment reservoir (Chapter 16). The contents of the reservoir are used for unrestricted irrigation in the Jordan Valley (the east bank of the River Jordan), and it is the microbiological quality of the reservoir effluent (rather than that of the ponds) that is important for its use for unrestricted irrigation.

Werribee, Melbourne

The Western Treatment Plant at Werribee in Melbourne, Australia commenced operations in 1892 as a 'sewage farm' (Penrose, 2001*). Currently it receives 530,000 m³ of wastewater per day from a population of 1.6 million (55 per cent of the city's total population) and from various industries (mainly distilleries, breweries, slaughterhouses and rendering plants, food processing factories, tanneries, paper mills and heavy industrial laundries) which contribute ~22 per cent of the flow and ~55 per cent of the BOD (Melbourne Water, 2002*). WSP systems were introduced in 1937; there are now three modern WSP systems (the '115E, 55E and 25W lagoons'), which together treat 69 per cent of the annual raw wastewater flow in a total pond area of 1667 ha. Each series comprises 10 ponds with an overall retention time of 50–120 days. The final effluent is discharged into Port Phillip Bay. Effluent quality is very high: unfiltered BOD, 10–43 mg/l; suspended solids, 30–62 mg/l; total N, 24–27 mg/l; total P, ~6 mg/l; and *E coli*, 50–500 per 100 ml. The mean temperature of the coldest month (July) is 13°C and the warmest month (January) 25°C.

The '55 East lagoon' system was upgraded in 2001. It comprises 10 ponds in series, each 200 x 1500 m (Figure 9.6). Pond 1 is a hybrid system: the first 400 m has a depth of 6 m and acts as an anaerobic pond, the first half of which is covered and the biogas collected (Chapter 13). The rest of Pond 1 is 1.9 m deep and is aerated by 50 30 kW surface aerators. Ponds 2–4 are maturation ponds, as are ponds 6–10. Pond 5 contains an activated sludge plant for nitrification and denitrification, which receives 30 per cent of its flow direct from the anaerobic pond and 70 per cent from Pond 4. Nitrification occurs in the aerated tanks and denitrification in the anoxic tanks. Secondary sedimentation tanks settle the activated sludge which is returned to the anoxic tanks; excess sludge is discharged into the aerated section of Pond 1. The clarified effluent is discharged into the remaining section of Pond 5 (200 x 900 m), and thence into Ponds 6–10. The final effluent is discharged into Port Phillip Bay.

Note: Photograph taken during the covering of the anaerobic section of Pond 1 and prior to the provision of the nitrification–denitrification activated sludge plant in Pond 5.
Source: Courtesy of Melbourne Water.

Figure 9.6 *The 55 East WSP Series at Werribee, Melbourne, Australia*

The WSP at Melbourne Water's Western Treatment Plant at Werribee have undergone several major modifications since their introduction in the late 1930s in response to changing environmental priorities. The recent addition of the nitrifying/denitrifying activated sludge unit was necessary as the regulator (the Environmental Protection Agency of the State of Victoria) required a maximum discharge into Port Phillip Bay of 3100 tonnes of total N per year (N, rather than P, is the limiting nutrient for eutrophication of the Bay), and it was not possible to guarantee this by conventional WSP within the land area available. Melbourne Water has shown that an 'enhanced lagoon system' (of which 55E is the largest example in the world) can meet stringent '21st century' environmental quality objectives.

Mangere, Auckland

The Mangere WSP in Auckland were commissioned in 1960 as secondary and tertiary treatment units following primary sedimentation. The WSP, which were built on land reclaimed from a tidal mudflat, comprised three facultative ponds in parallel and a single maturation pond in series which discharged into Manukau harbour at high tide (Figure 9.7). (Building the ponds in Manukau harbour destroyed a traditional Maori shellfishing area, but in 1960 this was not a major consideration – at least not to the local non-Maori decision makers. Today attitudes have changed and such an approach would be unthinkable.) The area of each facultative pond was 119–135 ha, and that of the maturation pond 125 ha – a total of 512 ha. The effluents from the facultative ponds were recirculated to their inlets, with a recirculation ratio of ~2.7. As the population grew, the ponds became overloaded and they were mechanically aerated until four large biofilters (Chapter 19) were installed in 1980. The WSP then received a variable mixture of primary and secondary effluents so that the surface BOD load on the facultative ponds could be controlled throughout the year, from 60–80 kg/ha day in winter to 110–140 kg/ha day in summer. This was necessary to control midge (*Chironomus zealandicus*) breeding and to prevent algal crashes with concomitant odour release (the algal crashes were due to infection with the fungal parasite *Pseudosphaerita euglenae* and grazing by predatory rotifers, *Brachionus* spp). The algal crashes occurred once or twice each year with major odour emissions which travelled 5–10 km and led, understandably, to complaints from local residents. Midge control was achieved by spraying the shallow margins of the ponds with Malathion; however, this was not always successful and swarms of midges also affected the local residents fairly regularly.

Recently, under the Resource Management Act 1991, the local regulator (Auckland Regional Council) set new effluent quality requirements for wastewater discharges into Manukau harbour; in particular, in order to prevent eutrophication (especially the proliferation of the red seaweed *Gracilliaria*) and to avoid fish toxicity problems, the ammonia consent level was reduced from ≤38 mg N/l to ≤5 mg N/l in winter and ≤3 mg N/l in summer. The existing plant, including the WSP, was unable to achieve this, and so the decision was taken to build a completely new land-based treatment system, to include nutrient removal, by 2003. The WSP could have been used for disinfection to achieve the required *E coli* count of ≤80 per 100 ml, but midge breeding and algal crashes followed by odour release would have remained a

Note: The maturation pond is at top right.
Source: Courtesy of Watercare Services Ltd, Auckland

Figure 9.7 *The Mangere WSP, Auckland, New Zealand, in 1996*

real risk (Lawty et al, 1996*). This risk was no longer acceptable and consequently the WSP were decommissioned in 2002; their site is now once again part of Manukau harbour (Watercare Services Ltd, 2002*). Disinfection is now achieved by UV radiation as the final unit process of the new land-based treatment plant.

The Mangere ponds served Auckland satisfactorily for over 40 years, despite the problems with midges and odour release. They demonstrated well the ability of WSP to meet their discharge requirements until it was decided to impose a very much stricter ammonia standard. Reclaiming more land from the harbour was not an option, and so the Mangere ponds had to be decommissioned. Over 4 million m^3 of sludge were painstakingly dredged from the ponds before the pond area was opened to the sea. Some 13 km of newly restored coastline has been landscaped and planted with native coastal species. The rapid recovery of the marine ecosystem in the large tidal embayment formerly occupied by the ponds has been well received by the regulator and environmentalists, and particularly by the local Maori people who have welcomed the return of their traditional fishing grounds.

High-altitude WSP

Pearson et al (1987a) studied the WSP at Cajamarca (2675 m above mean sea level) and Juliaca (3827 m) in the high Andes of Peru. The ponds at Cajamarca (three series, each comprising a facultative and a maturation pond) achieved a filtered COD (chemical oxygen demand) removal of ~85 per cent at a pond water temperature of 15–21°C (which remained reasonably constant despite the daily air temperature varying between 5 and 24°C, a diurnal range of 19 degC). Chlorophyll *a* levels (see Chapter 11) in the facultative ponds were ~1500 µg/l, and sludge accumulation was minimal: only 5 cm in the facultative ponds after five years of operation.

The WSP at Juliaca comprised eight facultative ponds in parallel. Filtered COD removal was ~80 per cent, and chlorophyll *a* levels were ~320 µg/l. In-pond temperatures were 6–9°C and the daily air temperature varied between –5 and 14°C (a diurnal difference also of 19 degC). Sludge accumulation was also minimal: 5.5 cm after three years.

Thus high-altitude WSP can be designed in the same way as low-altitude ponds (Chapters 10–12), although, of course, due to lower temperatures they are larger than low-altitude ponds (see also Juanicó et al, 2000*). Care must be taken, however, at altitudes above 3500 m as mean in-pond temperatures are around the same as mean air temperatures in the coldest month, rather than being 2–4 degC warmer. Interestingly, anaerobic activity in primary facultative ponds does not appear to be adversely affected by temperatures that are low throughout the year, presumably because the anaerobic bacteria have adjusted to them. In contrast, methanogenesis in low-altitude WSP decreases in the cool season.

WSP – or other treatment processes?

How well do WSP stand up against other treatment processes, such as constructed wetlands, UASBs and aerated lagoons?

WSP vs constructed wetlands

Constructed wetlands (Chapter 17) are secondary treatment units – that is they have to be preceded by a septic tank or an anaerobic pond to remove the solids that would otherwise clog the gravel bed of the wetland. As shown in the Design Example in Chapter 17, constructed wetlands require more land than a secondary facultative pond and a large amount of gravel. Moreover, Tanner (2001*) has demonstrated that the plants used in gravel-bed constructed wetlands (such as the common reed, *Phragmites australis*) are unnecessary for the removal of BOD, COD, suspended solids, phosphorus and *E coli* (see also Ayaz and Akça, 2001*; Regmi et al, 2003). This implies that the gravel bed itself, rather than the plants growing in it, is responsible for these removals and that a rock filter (Chapter 12) would therefore be more appropriate. Tanner did find, however, that the plants were needed for nitrogen removal; this suggests that constructed wetlands should only be considered for use when the regulator has specified a maximum effluent ammonia concentration (and they can be designed specifically for ammonia removal using equation 17.5). The question that designers must answer is: can WSP achieve the required ammonia level (equations 12.12–12.18) at lower cost than constructed wetlands?

WSP vs UASBs

Upflow anaerobic sludge blanket reactors (UASBs) (Chapter 18) are very efficient anaerobic reactors with short retention times (~8 hours). However, they are not significantly more efficient than anaerobic ponds, especially high-rate anaerobic ponds (Chapter 10), but they are much more expensive to construct, and overall the land area savings are small (see the Design Example in Chapter 18).

WSP vs aerated lagoons

Aerated lagoons (Chapter 20) are activated sludge units operated without sludge return. Retention times are 2–6 days, with 4 days being a typical value. The question to be answered is: is a 4-day aerated lagoon cheaper than a 1-day anaerobic pond and a 4-day secondary facultative pond? The answer to this question must include the annual cost of the electricity used to power the aerators. How much extra land could be purchased with this annual expenditure on electricity?

MACROPHYTE PONDS

Macrophytes are higher plants (whereas 'microphytes' are algae); they are occasionally, but generally inappropriately, used in or on WSP for algal and/or nutrient removal.

Floating macrophyte ponds

Macrophytes such as water hyacinth (*Eichhornia crassipes*) or water lettuce (*Pistia stratiotes*) are grown over the whole surface of a maturation pond in order to reduce algal suspended solids in the final effluent by depriving the algae of light. The roots of the plants also help to reduce nitrogen and phosphorus levels. However, they have the major disadvantage of encouraging mosquito breeding; this can be controlled by the introduction and maintenance of mosquito fish, such as *Gambusia*, which eat mosquito larvae, but this is an extra O&M task – making sure the fish stay alive. Moreover, the plants need regular harvesting every few months, otherwise they die in the pond and lead to a deterioration in effluent quality. As algae are vital for faecal bacterial and viral removal in WSP (Chapter 12), floating macrophyte ponds should only be used (if used at all) when *E coli* numbers have been reduced to the required level in the preceding unplanted maturation ponds.

Duckweeds of the family Lemnaceae are being increasingly recommended as a floating macrophyte for ponds (eg Skillicorn et al, 1993*; Iqbal, 1999*), since they are high in protein and also β-carotene (the pigment that gives egg yolks a deep gold colour). Harvested duckweeds can be used to feed certain species of carp and also hens (to ensure their eggs have golden yolks). However, they are troublesome to grow as they are so small (only a few mm) that they are easily blown by the wind into a corner of the pond unless wind action is minimized by placing lengths of bamboo across the pond surface. Fish yields are no higher than those from algal fishponds (Chapter 22), and golden-yolked eggs may not be as high a consumer preference in developing countries as it is in industrialized countries. Furthermore, nutrient removal in duckweed ponds is no higher than that in maturation ponds (Chapter 12) (see Zimmo, 2003).

Rooted macrophyte ponds

Rooted macrophytes of the type used in constructed wetlands (Chapter 17) can be planted in maturation ponds, which therefore become free-water-surface constructed wetlands. In France it used to be common practice to plant 50–100 per cent of the final maturation pond with the common reed (*Phragmites australis*), but this led to such massive mosquito breeding (especially of *Coquillittidia* spp and *Mansonia* spp, the larvae of which obtain their oxygen from the plants' lacunae, which transport oxygen from the leaves to the roots) that the practice had to be discontinued (Ringuelet, 1983).

ADVANCED POND SYSTEMS

There are two types of advanced pond systems: high-rate algal ponds, which were originally designed for algal production, and the 'Advanced Integrated Pond' system. They are included here for completeness, but they are not applicable in developing countries (although increasingly advocated as such).

High-rate algal ponds

High-rate algal ponds (HRAP) were devised by Professor William Oswald at the University of California at Berkeley in the 1960s (see Oswald, 1988a). They receive settled wastewater and they were originally designed to maximize algal production, rather than to optimize wastewater treatment, simply because algae are 50–60 per cent protein and protein yields from HRAP are so much greater than from conventional agriculture (~30,000 kg protein/ha year, compared with <1000 kg/ha year from soya beans), and algae are cheap to produce – around US$0.25/kg dry weight (Oswald, 1988b). In a food-short, especially protein-short, world HRAP are immediately attractive: even if the algae harvested from HRAP are not used for direct human consumption, they can be used as supplementary animal (commonly, chicken) feeds (but health food shops in industrialized countries have algal tablets on sale; they are held to be useful for dieting 'the natural way', and there is even a book called *Chlorella: The Emerald Food* – Bewicke and Potter, 1984).

The HRAP is arranged in a 'race track' configuration and its contents are gently stirred by electrically driven paddle wheels to prevent the algae from settling (the layout is essentially the same as that used for oxidation ditches – Figure 20.3), with a depth of 20–50 cm and a retention time of 2–6 days. Algal production is very high, around 15 g dry weight/m^2 day, equivalent to ~30 t protein/ha/year (see Oswald, 1995). The next two processes are algal harvesting and drying. The best way to harvest the algae from the HRAP effluent is dissolved air flotation. Drying can be done in the sun or, if the HRAP is preceded by a conventional primary sedimentation tank (rather than an anaerobic pond), the methane generated in an anaerobic digester treating the primary sludge can be burnt to heat air to dry the algae.

It will be apparent that the use of HRAP for maximal algal production is a complicated process, at least from the perspective of a wastewater treatment engineer (but not, perhaps, from that of an industrial microbiologist). However, the algae grown at high densities in HRAP are susceptible to fungal infections which can cause the population to 'crash'. In short, and despite their advantage of high protein yields, HRAP are too complicated a process for wastewater treatment in developing countries. There are very few full-scale HRAP even in industrialized countries, which suggests they might be just too complicated – full stop. Moreover, once the algae have been harvested and dried, they must be packaged and sold – otherwise there is no point in producing them in the first place. However, few, if any, wastewater treatment engineers in either industrialized or developing countries are likely to have the required marketing skills.

Advanced integrated pond systems

The 'Advanced Integrated Wastewater Ponding System' (AIWPS, which is a US registered trademark, so it should be written AIWPS®) was developed in California as a successor to HRAP (Oswald, 1991), presumably because of the difficulties encountered in practice with commercial algal production in HRAP. AIWPS is primarily a wastewater treatment process, and algal production is only a secondary consideration. It is also termed an 'Advanced Integrated Pond System' (Department of Energy, 1993). The AIWPS/AIPS consists of four or five ponds in series, as follows:

- a 4–5 m deep 'advanced' facultative pond which contains a solids 'digester pit'; the raw wastewater, after preliminary treatment (Chapter 8) is introduced at the base of the digester pit, which acts like an anaerobic pond within the facultative pond;

- an HRAP, part of the effluent from which is recirculated to the facultative pond to help keep its upper layer aerobic;
- an algal settling pond (the settled algae can be removed and used as fertilizer); and
- one or two maturation ponds for disinfection (optional).

Oswald (1991) reports the following retention times for the Advanced Integrated Pond System at St Helena, California: advanced facultative pond, 20 days; HRAP, 10 days; and algal settling pond, 5 days – a total of 35 days. For the AIPS at Hollister, California, the retention times are: advanced facultative pond 32 days; HRAP, 10 days; and algal settling pond, 7 days – a total of 49 days.

Advanced pond systems

'Advanced pond systems' are beginning to be used in New Zealand (a 'technology transfer' from California) (Craggs et al, 2003*). They have the same types of ponds as the Californian AIWPS/AIPS, but with different retention times, for example: HRAP, 7.5 days; algal settling pond, 2 days; maturation pond, 20 day. Two algal settling ponds (each with a 2-day retention time) are provided in parallel: one is operational while algae are removed from the other.

It appears, therefore, that these 'advanced' or 'advanced integrated' pond systems have no advantages over modern waste stabilization ponds designed as described in Chapters 10–12 or, in water-short regions, over the wastewater storage and treatment reservoirs (including the hybrid WSP–WSTR system) described in Chapter 16. (Of course, if an industrial microbiologist/ entrepreneur wishes to produce algae commercially, then these advanced pond systems could be very advantageous.)

10

Anaerobic Ponds

FUNCTION

Anaerobic ponds (Figure 10.1) are usually the first type of pond used in a series of ponds (Chapter 9). They are 2–5 m deep and receive such a high organic loading (usually >100 g BOD/m^3 day, equivalent to >3000 kg/ha day for a depth of 3 m) that they contain no dissolved oxygen and no algae, although occasionally a thin film of *Chlamydomonas* may be present at the surface. They function much like open septic tanks, and their primary function is BOD (biochemical oxygen demand) removal. Anaerobic ponds work extremely well: a properly designed and not significantly underloaded anaerobic pond will achieve >60 per cent BOD removal at 20°C. Retention times are short: for wastewater with a BOD of ≤300 mg/l, for example, 1 day is sufficient at a temperature of 20°C.

BOD removal is achieved by the sedimentation of settleable solids and their subsequent anaerobic digestion in the resulting sludge layer; this is particularly intense at temperatures above 15°C when the pond surface literally bubbles with the release of biogas (around 70 per cent methane and 30 per cent carbon dioxide). The bacterial groups involved are the same as those in any anaerobic reactor (Chapter 3), and those in anaerobic ponds are equally sensitive to the same toxicants, one of the most important of which is a pH below ~6.2.

Many compounds in industrial wastewaters are toxic to algae, and treatment in anaerobic ponds prior to facultative and maturation ponds (Chapters 11 and 12) is necessary to avoid this. Heavy metals are precipitated as metal sulphides, and many organic toxicants (eg phenol) are degraded to non-toxic forms. Floating materials (including oils) and scum, which block out the light needed in facultative ponds for algal photosynthesis, are retained in anaerobic ponds.

There is a gradual accumulation of digested solids in anaerobic ponds, so regular desludging once every 1–3 years is required (Chapter 14). Scum accumulates on the surface, but does not need to be removed (it helps keep the pond anaerobic), unless fly breeding reaches nuisance level (Chapter 14).

Figure 10.1 *Anaerobic Pond, with Partial Scum Coverage, at Ginebra, Valle del Cauca, Southwest Colombia*

Odour

Designers have in the past been afraid to incorporate anaerobic ponds in case they cause odour. Hydrogen sulphide, formed mainly by the anaerobic reduction of sulphate by sulphate-reducing bacteria such as *Desulfovibrio* spp, is the principal potential source of odour. However, in aqueous solution hydrogen sulphide is present as either dissolved hydrogen sulphide gas (H_2S) or the bisulphide ion (HS^-), with the sulphide ion (S^{2-}) only being formed in significant quantities at high pH (Figure 10.2). At the pH values normally found in well designed anaerobic ponds (around 7.5), most of the sulphide is present as the odourless bisulphide ion. Odour is only caused by escaping hydrogen sulphide molecules as they seek to achieve a partial pressure in the air above the pond which is in equilibrium with their concentration in it (Henry's law). Thus, for any given total sulphide concentration, the greater the proportion of sulphide present as HS^-, the lower the release of H_2S. Odour is *not* a problem if the recommended design loadings (Table 10.1) are not exceeded and if the sulphate concentration in the raw wastewater is <500 mg SO_4^{2-}/l (Gloyna and Espino, 1969). Sulphate concentrations are usually much less than this; they depend on the amount of sulphate in the local drinking water (for which the World Health Organization, 1993, recommends a limit of 250 mg/l as SO_4^{2-}), and on the local usage of detergents which contain large amounts (up to 40 per cent by volume) of sodium sulphate as a 'bulking' agent.

It is always worth checking the local drinking water – in parts of southern Spain, for example, the drinking water contains 600–1200 mg SO_4^{2-}/l and odour was a serious problem with anaerobic ponds until the sulphate concentration was reduced to <250 mg/l at the local *water* treatment plant. A further point to consider in coastal tourist areas is whether hotels use seawater for toilet flushing – seawater contains around 3000 mg SO_4^{2-}/l – so if the hotel wastewaters are treated in anaerobic and facultative ponds, there will be serious odour problems (Frederick-van Genderen, 1995).

Paing (2001) presents a model for odour release from anaerobic ponds in southern France receiving domestic wastewater with 100–220 mg SO_4^{2-}/l; in-pond temperatures were 8–26°C. It was found that sulphide was released to the atmosphere at rates of 25–710 mg S per m^2 of anaerobic pond surface area per day, which resulted in H_2S concentrations in the air of 0.3–8.5 mg S/m^3 and complaints from local residents.

A small amount of sulphide is beneficial as it reacts with heavy metals to form insoluble metal sulphides which precipitate out, but concentrations of 50–150 mg/l can inhibit methanogenesis (Pfeffer, 1970). A further important advantage of small concentrations (>3 mg/l) of sulphide in anaerobic ponds is that they are rapidly lethal to *Vibrio cholerae* (Oragui et al, 1993; Arridge et al, 1995*).

Designs now exist for covering anaerobic ponds to facilitate methane recovery (DeGarie et al, 2000*; see also Chapter 13 and Figure 16.3). This also provides additional security against odour release since, even if the methane is not to be used for power generation, the gases can be flared off.

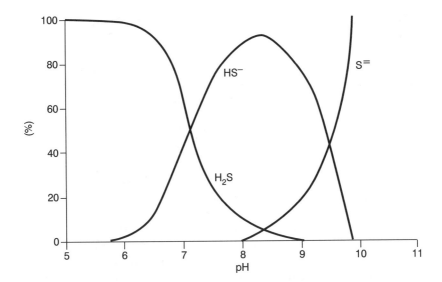

Source: Sawyer et al (2002)

Figure 10.2 *Variation of the Proportions of Hydrogen Sulphide, Bisulphide and Sulphide with pH in Aqueous Solutions*

DESIGN

Anaerobic ponds can be satisfactorily designed, without the risk of odour release, on the basis of volumetric BOD loading (λ_v, g/m^3 d), which is given by:

$$\lambda_v = L_i Q / V_a$$

(10.1)

where L_i is the influent BOD, mg/l (= g/m^3), Q is the flow, m^{3}d; and V_a is the anaerobic pond volume, m^3.

The permissible design value of λ_v increases with temperature, but there are too few reliable data to enable the development of a suitable design equation. Mara and Pearson (1998*) recommend the design values given in Table 10.1; these recommendations were based on those of Meiring et al (1968) that λ_v should lie between 100 and 400 g/m^3 day, the former in order to maintain anaerobic conditions and the latter to avoid odour release. However, in Table 10.1 the upper limit for design is set at 350 g/m^3 day in order to provide an adequate margin of safety with respect to odour.

Once a value of λ_v has been selected, the anaerobic pond volume is then calculated from equation 10.1. The mean hydraulic retention time in the pond (θ_a, d) is determined from:

$$\theta_a = V_a / Q$$

(10.2)

Retention times in anaerobic ponds greater than 1 day should not be used. If equation 10.2 gives a value of θ_a <1 day, a value of 1 day should be used. The corresponding value of V_a is Q m^3.

Anaerobic ponds are usually 2–5 m deep, with a value of 3 m usually being assumed for process design (and adjusted, if necessary, during the physical design stage – Chapter 13). The anaerobic pond area (A_a, m^2) is then given by:

$$A_a = Q\theta_a / D_a = L_i Q / \lambda_v D_a$$

(10.3)

where D_a is the anaerobic pond working (ie liquid) depth, m.

The performance of anaerobic ponds increases significantly with temperature, and the design assumptions for BOD removal (needed for the design of the receiving facultative pond) given in Table 10.1 can be confidently adopted. These are based on experience with anaerobic ponds in Germany in winter (T <10°C) (Bucksteeg, 1987), and in northeast Brazil at 25°C where little variation in BOD removal was found at retention times of 0.8–6.8 days (Table 10.2). Pearson et al (1996a*) also reported little variation of BOD removal with retention time at the Dandora ponds serving Nairobi, Kenya: 79–86 per cent removal at retention times of 2.5–9.5 days; the removal of

Table 10.1 *Design Values of Volumetric BOD Loadings on and Percentage BOD Removals in Anaerobic Ponds at Various Temperatures*

Temperature (°C)	Volumetric loading (g/m³ day)	BOD removal (%)
<10	100	40
10–20	20T − 100	2T + 20
20–25	10T + 100	2T + 20
>25	350	70

T = temperature,°C

79 per cent was achieved in the coldest month, July, when the mean monthly air temperature is 17°C – that is the removal was very much higher than the 56 per cent expected for 17°C from Table 10.1.

Design temperature

The design temperature for anaerobic ponds (and facultative ponds – Chapter 11) is usually taken as the mean *air* temperature of the coldest month. This is slightly conservative as the pond temperature is 1–2 degC higher than the air temperature in the coldest month.

The mean monthly temperature is the mean of the mean daily temperatures – that is the 28–31 day average of the mean of the daily maximum temperature and the daily minimum temperature (these are measured every day at meteorological stations, usually at 8 am).

Sludge accumulation

As noted in Chapter 13, the rate of accumulation of digested sludge in anaerobic ponds in warm climates is usually taken as 0.04 m³/person year. This is, however, only a rough estimate, and in northeast Brazil much lower rates were measured: of the order of 0.01 m³/person year (Silva, 1982). Initial rates of sludge accumulation are higher as the sludge volume comprises two zones: one for sludge digestion and one for the storage of digested sludge – initially the volume of the former is a higher proportion of the total, so

Table 10.2 *Variation of BOD Removal with BOD Loading and Retention Time in Anaerobic Ponds in Northeast Brazil at 25 °C*

Retention Time (days)	Volumetric BOD loading (g/m³ d)	BOD removal (%)
0.8	306	76
1.0	215	76
1.9	129	80
2.0	116	75
4.0	72	68
6.8	35	74

Source: Silva (1982)

accumulation rates are higher; as time passes its proportion of the total declines and accumulation rates become lower. Nelson (2002) describes a mechanistic model for sludge accumulation in primary facultative ponds; the model includes sedimentation of influent settleable solids, digestion of the settled solids and sludge compaction (a similar approach is taken by Metcalf and Eddy, Inc (1991) for the design of sedimentation ponds following aerated lagoons – Chapter 20). The management of sludge from anaerobic ponds is fully described by Franci (1999).

Drying beds

Sludge removed from anaerobic ponds can be conveniently dewatered in sludge drying beds. Moisture loss is by evaporation and percolation through the sand-gravel bed which comprises the base of the drying bed (300 mm of 0.3–0.75 mm sand over 300 mm of 5–25 mm gravel). The drying bed area should be ~0.025 m²/person, and the sludge should be applied at the start of the dry season (Chapter 13).

HIGH-RATE ANAEROBIC PONDS

High-rate anaerobic ponds are a recent development by Professor Miguel Peña Varón at the Universidad del Valle in Cali, Colombia (Peña Varón, 2002*; Peña Varón et al, 2002*). They combine the higher performance of upflow anaerobic sludge blanket reactors (UASBs – Chapter 18), which can achieve 70 per cent BOD removal at a retention time of only 6 hours, with the constructional and operational simplicity of anaerobic ponds. Several designs were evaluated by computer modelling, and some were then tested on a pilot scale. The best design, shown in Figure 10.3, introduces the wastewater at the base of the 'mixing pit' (as in a UASB) and separates solids digestion and solids settlement (as a UASB does); it achieved unfiltered and filtered COD (chemical oxygen demand) removals of 79 and 78 per cent, respectively, at a retention time of 0.6 day and a COD loading of 1115 g/m³ day (equivalent to ~450 g BOD/m³ day). A conventional (ie low-rate) anaerobic pond, operating at the same retention time and loading (and therefore overloaded) achieved unfiltered and filtered COD removals of only 15 and 22 per cent, respectively – thus clearly demonstrating the ability of the high-rate anaerobic pond to accept high loads and achieve very high treatment efficiency.

ANAEROBIC PONDS IN SERIES

With normal strength domestic wastewater it is not advantageous to have two (or more) anaerobic ponds in series. Silva (1982) found that a 0.8-day anaerobic pond reduced the BOD from 240 mg/l to 60 mg/l at 25°C in northeast Brazil, but a second 0.4-day anaerobic pond in series reduced it to only 46 mg/l. However, for the treatment of much stronger agro-industrial

Source: Peña Varón (2002*)

Figure 10.3 *High-rate Anaerobic Pond with a Mixing Pit*

wastewaters, a series of anaerobic ponds is very efficient. McGarry and Pescod (1970) used a series of five anaerobic ponds for the treatment of tapioca starch wastewater in Thailand; each pond was loaded at 224 g BOD/m³ day and the BOD was reduced from 3800 mg/l to 224 mg/l. Rao and Viraraghavan (1985) used two anaerobic ponds in series to treat distillery wastewater in southern India: the first pond reduced the BOD from 40,000 mg/l to 5000 mg/l and the second reduced it to 2000 mg/l (further treatment was provided in an oxidation ditch – Chapter 20, presumably because there was no space for more anaerobic ponds).

DESIGN EXAMPLE

Design an anaerobic pond to treat the following wastewater:

Q = 10,000 m³/day (ie 100,000 persons each producing 100 litres of wastewater per day),

$$L_i = 300 \text{ mg/l,}$$

$$T = 25°C.$$

Solution

From Table 10.1, λ_v = 350 g/m³ day for 25°C. Assume a depth of 3 m; then from equations 10.2 and 10.3:

$$A_a = L_i Q / \lambda_v D_a$$

$$= (300 \times 10,000)/(350 \times 3)$$

$$= 2860 \text{ m}^2$$

$$\theta_a = A_a D_a / Q$$

$$= (2860 \times 3)/10,000$$

$$= 0.86 \text{ day}$$

This is <1 day, the minimum retention time in anaerobic ponds. Therefore recalculate A_a from equation 10.3:

$$A_a = Q \theta_a / D_a$$

$$= 10,000 \times 1/3$$

$$= 3340 \text{ m}^2$$

From Table 10.2, the BOD removal is 70 per cent. Thus the effluent BOD is (0.3 x 300) = 90 mg/l. The anaerobic pond effluent requires further treatment in a secondary facultative pond (Chapter 11), a wastewater storage and treatment reservoir (Chapter 16) or a horizontal-flow constructed wetland (Chapter 17). If sufficient land for these natural wastewater treatment processes is not available, consideration should be given to treating the anaerobic pond effluent in a biofilter (Chapter 19), an aerated lagoon or an oxidation ditch (Chapter 20).

11

Facultative Ponds

FUNCTION

Facultative ponds are of two types: primary facultative ponds which receive raw wastewater (after preliminary treatment – Chapter 8 and see Figure 9.1), and secondary facultative ponds which receive settled wastewater (usually the effluent from anaerobic ponds). They are designed for BOD (biochemical oxygen demand) removal on the basis of a relatively low surface BOD loading in the range 100–400 kg/ha day (see equation 11.1 below) to permit the development of a healthy algal population, as the oxygen for BOD removal by the pond bacteria is mostly generated by algal photosynthesis. Facultative ponds are coloured dark green as a result of the large numbers of micro-algae in them, although they may occasionally appear red or pink (especially when slightly overloaded) due to the presence of anaerobic purple sulphide-oxidizing photosynthetic bacteria (see 'Purple ponds' later in this chapter). The algae that tend to predominate in the turbid waters of facultative ponds (Table 11.1) belong to motile genera (such as *Chlamydomonas*, *Pyrobotrys* and *Euglena*) as these can optimize their vertical position in the pond water column in relation to incident light intensity more easily than non-motile forms (such as *Chlorella*, although this is also common in facultative ponds). The concentration of algae in a facultative pond depends on loading and temperature (see Figure 11.5 below), but is usually in the range 500–2000 µg chlorophyll *a* per litre.

As a result of the photosynthetic activities of the pond algae, there is a diurnal variation in the concentration of dissolved oxygen (Figure 11.1). After sunrise, the dissolved oxygen level gradually rises, in response to photosynthetic activity, to a maximum in the mid-afternoon, after which it falls to a minimum during the night when photosynthesis ceases and algal (as well as bacterial) respiratory activity consumes oxygen. The position of the 'oxypause' (the depth at which the dissolved oxygen concentration reaches zero) similarly changes, as does the pH, since at peak algal activity carbonate and bicarbonate ions react to provide more carbon dioxide for the algae, so leaving an excess of hydroxyl ions with the result that the pH can rise to >9.4, which rapidly kills most faecal bacteria (Chapter 12).

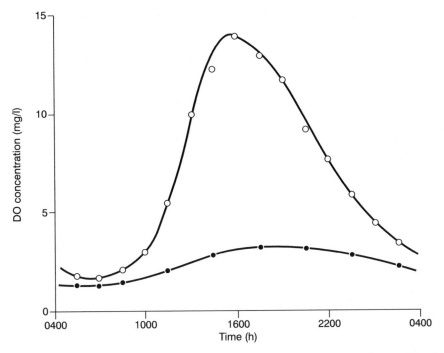

Figure 11.1 *Diurnal Variation of Dissolved Oxygen in a Facultative Pond:* ○ *top 200 mm of pond;* ●*, 800 mm below surface*

Mixing and stratification

Wind, heat and pond inlet design are the three factors of major importance that influence the degree of mixing that occurs within a pond. Mixing minimizes hydraulic short-circuiting and the formation of stagnant regions ('dead spaces') and it ensures a reasonably uniform vertical distribution of BOD, algae and oxygen. Mixing is the only means by which non-motile algae can be carried up into the zone of effective light penetration (the 'photic' zone); since the photic zone comprises only the top ~300 mm of the pond, much of the pond contents would remain in photosynthetic darkness if mixing did not occur. Mixing is also greatly influenced by the design of the inlet structure; this is discussed in greater detail in Chapter 13.

The depth to which wind-induced mixing is felt is largely determined by the horizontal distance over which the wind is in contact with the water (the 'fetch'): an unobstructed contact length of about 100 m is required for maximum mixing by wind action. The importance of wind action is clearly demonstrated by the following, admirably simple, experiment which was conducted on a facultative pond in Zambia: a 2-m high fence with no openings was erected around the pond and within a few days it turned anaerobic; when the fence was removed aerobic conditions were rapidly re-established (Marais, 1966).

Table 11.1 *Examples of Algal Genera Found in Facultative and Maturation Ponds*

Algae[a,b]	Facultative ponds	Maturation ponds
Euglenophyta		
*Euglena**	+	+
*Phacus**	+	+
Chlorophyta		
*Chlamydomonas**	+	+
*Chlorogonium**	+	+
Eudorina	+	+
*Pandorina**	+	+
*Pyrobotrys**	+	+
Ankistrodesmus	−	+
Chlorella	+	+
Micratinium	−	+
Scenedesmus	−	+
Selenastrum	−	+
*Carteria**	+	+
Coelastrum	−	+
Dictyosphaerium	−	+
Oocystis	−	+
*Volvox**	+	+
Chrysophyta		
*Navicula**	+	+
Cyclotella	−	+
Cryptophyta		
*Rhodomonas**	−	+
Cyanophyta[c]		
Oscillatoria	+	+
Anabaena	+	+

Notes:
[a] An identification key to pond algae is given in Mara (1997*) and Mara and Pearson (1998*)
[b] *, motile; +, present; −, absent
[c] The *Cyanophyta* (blue green algae) are strictly the cyanobacteria (blue green bacteria)

In the absence of mixing thermal stratification quickly occurs. The warm upper layers are separated from the colder lower layers by a thin static region of abrupt temperature change known as the 'thermocline'. Non-motile algae settle through the thermocline into photosynthetic darkness where they are unable to produce any oxygen; instead they exert an oxygen demand, with the result that conditions below the thermocline rapidly become anoxic. Above the thermocline the motile algae move away from the hot surface waters (which may have a temperature >30°C), and they usually form a dense layer about 300–500 mm below the surface. This algal band is an effective light barrier and the thermocline is usually just below the algae.

The diurnal mixing pattern in a 1.5 m deep facultative pond in Lusaka, Zambia, was thoroughly investigated by Marais (1966) and is typical of tropical and subtropical ponds:

1   In the morning, if there is any wind, there is a period of complete mixing in which the temperature is uniform throughout the pond but, owing to the absorption of solar radiation, gradually increases.
2   At some time, usually during a short lull in the wind, stratification develops abruptly and a thermocline forms. The temperature above the thermocline increases to a maximum and then decreases, while below the thermocline the temperature rapidly falls to a value approximately that of the earth and thereafter remains practically constant. A certain amount of mixing may take place above the thermocline.
3   In the afternoon and evening, a second period of mixing may be initiated as follows:
    (a) above the thermocline, under quiescent wind conditions, the top layers lose their heat more rapidly than the bottom layers. The cooler top layers sink, inducing mixing with the result that the temperature down to the thermocline remains approximately uniform but gradually decreases. The thermocline slowly sinks and, should the temperature above and below it become equal due to further cooling, mixing is initiated and sustained throughout the pond.
    (b) under windy conditions, usually during periods of decreasing temperatures, the energy imparted by the wind to the water above the thermocline at some stage overcomes the stratification forces and progressively mixes the warmer and colder layers adjacent to the thermocline, causing it to be displaced downwards until the temperature is uniform throughout and the whole pond is in a state of mixing.

This diurnal pattern of mixing and stratification also occurs in shallow lakes in the tropics, for example in Lake George in Uganda (Viner and Smith, 1973; see also Talling, 2001*). The same pattern occurs, but on an annual basis, in deep lakes in temperate regions.

Thermal stratification induces algal banding and this in turn, together with light attenuation, induces physicochemical stratification (see also Gu and Stefan, 1995*; Kayombo et al, 2002*), especially of pH which can rise to 9–10 and rapidly cause faecal bacterial die-off (Chapter 12). However, provided the effluent take-off point is below the maximum depth of algal banding (Chapter 13), stratification can minimize the daily effluent BOD and suspended solids concentrations as these are largely associated with the algae in the pond effluent (see below under the section 'Diurnal variation in effluent quality'). This increase in BOD and suspended solids removal may outweigh the disadvantages of any short-circuiting induced by stratification.

Sludge layer

Primary facultative ponds fulfil the functions of both anaerobic and secondary facultative ponds, and thus the settleable solids in the raw wastewater settle in primary facultative ponds to form a sludge layer. These solids are digested anaerobically with the evolution of biogas. Eventually the digested solids (the 'sludge') have to be removed, but this is necessary only very infrequently: in northern France primary facultative ponds are desludged once every ten years (see Figure 14.2); in warmer climates sludge accumulation is much lower due to more complete and more rapid digestion. Secondary facultative ponds (and maturation ponds – Chapter 12) should not require desludging during their design life.

Design

Conventional design

Facultative ponds are best designed on the basis of surface BOD loading (λ_s. kg/ha day), which is given by:

$$\lambda_s = \frac{10 L_i Q}{A_f}$$

(11.1)

where A_f is the facultative pond area, m^2. The factor 10 arises from the units used: $L_i Q$ is the mass of BOD entering the pond, g/day; so $10^{-3} L_i Q$ is in kg/day and the area in ha is $10^{-4} A_f$.

Surface loading is used for facultative ponds, rather than volumetric loading (as for anaerobic ponds – Chapter 10), because the light needed for algal photosynthesis arrives from the sun at the pond's surface. Thus algal oxygen production is a function of area, so the BOD loading (which is an oxygen demand) must also be a function of area.

The permissible design value of λ_s increases with temperature (T,°C) which is essentially a proxy for climate. The earliest relationship between λ_s and T is that given by McGarry and Pescod (1970), but their value of λ_s is the maximum that can be applied to a facultative pond before it fails (that is, becomes anaerobic). Their relationship, which is therefore an envelope of failure, is:

$$\lambda_s = 60 \ (1.099)^T$$

(11.2)

Equation 11.2 cannot be used for design as it does not incorporate a factor of safety. Mara (1987) gives the following global *design* equation:

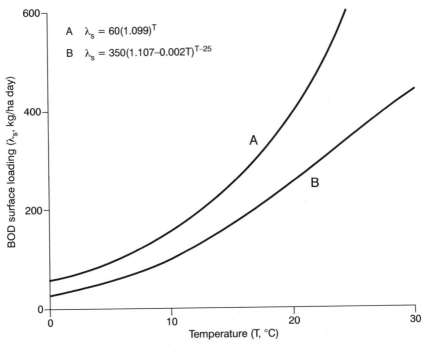

Figure 11.2 *Variation of Surface BOD Loading on Facultative Ponds with Temperature According to Equations 11.2 and 11.3*

$$\lambda_s = 350(1.107 - 0.002T)^{T-25}$$

(11.3)

Equation 11.3 is based on a loading of 80 kg/ha day at ≤8°C in European winters, a loading of 350 kg/ha day at 25°C in northeast Brazil, and an arbitrary loading of 500 kg/ha day at 35°C. Note that the reference temperature in equation 11.3 is 25°C. Equations 11.2 and 11.3 are shown graphically in Figure 11.2.

Once a suitable value of λ_s has been selected, the pond area is calculated from equation 11.1 and its retention time (θ_f, days) from:

$$\theta_f = A_f D / Q_m$$

(11.4)

where D is the pond depth, m (usually 1.5 m – but see below); and Q_m is the mean flow, m³/day. The mean flow is the mean of the influent and effluent flows (Q_i and Q_e), the latter being the former less net evaporation and seepage. Thus equation 11.4 becomes:

$$\theta_f = A_f D / [0.5(Q_i + Q_e)]$$

(11.5)

If seepage is negligible Q_e is given by:

$$Q_e = Q_i - 0.001eA_f$$

(11.6)

where e is the net evaporation rate, mm/day (meteorological stations usually record evaporation and rainfall in mm per month, so division by 28–31 days is necessary to obtain mm/day). Thus equation 11.5 becomes:

$$\theta_f = 2A_fD/(2Q_i - 0.001eA_f)$$

(11.7)

A minimum value of θ_f of 5 days should be adopted for temperatures <20°C, and 4 days for temperatures ≥20°C. This is to minimize hydraulic short-circuiting and to give the algae sufficient time to multiply (ie to prevent algal washout).

Depth

Facultative pond working (ie liquid) depths are usually in the range 1–1.8 m, with 1.5 m being the most commonly used. Depths <1 m do not prevent the emergence of vegetation. This must be avoided, as otherwise the pond becomes an ideal breeding ground for mosquitoes and midges. With depths >1.8 m the oxypause is too near the surface with the result that the pond is predominantly anaerobic rather than predominantly aerobic. This is undesirable, as the pond would have an unacceptably low factor of safety in normal operation and so be less able to cope with a fluctuating load or a sudden slug of heavy pollution. In arid climates evaporation rates are high and water losses can be minimized by increasing the depth to 2 m (even 2.5 m) and so reducing the surface area. In colder climates (eg at high altitude) similar depths can be used in order to preserve as much of the thermal energy of the influent wastewater as possible. These considerations are usually more important in these extremes of climate than those concerned with the position of the oxypause.

BOD removal

The BOD of the facultative pond effluent can be estimated from equation 5.7:

$$L_e = \frac{L_i}{1 + k_1\theta_f}$$

where L_i is the BOD of either the raw wastewater in the case of primary facultative ponds, or the anaerobic pond effluent (Chapter 10) in the case of secondary facultative ponds, mg/l; and k_1 is the first-order rate constant for BOD removal, day^{-1}, given by equation 5.8:

$$k_{1(T)} = k_{1(20)}(1.05)^{T-20}$$

Design values for $k_{1(20)}$ are 0.3 day^{-1} for primary facultative ponds and 0.1 day^{-1} for secondary facultative ponds (the value for the latter is much lower than that for the former as essentially all the BOD removal by sedimentation occurs in the preceding anaerobic pond).

The term L_e is the unfiltered BOD which includes the BOD of the algae present in the facultative pond effluent. This 'algal BOD' accounts for ~70–90 per cent of the total (ie unfiltered) BOD of the effluent. Thus the relationship between filtered and unfiltered BOD (ie non-algal and total BOD) is:

$$L_e(\text{filtered}) = F_{na}[L_e(\text{unfiltered})]$$

(11.8)

where F_{na} is the non-algal fraction of the total BOD (around 0.1–0.3, with a usual design value of 0.3). As noted in Chapter 4, a pond effluent with a filtered BOD of ≤25 mg/l is acceptable for surface water discharge in the European Union (and efforts should be made to persuade regulators in developing countries that this is also acceptable in their jurisdictions).

Diurnal variation in effluent quality

Due to the motility of many of the facultative pond algae, they are able to optimize their position in the pond water column with respect to incident light intensity and, when the pond is stratified, the algae form a band 10–20 cm thick in the top 50 cm of the pond. As a result of this algal movement in the pond, the quality of the effluent (which is drawn off from the pond at a fixed depth – Chapter 13) varies throughout the 24-hour day. Figure 11.3 shows this variation in effluent quality for a primary facultative pond in northeast Brazil that was receiving a BOD loading of 320 kg/ha day at 25°C. Effluent chlorophyll *a* concentrations varied between a few hundred to >10,000 µg/l, and changes in chlorophyll *a* were mirrored by corresponding changes in the concentrations of algae-associated parameters such as dissolved oxygen, pH, total phosphorus, BOD and suspended solids. (The significance of dissolved oxygen and pH changes in relation to faecal bacterial die-off is discussed in Chapter 12.)

These large variations in effluent quality parameters mean that a single 'grab' sample of effluent can only give information on effluent quality at the time the sample was collected. In general, therefore, 24-hour flow-weighted composite samples are required for most parameters to determine the mean daily effluent quality (Chapter 15).

Design based on uncertainty analysis

A significant contribution to facultative pond design, and to WSP design in general, was made by von Sperling (1996b*), who recognized that there is uncertainty about the values used for the design parameters, for example, we

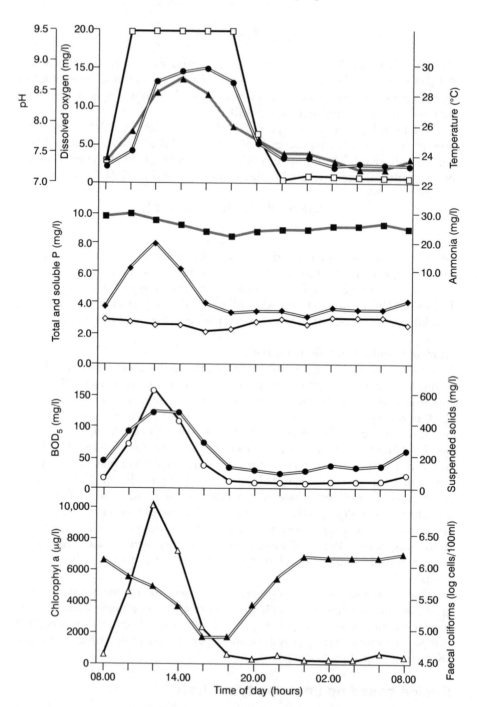

Note: □, dissolved oxygen; ▲, pH; ●, temperature; ■, ammonia; ◆, total and ◊, soluble phosphorus; ●, BOD; ○, suspended solids; △, chlorophyll *a*; and ▲, faecal coliforms.

Figure 11.3 *Diurnal Variation in Facultative Pond Effluent Quality*

may design for some future population P which has a wastewater generation of q l/person/day and a BOD contribution of B g/person day, and we then calculate the wastewater flow and BOD as $(10^{-3}Pq)$ m³/day and $(10^{3}B/q)$ mg/l, respectively. However, even though the values of P, q and B used in any one design are the design engineer's best estimates, they are in effect being used as 'certain' values which do not admit any variation. In practice, as recognized by von Sperling, there is some degree of uncertainty in their values; in other words, instead of taking P as, for example, 100,000, P is be allowed to be anywhere between, say, 80,000 and 120,000 – that is, there is an uncertainty in the value of P of, in this case, ± 20 per cent. This principle of uncertainty is applied to the values of all the parameters used for (in this case) facultative pond design. In equations 11.1, 11.3, 11.7, 5.7, 5.8 and 11.8, there are the following nine independent parameters used for facultative pond design:

- Population, P
- BOD contribution, B (g/person day)
- Wastewater flow, q (l/person day)
- Temperature, T (°C)
- Pond liquid depth, D (m)
- Net evaporation, e (mm/day)
- First-order rate constant for BOD removal at 20°C, k_1 (day^{-1})
- Arrhenius constant, ϕ
- Non-algal fraction of effluent BOD, F_{na}

Alternatively, in place of P, B and q, we could simply consider L_i and Q.

Each parameter is assigned a range of design values, rather than a single fixed (ie 'certain') value, although any parameter could be assigned a fixed value, for example, the depth D could be set at the single value of, say, 1.5 m. The range of values could be, for example:

- P 80,000–120,000
- B 35–45
- Q 100–140
- T 19–21
- D 1.5 (fixed value)
- e 4–6
- $k_1(20)$ 0.08–0.12
- ϕ 1.04–1.06
- F_{na} 0.1–0.3

A multi-trial Monte Carlo design simulation is now established. This procedure selects at random a value for each design parameter within the specified range and then determines the design – that is, it calculates, for example, the pond mid-depth area and the pond effluent filtered BOD. It then repeats this 'random value design procedure' any required number of times; usually a 1000-trial design is used. Clearly this cannot be done manually, so an Excel-based design program is used (Sleigh and Mara, 2003a*). The program completes the 1000 designs and the output can be analysed to provide frequency histograms and cumulative frequency curves for the pond area, retention time and the pond effluent filtered BOD. The pond area and retention time which correspond to the achievement of the required effluent filtered BOD on either a 50-percentile or a 95-percentile basis (depending on the regulator's requirement) are selected as the design values, and this area and retention time will be sufficient *for the parameter ranges chosen* to produce an effluent filtered BOD of the required value for 50 or 95 per cent of the time. The procedure is illustrated in the second Design Example at the end of this chapter.

Microbiological quality

At this stage in the design of a WSP system (ie after the design of the anaerobic and secondary facultative ponds, or of the primary facultative pond), it is often worthwhile to assess effluent quality in terms of suitability for re-use in 'restricted' irrigation (Chapter 4) – that is for numbers of human intestinal nematode eggs and *E coli*.

Human intestinal nematode egg removal

The World Health Organization (1989*, 2004*) recommends that treated wastewaters used for crop irrigation should contain ≤ 1 human intestinal nematode egg/l or, when children under 15 years are exposed, ≤ 0.1 egg/l (Chapters 4 and 21).

Using data from WSP in Brazil, India and Kenya, Ayres et al (1992*) found that there was no statistically significant difference between egg removal in anaerobic, facultative and maturation ponds (this is to be expected as their removal mechanism is sedimentation – Chapter 12) (see also von Sperling et al, 2002). They derived the following equation for percentage egg removal:

$$R = 100[1 - 0.14\exp(- 0.38\theta)]$$

$$(11.11)$$

where R is the percentage egg removal in anaerobic, facultative or maturation ponds; and θ is the retention time in the pond, days. The equation corresponding to the lower 95 per cent confidence interval for the data used to derive equation 11.11 is:

$$R = 100[1 - 0.41\exp(- 0.49\theta + 0.0085\theta^2)]$$

$$(11.12)$$

Equation 11.12 is recommended for use in design. It is applied sequentially to each pond in the series – at this stage in the design first to the anaerobic pond and then to the secondary facultative pond. Its use is illustrated in the first Design example at the end of this chapter.

E coli removal

If the number of human intestinal nematode eggs in the effluent from the facultative pond is determined from equation 11.12 as ≤1 per litre, or ≤0.1 per litre if children under the age of 15 are exposed, then the number of *E coli* in the facultative pond effluent should be determined as described in Chapter 12. For restricted irrigation *E coli* numbers should be ≤105 per 100 ml (World Health Organization, 2004*).

ALGAL BIOMASS

The algal biomass in healthy facultative ponds is ~500–2000 mg chlorophyll *a* per litre, and thus healthy (ie not overloaded) facultative ponds are dark green in colour. The concentration of chlorophyll *a* ($C_{55}H_{72}N_4O_5Mg$) is used as algae vary considerably in volume, by up to three orders of magnitude, so that algal cell counts are not very informative. As all WSP algae are composed of ~1.5 per cent chlorophyll *a* by weight, expression of algal biomass in terms of chlorophyll *a*, their principal photosynthetic pigment, is more meaningful and, as chlorophyll *a* is easily measured, more reproducible (Pearson, 1987*, details a method for determining chlorophyll *a* concentrations based on a membrane filtration, chlorophyll extraction in 90 per cent methanol and measurement of absorbance at 663 nm).

Chlorophyll *a* absorbs photons of violet–indigo–blue and orange–red light of wavelengths ~350–450 and ~650–700 nm (absorption of light of wavelengths 450–650 nm – that is mainly green light, is very weak – hence the green colour of algae and most higher plants). This absorbed light energy is used to fix carbon dioxide and to produce oxygen (as a by-product of photosynthesis) from water. A more complete equation for algal photosynthesis than the simple equation given in Chapter 9 is (Oswald, 1988b):

$$106CO_2 + 236H_2O + 16NH_4^+ + HPO_4^{2-} \xrightarrow{light} C_{106}H_{181}O_{45}N_{16}P + 118O_2 + 171H_2O + 14H^+$$

This equation shows that 1 g of algae produces (3776/2429) = 1.55 g of oxygen. This quantity of oxygen is sufficient to satisfy the oxygen demand of 1.55 g of BOD_u, which approximately equals 1 g of BOD_5 (Chapter 1).

Algal productivity

In-pond algal productivity can be estimated by the 'light-and-dark-bottle' technique (American Public Health Association, 1998 – method 10200 J.2): samples are taken from the pond at 15-cm depth intervals and each is used to completely fill three BOD bottles – one is used to measure the dissolved oxygen (DO) concentration immediately (ie at zero time); one of the other two is covered in aluminium foil (the 'dark bottle'), and this and the remaining bottle (the 'light bottle') are resuspended in the pond at the depth from which the samples they contain were collected. After a certain time t they are removed from the pond and the DO concentration in their contents is measured (the time t that the bottles are immersed in the pond has to be chosen carefully, usually by trial and error, so that the DO concentration in the dark bottle is not zero after t minutes and the DO concentration in the light bottle is not higher than the maximum DO meter reading – usually 20 mg/l; t also depends on the time of day: longer times are needed early in the morning, or late in the afternoon, than at midday). The increase in DO in the light bottle (which is due to algal photosynthesis less bacterial respiration) plus the decrease in the dark bottle (due to algal and bacterial respiration) is the gross algal DO production at that level in the pond and at that time of day. The gross DO production in the pond water column at that time of day is the sum of the values obtained at each depth; if this is denoted by $\Sigma(GDOP)$ in mg O_2 per litre, then on an areal basis in kg O_2/ha day the gross algal oxygen production (GAOP) is given by:

$$GAOP = \frac{\Sigma(NDOP)}{10^6} \times \frac{V}{1000} \times \frac{10^8}{A} \times \frac{24 \times 60}{t}$$

where V is the volume of the sample bottle, ml; A is the cross-sectional area of the sample bottle, cm^2; and t is the time of immersion of the bottles in the pond, min. The factor 10^6 converts mg/l to kg/l; 1000 converts ml to l; 10^8 converts cm^2 to ha; and (24×60) converts minutes to days – so that GAOP is expressed in kg/ha day.

The test needs to be repeated at different times of the day to obtain an estimate of total daily gross algal oxygen production. For a facultative pond in northeast Brazil loaded at 250 kg BOD/ha day at 25°C, this was just over 400 kg O_2/ha day; and in a maturation pond loaded at 50 kg BOD ha day it was nearly 300 kg O_2/ha day.

The light-and-dark-bottle test described above can be rather 'tricky' and experience is needed to obtain good results.

Algal biomass concentration

Algal biomass concentrations in facultative ponds, and to a lesser extent in maturation ponds, are influenced by several factors, including light intensity, the BOD loading on the pond (λ_s), the un-ionized ammonia (ie NH_3) concentration and the un-ionized H_2S concentration. If there are industrial effluents present in the wastewater, the algae may be adversely affected, even killed, by industrial toxicants, although many of these are degraded or removed in anaerobic ponds (Chapter 10).

Light intensity

Light intensity can be expressed in several ways, but in relation to photosynthesis it is best to express irradiance (radiant solar energy flux density,

W/m^2) in terms of photon flux density – that is, the number of photons (quanta of light) falling on a surface of unit area per unit of time. The 'photosynthetic photon flux density' (PPFD) is the number of photons of photosynthetically active radiation (PAR) – that is, light in the 400–700 nm wavelength range – falling on 1 m^2 of the earth's surface per second. The units of PPFD are einsteins/m^2 second (but usually μE/m^2 s), where one einstein is 6.023 x 10^{23} photons (6.023 x 10^{23} is Avogadro's number). The energy (E, joules) of one einstein depends on the wavelength of the photons which comprise it:

$$E = 6.023 \times 10^{23}(hc/\lambda)$$

(11.9)

where h is Planck's constant (6.626 x 10^{-34} J s); c is the speed of light (3 x 10^8 m/s); and λ is the wavelength of the light, m. For example, for light of wavelength 663 nm , (ie 6.63 x 10^{-7} m) the energy of one einstein is given by:

$$E = (6.023 \times 10^{23})(6.626 \times 10^{-34})(3 \times 10^8)/(6.63 \times 10^{-7}) = 0.18 \text{ MJ}$$

Once the photons enter water (eg a facultative or maturation pond) their speed decreases by a factor of 1.33 (the refractive index of water), so the energy of one einstein of red light at 663 nm is 0.14 MJ. However, the light available for photosynthesis in water bodies (including WSP) covers the whole PAR spectrum of 400–700 nm, and the energy of one einstein of underwater PAR is ~0.24 MJ (Kirk, 1994).

The chemical free energy needed to convert one mole (ie gram molecule, which is the molecular weight in daltons expressed in grams) of CO_2 to carbohydrate is given by:

$$4 \times 1.25 \times 0.0964 = 0.48 \text{ MJ}$$

where 4 is the number of electrons involved in the reaction; 1.25 is the redox potential difference between CO_2 fixation and O_2 evolution, V; and 0.0964 converts energy expressed in eV (electron volts) to energy in megajoules (MJ).

Two photons of light energy are needed per electron, so the light energy needed by the WSP algae to fix one mole of CO_2 is 8 einsteins, which is (8 x 0.24) = 1.92 MJ. Thus the efficiency of algal photosynthesis is 100(0.48/1.92) = 25 per cent. This efficiency is only for CO_2 fixation, but the algae have to use additional light energy to produce organic compounds such as proteins, lipids and nucleic acids, and so need more than 8 einsteins of light energy per mole of CO_2 fixed, and thus their efficiency is well below 25 per cent. In the 'real world' of facultative ponds, characterized by high turbidity (which is mostly due to the algae themselves), this efficiency can be as low as 10 per cent – that is, a requirement of 20 einsteins of underwater PAR per mole of CO_2 fixed. Since 1 mole of CO_2 fixed is accompanied by the production of 1 mole (ie 32 g) of O_2, 20 einsteins of light produces enough oxygen to remove 32 g of BOD$_u$ equivalent to 21 g of BOD$_5$. Thus a

BOD_5 removal of 1 kg/ha day requires 950 (ie ~1000) einsteins of underwater PAR/ha day.

Meteorological stations generally measure solar radiation intensity in W/m^2 (using an instrument called a pyranometer). One $W/m^2 = 1$ J/m^2 s = 864 MJ/ha day. Only ~40 per cent of total solar radiation incident on a calm water surface becomes underwater PAR, so 1 W/m^2 becomes ~346 MJ of underwater PAR/ha day or, as 1 einstein of underwater PAR = 0.24 MJ, ~1440 einsteins of underwater PAR/ha day. Since ~1000 einsteins of underwater PAR are required per kg BOD_5 removed, the removal of 1 kg BOD_5/ha day requires ~0.7 W/m^2. Thus, in the warm tropics (25°C), a design BOD_5 loading of 350 kg/ha day, with an expected non-algal BOD_5 removal of 90 per cent, requires ~220 W/m^2 – a level of total solar radiation always exceeded in these regions. In temperate climates (for example, Europe or New Zealand, with a winter design temperature of ≤8°C – Abis and Mara, 2003*), a loading of 80 kg/ha day with a similar removal requires ~50 W/m^2, which is almost always exceeded, even in winter. (Some meteorological stations may still measure solar radiation intensity in the old units of langleys/day. One langley/day = 1 $kcal/cm^2$ day = 4.168 J/cm^2 day = 0.48 W/m^2.)

The relationship between light intensity and algal photosynthesis is similar to that between substrate concentration and bacterial growth rate (equation 3.4). Light at too low an intensity limits photosynthesis, and light at too high an intensity also limits photosynthesis ('photoinhibition'). In tropical and subtropical facultative and maturation ponds the algae are 'light-saturated' (ie light intensity does not limit photosynthesis) at ~50 W/m^2, and photoinhibition sets in at ~300 W/m^2 (this level of photoinhibition explains why the algal band in stratified facultative ponds moves up and down within the top 50 cm of the pond as the algae seek to remove themselves from inhibitory light intensities).

BOD loading

The BOD loading applied to facultative ponds has a major influence on the in-pond algal biomass. In primary facultative ponds in northeast Brazil at 25°C chlorophyll *a* levels fell sharply with increasing BOD load up to ~450 kg/ha day, above which they were essentially constant at ~200 μg/l (Figure 11.4). This was the reason for selecting a design BOD loading rate of 350 kg/ha day at 25°C (equation 11.3). Along with higher BOD loads, higher BOD loading rates also bring higher loadings of sulphate and ammonia.

Sulphide toxicity

Sulphates in raw wastewater are reduced in anaerobic ponds and primary facultative ponds by the obligately anaerobic sulphate-reducing bacteria to sulphides, and these are also present in secondary facultative ponds which receive them in the anaerobic pond effluent. Un-ionized H_2S is highly toxic to pond algae and, as shown in Figure 10.2, the amount of total sulphide present as dissolved H_2S gas increases as the pH decreases. Dissolved H_2S rapidly passes through the algal cell membrane to attack its photosynthetic apparatus; hence algal growth and algal oxygen production are inhibited, and the pond

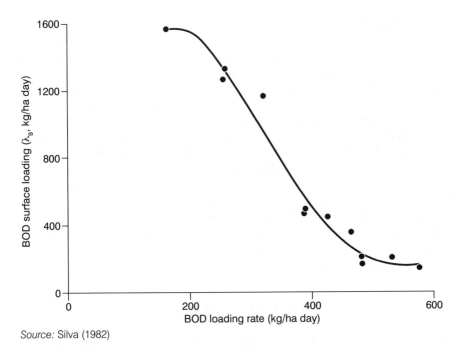

Source: Silva (1982)

Figure 11.4 *Variation of Chlorophyll* a *with Surface BOD Loading on Primary Facultative Ponds in Northeast Brazil*

quickly turns anaerobic or at least anoxic. This toxicity increases with decreasing pH. Experiments with strains of four common facultative pond algae – *Chlamadomonas, Chlorella, Euglena* and *Scenedesmus* – showed that photosynthesis is inhibited by 50 per cent (relative to that in the absence of H_2S) by very low levels of H_2S which vary from alga to alga: *Chlamadomonas* (45 μM), *Chlorella* (30 μM), *Scenedesmus* (22 μM) and *Euglena* (10 μM) (1 μM H_2S = 34 μg H_2S/l) (Pearson et al, 1987b). The comparatively high tolerance of *Chlamadomonas* to H_2S most probably explains why it is sometimes found as a surface film on anaerobic ponds (Chapter 10).

In primary facultative ponds in northeast Brazil loaded at 160–580 kg BOD/ha day at 25°C, Silva (1982) found a linear relationship between chlorophyll *a* and sulphide:

$$[Chl.a, μg/l] = 2550 - 346[S, mg/l]$$

$$(11.10)$$

This low tolerance of facultative pond algae to sulphide indicates that anaerobic pond effluent should not be introduced at or near the surface of a secondary facultative pond, since this is where the algae are. Instead it should be introduced in the lower part of the pond (at least 0.8 m below the surface) where the H_2S it contains (5–15 mg/l) can be oxidized by anaerobic photosynthetic bacteria (see below under 'Purple ponds').

Ammonia toxicity

Ammonia is present in aqueous solution as dissolved ammonia gas (NH_3 – ie un-ionized ammonia) and the ammonium ion (NH_4^+). As with sulphide, it is the un-ionized ammonia that is toxic to algae, but with one important difference: as the pH increases, the proportion of total ammonia present as NH_3 also increases, thus ammonia toxicity increases with increasing pH. Pearson et al (1987b) found that 50 per cent inhibition of photosynthesis in the four pond algae occurred in a different order from that caused by H_2S: *Chlorella* (3.9 mM), *Scenedesmus* (1.6 mM), *Euglena* and *Chlamadomonas* (both 0.9 mM) (1 mM NH_3 = 14 mg NH_3–N/l).

As ammonia toxicity increases with pH, it can be self-correcting at sublethal concentrations. This is because rapid photosynthesis leads to a high pond pH (often 9–10), ammonia toxicity thus increases and therefore photosynthesis decreases; the pH falls and the ammonia toxicity decreases – this leads to increased photosynthesis, an increase in pH and therefore in ammonia toxicity, and so the cycle repeats itself.

PURPLE PONDS

When facultative ponds are overloaded, either permanently or transiently, they often appear purple in colour (although the precise colour can vary from pink, through red and purple, to light brown). This is due to the toxic effects of mainly sulphide on the algae and the consequent predominance of purple and green anaerobic photosynthetic bacteria. These bacteria use light energy to fix carbon dioxide with the concomitant oxidation of hydrogen sulphide to sulphur and sulphate:

$$21H_2S + 10CO_2 + 2NH_3 \xrightarrow{\text{light}} 2(C_5H_8O_2N) + 21S + 16H_2O$$

$$21S + 30CO_2 + 6NH_3 + 36H_2O \xrightarrow{\text{light}} 6(C_5H_8O_2N) + 21H_2SO_4$$

These equations are for 'photo-autotrophic' growth (ie light-enabled growth on carbon dioxide). The green and purple photosynthetic bacteria can also utilize simple organic compounds, such as acetate, for 'photoheterotrophic' growth:

$$H_2S + 5CH_3OOH + 2NH_3 \xrightarrow{\text{light}} 2(C_5H_8O_2N) + S + 6H_2O$$

$$S + 15CH_3COOH + 6NH_3 \xrightarrow{\text{light}} 6(C_5H_8O_2N) + H_2SO_4 + 14H_2O$$

Anaerobic bacterial photosynthesis does not result in the production of oxygen (ie it is 'anoxygenic') as H_2S is oxidized, rather than H_2O as in the case of algal photosynthesis.

There are many photosynthetic bacteria, but two main groups are important in facultative ponds: the purple sulphur bacteria belonging to the

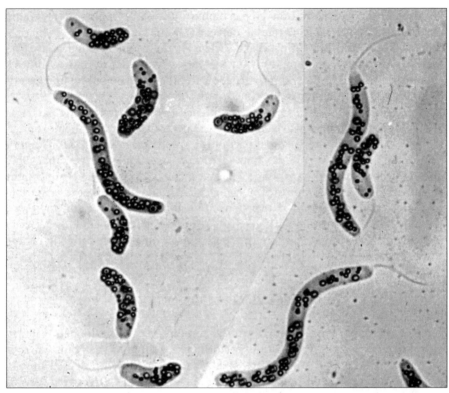

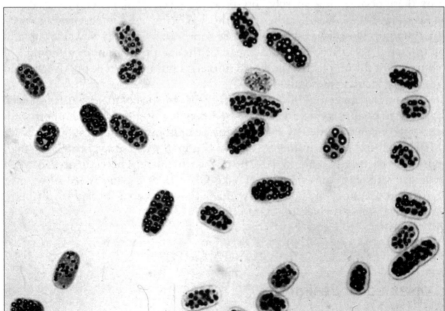

Figure 11.5 *Photosynthetic Purple Sulphur Bacteria:* top, Thiopedia *sp;*
bottom, Chromatium *sp*

family Chromatiaceae, and the green sulphur bacteria belonging to the family Chlorobiaceae. The Chromatiaceae deposit sulphur granules inside their cells (Figure 11.5), and the Chlorobiaceae deposit them outside their cells (the pathways in the second equations in the above two pairs of photosynthesis equations are only used when hydrogen sulphide is unavailable; in times of H_2S plenty, S is stored for use in times of H_2S famine).

Bacteriochlorophylls (the principal pigments of photosynthetic bacteria) absorb light of a longer wavelength than that absorbed by algal chlorophyll (750–900 nm – ie in the infra-red part of the spectrum, rather than <700 nm). Thus, in facultative ponds that are *not* overloaded, the anaerobic photosynthetic bacteria are found below the algae (longer-wavelength light penetrates deeper than shorter-wavelength light) and closer to the anaerobic sulphate-reducing bacteria that produce the sulphide – that is, they act as a sulphide 'filter', protecting the algae from the toxic effects of sulphide and also reducing odour release. They are thus very important in both correctly loaded and overloaded facultative ponds.

WIND-POWERED POND MIXERS

Gently mixing (stirring, circulating) the contents of an overloaded primary facultative pond can greatly aid its performance – often to the point where it no longer acts as if it were overloaded. The use of wind-powered mixers (sometimes called 'wind-powered aerators') can be a cost-effective means to mix these ponds; alternatively, low-powered electric mixers can be used (the power input is <1 W/m^3, rather than the 3–6 W/m^3 used in aerated lagoons – Chapter 20). However, a generally more appropriate strategy in warm climates is to install an anaerobic pond ahead of the facultative pond, although, of course, wind- or electric-powered mixers could be used on overloaded secondary facultative ponds.

Viraraghavan et al (2002) studied the performance of a 5.2-ha, 1.5-m deep facultative pond, serving a village of 565 people in central Canada, both with and without two 'Little River Pond Mills' wind-powered mixers (Sunset Solar Systems, 2002*). The influent BOD of 170 mg/l was reduced to 40–80 mg/l without the mixers and to 10–20 mg/l with them. The estimated oxygen transfer rate was equivalent to ~1.5 kg O_2/kWh at a wind speed of ~5 m/s. Further discussion on the use of wind/electric-powered mixers for primary facultative ponds is given by Mara (2003*).

DESIGN EXAMPLES

Conventional design

Design (a) a primary facultative pond to treat the wastewater detailed in the Design example in Chapter 10; and (b) a secondary facultative pond to treat the effluent from the anaerobic pond designed in Chapter 10.

Additional design parameters: $e = 5$ mm/d; $E_i = 500$ human intestinal nematode eggs/l; and $N_i = 5 \times 10^7$ *E coli* per 100 ml.

Primary facultative pond

From equation 11.3 $\lambda_s = 350$ kg/ha day for 25°C. Thus from equations 11.1 and 11.7 and assuming a depth of 1.5 m:

$$A_f = 10L_iQ/\lambda_s$$

$$= (10 \times 300 \times 10{,}000)/350$$

$$= 85{,}720 \text{ m}^2 \text{ (ie 8.6 ha)}$$

$$\theta_f = 2A_fD_f/(2Q - 0.001eA_f)$$

$$= (2 \times 85{,}720 \times 1.5)/[(2 \times 10{,}000) - (0.001 \times 5 \times 85\ 720)]$$

$$= 13 \text{ days}$$

Secondary facultative pond

With $L_i = 90$ mg/l (the BOD of the anaerobic pond effluent), equations 11.1 and 11.7 give:

$$A_f = 25{,}720 \text{ m}^2$$

$$\theta_f = 3.88 \text{ days}$$

The retention time is <4 days, the minimum retention time in facultative ponds. Therefore recalculate A_f from equation 11.7 with $\theta_f = 4$ days:

$$A_f = 2Q\theta_f/(2D + 0.001e\theta_f)$$

$$= (2 \times 10{,}000 \times 4)/[(2 \times 1.5) + (0.001 \times 5 \times 4)]$$

$$= 26{,}500 \text{ m}^2 \text{ (ie 2.7 ha)}$$

Check for BOD and helminth egg removal in the anaerobic and secondary facultative ponds:

BOD removal: from equations 5.7 and 5.8, the BOD of the effluent from the secondary facultative pond is:

$$k_1 = 0.1 \ (1.05)^{T-20}$$

$$= 0.1 \ (1.05)^{25-20}$$

$$= 0.13 \text{ days}^{-1}$$

$$L_e = L_i/(1 + k_1\theta_f)$$

$$= 90/[1 + (0.13 \times 4)]$$

$$= 60 \text{ mg/l (unfiltered BOD)}$$

Thus the filtered BOD is given by equation 11.8 as:

$$L_e \text{ (filtered)} = 0.3 \, (L_e, \text{ unfiltered})$$

$$= 0.3 \times 60$$

$$= 18 \text{ mg/l}$$

Thus the effluent from the secondary facultative pond is suitable for surface water discharge.

Egg removal: using equation 11.12, the egg removal in the 1-day anaerobic pond is 75 per cent, and in the 4-day secondary facultative pond 93 per cent. Thus the number of eggs in the effluent from the latter is:

$$E_e = 500(1 - 0.75)(1 - 0.93)$$

$$= 9 \text{ per litre}$$

This is >1 per litre, the guideline level for restricted irrigation, and >>0.1 per litre, the recommended level for restricted irrigation when children under the age of 15 years are exposed (Chapter 21). Thus this particular secondary facultative pond effluent is not suitable for restricted irrigation, and it requires further treatment in maturation ponds (Chapter 12).

Effluent flow: the flow from the secondary facultative pond, which is required for the design of the maturation ponds, is given by:

$$Q_e = Q_i - 0.001eA_f$$

$$= 10,000 - (0.001 \times 5 \times 26,500)$$

$$= 9868 \text{ m}^3/\text{day}$$

Land saving achieved by anaerobic ponds
The areas calculated above are:

1   anaerobic and secondary facultative ponds: 3340 + 26,500 = 29,840 m^2
2   primary facultative pond: 85,720 m^2.

Thus the primary facultative pond requires 187 per cent more land than the anaerobic and secondary facultative ponds combined. This illustrates very well the following observation of Marais (1970): '*Anaerobic pretreatment is so advantageous that the first consideration in the design of a series of ponds should always include the possibility of anaerobic pretreatment*'.

Design based on uncertainty

This design procedure is based on von Sperling (1996b*). The following ranges of parameter values were used for the design of the secondary facultative pond (of course, different ranges could be used and different designs obtained):

- Q 8000–10,000 m3/day
- L_i 90–112 mg/l
- T 24–26°C
- D_f 1.5 m (fixed value)
- e 4–6 mm/day
- $k_{1(20)}$ 0.09–0.11 day^{-1}
- ϕ 1.05–1.06
- F_{na} 0.1–0.3

The three equations of interest are equations 11.1 and 11.3 combined, equation 11.7, and equations 5.7, 5.8 and 11.8 combined – that is:

$$A_f = 10L_iQ/[350(1.107 - 0.002T)^{T-25}]$$

$$\theta_f = 2A_fD_f/(2Q - 0.001eA_f)$$

$$L_e \text{ (filtered)} = F_{na}L_i/[1 + (k_{1(20)}\phi^{T-20}\theta_f)]$$

The Monte Carlo programme (Sleigh and Mara, 2003a*) produced the following results after 1000 trials (each 1000-trial run produces slightly different results):

1   Mean area = 26,046 m^2 and mean filtered L_e = 6 mg/l, and
2   95-percentile area = 30,524 m^2 and 95-percentile filtered L_e = 7 mg/l.

If the regulator requires compliance with a mean effluent filtered BOD, then the pond area is 2.6 ha. If, however, compliance were required on a 95-percentile basis, the area would be 3.1 ha.

12

Maturation Ponds

FUNCTION

The main function of maturation ponds is to reduce the number of excreted pathogens, principally faecal bacteria and viruses, present in the effluent of facultative ponds (Chapter 11) to a level suitable for agricultural and/or aquacultural re-use (Chapters 21 and 22). BOD and suspended solids are removed only very slowly, and nutrient (nitrogen and phosphorus) removal is also quite slow, although in a well-designed and properly operated and maintained series of WSP (anaerobic, facultative and several maturation ponds), cumulative removals of BOD, suspended solids and nutrients are high, as shown in Table 12.1. The extremely high removal of $E\ coli$ in WSP is also shown in Table 12.1: from $5 \times 10^7/100$ ml in the raw wastewater to 30/100 ml in the effluent of the third maturation pond – a removal of 6 log units, or 99.9999 per cent (the effluent of the second maturation pond contained <1000 $E\ coli$ per 100 ml, and so would be suitable for unrestricted irrigation – Chapters 4 and 21; thus there would be no point in practice in having the third maturation pond, the effluent of which contained only 30 $E\ coli$ per 100 ml – better bacteriologically than the water used for drinking by many millions of people in developing countries).

Maturation ponds are typically aerobic throughout their depth, and they show less stratification than facultative ponds. They contain a greater diversity of algal genera (Table 11.1), but algal biomass is lower. In a series of maturation ponds, algal diversity increases, but algal biomass decreases, from pond to pond. Depths are typically 1 m; shallower ponds achieve higher faecal bacterial and viral removals due to greater light penetration, but unlined ponds with depths of less than 1 m are likely to contain emergent macrophytes (rooted plants growing up from the pond base) – these provide a suitably shaded habitat for mosquito breeding, and so should be avoided by having depths ≥1 m unless the ponds are lined (Chapter 13).

Table 12.1 *Performance of a Series of Five WSP in Northeast Brazil*

Parameter (mg/l)[a]	Raw wastewater	Anaerobic pond effluent	Facultative pond effluent	1st Maturation pond effluent	2nd Maturation pond effluent	3rd Maturation pond effluent	Cumulative percentage removal
BOD	240	63	45	25	19	17	93
COD	601	175	190	135	103	109	82
SS	305	56	74	61	43	45	85
Ammonia-N	45	32	27	20	14	8	82
Phosphorus[b]	6.6	4.0	3.7	3.4	3.2	2.4	64
Chlorophyll[a]	–	–	1120	480	270	420	–
Faecal coliforms	5×10^7	3×10^6	3×10^5	2×10^4	450	30	99.9999

Notes: The ponds had retention times of 5.5 d, except the anaerobic pond (6.8 d) and maturation pond 3 (5.8 d). The results are mean values over a 24-month period.
[a] Except chl.a (μg/l) and FC (per 100 ml)
[b] Total P for raw wastewater and anaerobic pond effluent; soluble (ie, non-algal) P for others
Source: Silva (1982)

PATHOGEN REMOVAL MECHANISMS

Viruses

The mechanisms underlying viral die-off and removal in WSP are not fully understood, but it is believed that they are removed mainly by sedimentation following adsorption on to solids, including algae (which settle out when they die). Few studies have been done on viral removal in WSP (as counting viruses is expensive and requires a highly skilled microbiologist). Oragui et al (1995*) studied rotavirus and faecal coliform removal in several WSP series in northeast Brazil, each of which comprised an anaerobic pond, a secondary facultative pond and three maturation ponds, with overall retention times of 10–25 days. Rotaviruses were reduced from 1×10^4/l of raw wastewater to <2/l of final effluent – a removal of 99.997 per cent; the corresponding faecal coliform removal was from 3×10^7/100 ml to ~50/100 ml, a removal of 99.9998 per cent. Rotavirus removal was best in the 0.6 m deep tertiary maturation ponds which had retention times of 5 days: rotavirus numbers decreased from 1500 per litre to <2/l, a removal of ~99.9 per cent. The data in Table 12.2 for rotavirus removal indicate first-order rate constant values (for use in equation 12.1 below) of ~3 day^{-1} in the anaerobic pond and ~0.3–0.5 day^{-1} in the facultative and maturation ponds at 25°C.

Bacteriophages, which are viruses that attack bacteria, can be used as surrogates for human viral removal in WSP. Vorkas and Lloyd (2000*), working on WSP near Cali, Colombia, showed that phages of *Erwinia*,

Pseudomonas and *Serratia* were good models for viral transport through, and removal in, WSP. Phage die-off was higher at in-pond pH values >8.5 and was accelerated by the same sunlight-mediated effects that Curtis et al (1992a) found for faecal bacterial removal in WSP (see below).

Bacteria

The faecal bacteria of interest are the pathogens which cause infectious intestinal disease, such as *Campylobacter*, diarrhoeagenic *Escherichia coli*, *Salmonella*, *Shigella* and *Vibrio cholerae* (Chapter 2), and *E coli* which is used as a bacterial and viral pathogen indicator organism (Chapter 3). The removal of faecal bacteria in WSP has been studied by many research workers, and it is almost always found that their removal is very high in a well designed, properly operated and maintained series of WSP. As an example of this huge research effort over the past 30 or so years, the removal data of Oragui et al (1987) for a 5-pond series in northeast Brazil are given in Table 12.2. This data set is unique in that it contains data from the same series of WSP and at the same time on the removal of faecal coliforms, two bacterial pathogens and two viral pathogens. It is also highly supportive of the World Health Organization's (WHO, 1989*, 2004*) guidelines for unrestricted irrigation (Chapters 4 and 21) as it shows that, when the faecal coliform count was reduced to 7000/100 ml, both bacterial pathogens had been completely removed and that only very low numbers of the viral pathogens were present – thus demonstrating that the WHO guideline level of ≤1000 *E coli* per 100 ml is perfectly adequate (this point is discussed in greater detail in Chapter 21).

Oragui et al (1993) were able to monitor the removal of *V cholerae* O1 in WSP when the seventh cholera pandemic arrived in northeast Brazil. The (slightly unusual) WSP series comprised a 1-day anaerobic pond followed by nine 2-day ponds. The raw wastewater contained 485 *V cholerae* per litre and 2×10^7 faecal coliforms per 100 ml. Most (94 per cent) of the *V cholerae* were removed in the anaerobic pond (Chapter 10), and complete (ie 100 per cent) removal was achieved in the effluent of the fifth 2-day pond (ie after 11 days); the corresponding faecal coliform count was 6×10^4/100 ml – again supporting the WHO *E coli* guideline for unrestricted irrigation.

Several factors have been proposed to explain the die-off of faecal bacteria in WSP, and they can be conveniently grouped into 'dark-mediated' processes and 'light-mediated' processes. The dark-mediated processes (which are really 'light-independent' processes, as they occur in both the light and the dark), include sedimentation of the faecal bacteria adsorbed on to settleable solids or contained within flocs of settleable solids; predation (ie consumption) by free-living protozoa and micro-invertebrates such as *Daphnia* and *Moinia* (water fleas); and death due to starvation and senescence. There are external factors which aid these dark-mediated factors, for example, pond depth (the deeper a pond, the greater the proportion of it that is in darkness), and organic loading (the greater the loading, the more anaerobic the pond and the effects of the light-mediated factors are reduced).

Table 12.2 *Bacterial and Viral Removals in a Series of Five WSP in Northeast Brazil*

Organism[a]	Raw wastewater	Anaerobic pond effluent	Facultative pond effluent	1st maturation pond effluent	2nd maturation pond effluent	3rd maturation pond effluent
Faecal coliforms	2×10^7	4×10^6	8×10^5	2×10^5	3×10^4	7×10^3
Campylobacter	70	20	0.2	0	0	0
Salmonella	20	8	0.1	0.02	0.01	0
Enteroviruses	1×10^4	6×10^3	1×10^3	400	50	9
Rotaviruses	800	200	70	30	10	3

Notes: The anaerobic pond had a retention time of 1 day, each of the others 5 days.
[a] Bacterial numbers per 100 ml, viral numbers per 10 l.
Source: Oragui et al (1987)

The most important of the light-mediated factors are:

- **Time and temperature:** these are taken as light-mediated factors as the pond temperature is the result of the sunlight intensity at the pond surface, and the longer the time that the pond is exposed to the light-mediated factors, the greater the faecal bacterial die-off. (There is potential for confusion here, as we know that bacterial growth rates increase with temperature, but so do bacterial death rates. Whatever the cells are going to do – grow or die – they do it more quickly at higher temperatures.) Time and temperature are the two factors included in Marais' (1974) model for *E coli* die-off in WSP (see equations 12.1 and 12.2 below).
- **High pH:** in-pond pH values ≥9.4 induce very rapid faecal bacterial die-off (Parhad and Rao, 1974; Pearson et al, 1987c), except that of *V cholerae* (for which pH 9 is used in isolation media to inhibit other faecal bacteria; as noted in Chapter 10, *V cholerae* is very sensitive to sulphide concentrations ≥3 mg/l which occur in anaerobic ponds). High pH is a light-mediated factor as it is induced by the pond algae. When algae are photosynthesizing rapidly, their demand for CO_2 outstrips its supply from bacterial metabolism and transfer across the pond surface; this absence of dissolved CO_2 in the pond disturbs the CO_2–bicarbonate–carbonate equilibrium, and consequently bicarbonate and carbonate ions dissociate, as follows:

$$2HCO_3^- \rightarrow CO_3^{2-} + H_2O + CO_2$$

$$CO_3^{2-} + H_2O \rightarrow 2OH^- + CO_2$$

The resulting CO_2 is fixed by the algae, and the hydroxyl ions (OH^-) accumulate to raise the pH. High pH values ≥9.4, even >10, occur on sunny days close to the pond surface, which is therefore where the most rapid faecal bacterial die-off occurs. A high in-pond (ie extracellular) pH kills faecal bacteria by making them unable to maintain their optimal intracellular pH of 7.4–7.7.

- **High light intensity and high dissolved oxygen:** the role of light in mediating faecal bacterial die-off was elucidated by Curtis (1990) (see also Curtis et al, 1992a, 1992b, 1994; see also Davies-Colley et al, 2000*). Curtis found that light of wavelengths up to 700 nm could damage faecal bacteria; however, light of wavelengths below 425 nm (ie including UV light) was unimportant in WSP as it is almost wholly absorbed in the first few mm of the pond. Light of wavelengths >425 nm could only damage faecal bacteria in the presence of both a dissolved sensitizer such as the humic substance gilvin ('dissolved yellow matter') and dissolved oxygen – both gilvin and oxygen are required for light-induced damage of faecal bacteria ('photo-oxidation'). Gilvin is present in almost all waters, including wastewaters and WSP (it is measured by the absorbance of a 0.2-μm filtrate of the water sample at 440 nm). The light–oxygen–gilvin damage is enhanced by intracellular pH values >7.7, so the pond algae are crucial for the die-off of faecal bacteria in WSP: they produce high dissolved oxygen levels and induce high in-pond pH values which induce an intracellular pH >7.7, which in turn and in conjunction with high light intensities (>~500 W/m^2) achieves rapid faecal bacterial die-off. The way in which the combination of high light intensity, high dissolved oxygen, high pH and gilvin kills faecal bacteria appears to be as follows: gilvin absorbs the light and then reacts with oxygen to form oxygen radicals (eg hydrogen peroxide) which damage the cell membrane and so cause the cell to die; and the high pH enhances cell damage in the way explained above.

Helminth eggs and protozoan cysts

Eggs and cysts are removed in WSP by sedimentation, and thus their removal occurs mainly in the first ponds in a series – anaerobic and facultative ponds. Settling velocities for eggs and cysts are given in Table 12.3. Cysts are smaller and settle more slowly than eggs, and hence their removal requires a longer retention time. Grimason et al (1993) studied the removal of *Cryptosporidium*

Table 12.3 *Settling Velocities for Parasite Eggs and Cysts*

Parasite	Egg/cyst size (μm)	Relative density	Settling velocity (m/h)
Ascaris	55 x 40	1.11	0.65
Trichuris	22 x 50	1.15	1.53
Hookworms	60 x 40	1.06	0.39
Giardia	14	1.05	0.02
Cryptosporidium	6	1.08	0.004

Sources: Shuval et al (1986*) and Department of the Environment and Department of Health (1990)

Table 12.4 *Helminth Egg Removal in Waste Stabilization Ponds in Northeast Brazil*

	Raw wastewater	Anaerobic pond effluent	Facultative pond effluent	1st maturation pond effluent	2nd maturation pond effluent	3rd maturation pond effluent
Egg numbers per litre	804	29	1	0	0	0
Retention time, days	–	6.8	5.5	5.5	5.5	5.8
Egg numbers per litre	1489	48	10	14	10	4
Retention time, days	–	4.0	3.2	3.2	3.2	3.4

Source: Silva (1982)

oocysts and *Giardia* cysts in 11 WSP systems in Kenya with overall retention times of 14–133 days. The raw wastewaters contained 13–73 oocysts and 213–6213 cysts/l, but none was found in the final effluents, except at one location – the overloaded WSP at Eldoret (actual retention time 22 days; design value 33 days), the effluent of which had 40–50 *Giardia* cysts/l. Amahmid et al (2002*) found complete removal of *Giardia* cysts in the WSP at Marrakech, Morocco which had a retention time of 16 days.

Helminth eggs are completely removed in WSP within around 5–15 days (Table 12.4), depending on the number of eggs in the raw wastewater. Equation 11.11 of Ayres et al (1992*), based on egg removal in WSP in Brazil, India and Kenya, describes egg removal very well (this was independently confirmed by von Sperling et al, 2002b), but for design purposes equation 11.12 should be used.

DESIGN FOR *E COLI* REMOVAL

Marais' method

Marais (1974) refined the earlier model of Marais and Shaw (1961) for *E coli* removal in WSP which was modelled on first-order kinetics in a completely mixed reactor (Chapter 5). The resulting equations for a single pond are the following modifications of equations 5.7 and 5.8:

$$N_e = \frac{N_i}{1 + k_{B(T)}\theta}$$

$$(12.1)$$

$$k_{B(T)} = 2.6(1.19)^{T-20}$$

$$(12.2)$$

where N_e and N_i are the numbers of E coli per 100 ml of the pond effluent and influent, respectively; $k_{B(T)}$ is the first-order rate constant for E coli removal at T°C in a completely mixed reactor, day^{-1}; θ is the mean hydraulic retention time in the pond, days; and T is the design temperature, °C.

The design temperature is the mean temperature of the coolest month in the season in which the maturation ponds have to produce an effluent of the required microbiological quality. This is the irrigation season if the effluent is to be re-used in agriculture. The design temperature is the mean temperature of the coolest month if the effluent is used for fishpond fertilization or if it is discharged into bathing waters or near shellfisheries (as these are year-round activities).

Equation 12.2 gives the value of $k_{B(T)}$ as 2.6 day^{-1} at 20°C, and its value is highly temperature-dependent: it changes by 19 per cent for each change in temperature of 1 degC.

For a series of WSP comprising an anaerobic pond, a secondary facultative pond and n equally sized maturation ponds, equation 12.1 is rewritten as:

$$N_e = \frac{N_i}{(1 + k_{B(T)}\theta_a)(1 + k_{B(T)}\theta_f)(1 + k_{B(T)}\theta_m)^n}$$

$$(12.3)$$

where N_e and N_i are now the E coli numbers per 100 ml of the final effluent and the raw wastewater, respectively; the subscripts a, f and m refer to the anaerobic, facultative and maturation ponds; and n is the number of equally sized maturation ponds.

In this chapter it is assumed that it is possible to have n equally sized maturation ponds. However, if during the physical design stage (Chapter 13), site conditions are such that this is not possible, then a redesign is necessary with the term $(1 + k_{B(T)}\theta_m)^n$ in equation 12.3 replaced by:

$$(1 + k_{B(T)}\theta_{m1})(1 + k_{B(T)}\theta_{m2})...(1 + k_{B(T)}\theta_{mn})$$

The value of θ_m is subject to the following three constraints:

1   $\theta_m \not> \theta_f$,
2   $\theta_m \not< \theta_m^{min}$, and
3   $\lambda_{s(m1)} \not> 0.75\lambda_{s(f)}$

The first constraint simply states that the retention time in the maturation pond should not be greater than that in the facultative pond. There is no theoretical reason for this, but it seems sensible (ie it is based on 'engineering judgement'). The second constraint sets a minimum value for the retention time in the maturation ponds to permit algal reproduction and to minimize hydraulic short-circuiting. Marais (1974) recommends a value of 3 days for θ_m^{min}. The third constraint, which is the critical one to consider first, sets a limit on the BOD surface loading on the first maturation pond; clearly this should not be more than that on the facultative ponds, and it is better if it is less; here it is set at 75 per cent of the latter.

Equation 11.1 for surface loading can be rewritten with $Q/A = D/\theta$ for the first maturation pond as:

$$\lambda_{s(m1)} = 10L_iD_{m1}/\theta_{m1}$$

(12.4)

Here, L_i is the unfiltered BOD of the influent into the first maturation pond – that is, that of the effluent from the facultative pond ($L_{e(fac)}$) as determined by equations 5.7 and 5.8 (with $k_{1(20)} = 0.1$ day^{-1} for secondary facultative ponds, or 0.3 day^{-1} for primary facultative ponds, and $\phi = 1.05$). Thus equation 12.4 becomes:

$$\theta_{m1} = 10L_{e(fac)}D_m1/0.75\lambda_{s(fac)}$$

(12.5)

and equation 12.3 is rewritten as:

$$N_e = N_i/(1 + k_{B(T)}\theta_a)(1 + k_{B(T)}\theta_f)(1 + k_{B(T)}\theta_{m1})(1 + k_{B(T)}\theta_m)^n$$

(12.6)

where θ_m is now the retention time in the second and subsequent maturation ponds of which there are now n.

At this stage in the design all the terms in equation 12.6 are known or assumed, except θ_m and n: N_e is the effluent quality required (eg 1000 *E coli*/100 ml for unrestricted irrigation – Chapter 21); N_i is either known or taken as 5×10^7 per 100 ml; θ_a and θ_f are known from the designs for the anaerobic and facultative ponds (Chapters 10 and 11); and θ_{m1} is calculated from equation 12.5 and $k_{B(T)}$ from equation 12.2.

A more convenient form of equation 12.6 is:

$$\theta_m = \{[N_i/N_e(1 + k_{B(T)}\theta_a)(1 + k_{B(T)}\theta_f)(1 + k_{B(T)}\theta_{m1}]^{1/n} - 1\}/k_{B(T)}$$

(12.7)

Equation 12.7 is solved first for $n = 1$, then for $n = 2$, and so on, until the calculated value of θ_m is $<\theta_m^{min}$; assume this happens when $n = \tilde{n}$. Consider only values of θ_m which are $<\theta_f$ and $>\theta_m^{min}$, but also θ_m^{min} itself; and choose the combination of n and θ_m, including $\tilde{n}$ and θ_m^{min}, which has the least overall retention time and therefore the least land area requirement. As an example (and *only* as an example), suppose the following solutions to equation 12.7 were obtained:

- for $n = 1$, $\theta_m = 256$ days;
- $n = 2$, $\theta_m = 27$ days;
- $n = 3$, $\theta_m = 4$ days; and
- $n = 4$, $\theta_m = 1.9$ days (ie $\tilde{n} = 4$).

Assuming $\theta_f < 27$ days, then the two combinations to consider are $n = 3$ and θ_m = 4 days, and $\tilde{n} = 4$ and $\theta_m^{min} = 3$ days. Both give an overall retention time of 12 days; in this case it is better to have three 4-day maturation ponds rather than four 3-day ones in order to minimize embankment construction.

Values of $k_{B(20)}$ and ϕ

The values of $k_{B(20)}$ and ϕ given by Marais in equation 12.2 are 2.6 day^{-1} and 1.19, respectively. Marais derived these values from his analysis of the faecal coliform data from the primary facultative and maturation ponds serving 'Community C' (in the USA) reported by Slanetz et al (1970). The temperature range for these ponds was 2–21°C; the BOD loading on the primary facultative pond was not stated, but was presumably ~50 kg/ha day or less.

However, the value of k_B is highly dependent on the BOD loading. Figure 12.1 shows a steep decline in the value of k_B in primary facultative ponds at 25°C in northeast Brazil up to a BOD loading of 400 kg/ha day, above which it was essentially constant at ~2.8 day^{-1}, which is its value in anaerobic ponds at 25°C (equation 12.8 below). Figures 11.4 and 12.1, which have the same shape, together provide direct experimental evidence that the value of k_B is controlled by the algal concentration (see Figure 12.2), which in turn is controlled by the BOD loading.

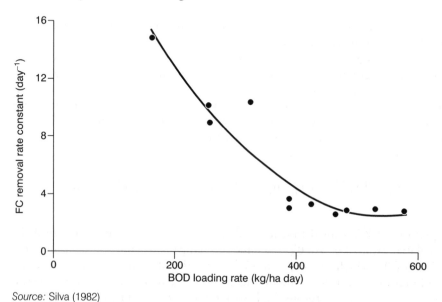

Source: Silva (1982)

Figure 12.1 *Variation of* k_B *with Surface BOD Loading on Primary Facultative Ponds in Northeast Brazil*

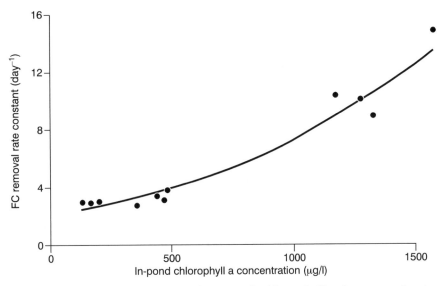

Figure 12.2 *Variation of* k_B *with In-pond Chlorophyll a Concentration in Primary Facultative Ponds in Northeast Brazil*

As noted by Catunda (1994) and Mendonça (2000), several research workers have found $k_{B(20)}$ values <2.6 day^{-1} and ϕ values <1.19. Examples are given in Table 12.5. Catunda also reported k_B values at 25°C from WSP in the same city in northeast Brazil that varied significantly with the pond depth: from 7.3 day^{-1} in 0.3 m deep ponds to 0.8 day^{-1} in 3 m deep ponds. Thus the original method of Marais with $k_{B(20)}$ = 2.6 day^{-1} and ϕ = 1.19 may not be generally applicable. A more generally applicable method is that of von Sperling, which is now discussed.

von Sperling's method

As noted in Chapter 5, von Sperling (1999*, 2002*, 2003*) recommends the use of the dispersed flow model (equation 5.13) for *E coli* removal in WSP, with equation 5.14 for δ and equations 5.8 and 5.15 for k_B. For convenience these equations are repeated here:

- The 'abbreviated' Wehner–Wilhelm equation for dispersed flow rewritten in terms of *E coli* numbers:

$$N_e = N_i[4a/(1 + a)^2]\exp[(1 - a)/2\delta]$$

(5.13)

- where $a = \sqrt{(1 + 4k_{B(T)}\theta\delta)}$ and $\theta = V/Q$ (ie the nominal mean hydraulic retention time), days.
- von Sperling's equation for δ:

Table 12.5 *Reported Values of* $k_{B(20)}$ *and* ϕ *for Use in Equation 12.2*

Source	$k_{B(20)}$ (day^{-1})	ϕ
Klock (1971)	1.1	1.07
Marais (1974)	2.6	1.19
Skerry and Parker (1979)	1.5	1.06
Arceivala (1981)	1.2	1.19
Mills et al (1992)	0.7	1.17
Yanez (1993)	1.1	1.07
Mayo (1995*)	1.9	1.08
Mara et al (2001b*)[a]	2.6	1.15

Note
[a] For temperatures >20°C

$$\delta = (L/B)^{-1}$$

(5.14)

- von Sperling's equations for k_B:

$$k_{B(20)} = 0.92D^{-0.88}\theta^{-0.33}$$

(5.15)

$$k_{B(T)} = k_{B(20)}(1.07)^{T-20}$$

(5.8)

where L, B and D are the pond length, breadth and depth, respectively, m.

Equation 5.15 was derived by von Sperling from the faecal coliform removal data from 33 facultative and maturation systems in tropical and subtropical Brazil (latitude 7–24° South). It thus represents a very wide range of conditions and can be recommended in preference to Marais' method, particularly since more recent workers have, as noted above, found complete-mix values of $k_{B(20)}$ <2.6 day^{-1} and ϕ <1.19.

   This design procedure must include the three constraints for the retention times in the maturation ponds and the judicious selection of the combinations of retention time in, and number of, maturation ponds (as described above under 'Marais' method'). As recommended by von Sperling (2003*), the whole procedure can also be subjected to 'uncertainty' analysis as described in Chapter 11 for facultative ponds (see also Gawasiri, 2003).

   However, Pearson et al (1995*, 1996b*) found that the performance of secondary facultative and secondary maturation ponds in northeast Brazil at 25°C was not influenced by either depth (1–2 m for facultative ponds, 0.4–0.9 m for maturation ponds) or length-to-breadth ratio (1–6.5 to 1 for facultative pond, 2.8–8 to 1 for maturation ponds) (Table 12.6). The actual faecal coliforms removals in these ponds were very close to those predicted by Marais' equations. These ponds in northeast Brazil were optimally loaded, as

Table 12.6 *Performance Data for WSP with Different Depths and Length-to-Breadth Ratios in Northeast Brazil at 25 °C*

Pond reference no	Length-to-breadth ratio	Depth (m)	Retention time (day)	BOD loading (kg/ha day)	In-pond chl a (mg/m²)[a]	Faecal coliforms (per 100 ml)	Unfiltered BOD (mg/l)	Ammonia-nitrogen (mg/l)
(a) Secondary facultative ponds							
F21	6.5 to 1	1.00	3	230	435	11×10^5	32	37
F22	6.5 to 1	1.33	4	230	722	9×10^5	29	36
F23	6.5 to 1	1.67	5	230	655	9×10^5	28	36
F24	6.5 to 1	2.00	6	230	716	8×10^5	24	35
F25	1 to 1	2.00	6	247	706	9×10^5	25	35
(b) Secondary maturation ponds							
M20	8 to 1	0.39	1	70	201	1600	25	17
M19[b]	2.8 to 1	0.39	3	24	361	630	26	9
M18	2.8 to 1	0.39	3	24	351	760	25	8
M17	2.8 to 1	0.64	5	24	392	680	21	7
M16	2.8 to 1	0.90	7	24	447	550	22	7

Notes:
[a] Chlorophyll a units are mg/m² – ie the algal biomass in the water column below 1 m² of pond surface area
[b] Ponds M18 and M19 were identical (internal experimental controls)
Source: Pearson et al (1995*, 1996b*)

were the ponds in the US that Marais used to derive his equations; in contrast, many of the pond systems used by von Sperling were not optimally loaded, as was the case for many of those referred to in Table 12.5. Nevertheless, von Sperling's method for *E coli* removal in tropical and subtropical WSP may be the most generally applicable model since, in practice, most pond systems are, or become, overloaded.

For anaerobic ponds, which are often square (ie $L/B = 1$ and, from equation 5.14, δ also = 1), the complete-mix equation can be used for *E coli* removal (equation 12.1), with $k_{B(T)}$ given by:

$$k_{B(T)} = 2.0(1.07)^{T-20}$$

(12.8)

Equation 12.8 was derived from faecal coliform removal data reported by Silva (1982) for anaerobic ponds in northeast Brazil that had retention times of 0.8–6.8 days.

Light intensity

Xu et al (2002*) also used the dispersed flow model, but they correlated $k_{B(T)}$ with solar radiation intensity (see Chapter 11) as well as with temperature, as follows:

$$k_{B(T)} = k_{B(20)}(0.915)^{T-20}\exp(aI_m)$$

(12.9)

where a is a constant (for values, see below); and I_m is the depth-averaged in-pond solar radiation intensity, J/cm² day, given by:

$$I_m = I_0\,(1 - e^{-KD})/KD$$

(12.10)

where I_0 is the solar radiation intensity at the pond surface, J/cm² day; D is the pond depth, m; and K is the light extinction coefficient, m^{-1}, given by:

$$K = 24.1 + 0.69(SS)$$

(12.11)

where SS is the in-pond suspended solids concentration, mg/l. The in-pond SS in equation 21.11 is basically a surrogate for the in-pond algal concentration as almost all the SS in maturation ponds are algae.

Equation 12.9 was derived for secondary and tertiary maturation ponds on the island of Noirmoutier off the French Atlantic coast (temperature, 6–22°C; solar radiation intensity, 300–2400 J/cm² day – ie 35–280 W/m²); $k_{B(20)}$ was found to be 0.019 day^{-1} and a 0.170 for the 1.4-m deep secondary pond, and 0.065 day^{-1} and 0.191 for the 2.2-m deep tertiary pond. It shows that, at least in this location, solar radiation intensity is more important than temperature in *E coli* removal in maturation ponds. Research is clearly needed to develop a form of equation 12.9 for tropical and subtropical maturation ponds.

DESIGN FOR HELMINTH EGG REMOVAL

If the facultative pond effluent contains >1 egg/l or, if children under the age of 15 years are exposed (see Chapter 21), >0.1 egg/l, then one or two maturation ponds are required to reduce the egg count to one of these levels in order that the effluent can be used for restricted irrigation. The retention time in the first of these maturation ponds is determined from equation 12.5 and the egg removal from equation 11.12.

If the effluent is to be used for unrestricted irrigation, then by the time the *E coli* numbers are reduced to ≤1000 per 100 ml, the eggs will have been reduced to <<1 (even <0.1) egg/l – but this should always be checked.

BOD REMOVAL

BOD removal in maturation ponds is much slower than in facultative ponds (Table 12.1). Equation 5.7 for unfiltered BOD can be used with a value of k_1

of ~0.05 day^{-1} for temperatures of 15–25°C, as there is little variation of BOD removal in maturation ponds with temperature. The non-algal (ie filtered) BOD is then estimated from equation 11.8 with F_{na} = 0.1 (ie assuming that 90 per cent of the BOD is algal).

NUTRIENT REMOVAL

Total nitrogen

There is no total nitrogen removal in anaerobic ponds, only nitrogen transformation with some of the organic nitrogen (principally urea and amino acids) being converted to ammonia (a process called 'ammonification'). Nitrogen removal occurs in facultative and maturation ponds, mainly through the incorporation of ammonia into algal cells. Reed (1985) gives the following equation for total nitrogen removal in facultative and maturation ponds:

$$C_e = C_i \exp\{- [0.0064(1.039)^{T-20}][\theta + 60.6(\text{pH} - 6.6)]\}$$

(12.12)

where C_e and C_i are the effluent and influent total nitrogen concentrations, respectively, mg N/l. If the pond pH is unknown, it may be estimated from the equation:

$$\text{pH} = 7.3\exp(0.0005A)$$

(12.13)

where A is the alkalinity, mg $CaCO_3$/l.

The range of temperature used in the derivation of equation 12.12 was 1–28°C, so it can be confidently used in developing countries. It has direct application in the design of wastewater-fed fishponds (Chapter 22).

Ammonia

Ammonia is principally removed in facultative and maturation ponds by incorporation into algal biomass, although at high pH it may also be lost by volatilization to the atmosphere. Pano and Middlebrooks (1982) give two equations for ammonia removal in facultative and maturation ponds:

- for T ≤20°C:

$$C_e = C_i/\{1 + [(A/Q)(0.0038 + 0.000134T)\exp((1.041 + 0.044T)(\text{pH} - 6.6))]\}$$

(12.14)

- for $T > 20°C$:

$$C_e = C_i/\{1 + [5.035 \times 10^{-3}(A/Q)][\exp(1.540 \times (pH - 6.6))]\}$$

(12.15)

where C_e and C_i are the effluent and influent ammonia concentrations, respectively, mg N/l. The pH is estimated from equation 12.13.

Both these equations are in fact versions of equation 5.7. Since $A/Q = \theta/D$, k_1 (here the first-order rate constant for ammonia-N removal) is given for equation 12.14 by:

$$k_1 = (1/D)(0.0038 + 0.000134T)\exp[(1.041 + 0.044T)(pH - 6.6)]$$

(12.16)

Equation 12.14 or 12.15 is also used in the design of wastewater-fed fishponds (Chapter 22).

Recent research on ammonia removal in WSP in northeast Brazil

Pano and Middlebrooks (1982) derived their equations for ammonia removal in facultative ponds which were receiving BOD loads of only 10–40 kg/ha day, much less than those used in warm climates (Chapter 11). Silva et al (1995*) investigated nitrogen removal in WSP in northeast Brazil: they found that the Pano and Middlebrooks model was satisfactory for ammonia removal in facultative and primary maturation ponds, but not for removal in secondary and tertiary maturation ponds. Results for all facultative and maturation ponds showed that ammonia removal at 25–27°C was very well predicted by the equation:

$$C_c = C_i/[1 + 8.65 \times 10^{-3}(A/Q)\exp(1.727(pH - 6.6))]$$

(12.17)

where C_c is the in-pond column-sample ammonia concentration, mg N/l (see Chapter 14 for details of in-pond column sampling). The range of BOD loadings on the ponds used to derive equation 12.17 was 20–220 kg/ha day. Ammonia removal in a five-pond series with an overall retention time of 19 days was 91 per cent. Silva et al (1995*) also give the following equation for TKN removal in facultative and maturation ponds (TKN is total Kjeldahl nitrogen, which is organic N + ammonia N):

$$C_c = [(0.19/\lambda_s^{TKN}) - 0.063]^{-1}$$

(12.18)

where C_c is the in-pond TKN concentration, mg N/l; and λ_s^{TKN} is the TKN loading, kg N/ha/day (range 20–170 kg N/ha day).

Nitrification

Nitrification, the obligately aerobic autotrophic oxidation of ammonia to nitrite and then nitrate (Chapter 3), does not appear to be common in WSP; nitrifying bacterial populations are small (but they are present). However, strong claims for nitrification occurring in the WSP at the Western Treatment Plant in Melbourne, Australia (Chapter 9) have been made by Hurse and Connor (1999*; see also Lai and Lam, 1997*), with up to 10^7 nitrifying bacteria per millilitre in the water column in Ponds 6–10 of the 10-pond system which had an average overall retention time of 80 days; the annual mean temperature variation was 8–23°C. This may explain why WSP in warm climates do not nitrify – overall retention times are commonly <<40 days.

Phosphorus

Phosphorus removal in facultative and maturation ponds occurs mainly through precipitation as calcium hydroxyapatite at pH >9. However, overall P removal in a series of WSP is often only ~50 per cent, with effluent concentrations usually >3 mg P/l. If lower concentrations are required by the regulator, in-pond dosing with aluminium sulphate ('alum') or ferric chloride can be effective in reducing P levels from up to 15 mg/l to ~1 mg/l, without causing significant sludge accumulation (Surampalli et al, 1995*).

POND EFFLUENT POLISHING

When WSP effluents are discharged to inland waters, it may be necessary to remove the algal suspended solids so that the effluent can comply with the required quality for suspended solids. In the European Union this is ≤150 mg SS/l for WSP effluents (Chapter 4), and so algal removal would not be necessary. However, if a requirement of <50 mg/l is set, then it may be necessary to remove the algal solids (but see Table 12.1 which shows a final suspended solids concentration of 45 mg/l). If algal solids removal is necessary, it is best done in rock filters (Middlebrooks, 1988, 1995*; Environmental Protection Agency, 2002*; Neder et al, 2002*), although a final deep maturation pond may achieve the same effect as light penetration is lower, and algal solids are correspondingly lower, at greater depths.

Rock filters consist of a bed of rock which is full of pond effluent and within which the algae settle out as the effluent flows horizontally through the filter. The algae decompose releasing nutrients which are utilized by bacteria growing on the surface of the rocks. Rock filters can be in-pond filters within the final maturation pond, but it is operationally better (for ease of maintenance) to have them as separate units following the final maturation pond. Rock size is ~50–100 mm (~100–200 mm is also used), with a bed depth of 0.5–1 m. The rocks should extend at least 100 mm above the water level in the filter so as to avoid mosquito breeding and odours due to cyanobacteria (blue green algae) growing on wet rocks exposed to sunlight.

Rock filter design

Rock filters are designed on the basis of hydraulic loading rate, expressed as m^3 of pond effluent per m^3 gross rock filter volume (ie ignoring the space occupied by the rocks) per day; its units are thus day^{-1}. Early work in the US produced the following equations for percentage BOD and SS removal (Swanson and Williamson, 1980; see also Johnson and Mara, 2002):

$$R_{BOD} = 72 - 109(HLR)$$

(12.19)

$$R_{SS} = 97 - 137(HLR)$$

(12.20)

where HLR is the hydraulic loading rate, day^{-1}.

The range of HLR investigated by Swanson and Williamson was 0.06–0.34 day^{-1}, which is low for warm climates. In northeast Brazil, Mara et al (2001b*) found that rock filters receiving primary maturation pond effluent at an HLR of 1 day^{-1} achieved BOD and SS removals of 46 and 62 per cent at 25°C, respectively, but at an HLR of 2 day^{-1} the removals were only 14 and 53 per cent. In Amman, Jordan, Saidam et al (1995*) used rock filters to treat the final pond effluent; they found that rock filters of 20–230 mm 'wadi gravel' achieved BOD and SS removals of 49 and 46 per cent at an HLR of 0.27 day^{-1} at 25°C, but at an HLR of 0.39 day^{-1} the removals of both were reduced to 41 per cent. The following equation was derived for SS removal:

$$SS_e = 0.88SS_i - 1.92\theta T$$

(12.21)

where SS_e and SS_i are the effluent and influent suspended solids respectively, mg/l; θ is the rock filter retention time, days; and T is the temperature, °C. The retention time is given by:

$$\theta = \varepsilon V_{rf}/Q$$

(12.22)

where ε is the porosity of the rock medium (around 0.4), and V_{rf} is the gross rock filter volume, m^3.

DESIGN EXAMPLE

Design a maturation pond system to treat the effluent from the secondary facultative pond calculated in Chapter 11 to produce (a) ≤1 egg/l and ≤0.1 egg/l/, and (b) ≤1000 *E coli*/100 ml by the methods of Marais (1974) and von Sperling (1999*, 2002*, 2003*).

Solution

Helminth eggs
A single maturation pond with the minimum retention time of 3 days achieves a 90 per cent egg reduction (equation 11.12). Therefore:

$$E_e = 9(1 - 0.90)$$

$$= 0.9 \text{ egg/l}$$

This complies with the World Health Organization's (1989*, 2004*) guideline of ≤1 egg/l. For compliance with ≤0.1 egg/l when children under 15 years are exposed, a second 3-day maturation pond would be required:

$$E_e = 0.9(1 - 0.90)$$

$$= 0.09 \text{ egg/l}$$

The surface BOD loading on the first 3-day maturation pond is given by equation 11.1 as:

$$\lambda s = 10L_i Q/A_m$$

$$= 10L_i D_m/\theta_m$$

$$= 10 \times 60 \times 1/3$$

$$= 200 \text{ kg/ha day}$$

This is less than 70 per cent of the loading of 350 kg/ha day on the secondary facultative pond, and therefore satisfactory.

E coli removal – Marais' method
The *E coli* count in the effluent of the secondary facultative pond is given by equations 12.3 and 12.2:

$$k_{B(T)} = 2.6(1.19)^{T-20} = 6.2 \text{ day}^{-1} \text{ for } T = 25°C$$

$$N_e = N_i/(1 + k_{B(T)}\theta_a)(1 + k_{B(T)}\theta_f)$$

$$= 5 \times 10^7/[1 + (6.2 \times 1)][1 + (6.2 \times 4)]$$

$$= 2.7 \times 10^5 \text{ per } 100 \text{ ml}$$

The *E coli* count in the effluent of the first 3-day maturation pond is given by equation 12.1 as:

$$N_e = 2.7 \times 10^5/[1 + (6.2 \times 3)]$$

$$= 1.4 \times 10^4 \text{ per } 100 \text{ ml}$$

This is $<10^5/100$ ml, the guideline value for restricted irrigation (Chapter 21). The second 3-day maturation pond reduces the *E coli* count to:

$$N_e = 1.4 \times 10^4/[1 + (6.2 \times 3)]$$

$$= 700/100 \text{ ml}$$

This is $<1000/100$ ml, the guideline value for unrestricted irrigation.

Thus to produce an effluent for unrestricted irrigation requires – *in this case and with Marais' model* – a total retention time of only 11 days (1 day in the anaerobic pond, 4 days in the secondary facultative pond and 3 days in each of the two maturation ponds).

The area of the first maturation pond is:

$$A_{m1} = 2Q_i\theta_m/(2D_m + 0.001e\theta_m)$$

where Q_i is the effluent flow from the secondary facultative pond, $= 9868$ m³/day.

$$A_{m1} = 2 \times 9868 \times 3/[(2 \times 1) + (0.001 \times 5 \times 3)]$$

$$= 29{,}380 \text{ m}^2$$

$$Q_e = 9868 - (0.001 \times 5 \times 29{,}380)$$

$$= 9721 \text{ m}^3/\text{day}$$

The area of the second maturation pond is:

$$A_{m2} = 2 \times 9721 \times 3/[(2 \times 1) + (0.001 \times 5 \times 3)]$$

$$= 28{,}950 \text{ m}^2$$

$$Q_e = 9721 - (0.001 \times 5 \times 29\,380)$$

$$= 9576 \text{ m}^3/\text{day}$$

Thus the total area required for treatment to ≤ 1000 *E coli*/100 ml is:

- Anaerobic pond   3340 m²
- Secondary facultative pond   26, 500 m²
- First maturation pond   29, 380 m²

- Second maturation pond   28, 950 m²
- Total pond area   88, 170 m²

For the population served of 100,000, this equals 0.88 m²/person, or 88 ha/million people. Allowing for embankments, etc, the overall area would be ~(1.25 x 88), = ~110 ha/million people.

Note
The above design example is very straightforward. To illustrate the general design procedure in greater detail, consider a design temperature of 15°C (rather than 25°C).

- *Anaerobic pond*: the retention time is now 1.5 days and the BOD removal 50 per cent.
- *Secondary facultative pond*: the design surface BOD loading is 170 kg/ha day; the retention time is now 13.5 days and the effluent BOD is 72 mg/l.
- *Primary maturation pond*: the retention time in the first maturation pond is given by equation 12.5 as:

$$Q_{m1} = 10L_{e(f)}D_m/0.75\lambda_{s(f)}$$

$$= (10 \times 72 \times 1)/(0.75 \times 170)$$

$$= 5.7 \text{ days}$$

- *E coli* removal: the value of k_B at 15°C is given by equation 12.2 as 1.09 day^{-1}; therefore the number of *E coli*/100 ml of the primary maturation pond effluent, as given by equation 12.3 is:

$$N_e = N_i/(1 + k_B\theta_a)(1 + k_B\theta_f)(1 + k_B\theta_{m1})$$

$$= 5 \times 10^7/[1 + (1.09 \times 1.5)][1 + (1.09 \times 13.5)][1 + (1.09 \times 5.7)]$$

$$= 1.7 \times 10^5 \text{ per } 100 \text{ ml}$$

- Subsequent maturation ponds: the following version of equation 12.7 is used:

$$\theta_m = [(N_i/N_e)^{1/n} - 1]/k_B$$

This equation, with $N_i = 1.7 \times 10^5/100$ ml and $N_e = 1000/100$ ml, is now solved for $n = 1, 2$, etc until the calculated value of θ_m is <3 days:

- for $n = 1$, $\theta_m = 155$ days
- for $n = 2$, $\theta_m = 11$ days
- for $n = 3$, $\theta_m = 4.2$ days
- for $n = 4$, $\theta_m = 2.4$ days – thus ñ = 4

Consider, therefore, the combinations of 3 ponds @ 4.2 days and 4 ponds @ 3 days (θ_m^{min}). Choose the former, as it is only 0.6 days more but will minimize embankment construction. The areas of all four maturation ponds (ie including the primary maturation pond) are calculated as shown above.

E coli removal – von Sperling's method

- *Anaerobic pond*: the *E coli* count in the anaerobic pond effluent is given by equations 12.1 and 12.8 as:

$$k_{B(25)} = 2.0(1.07)^5 = 2.8 \text{ day}^{-1}$$

$$N_e = 5 \times 10^7/[1 + (2.8 \times 1)] = 1.3 \times 10^7/100 \text{ ml}$$

- *Secondary facultative pond*: assume a retention time of 4 days, a length-to-breadth ratio of 3 to 1 and a depth of 1.5 m. Equations 5.8 and 5.13–5.15 give:

$$k_{B(20)} = 0.92(1.5)^{-0.88}(4)^{-0.33} = 0.41 \text{ day}^{-1}$$

$$k_{B(25)} = 0.41(1.07)^5 = 0.56 \text{ day}^{-1}$$

$$\delta = 0.33$$

$$a = [1 + (4 \times 0.56 \times 4 \times 0.33)]^{0.5} = 1.99$$

$$N_e = [1.3 \times 10^7][(4 \times 1.99)/(1 + 1.99)^2]\exp[(1 - 1.99)/(2 \times 0.33)]$$

$$= 2.6 \times 10^6 \text{ per } 100 \text{ ml}$$

- *Maturation ponds*: take $\theta_m = \theta_m^{min} = 3$ days and a depth of 1 m; assume that the ponds are baffled to give a length-to-breadth ratio of 10 to 1. Equations 5.8 and 5.13–5.15 give for each pond:

$$k_{B(20)} = 0.92(1)^{-0.88}(3)^{-0.33} = 0.64 \text{ day}^{-1}$$

$$k_{B(25)} = 0.64(1.07)^5 = 0.90 \text{ day}^{-1}$$

$$\delta = 0.1$$

$$a = [1 + (4 \times 0.90 \times 3 \times 0.1)]^{0.5} = 1.44$$

$$N_e = N_i[(4 \times 1.44)/(1 + 1.44)^2]\exp[(1 - 1.44)/(2 \times 0.1)]$$

$$= N_i \times 0.107$$

For the effluent from the fourth maturation pond:

$$N_e = 2.6 \times 10^6 \times (0.107)^4 = 360/100 \text{ ml}$$

Thus, for unrestricted irrigation, the WSP series comprises a 1-day anaerobic pond, a 4-day secondary facultative pond and four 3-day maturation ponds, giving a total retention time of 17 days.

Note

The von Sperling design has a total retention time of 17 days and the Marais design 11 days. This discrepancy can be explained (at least partially) by the fact that Marais' equation for $k_{B(T)}$ was derived from a single WSP series close to its optimal loading, whereas von Sperling's equations were derived from many WSP systems which were not all optimally loaded. In practice, of course, it would be unusual for WSP systems to be at their optimal (ie correct design) loading – for most of the time they are either underloaded or, more commonly, overloaded. Von Sperling's method may therefore reflect actual (as opposed to optimal) faecal coliform removal in a series of WSP.

13

Physical design of WSP

The WSP process design prepared as described in Chapters 10–12 must be 'translated' into a physical design. Actual pond dimensions, consistent with the available site, must be calculated; embankments and pond inlet and outlet structures must be designed; and decisions taken regarding preliminary treatment (Chapter 8), how many parallel pond series to have, and whether or not to line the ponds. By-pass pipework, security fences and notices are generally required, and operator facilities should be provided.

The physical design of WSP must be carefully done: it is at least as important as process design and can significantly affect treatment efficiency (Bernhard and Degoutte, 1990; Drakides and Trotouin, 1991). Advice on the preparation of engineering drawings for WSP is given by the Agency for International Development (1982*).

POND LOCATION

Ponds should be located at least 200 m (preferably 500 m) downwind from the community they serve and away from any likely area of future expansion; this is to discourage people from visiting the ponds. Odour release, even from anaerobic ponds, is most unlikely to be a problem in a well-designed and properly maintained system, but the public may need assurance about this at the planning stage, and a minimum distance of 200–500 m normally allays any fears (in some parts of the developing world people live immediately adjacent to WSP, and they generally like the location of their house – it has a nice view!).

There should be vehicular access to and around the ponds and, in order to minimize earthworks, the site should be flat or gently sloping. The soil must also be suitable. Ponds should not be located within 2 km of airports, as birds attracted to the ponds constitute a risk to air navigation.

GEOTECHNICAL CONSIDERATIONS

Geotechnical aspects of WSP design are very important. In France, for example, a third of the WSP systems that malfunction do so because of geotechnical problems which could have been avoided at the design stage (Bernhard and Kirchgessner, 1987). Poor geotechnical design is also common in Mexico (Mantilla et al, 2002) and presumably elsewhere.

The principal objectives of a geotechnical investigation are to ensure correct embankment design and to determine whether the soil is insufficiently impermeable to require the pond to be lined. The maximum height of the groundwater table should be determined, and the following properties of the soil at the proposed pond location must be measured:

1 particle size distribution,
2 maximum dry density and optimum moisture content (modified Proctor test),
3 Atterberg limits,
4 organic content, and
5 coefficient of permeability.

At least one soil sample should be taken per hectare and the samples should be as undisturbed as possible. They should be representative of the soil profile to a depth 1 m greater than the envisaged pond depth.

Organic and plastic soils and medium-to-coarse sands are not suitable for embankment construction. If there is no suitable local soil with which at least a stable and impermeable embankment core can be formed, it must be brought to the site at extra cost and the local soil, if suitable, used for the embankment slopes.

Ideally, of course, embankments should be constructed from the soil excavated from the site, and there should be a balance between cut and fill, although it is worth noting that ponds constructed completely in cut may be a cheaper alternative, especially if embankment construction costs are high. The soil used for embankment construction should be compacted in 150–250 mm layers to 90 per cent of the maximum dry density as determined by the modified Proctor test. Shrinkage of the soil occurs during compaction (by 10–30 per cent) and excavation estimates must take this into account. After compaction, the soil should have an *in situ* coefficient of permeability of $<10^{-7}$ m/s. Wherever possible and particularly at large pond installations, embankment design should allow for vehicular access to facilitate maintenance.

Embankment slopes are commonly 1 to 3 internally and 1 to 1.5–2 externally. Steeper slopes may be used if the soil is suitable; slope stability should be ascertained according to standard soil mechanics procedures for small earth dams. Embankments should be planted with grass to increase stability; a slow-growing rhizomatous species (eg Bermuda grass) should be used to minimize maintenance.

External embankments should be protected from stormwater erosion by providing adequate drainage. Internal embankments require protection against erosion by wave action, and this is best achieved by lean concrete cast *in situ*, precast concrete slabs or stone rip-rap at top water level (see Figures

Figure 13.1 *Embankment Protection by Concrete Cast* in situ

13.1–13.3). Such protection also prevents vegetation from growing down the embankment into the pond, so preventing the development of a shaded habitat suitable for mosquito or snail breeding.

Figure 13.2 *Embankment Protection by Precast Concrete Slabs*

Figure 13.3 *Embankment Protection by Stone Rip-rap*

POND LINING

Ponds should be lined if the soil is too permeable. As a general guide the following interpretations can be given to the values obtained for the *in situ* coefficient of permeability, k:

- $k > 10^{-6}$ m/s: the soil is too permeable and the ponds must be lined,
- $k < 10^{-7}$ m/s: some seepage may occur but not sufficiently to prevent the ponds from filling,
- $k < 10^{-8}$ m/s: the ponds will seal naturally, and
- $k < 10^{-9}$ m/s: there is no risk of groundwater contamination (if $k > 10^{-9}$ m/s and the groundwater is used for potable supplies, a detailed hydrogeological investigation will be required).

A variety of lining materials can be used when k is $>10^{-6}$ m/s; local availability and costs will determine which should be used. Plastic liners are commonly used (Figures 13.4 and 13.5); alternatively a 300-mm thick clay liner can be used. Advice on pond lining is given by Environment Protection Agency (2002*).

Figure 13.4 *Anaerobic Pond Lined with an Impermeable Plastic Membrane*

POND GEOMETRY

There has been little rigorous work done on determining optimal pond shapes. The most common shape is rectangular, although there is much variation in the length-to-breadth ratio. Clearly, the optimal pond geometry, which includes not only the shape of the pond but also the relative positions of its inlet and outlet, is that which minimizes hydraulic short-circuiting (Persson, 2000*).

In general, anaerobic and primary facultative ponds should be rectangular, with length-to-breadth ratios of 2–3 to 1 so as to avoid sludge banks forming near the inlet. However, the geometry of secondary facultative and maturation ponds is less important than previously thought (Pearson et al, 1995*); they can have higher length-to-breadth ratios (up to 10 to 1) so that they better approximate plug flow conditions. Ponds do not need to be strictly rectangular; they can be gently curved if necessary or if desired for aesthetic reasons. A single inlet and outlet are usually sufficient, and these should be located in diagonally opposite corners of the pond (the inlet should *not* discharge centrally in the pond as this maximizes hydraulic short-circuiting). To minimize hydraulic short-circuiting, the inlet should be located such that the wastewater flows into the pond against the prevailing wind.

Baffles should only be used with caution. In facultative ponds, when baffles are needed because the site geometry is such that it is not possible to locate the inlet and outlet in diagonally opposite corners, care must be taken in locating

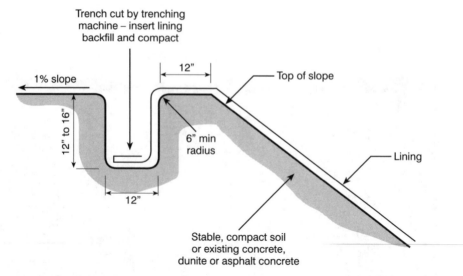

Source: Environmental Protection Agency (1983)

Figure 13.5 *Anchoring the Pond Liner at the Top of the Embankment*

the baffle(s) in order to avoid too high a BOD loading in the inlet zone (and the consequent possible risk of odour release). In maturation ponds baffling is advantageous as it helps to maintain the surface zone of high pH, which facilitates the removal of faecal bacteria (Pearson et al, 1995*; Lloyd et al, 2003*). Recent research into pond hydraulics by Shilton (2001*) and Shilton and Harrison (2003a*), which involved computer modelling, laboratory investigations and testing on full-scale ponds, has demonstrated that the energy (ie momentum) of the pond influent flow is more important than wind effects in determining flow patterns within the pond and hence the degree of hydraulic short-circuiting induced. It was found that short 'stub' baffles near the inlet and outlet were as effective as two long baffles, each extending 70 per cent of the pond width, in reducing *E coli* levels. Persson (2000*) found that a small island (with 2 per cent of the pond area) located near the inlet achieved very little short-circuiting, with the effective pond volume being 96 per cent of the actual pond volume. Persson's inlet island and Shilton and Harrison's inlet stub baffle are essentially the same hydraulic device (as is the inlet scum box shown in Figure 13.8). Pond hydraulics are discussed in detail by Shilton and Harrison (2003b*), which should be consulted for further details.

The areas calculated by the process design procedures described in Chapters 10–12 are mid-depth areas, and the dimensions calculated from them are thus mid-depth dimensions. These need to be corrected for the slope of the embankment, as shown in Figure 13.6. A more precise method is advisable for anaerobic ponds, as these are relatively small; the following formula is used (Environmental Protection Agency, 1983):

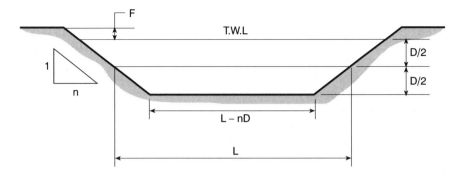

Figure 13.6 *Calculation of Top and Bottom Pond Dimensions from those Based on Mid-depth*

$$V_a = [(LW) + (L - 2sD)(W - 2sD) + 4(L - sD)][D/6]$$

(13.1)

where V_a is the anaerobic pond volume, m³; L is the pond length at top water level (TWL), m; W is the pond width at TWL, m; s is the horizontal slope factor (ie a slope of 1 in s); and D is the pond liquid depth, m. With the substitution of L as nW, based on a length-to-breadth ratio of n to 1, equation 13.1 becomes a simple quadratic in W.

The dimensions and levels that the contractor needs to know are those of the base and the top of the embankment; the latter includes the effect of the freeboard. The minimum freeboard that should be provided is decided on the basis of preventing wind-induced waves from overtopping the embankment. For small ponds (<1 ha in area) 0.5 m freeboard should be provided; for ponds between 1 ha and 3 ha, the freeboard should be 0.5–1 m, depending on site considerations. For larger ponds the freeboard may be calculated from the equation (Oswald, 1975):

$$F = (\log_{10}A)^{1/2} - 1$$

(13.2)

where F is the freeboard, m; and A is the pond area at TWL, m².

Pond liquid depths are commonly in the following ranges:

- anaerobic ponds: 2–5 m
- facultative ponds: 1–2 m
- maturation ponds: 1–1.5 m

The depth chosen for any particular pond depends on site considerations (eg the presence of shallow rock, minimization of earthworks). The depth of facultative and maturation ponds should be ≥1 m so as to avoid vegetation growing up from the pond base, with the consequent hazard of mosquito and snail breeding.

At WSP systems serving >10,000 people, it is often sensible (so as to increase operational flexibility) to have two or more series of ponds in parallel. The available site topography may in any case necessitate such a subdivision, even for smaller systems. Usually the series are equal, that is to say they receive the same flow, and arrangements for splitting the raw wastewater flow into equal parts after preliminary treatment must be made (see Stalzer and von der Emde, 1972). This is best done by providing weir penstocks ahead of each series.

It is very important to divide the total area for each type of pond, as calculated from the process design equations in Chapters 10–12, in *parallel* and not in series. Thus, if it is decided to have n series of ponds at a particular site, each anaerobic pond has an area of A_a/n, each facultative pond one of A_f/n, and so on. (If they are divided in series, then the loading on the first pond is n times higher than it should be and pond failure is guaranteed.)

INLET AND OUTLET STRUCTURES

There is a wide variety of designs for the inlet and outlet structures, and provided they follow certain basic concepts, their precise design is relatively unimportant. First, they should be simple and inexpensive. While this should be self-evident, it is all too common to see unnecessarily complex and expensive structures. Second, they should permit samples of the pond effluent to be taken with ease. The inlet to anaerobic and primary facultative ponds

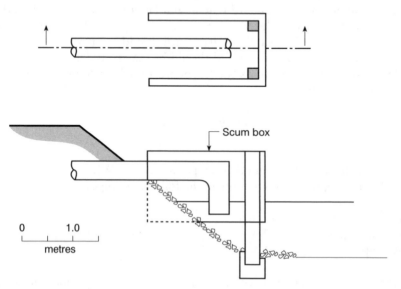

Note: The scum box retains most of the floating solids, so easing pond maintenance; it also improves pond hydraulics.
Source: ABLB and CTGREF (1979)

Figure 13.7 *Inlet Structure for Anaerobic and Primary Facultative Ponds*

Figure 13.8 *Inlet Structure on a Facultative Pond with Integral Scum Box*

should discharge well below the liquid level so as to minimize short-circuiting (especially in deep anaerobic ponds) and reduce the quantity of scum (which is important in facultative ponds). Inlets to secondary facultative and maturation ponds should also discharge below the liquid level, preferably at mid-depth in order to reduce the possibility of short-circuiting. Some simple inlet designs are shown in Figures 13.7–13.9.

Single inlets and outlets in diagonally opposite corners are best. Occasionally multi-inlets and multi-outlets are used in the mistaken belief that they improve pond hydraulics. However, what often happens is that, due to poor construction, one of the outlets settles and its discharge level is then lower than those of the others, with the result that all the pond effluent discharges through this outlet and the others are left, literally, high and dry.

All outlets should be protected against the discharge of scum by the provision of a scum guard. The take-off level for the effluent, which is controlled by the scum guard depth, is important as it has a significant influence on effluent quality. In facultative ponds, the scum guard should extend just below the maximum depth of the algal band when the pond is stratified so as to minimize the daily quantity of algae, and hence BOD, leaving the pond. In anaerobic and maturation ponds, where algal banding is irrelevant, the take-off should be nearer the surface: in anaerobic ponds it should be well above the maximum depth of sludge but below any surface crust, and in maturation ponds it should be close to the surface to give the best possible microbiological quality. The following effluent take-off levels are recommended:

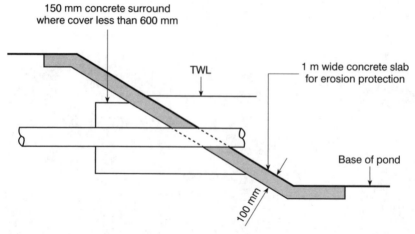

Note: This would receive the discharge from the outlet structure shown in Figure 13.10.

Figure 13.9 *Inlet Structure for Secondary Facultative and Maturation Ponds*

- Anaerobic ponds: 300 mm
- Facultative ponds: 600 mm
- Maturation ponds: 50 mm

The installation of a variable height scum guard is recommended, since it permits the optimal take-off level to be set once the pond is operating.

A simple outlet weir structure is shown in Figure 13.10. The following formula should be used to determine the head over the weir and so, knowing the pond depth, the required height of the weir above the pond base can be calculated:

$$q = 0.0567h^{3/2}$$

(13.3)

where q is the flow per metre length of weir, l/s; and h is the head of water above weir, mm.

The outlet from the final pond in a series should discharge into a simple flow-measuring device such as a triangular or rectangular notch. Since the flow into the first pond is also measured, this permits the rate of evaporation and seepage to be calculated or, if evaporation is measured separately, the rate of seepage.

BY-PASS PIPEWORK

It is necessary to by-pass anaerobic ponds so that facultative ponds may be commissioned first and also during desludging operations. Figure 13.11 shows a by-pass arrangement for two series of WSP in parallel.

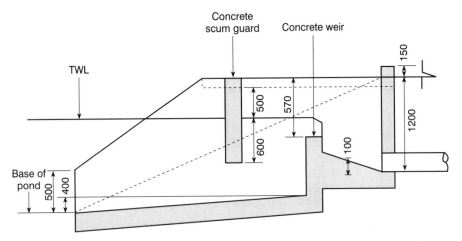

Note: The weir length is calculated from equation 13.3. The discharge pipe would connect with the inlet structure shown in Figure 13.9. The concrete scum guard depth should be appropriate for the type of pond it is in (here, it is 600 mm, suitable for facultative ponds); as an alternative a variable-depth wooden scum guard may be used.

Figure 13.10 *Outlet Weir Structure*

ANAEROBIC POND COVERS

Covering an anaerobic pond allows the biogas to be collected and used (commonly for electricity generation), and it also minimizes any potential odour problem (Figures 13.12 and 16.3). DeGarie et al (2000*) describe a floating composite cover for the anaerobic section of the first pond in the large WSP systems at the Western Treatment Plant in Melbourne, Australia, each of which receives a wastewater flow of 120,000 m^3/day (Chapter 9). The cover is composed of three layers: a high-tensile-strength UV-resistant geomembrane for biogas recovery at the top, a 12.5-mm polyfoam insulation and flotation layer in the middle which is welded to a base layer of high-density polyethylene. The cover measures 171 x 200 m (ie an area of 3.4 ha). The biogas collected from the ponds is used to generate 6000 kW of electricity 8–16 hours per day, 365 days per year, which is worth around Aus$1.8 million (US$1.1 million) per year.

Only anaerobic ponds at large WSP systems are suitable for biogas collection and energy generation. Methane, which comprises around 70 per cent of the biogas, is a powerful greenhouse gas, so its utilization for energy generation at large WSP systems is, environmentally, a very sensible option.

TREEBELT

In desert areas a treebelt should be provided to prevent wind-blown sand from being deposited in the ponds. Treebelts may also be desired for aesthetic

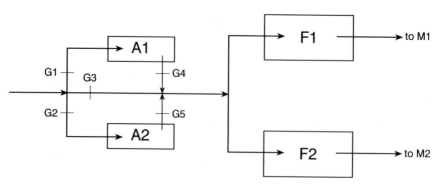

Note: During normal operations, gate G3 is closed and the others open; to by-pass the anaerobic ponds gate G3 is opened and the others closed

Figure 13.11 *By-pass Pipework for Anaerobic Ponds*

reasons if the WSP site is close to human habitation. They should be planted upwind of the WSP and comprise up to five rows, as follows (from the upwind side):

1   1–2 rows of mixed shrubs such as *Latana, Hibiscus* and *Nerium oleander* (none of which is eaten by goats);
2   1–2 rows of *Casuarina* trees; and
3   1 row of a mixture of taller trees such as *Poinciana regia* (flame trees), *Tipuana tipu, Khaya senegalensis* and *Albizia lebbech.*

Figure 13.12 *Covered Anaerobic Pond at the Western Treatment Plant, Melbourne, Australia*

Local botanists will be able to advise on which species are most appropriate (see also Wickers et al, 1985); those given above are suitable for use in North Africa. Such a treebelt is around 40–60 m wide. It should be irrigated with final effluent.

If food trees (for example, olive trees) are also grown, then sale of the produce (either directly or by concession) can contribute significantly to operation and maintenance (O&M) costs. For example, at the large WSP system at Al Samra, serving the cities of Amman and Zarqa (combined population: 2.6 million) in Jordan, over 1.5 million trees were planted around the site (which is a desert), and they are irrigated with 2–3 per cent of the final effluent. Some 60,000 mature olive trees are leased to a local farmer who pays US$12,000 per year for this, which contributes significantly to the O&M costs (Figure 13.13).

SECURITY

Ponds (other than at very remote locations) should be surrounded by a chain-link fence with gates which should be kept padlocked. Warning notices in the appropriate local language(s) (Figure 13.14), advising that the ponds are a wastewater treatment facility and therefore potentially hazardous to health, are essential to discourage people from visiting the ponds, which if properly maintained can appear as pleasant, inviting bodies of water. Children are especially at risk, as they may be tempted to swim or play in the ponds.

In many parts of the developing world particular attention must be paid to keeping wild animals away from the ponds, especially hippopotamuses and crocodiles. Low-voltage electric fences (12 V DC) are effective in keeping hippos out (and this is important: an operator at the Dandora WSP in Nairobi was killed by a hippo in 1989). To keep out crocodiles, the chain link fence should extend 50 cm below ground level; this section and the first 50 cm above ground level should be in small-aperture chain-link fencing to keep out baby crocodiles.

Figure 13.13 *Partial View of the Al Samra WSP Showing some of the Olive Trees, the Produce from which helps Pay for the System's O&M*

Figure 13.14 *Fence and Warning Notice in English and Kiswahili at a Pond Site in Nairobi, Kenya*

OPERATOR FACILITIES

The facilities to be provided for the team of pond operators depend partly on their number (Chapter 14), but would normally include the following:

1   a first-aid kit (which should include a snake-bite kit);
2   strategically placed lifebuoys;
3   a wash-hand basin and toilet; and
4   storage space for protective clothing, grass-cutting and scum-removal equipment, screen rakes and other tools, a sampling boat (if provided) and life-jackets.

With the exception of the lifebuoys, these can be accommodated in a simple building. This can also house, if required, sample bottles and, if electricity is available, a refrigerator for sample storage. Laboratory facilities, offices and a telephone may also be provided at large installations. There should be vehicular access and space for parking.

UPGRADING AND EXTENDING EXISTING WSP

Prior to upgrading or extending a WSP system, its performance should be evaluated as described in Chapter 15, as this will generally permit the correct decision about how to upgrade and/or extend the system to be made.

A number of strategies can be used to upgrade and extend WSP systems (Environmental Protection Agency, 1977). In addition to any rehabilitation measures needed (Chapter 14), these include:

1 the provision of anaerobic ponds;
2 the provision of additional maturation ponds;
3 the provision of one or more additional series of ponds; and/or
4 the alteration of pond sizes and configuration – for example, the removal of an embankment between two ponds to create a larger one.

Original design:

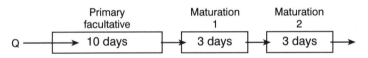

Upgraded system:

Note: The embankment between the original maturation ponds becomes a baffle in the upgraded first maturation pond. The total retention time is increased only from 16 to 16.4 days. The improvement in microbiological quality can be illustrated as follows, by using equation 12.3 with $N_i = 5 \times 10^7$ per 100 ml and $k_T = 2.6$ day^{-1} (ie for 20°C):

$$\text{Original design: } N_e = 5 \times 10^7 / [(1 + (2.6 \times 10)) (1 + (2.6 \times 3))^2]$$

$$= 24{,}000 \text{ per } 100 \text{ ml}$$

$$\text{Upgraded system: } N_e = 5 \times 10^7 / [(1 + (2.6 \times 1)) (1 + (2.6 \times 5)) (1 + (2.6 \times 3)) (1 + (2.6 \times 3.7))^2]$$

$$= 11{,}000 \text{ per } 1000 \text{ ml}$$

Figure 13.15 *Upgrading a WSP Series to Treat Twice the Original Flow*

Figure 13.15 shows how (1), (2) and (4) above can be combined to upgrade a single series of WSP to receive twice its original design flow, with the production of a higher quality effluent which meets the World Health Organization's (1989*, 2004*) guideline value for unrestricted irrigation.

14

Operation and Maintenance of WSP

START-UP PROCEDURES

WSP systems should preferably be commissioned at the beginning of the hot season in order to establish as quickly as possible the necessary microbial populations to effect waste stabilization. Prior to commissioning, all ponds should be free from vegetation. Facultative ponds should be commissioned before anaerobic ponds in order to avoid odour release when an anaerobic pond effluent is discharged into an empty facultative pond. It is best to fill facultative and maturation ponds first with river or lake water so as to permit the gradual development of the algal and heterotrophic bacterial populations. If such water is unavailable, facultative ponds should be filled with raw wastewater and left for 3–4 weeks to allow the microbial populations to develop; a little odour release may occur during this period.

Anaerobic ponds should be filled with raw wastewater and seeded, where possible, with digesting sludge from, for example, local septic tanks. The ponds should then be gradually loaded up to the design loading rate over the following week (or month if the ponds are not seeded). Care should be taken to maintain the pond pH above 7 to permit the development of methanogenic bacteria, and it may be necessary during the first month or so to dose the pond with lime or soda ash. If, due to an initially low rate of sewer connections in newly sewered towns, the wastewater is weak or its flow low, it is best to by-pass the anaerobic ponds (Figure 13.11) until the wastewater strength and flow is such that a BOD loading of at least 50 g/m^3 day can be applied to them. (If it is planned to by-pass the anaerobic ponds during desludging (see below), then the by-pass should be a permanent facility.)

ROUTINE MAINTENANCE

The maintenance requirements of ponds are very simple, but they *must* be carried out regularly. Otherwise, there may be serious odour, fly and mosquito nuisance. Maintenance requirements and responsibilities must therefore be clearly defined at the design stage so as to avoid problems later. Routine maintenance tasks are as follows:

1   the removal of screenings and grit from the preliminary treatment processes (Chapter 8);
2   cutting the grass on the embankments and removing it so that it does not fall into the pond (this is necessary to prevent the formation of mosquito-breeding habitats);
3   the removal of floating scum and floating macrophytes, such as *Lemna* (duckweed), from the surface of facultative and maturation ponds (this is required to maximize photosynthesis and surface reaeration and to prevent fly and mosquito breeding);
4   spraying the scum on anaerobic ponds (which should not be removed as it aids the treatment process), as necessary, with clean water or pond effluent, or a suitable biodegradable larvicide, to prevent fly breeding;
5   the removal of any accumulated solids in the inlets and outlets;
6   repairing any damage to the embankments caused by rodents, rabbits or other animals; and
7   repairing any damage to the external fences and gates.

The operators must be given precise instructions on the frequency with which these tasks should be done, and their work should be constantly supervised. The operators, after suitable training, may also be required to take samples for subsequent laboratory analyses (Chapter 15).

DESLUDGING AND SLUDGE DISPOSAL

Anaerobic ponds require desludging when they are around one-third full of sludge (by volume). This occurs every n years where n is given by:

$$n = V_a/3Ps$$

$$(14.1)$$

where V_a is the volume of anaerobic pond, m³; P is the population served; and s is the sludge accumulation rate, m³/person year.

A good design value for s in warm climates is 0.04 m³/person year. The precise requirement for desludging can be determined by the 'white towel' test of Malan (1964). White towelling material is wrapped along one-third of a sufficiently long pole, which is then lowered vertically into the pond until it reaches the pond bottom; it is then slowly withdrawn. The depth of the sludge layer is clearly visible since some sludge particles will have been entrapped in the towelling material (Figure 14.1). The sludge depth should be measured at various points throughout the pond, away from the embankments, and its mean depth calculated.

While an anaerobic pond must be desludged when it is one-third full of sludge, which occurs every n years as given by equation 14.1, it may be operationally easier to desludge it partially in the same month of every year. A task that has to be done every February, for example, has a better chance of

Figure 14.1 *Sludge Depth Measurement by the 'White Towel' Test*

Figure 14.2 *Pond Desludging in Northern France using a Raft-mounted Sludge Pump – detail: sludge suction head*

being carried out than one to be done every *n* years (as it is often forgotten exactly when the task was last undertaken).

Sludge can be readily removed by using a raft-mounted sludge pump. These are commercially available (eg Brain Associates Ltd, Narberth, Pembrokeshire SA67 7ES, UK), or they can be assembled locally: Figure 14.2 shows one such unit being used on a primary facultative pond in France. The sludge is discharged into either adjacent sludge drying beds or tankers to transport it to a landfill site, agricultural land or other suitable disposal location. Although pond sludge has a better microbiological quality than that from conventional treatment works, its disposal must be carried out in accordance with any local regulations governing sludge disposal.

STAFFING LEVELS

In order that the routine operation and maintenance (O&M) tasks can be properly done, WSP installations must be adequately staffed. The level of staffing depends on the type of inlet works (for example, mechanically raked screens and proprietary grit removal units require an elctromechanical technician, but manually raked screens and manually cleaned grit channels do not), whether there are on-site laboratory facilities, and how the grass is cut (manually or by mechanical mowers). Recommended staffing levels are given in Table 14.1 for WSP systems serving populations up to 250,000; for larger systems the number of staff should be increased pro rata.

Table 14.1 *Recommended Staffing Levels for WSP Systems*

Population served	10,000	25,000	50,000	100,000	250,000
Foreman/supervisor	–	–	1	1	1
Mechanical engineer[a]	–	–	–	1	1
Laboratory technician[b]	–	1	1	1	2
Assistant foreman	–	1	2	2	2
Labourers	1	2	4	6	10
Driver[c]	–	1	1	1	2
Watchman[d]	1	1	2	3	5
Total	2	6	11	15	23

Notes:
[a] Depends on amount of mechanical equipment used
[b] Depends on existence of laboratory facilities
[c] Depends on use of vehicle-towed lawn mowers, etc
[d] Depends on location and value of equipment used
Source: Arthur (1983*)

POND REHABILITATION

If good pond O&M is not routinely carried out, the effects can become very serious: odour release from both anaerobic and facultative ponds; fly breeding in anaerobic ponds; floating macrophytes and/or emergent vegetation in facultative and maturation ponds leading to mosquito breeding (Figure 14.3); and in extreme cases the ponds can silt up and completely 'disappear'. Agunwamba (2001*) describes a very poorly maintained WSP system at a university campus in West Africa: the wastewater flow and BOD had increased over a 20-year period by 62 and 426 per cent, respectively, with the result that odour release and mosquito breeding were occurring, and also flooding; some livestock had drowned in the ponds, which were ~80 per cent full of sludge. Examples, like this, of grossly poor pond maintenance are not, unfortunately, uncommon (and they are often used to advocate that other, usually more 'sophisticated', wastewater treatment systems be used instead of WSP – but if WSP cannot be maintained properly, what chance do other systems have?).

Pond rehabilitation is then necessary. This is achieved by a combination of the following:

1   a complete overhaul (or redesign) of the inlet works, replacing any units that cannot be satisfactorily repaired;
2   repairing or replacing any flow-measuring devices;
3   ensuring that any flow-splitting devices actually split the flow into the required proportions;
4   desludging the anaerobic or primary facultative ponds, and any subsequent ponds if necessary;
5   unblocking, repairing or replacing pond inlets and/or outlets;
6   relocating any improperly located inlets and/or outlets, so that they are in diagonally opposite corners of each pond (or providing a baffle if relocation is not feasible);
7   repairing, replacing or providing effluent scum guards;
8   preventing 'surface streaming' of the flow by discharging the influent at mid-depth;
9   removing scum and floating or emergent vegetation from the facultative and maturation ponds;
10 checking embankment stability, and repairing, replacing or installing embankment protection;
11 checking for excessive seepage (>10 per cent of inflow) and lining (or relining) the ponds if necessary;
12 cutting the embankment grass; and
13 repairing or replacing any external fences and gates; fences may need to be electrified to keep out wild and domestic animals.

As rehabilitation is commonly very expensive, good routine O&M is very much more cost-effective.

Figure 14.3 *A very Badly Neglected Facultative Pond in Eastern Africa*

15

Monitoring and Evaluation of WSP

Once a WSP system has been commissioned, a routine monitoring programme should be established so that the actual quality of its effluent can be determined. This permits a regular assessment to be made of whether the effluent is complying with local discharge or re-use standards. Moreover, should a pond system suddenly fail or its effluent start to deteriorate, the results of such a monitoring programme often give some insight into the cause of the problem and so indicate what remedial action is required.

The evaluation of pond performance and behaviour, although a much more complex procedure than the routine monitoring of effluent quality, is nonetheless extremely useful as it provides information on how underloaded or overloaded the system is, and thus by how much, if any, the loading on the system can be safely increased as the community it serves expands, or whether further ponds in parallel and/or in series are required (Chapter 13). It also indicates how the design of future pond installations in the region can be improved to take account of local conditions.

EFFLUENT QUALITY MONITORING

Effluent quality monitoring programmes should be simple and the minimum required to provide reliable data. Two levels of effluent monitoring are recommended:

1   *Level 1*: representative samples of the final effluent should be taken regularly (at least monthly) and analysed for those parameters for which effluent discharge or re-use requirements exist.
2   *Level 2*: when Level 1 monitoring shows that a pond effluent is failing to meet its discharge or re-use quality, a more detailed study is necessary. Table 15.1 gives a list of the parameters whose values are required, together with recommendations for the types of samples that should be taken.

Since pond effluent quality shows a significant diurnal variation (although this is less pronounced in anaerobic and maturation ponds than in facultative ponds), 24-hour flow-weighted composite samples are preferable for most parameters, although grab samples are necessary for some (pH, temperature and *E coli*). Composite samples should be collected in one of the following ways:

1   in an automatic sampler which takes grab samples every 1–2 hours, with subsequent manual flow-weighting if this is not done automatically by the sampler;
2   by taking grab samples every 1–3 hours with subsequent manual flow-weighting; or
3   by taking a column sample near the outlet of the final pond; this can be done at any time of day and gives a good approximation (± ~20 per cent) to the mean daily effluent quality (Pearson et al, 1987d).

Flow-weighting is used in order to determine more accurate estimates of mean daily parameter values such as BOD and suspended solids. Grab samples are taken every 1–3 hours for 24 hours, and the volume of each grab sample used to make the 24-hour composite sample depends on the wastewater flow at the time it was taken, for example, if at any time the flow were 10,000 m³/day, then 100 ml of the grab sample taken at that time would be used to make the 24-hour composite; 150 ml would be used for a flow of 15,000 m³/day, and 230 ml for a flow of 23,000 m³/day, and so on. Thus the greater the flow, the more 'weight' is given to the sample – hence the term 'flow-weighting'.

EVALUATION OF POND PERFORMANCE

A full evaluation of the performance of a WSP system is a time-consuming and expensive process, and it requires experienced personnel to obtain and interpret the data. However, it is the only means by which pond designs can be optimized for local conditions. It is often, therefore, a highly cost-effective exercise. The recommendations given below constitute a Level 3 monitoring programme, and they are based on the guidelines for the minimum evaluation of pond performance given by Pearson et al (1987e).

It is not intended that all pond installations be studied in this way, but only one or two representative systems in each major climatic region. This level of investigation is most likely to be beyond the capabilities of local organizations, and it would need to be carried out by a state or national body, or by a university under contract to such a body. This type of study is also necessary when it is required to know how much additional loading a particular system can receive before it is necessary to extend it (Chapter 13).

Samples should be taken and analysed on seven days over a seven-week period at both the hottest and coldest times of the year. Samples are required of the raw wastewater and of the effluent of each pond in the series and, so as to take into account the weekly variation in influent and effluent quality, samples should be collected on Monday in the first week, Tuesday in the second week

Table 15.1 *Parameters to be Determined for Level 2 Pond Effluent Quality Monitoring*

Parameter	Sample type[a]	Remarks
Flow	–	Measure both raw wastewater and final effluent flows
BOD	C	Unfiltered samples[b]
COD	C	Unfiltered samples[b]
Suspended solids	C	
pH		
Temperature	G	Take two samples, one at 08.00 – 10.00 h
	G	and the other at 14.00 – 16.00 h
E. coli	G	Take sample between 08.00 and 10.00 h
Total nitrogen	C	
Total phosphorus	C	
Chloride	C	
Electrical conductivity	C	Only when effluent being used (or being
Ca, Mg, Na	C	assessed for use) for crop irrigation. Ca,
Boron	C	Mg and Na are required to calculate the
Helminth eggs	C	sodium absorption ratio (Chapter 22)

Notes:
a C = 24-hour flow-weighted composite sample; G = grab sample
b Also on filtered samples if the discharge requirements are so expressed

and so on. Table 15.2 lists the parameters whose values are required. Generally the analytical techniques described in the latest edition of *Standard Methods* (American Public Health Association, currently 1998) are recommended, although the modified Bailenger technique should be used for counting the number of nematode eggs (Ayres and Mara, 1996*) and *E coli* is best counted using modern selective media (such as chromogenic media, Chromagar, 2002*; see also Environment Agency, 2002*).

Composite samples are necessary for most parameters, but grab samples are required for temperature, pH and *E coli*, and samples of the entire pond water column should be taken for algological analyses (chlorophyll *a* and algal genera determination), using the pond column sampler shown in Figure 15.1. Pond column samples should be taken from a boat or from a simple sampling platform that extends beyond the embankment base (or from the outlet structure if this extends sufficiently far into the pond). Data on at least daily maximum and minimum air temperatures, rainfall and evaporation should be obtained from the nearest meteorological station.

On each day that samples are taken, the mean mid-depth temperature of each pond, which closely approximates the mean daily pond temperature, should be determined by suspending a maximum-and-minimum thermometer at the mid-depth of the pond at 8–9 am and reading it 24 hours later.

On one day during each sampling period, the depth of sludge in the anaerobic and facultative ponds should be determined by the 'white towel' test

Table 15.2 *Parameters to be Determined for the Minimum Evaluation of WSP Performance*

Parameter	To be determined for[a]	Sample type[b]	Remarks
Flow	RW, FE	–	
BOD	RW, all pond effluents	C	Unfiltered and filtered samples
COD	RW, all pond effluents	C	Unfiltered and filtered samples
Suspended solids	RW, all pond effluents	C	
E. coli	RW, all pond effluents	G	
Chlorophyll *a*	All F and M pond contents	P	
Algal genera	All F and M pond contents	P	
Ammonia	RW, all pond effluents	C	
Nitrate	RW, FE	C	
Total phosphorus	RW, FE	C	
Sulphide	RW, A pond effluent, F pond contents or depth profile	G, P	Only if odour nuisance present or facultative pond effluent quality poor. A depth profile is preferable
pH	RW, all pond effluents	G	
Temperature (mean daily)	RW, all ponds	–	Use maximum–minimum thermometers suspended in RW flow and at mid-depth in ponds
Dissolved oxygen[c]	Depth profile in all F and M ponds	–	Measure at 08.00, 12.00 and 16.00 h on at least three occasions
Sludge depth	A and F ponds	–	Use 'white towel' test
Electrical conductivity	FE	C	Only if effluent used or to be used for crop irrigation. Ca, Mg and Na required to calculate the sodium absorption ratio (Chapter 22)
Chloride	RW, FE	C	
Ca, Mg and Na	FE	C	
Boron	FE	C	
Helminth eggs	RW, all pond effluents	C	

Notes:
[a] RW, raw wastewater; FE, final effluent of pond series; A, anaerobic; F, facultative; M, maturation.
[b] C, 24 hour flow-weighted composite sample; G, grab sample taken when pond contents most homogeneous; P, pond column sample.
[c] Measure depth profiles of pH and temperature at same times, if possible.

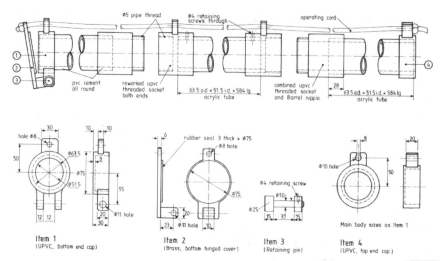

Figure 15.1 *Details of Pond Column Sampler*

Note: The overall length (here 1.7 m) may be altered as required. The design shown is a three-piece unit for ease of transportation, but this feature may be omitted. Alternative materials may be used (eg PVC drainage pipe).

(Figure 14.1). The sludge depth should be measured at various points throughout the pond, away from the embankment base, and the mean depth calculated.

It is also useful to measure on at least one occasion during each sampling season the diurnal variation in the vertical distribution of pH, dissolved oxygen and temperature. Profiles should be obtained at 08.00, 12.00 and 16.00 h. If submersible electrodes are not available, samples should be taken manually every 15–20 cm.

DATA STORAGE AND ANALYSIS

It is advisable to store all data in a PC using a spreadsheet such as Excel, so that simple data manipulations can be performed. From the data collected in each sampling season (or month if sampling is done throughout the year), mean values should be calculated for each parameter. Values, based on these means, can then be calculated for:

1   the mean hydraulic retention time (= volume/flow) in each pond;
2   the volumetric BOD and COD loadings on anaerobic ponds;
3   the surface BOD and COD loadings on facultative ponds; and
4   the percentage removals of BOD, COD, suspended solids, nitrogen, phosphorus, *E coli* and nematode eggs in each pond and in each series of ponds.

A simple first-order kinetic analysis may be undertaken if desired (Chapter 5). The responsible local or central governmental agency should record and store all the information on, and all the data collected from, each pond complex, together with an adequate description of precisely how they were obtained, in such a way that design engineers and research workers can have ready and meaningful access to them.

16

Wastewater Storage and Treatment Reservoirs

SINGLE RESERVOIRS

Wastewater storage and treatment reservoirs (WSTR), also called effluent storage reservoirs, were developed in Israel to enable the whole year's treated wastewater to be used for crop irrigation during the irrigation season (Juanicó and Shelef, 1991, 1994; Juanicó and Dor, 1999; see also Barbagallo et al, 2003*; Friedler et al, 2003*). With an irrigation season of four months in Israel, this means that three times the land area can be irrigated, and three times the quantity of crops produced. In water-short areas, such as Israel and also many parts of the developing world, this is a major agricultural advantage. The use of WSTR thus maximizes the potential of wastewater re-use for crop production (Chapter 21).

Single WSTR (Figures 16.1 and 16.2a) are mostly used in Israel as the main crop is cotton – that is, the practice is restricted irrigation (Chapter 21) and the principal microbiological quality for the treated wastewater is ≤1 or ≤0.1 human intestinal nematode eggs/l (Chapter 4). Israeli practice with single WSTR is to treat the wastewater first in an anaerobic pond (Chapter 10). The WSTR have a depth of 5–25 m and a volume equal to the volume of effluent produced in the 8-month non-irrigation season, so that it is full immediately before the irrigation season. During the irrigation season, the WSTR contents are pumped out to the fields to be irrigated, while at the same time there is still a continuous inflow of anaerobic pond effluent. As the irrigation season progresses, there is a progressive deterioration in the quality of the WSTR contents as the retention time in the reservoir of the anaerobic pond effluent becomes correspondingly shorter (Liran et al, 1994). For restricted irrigation, certainly for the irrigation of cotton, this does not matter, but for unrestricted irrigation it would be a serious problem.

Figure 16.1 *Single WSTR in Israel*

SEQUENTIAL BATCH-FED RESERVOIRS

If the local farmers wish to practise unrestricted irrigation – that is including the irrigation of salad crops and vegetables eaten uncooked – then single WSTR are inappropriate as the treated wastewater must contain no more than 1000 *E coli*/100 ml throughout the irrigation season (as well as meeting the nematode egg guideline level) (Chapters 4 and 21). 'Sequential batch-fed WSTR' are easily able to achieve this *E coli* requirement (Mara and Pearson, 1992; Juanicó, 1996*).

Depending on the length of the irrigation season, three or four sequential batch-fed WSTR are used to store and treat the anaerobic pond effluent (Figure 16.2b). The WSTR are in parallel, and each is operated on a cycle of 'fill–rest–use'. As soon as the contents of one reservoir are used, another is brought into irrigation service and the one just emptied is refilled in readiness for the next irrigation season (Table 16.1). *E coli* numbers decline rapidly during the rest phase: in studies in northeast Brazil Pearson et al (1996c*) found that in WSTR which received organic loadings of 126–162 kg BOD/ha day during the fill phase, *E coli* numbers dropped from 10^6–10^7/100 ml of anaerobic pond effluent to <1000/100 ml during the first 14 days of the rest phase at 25°C.

Sequential batch-fed WSTR are an integral component of Shelef and Azov's (2000*) vision of high-efficiency pond systems for the 21st century. Figure 16.3 shows the sequential batch-fed WSTR system for the town of Arad (population 22,000) in the Negev desert, Israel.

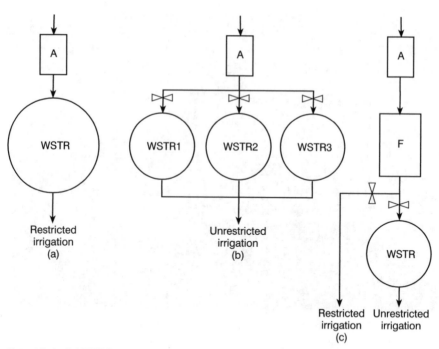

Note: (a) single WSTR for restricted irrigation; (b) sequential batch-fed WSTR for unrestricted irrigation; and (c) hybrid WSP–WSTR system for both restricted and unrestricted irrigation. A, anaerobic pond; F, facultative pond.

Figure 16.2 *Wastewater Storage and Treatment Reservoir Systems*

HYBRID WSP–WSTR SYSTEM

Given that farmers often want treated wastewater for both restricted and unrestricted irrigation, a hybrid pond–reservoir system is an appropriate alternative to sequential batch-fed WSTR which only produce treated wastewater for unrestricted irrigation – that is, it is of too high a quality for restricted irrigation. In the hybrid system (Figure 16.1c) the wastewater is treated in anaerobic and facultative ponds. During the non-irrigation season, the facultative pond effluent is used to fill a single WSTR. During the irrigation season the facultative pond effluent is used for restricted irrigation, and the WSTR contents for unrestricted irrigation (Mara and Pearson, 1999*).

If the number of nematode eggs in the facultative pond exceeds 1/l (or 0.1/l when children under 15 years are exposed), then an additional short-retention-time maturation pond would be required (Chapters 11 and 12).

DESIGN EXAMPLES

Design a wastewater storage and treatment reservoir system for the wastewater detailed at the end of Chapter 10. Assume the irrigation season is 6 months.

Table 16.1 *Operational Strategy for Three Sequential Batch-fed WSTR for an Irrigation Season of Six Months*

Month[a]	WSTR 1	WSTR 2	WSTR 3
January	Rest	Fill (1/2)	Fill (1/2)
February	Rest	Fill (1/2)	Fill (1/2)
March	Rest	Rest	Fill (1)
April	Rest	Rest	Fill (1)
May	**Use**	Rest	Fill (1)
June	**Use**	Rest	Fill (1)
July	Fill (1)[b]	**Use**	Rest
August	Fill (1)	**Use**	Rest
September	Fill (1/2)	Fill (1/2)	**Use**
October	Fill (1/2)	Fill (1/2)	**Use**
November	Fill (1/3)	Fill (1/3)	Fill (1/3)
December	Fill (1/3)	Fill (1/3)	Fill (1/3)
Volume[c]	4	4	4

Notes:
[a] July and August are the hottest months, so WSTR No 3 has the minimum rest period of two months at this time. The other two WSTR have rest periods of four months to ensure *E. coli* die-off to <1000 per 100 ml during the cooler months
[b] Proportion of monthly flow discharged into each WSTR
[c] WSTR volume expressed as multiple of monthly wastewater flow

Solutions

Restricted irrigation

Pretreat the wastewater in the anaerobic pond calculated in Chapter 10. Choose a single WSTR (Figure 16.2a), which must be full at the start of the irrigation season and empty at the end of it. Thus the WSTR volume is equal to 6 months wastewater flow:

$$V = (365/2) \times 10,000$$

$$= 1,825,000 \text{ m}^3$$

Assuming a depth of 10 m, the WSTR mid-depth area is 18.25 ha.

Unrestricted irrigation

Pretreat the wastewater in the same anaerobic pond, and choose three sequential batch-fed WSTR in parallel as shown in Figure 16.2b. The volume of each WSTR is equal to four months wastewater flow (Table 16.1):

$$V = (365/3) \times 10,000$$

$$= 1,216,700 \text{ m}^3$$

Note: (a) view of Arad town in the Negev desert, (b) covered anaerobic pond, (c) WSTR in rest phase, and (d) WSTR in use phase.

Figure 16.3 *Sequential Batch-fed WSTR at Arad, Israel*

Assuming a depth of 10 m, the mid-depth area of each WSTR is 12.17 ha. The total mid-depth area, including that of the anaerobic pond, is 37 ha.

Restricted and unrestricted irrigation

Assume that the local farmers wish to use half the treated wastewater for restricted irrigation and half for unrestricted irrigation. Choose the hybrid WSP–WSTR system shown in Figure 16.2c. This comprises the anaerobic and secondary facultative ponds calculated in Chapters 10 and 11, and the single WSTR calculated above. The total mid-depth area is 22 ha.

17

Constructed Wetlands

Many natural wetlands have received domestic wastewater pollution for a long time, and their productivity is increased as they have a large capacity for absorbing domestic wastewater. Constructed wetlands are the engineer-made equivalent of natural wetlands, and they are designed to reproduce and intensify the wastewater treatment processes that occur in natural wetlands. Thus rooted aquatic plants, often termed 'macrophytes', are grown either in soil or, now more commonly, gravel beds which receive domestic wastewater after primary treatment in, for example, an anaerobic pond. Constructed wetlands are also called 'reedbeds' after the aquatic macrophyte most commonly grown in them – *Phragmites australis*, the common reed. Other plants commonly used include *Schoenoplectus lacustris* (bulrush), *Typha latifolia* (cattail) and *Juncus effusus* (soft rush). Constructed wetlands are long, narrow, shallow (ie almost plug flow) reactors (Figure 17.1) in which the partially treated wastewater is treated further by natural wetland processes. Fully comprehensive reviews of constructed wetlands for wastewater treatment are given by IWA Specialist Group (2000) and Sundaravadivel and Vigneswaran (2001*).

In industrialized countries, constructed wetlands are sometimes used to create wildlife habitats (often with public access and visitor facilities) following their use for wastewater treatment (eg Environmental Protection Agency, 1993*). There is nothing inherently wrong in this, of course, but it should be realized that this is *not* wastewater treatment and therefore should be funded separately – unless the wastewater treatment authority has the necessary funds and wishes to derive some public-relations benefit from so doing. Wildlife habitat creation is really an example of treated wastewater re-use.

In this chapter only gravel-based 'subsurface-flow' wetlands are discussed, principally because of the major risk of mosquito (especially *Coquillittidia* spp and *Mansonia* spp) breeding in 'surface-flow' wetlands in developing countries.

SUBSURFACE-FLOW WETLANDS

There are two types of subsurface-flow wetlands: horizontal-flow and vertical-flow units. Horizontal-flow wetlands are the most common; vertical-flow

Figure 17.1 *A 100-m Long Subsurface-flow Constructed Wetland in Egypt*

wetlands are occasionally used in temperate climates as a secondary stage to horizontal-flow wetlands. Only horizontal-flow wetlands are considered here.

Horizontal-flow wetlands

BOD, suspended solids and nutrients (N and P) are removed in subsurface-flow wetlands by a combination of the mechanisms occurring in rock filters treating effluents from waste stabilization ponds (Chapter 12) and mechanisms due to the plants. Tanner (2001*) found no improvement in BOD, suspended solids, phosphorus and faecal bacterial removals in planted wetlands compared with unplanted control systems (which functioned therefore as rock/gravel filters). There was, however, better nitrogen removal in the planted beds than in the unplanted beds, but this was not primarily due to uptake by the plants, but more to the accumulation of organic nitrogen in the bed sediments and to the release of oxygen by the plants around their roots which is then used for ammonia removal by nitrification, with removal of the nitrate so formed by denitrification in the bulk anoxic zone of the gravel bed. Similar results were reported by Ayaz and Akça (2001*) and Regmi et al (2003).

Horizontal subsurface-flow constructed wetlands are normally designed for BOD removal, which is modelled by equation 5.10 for plug flow reactors, but with the retention time given by:

$$\theta = V_{cw}/Q = \varepsilon A_{cw}D_{cw}/Q$$

$$(17.1)$$

where ε is the porosity of the planted gravel bed (typically 0.4 for 25-mm gravel), and Q is the mean flow, m^3/day, given by equation 11.6 with e (net evaporation) being taken here as the net evapotranspiration, mm/d. Thus equation 5.10 becomes:

$$L_e = L_i exp\{- k_1[2\varepsilon A_{cw}D_{cw}/(2Q_i - 0.001eA_{cw})]\}$$

$$(17.2)$$

The value of k_1 depends not only on temperature, but also on the porosity as bacterial growth occurs on the surface of the gravel in the gravel bed and the amount of bacterial growth present changes with porosity, and also with temperature, as follows (Reed et al, 1988; Corea, 2001*):

$$k_1 = 68.6\varepsilon^{4.172}(1.06)^{T-20}$$

$$(17.3)$$

Corea (2001*) used equations 17.2 and 17.3 to determine the size of on-site wetland systems for hotels in Sri Lanka treating the effluent from septic tanks and anaerobic filters. For L_i = 100 mg/l, L_e = 10 mg/l, ε = 0.4, D_{cw} = 0.6 m (the value most commonly used), T = 27°C, e = 0 and Q = 0.15 m^3/day (the wastewater flow per person), he determined the wetland area to be 0.64 m^2 per person (this is close to the value of 0.66 m^2 per person found in Egypt by Williams et al, 1995). In the case of housing estates with only septic tanks, Corea determined for L_i = 150 mg/l and L_e = 30 mg/l (the Sri Lankan effluent BOD standard for surface water discharge) a wetland area of 0.45 m^2 per person.

Reeds were used in the wetland systems for housing estates by Corea (2001*), but for the hotel systems a variety of ornamental plants was used (Figure 17.2); broad-leaved plants were used to reduce the effluent flow as their evapotranspiration is high, but if the effluent was required to water the hotel gardens, other plants were used and the effluent was treated further in a small vertical-flow wetland prior to its use. Corea (2001*) should be consulted for further details of these on-site hotel systems.

Suspended solids removal
Suspended solids are removed in subsurface-flow constructed wetlands by entrapment in the gravel interstices and sedimentation. Reed and Brown (1995) give the following equation for SS removal:

$$(SS)_e = (SS)_i[0.106 + 0.11(AHLR)]$$

$$(17.4)$$

Source: Corea, 2001*

Figure 17.2 *A Horizontal-flow Constructed Wetland at a Hotel in Kandy, Sri Lanka, Planted with Ornamentals*

where $(SS)_e$ and $(SS)_i$ are the effluent and influent suspended solids concentrations, respectively, mg/l; and AHLR is the areal hydraulic loading rate $(= Q_i/A_{cw})$, m/day.

Ammonia removal

Ammonia is removed in subsurface-flow constructed wetlands by several factors, such as nitrification (and subsequent denitrification), plant uptake and accumulation of organic nitrogen in the bed sediments. Huang et al (2000*) give the following equation for ammonia-N removal in constructed wetlands:

$$C_e = C_i \exp[-0.126(1.008)^{T-20}\theta]$$

$$(17.5)$$

where C_e and C_i are the effluent and influent ammonia concentrations, respectively, mg N/l; and θ is given by equation 17.1. Equation 17.5 was derived from constructed wetlands in the US, planted with *Schoenoplectus* and *Typha* and treating septic tank effluent; bed temperatures were 6°C in winter and 20°C in summer.

Helminth egg removal

Helminth egg removal in the gravel bed of horizontal-flow wetlands is very efficient: Stott et al (1999*) found that all eggs were removed in a 100-m long reedbed in Egypt, with most being removed in the first 25 m.

WETLANDS OR WASTE STABILIZATION PONDS?

Horizontal-flow constructed wetlands are secondary treatment units – that is, they must be preceded by a septic tank or anaerobic pond. Therefore their area should be compared with that of a secondary facultative pond (Chapter 11).

Wetland area
- L_i = 90 mg/l (the BOD of the effluent of the anaerobic pond detailed in Chapter 10),
- L_e = 18 mg/l (the same as the filtered BOD of the effluent of the secondary facultative pond detailed in Chapter 11),
- T = 25°C,
- e = 5 mm/day,
- ε = 0.4,
- D_{cw} = 0.6 m,
- Q_i = 10, 000 m³/day, and
- Population served = 100, 000

Using equations 17.2 and 17.3 with the design parameter values used in Chapter 11, the area of the wetland is calculated as follows, assuming evapotranspiration = evaporation:

1   from equation 17.3:

$$k_1 = 68.6 \, (0.4)^{4.172}(1.06)^5 = 2.0 \text{ day}^{-1}$$

2   rearranging equation 17.2:

$$A_{cw} = [-2Q_i \ln(L_e/L_i)]/[2k_1 \varepsilon \, D_{cw} - (0.001e\ln(L_e/L_i))]$$

$$= [-2 \times 10000 \ln(18/90)]/[(2 \times 2 \times 0.4 \times 0.6) - (0.001 \times 5 \ln(18/90))]$$

$$= 33 \, 250 \text{ m}^2 = 0.33 \text{ m}^2 \text{ per person}$$

Secondary facultative pond
The area of the secondary facultative pond detailed in Chapter 11 is 26,500 m² – that is 0.27 m² per person.

The horizontal-flow constructed wetland thus requires 22 per cent more area than the secondary facultative pond; it also requires ~53 t of gravel. In general, therefore, ponds are preferable to wetlands. Calculations of the kind done above are necessary to demonstrate the preference for WSP over constructed wetlands in developing countries, so that preferences to the contrary (eg Juwarkar et al, 1995*; Haberl, 1999*; Kivaisi, 2001*) can be logically rebutted. An exception to this is, for example, the small on-site hotel systems with ornamental plants described by Corea (2001*).

18

Upflow Anaerobic Sludge Blanket Reactors

TREATMENT PRINCIPLES

Upflow anaerobic sludge blanket reactors (UASBs) are high-rate anaerobic wastewater treatment units. They were developed in the 1970s by Professor Gatze Lettinga at the University of Wageningen in The Netherlands, and they have been extensively tested at full-scale in tropical and subtropical regions, particularly in Brazil, Columbia and India (van Haandel and Lettinga, 1994; Foresti, 2002*; for an excellent on-line introduction to UASBs, see Field and Sierra, 2002*). They are used for the primary treatment of domestic wastewaters and high-strength biodegradable industrial and agro-industrial wastewaters. They have also been found satisfactory for the treatment of mixed domestic and industrial wastewaters in Mauritius (Dean and Horan, 1995*). However, an alternative view of their performance and applicability in developing countries (at least in Kanpur, India) is given by Sharma (2002*).

UASBs are reinforced-concrete structures (Figure 18.1), with a short hydraulic retention time, of the order of 6–12 hours. As shown in Figure 18.2, the raw wastewater, after screening and grit removal (Chapter 8), is distributed as evenly as possible across the base of the reactor. It then flows upwards through the sludge layer (termed the sludge 'blanket'); this ensures intimate contact between the wastewater and the anaerobic bacteria in the sludge blanket, so aiding the anaerobic biochemical reactions detailed in Chapter 3 and thus increasing the efficiency of BOD removal in the reactor. The wastewater, together with some active sludge particles, then rises through the reactor, and, during this time, further BOD reduction occurs. The wastewater–sludge suspension then reaches the 'phase separator', which is the important characteristic of this type of anaerobic reactor: it divides the reactor into its two constituent zones – the lower digestion zone and the upper settling zone. As the wastewater–sludge suspension rises through the settling zone, its upflow velocity decreases since, due to the outwardly inclined surface of the phase separator, the flow area increases and the suspended sludge particles settle out, mainly on to the inclined sides of the phase separator. Eventually the weight of the accumulated sludge particles exceeds the frictional force

Note: Top, general view; bottom, view showing top of UASB, including effluent overflow weirs.

Figure 18.1 *An UASB at Ginebra, Valle del Cauca, Southwest Colombia, Treating 10 l/s of Domestic Wastewater*

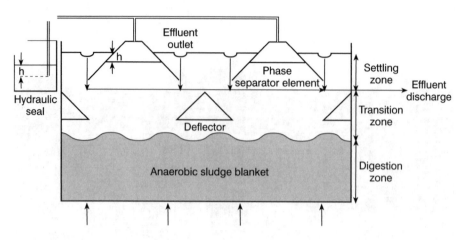

Source: van Haandel and Lettinga (1994)

Figure 18.2 *Schematic Diagram of an UASB*

keeping them on the inclined surfaces, and they settle down to the sludge layer. The phase separator thus maintains a high concentration of sludge particles in the lower zone of the reactor, and enables an effluent with a very low suspended solids concentration to be discharged from the reactor.

Biogas bubbles are collected under the phase separator, from where the gas is easily extracted either for use (to generate electricity, for example) or for flaring-off. Deflectors are placed between the phase separator units to prevent any biogas bubbles entering the settling zone where they would hinder sedimentation.

UASBs are very efficient, as shown by the following equation for COD removal (van Haandel and Lettinga, 1994):

$$R = 100(1 - \theta^{-0.68})$$

$$(18.1)$$

where R is the percentage COD removal (which essentially equals the percentage BOD removal for domestic wastewaters); and θ is the mean hydraulic retention time, hours. Thus for $\theta = 6$ h (the value recommended by van Haandel and Lettinga for domestic wastewaters in the single-compartment UASBs considered here), $R = 70$ per cent.

DESIGN

UASB design is described in full by van Haandel and Lettinga (1994), which should be consulted for greater detail than the brief outline given here.

The upflow velocity (V_{up}, m/h) of wastewater in UASBs, which should not exceed 1 m/h, is given by:

$$V_{up} = Q/A = QD/AD = D/\theta$$

$$(18.2)$$

where Q is the wastewater flow, m³/h; A is the surface area of the reactor, m²; and D is the depth of wastewater in the reactor, m.

Thus, for V_{up} = 1 m/h and for θ = 6 h, D = 6 m. In practice the range of D used is 4–6 m, so V_{up} is ≤1 m/h.

UASB reactor size is normally limited to 1000 m³. An UASB of this volume with a retention time of 6 h can treat 4000 m³ of wastewater per day; for larger flows additional UASB reactors are provided in parallel. UASBs are normally rectangular in plan with a length-to-breadth ratio less than 4 to 1. Parallel units share longitudinal walls.

Influent distribution

The raw wastewater, after screening and grit removal (Chapter 8), has to be distributed as evenly as possible over the reactor base. Influent outlet devices are located on the reactor base at the rate of one per 3–4 m² of reactor base area. Each of these devices has to receive an equal proportion of the raw wastewater flow; this is ensured by having an influent distribution channel which is closed at the far end and which has a number of 90° V-notches along one side, with the number of notches being equal to the number of outlet devices on the reactor base. The distribution channel is designed for a liquid level in the channel 125 mm higher than the apex of the V-notch. Figure 18.3 shows the general arrangement of the influent distribution channel and distribution boxes.

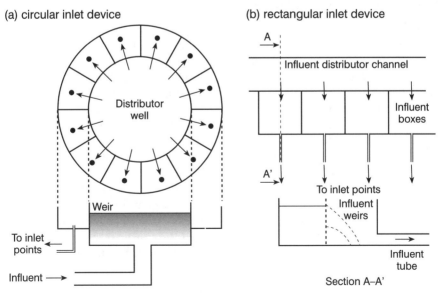

Source: Adapted from van Haandel and Lettinga (1994)

Figure 18.3 *Influent Distribution Channel and Distribution Boxes*

Phase separators

The phase separators divide the reactor into its two zones, the settling zone and the sludge zone, and they separate the three phases occurring in the reactor – gas, liquid and solid. Often the separators are submerged (Figure 18.4) as this keeps the biogas under a small positive pressure. The sides of the separators are inclined at 45–60° to the horizontal, and there should be an overlap of at least 100 mm between the lower edge of the separator and the deflector in order to prevent any escape of biogas into the settling zone. The volume of the settling zone (ie the liquid volume outside the separators and above their base) is 15–20 per cent of the total reactor volume.

The total base width of the separator units is around two-thirds of the total width of the reactor (Figure 18.4). Thus the upflow velocity of the rising wastewater–sludge suspension increases to $3V_{up}$ at the separator base level as it passes between adjacent separator units, and then decreases to V_{up} at the discharge level.

Effluent collection

The treated effluent is collected in a horizontal gutter which has regular V-notches (two notches per m^2 of reactor surface area for V_{up} = 1 m/h). A scum guard is installed to prevent any floating solids leaving the reactor. The general arrangement is the same as that used on primary and secondary sedimentation tanks in conventional wastewater treatment plants (see Metcalf and Eddy, Inc, 1991).

Sludge production and drying

UASBs produce quite large amounts of waste sludge, ~0.2 kg/kg of BOD removed. This is much less than is produced in conventional activated sludge plants (~0.8 kg/kg), but much more than in anaerobic ponds (Chapter 10); and UASBs produce waste sludge which needs to be disposed of continuously (see Cavalcanti et al, 1999*), whereas anaerobic ponds only produce waste sludge intermittently.

In warm climates, UASB waste sludge can be simply dewatered on drying beds. Drying bed design is covered in detail by van Haandel and Lettinga (1994); in essence the drying bed area required at temperatures ≥20°C is in the range 0.01–0.015 m^2 per person. The total drying bed area is divided into 3–5 individual beds; these can be covered with a simple roof to aid drying in the rainy season. Sludge is wasted once every 1–2 weeks; it dries quite quickly and without odour release, usually within 3–4 weeks. As it will contain some viable *Ascaris* eggs, the dried sludge should be stored for at least three months before it is applied to agricultural land. Alternatively, it can be landfilled immediately.

(a) Submerged separator

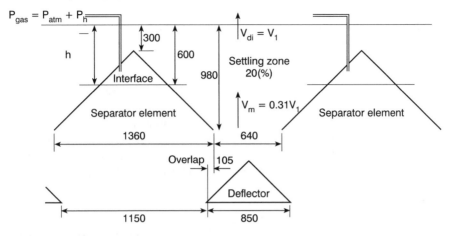

(b) Separator with gas under atmospheric pressure

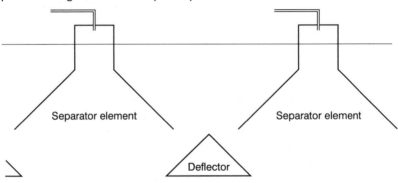

(c) Hybrid separator with opening for maintenance

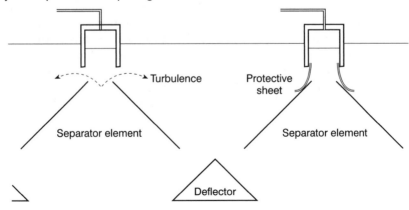

Source: van Haandel and Lettinga (1994)

Figure 18.4 *Details of a Submerged Phase Separator*

UASBs OR ANAEROBIC PONDS?

A 6-h UASB achieves a 70 per cent removal of BOD, but this is also achieved by a 1-day anaerobic pond at 25°C (Chapter 10). Which is 'better'? (This question was asked, and answered, by Peña Varón et al, 2000*.) The UASB is clearly smaller: it has only one quarter of the volume of the anaerobic pond. However, it costs more to construct a 6-h UASB in reinforced concrete (even reinforced brickwork) than it costs to construct (essentially excavate) a 1-day anaerobic pond. Furthermore, the saving in land area is insignificant when the area of the secondary facultative pond needed to treat the anaerobic effluent (from either the UASB or the anaerobic pond) and the area of the drying beds for the UASB sludge are taken into account. This can be illustrated as follows:

UASB and facultative pond

For a wastewater flow of 10,000 m^3/day, a 4-m deep 6-h UASB has an area of 625 m^2; the drying beds for the UASB sludge have an area of (100,000 persons x0.15 m^2/person) = 1500 m^2; and the secondary facultative pond designed in Chapter 11 has an area of 26,500 m^2 – that is a total mid-depth area of 28,000 m^2.

Anaerobic and facultative ponds

For the same wastewater flow, a 3-m deep 1-day anaerobic pond has an area of 3340 m^2 giving, with the same facultative pond, a total mid-depth area of 29,840 m^2 – only 6.6 per cent more than the UASB–facultative pond combination. If maturation ponds are used, then the land saving due to using UASBs, rather than anaerobic ponds, is even less.

Thus, in almost all situations anaerobic ponds, and in particular high-rate anaerobic ponds (Chapter 10), will be preferred to UASBs. An exception to this will be when high-strength industrial or agro-industrial wastewaters are to be treated, or pretreated prior to discharge to sewer; in such cases the finance for construction and the skilled personnel for operation and maintenance are more readily available – as, for example, at the potato chip factory in Egypt reported by El-Gohary and Nasr (1999*; see also Field and Sierra, 2002*). UASBs are also useful to treat wastewaters with a high sulphate concentration as the resulting hydrogen sulphide in the biogas can be readily removed in a chemical scrubber or a 'bioscrubber' (Nishimura and Yoda, 1997*).

19

Biofiltration

FUNCTION

Biofilters (also called trickling filters, percolating filters and bacteria beds) are an old process for the secondary treatment of domestic wastewater dating from the beginning of the 20th century (Institution of Water and Environmental Management, 1988), and there are many thousands of biofilters in use in both industrialized and developing countries. However, for use in warm climates (whether in industrialized or developing countries) they should now only be used with modern fly control techniques (see below). Biofilters produce high quality effluents (eg <20 mg BOD/l and <30 mg SS/l) without requiring large areas of land or consuming vast quantities of electricity. In many situations in developing countries they are much more appropriate than activated sludge.

Biofilters comprise a 2–3 m deep bed of 50–100 mm rock (Figure 19.1). The settled wastewater – that is, the effluent from either a primary sedimentation tank, or in developing countries more appropriately an anaerobic pond (Broome et al, 2003*) – is distributed mechanically over the rock medium (Figure 19.2) and it percolates down through the medium to be collected in an underdrain system at the base of the bed. A microbial film develops on the surface of the rock and the bacteria in this 'biofilm' oxidize the wastewater organics (ie remove the BOD) as the settled wastewater trickles down through the bed.

The biofilm develops in thickness as the bacteria in it grow on the settled wastewater. Eventually it becomes too thick and some is sheared off (often described as 'sloughed off') by the wastewater flow. The solids (sometimes called 'humus solids' or simply 'humus') have to be removed in a secondary sedimentation tank (a 'humus tank') or in a sedimentation or maturation pond, so that the final effluent has a sufficiently low suspended solids concentration.

DESIGN

Biofilters are plug flow reactors in which BOD removal is reasonably well represented by first-order kinetics (Chapter 5). The effluent BOD (after sedimentation) is thus given by equation 5.10:

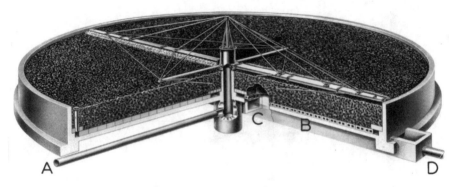

Note: A, inlet pipe; B, underdrain blocks; C, effluent channel; D, outlet pipe.

Figure 19.1 *Sectional Perspective View of a Circular Biofilter Showing the Rotating Wastewater Distributor and Filter Medium*

$$L_e = L_i e^{-k_1 \theta}$$

The retention time is a function of the specific surface area S of the filter medium (its surface area per unit volume, m^2/m^3), the gross filter volume V (m^3) and the flow rate Q (m^3/day), and is equal to distance/velocity. The distance travelled is a slightly zigzag path which is proportional to the depth (D, m) of the biofilter – let this be αD (where $\alpha > 1$). To calculate the velocity (= flow/unit area), consider a 1-m cube of the filter medium:

1 the flow applied to the cube is Q/A, where A is the cross-sectional area of the biofilter (m^2), and
2 the cross-sectional area available for effective flow is the area immediately adjacent to the film of the microbial growth. In the 1-m cube there are S m^2 of surface area. Since the depth of the cube is 1 m, its effective linear cross-sectional dimension (ie 'flow perimeter') is S m. If the flow thickness is d m, the cross-sectional area used for the flow is xSd, where x is <1 and is a combined measure of the non-availability and non-use of the theoretical flow area (Sd) for actual flow (non-availability arises from the presence of the microbial film and non-use is due to the non-ideal distribution of the wastewater over the whole cross-section).

The flow velocity is flow/area – that is $(Q/A)/(xSd)$, and the retention time θ is distance/velocity, so that:

$$\theta = \frac{\alpha D}{(Q/A) / xSd}$$

$$(19.1)$$

Figure 19.2 *Distribution of Settled Wastewater on to a Rectangular Biofilter*

Equation 5.10 therefore becomes:

$$L_e = L_i \exp(-KVS/Q)$$

$$(19.2)$$

where K is a 'modified rate constant' ($= k_1 \alpha x d$), m/day; and V is the biofilter volume ($= AD$), m^3.

Since k_1 is temperature-dependent (equation 5.8), K must also vary with temperature. Studies at pilot-scale in England (Water Pollution Research Board, 1973) showed that:

$$K_T = 0.037(1.08)^{T-15}$$

$$(19.3)$$

Recirculation

The proportion of voids ('porosity') in a filter comprising 50–100 mm aggregate is ~40 per cent of the gross volume. When a strong wastewater is applied to such a filter, excessive biofilm growth occurs and this can lead to blockage of the filter and 'ponding' of the wastewater on the surface of the filter. Experience has shown that, if a final effluent of BOD ≤20 mg/l and SS ≤30 mg/l is required, the BOD loading that can be safely be applied to a single-pass filter is ≤15 kg/m^{3}day. However, if some of the clarified effluent is returned to the filter inlet, 2–3 times the normal loading for a single-pass filter can be applied with the production of a satisfactory effluent.

Recirculation serves not only to dilute the settled wastewater but, more importantly, to reduce the rate of biofilm growth and to increase the hydraulic stripping of the film. It also ensures that more of the available surface area is used for waste oxidation by providing a more uniform hydraulic distribution across the filter and also a more uniform vertical distribution of the microbial film. The recirculation ratio (ie the ratio of the recycled flow to the settled wastewater flow) is generally in the range 0.5–6, with 1 being most commonly used.

Alternative design equations

There are several empirical or semi-empirical design equations for biofilters, mainly derived from biofilter plants in the US (see Baker and Graves, 1968; Horan, 1990; Metcalf and Eddy, Inc, 1991). One of the most commonly used is the National Research Council (1946) equation; its original form, in US customary units, is:

$$E_{20} = \frac{100}{1 + 0.0561(W/VF)^{0.5}}$$

(19.4)

where E_{20} is the BOD removal efficiency at 20°C; W is the BOD load applied to the filter, lb/day; V is the filter volume, 1000 ft³; and F is the corrected recirculation factor (dimensionless) given by:

$$F = \frac{1 + R}{(1 + 0.1R)^2}$$

(19.5)

where R is the ratio Q_r/Q_i (Q_r is the recirculation flow rate and Q_i is the influent wastewater flow rate prior to recirculation). If there is no recirculation, then $F = 1$.

The efficiency at T°C is given by Metcalf and Eddy, Inc (1991) as:

$$E_T = E_{20}(1.035)^{T-20}$$

(19.6)

In metric units, equation 19.4 becomes:

$$E_{20} = \frac{100}{1 + 0.225(W/VF)^{0.5}}$$

(19.7)

where W is now in g/day and V in m³ (1 lb = 454 g and 1000 ft³ = 28.32 m³). Note that $W/V = L_iQ_i/V$ (where L_i is the influent BOD before recirculation, mg/l; and Q_i is in m³/day) = λ_v, g/m³ day (equation 10.1).

Equations 19.5–19.7 are used for design.

FLY CONTROL

Bacteria are not the only organisms to live in biofilters. There is a whole complex ecosystem of protozoa, metazoa, worms – and fly larvae. Unless controlled, swarms of newly emergent adult 'filter flies' (such as *Psychoda* and *Sylvicola*) and chironomid midges can make life unpleasant for nearby residents (*Surrey Advertiser*, 1998*).

Fly control is best achieved by covering the rock medium with high-density polyethylene netting (Palmhive Technical Textiles, 2002*) (Figure 19.3), which prevents gravid female flies from entering the biofilter to lay their eggs – no eggs, no larvae, no flies (Burridge, 2000). Of course, a few flies will get in and lay their eggs; the resulting newly emergent flies are best attracted to, and killed by, electronic fly killers (P & L Systems, 2002*).

HUMUS REMOVAL

The humus (suspended solids) in the biofilter effluent must be removed prior to discharge. This is achieved in secondary sedimentation tanks (for the design of these, see Metcalf and Eddy, Inc, 1991 and Horan, 1990) or in sedimentation ponds (Chapter 20). If the biofilter effluent is to be used for restricted crop irrigation, a sedimentation pond is used (rather than a secondary sedimentation tank) in order to achieve ≤1 nematode egg/l or ≤0.1 egg/l if children under 15 years are exposed. If it is to be used for unrestricted irrigation, a series of maturation ponds (Chapter 12) is necessary to reduce the *E coli* count to ≤1000/100 ml; the first maturation pond should be 0.5 m deeper than the others to allow for settlement, digestion and storage of the humus solids.

Figure 19.3 *Rectangular Biofilters Covered with High-density Polyethylene Netting to Control Fly Nuisance*

DESIGN EXAMPLE

Design a biofilter to treat the effluent of the anaerobic pond designed in Chapter 10.

Solution
At 25°C KT is given by equation 19.3 as:

$$K_{25} = 0.037(1.08)^{25-15}$$

$$= 0.08 \text{ m/day}$$

Rearrangement of equation 19.2 gives:

$$V = - [Q \ln(L_e/L_i)][K_T S]^{-1}$$

For L_e = 30 mg/l and S = 40 m²/m³ (a typical value for 50–100 mm rock)

$$V = - [10\,000 \times \ln(30/90)][0.08 \times 40]^{-1}$$

$$= 3500 \text{ m}^3$$

Choose two biofilters in parallel, each 36 m in diameter and 1.8 m deep.

20

Simple Activated Sludge Variants

AERATED LAGOONS

Aerated lagoons are activated sludge units operated without sludge return. Historically they were developed from waste stabilization ponds in the northern US, where mechanical aeration was used to supplement the algal oxygen supply in winter. It was found, however, that soon after the aerators were put into operation the algae disappeared and the microbial community quickly came to resemble that of activated sludge. Aerated lagoons (Figure 20.1), especially those operating at short retention times in warm climates, are designed as completely mixed non-return activated sludge units. Floating aerators (Figure 20.2) are used to supply the necessary oxygen and mixing power.

Aerated lagoons can treat either raw wastewater (after preliminary treatment – Chapter 8), or settled wastewater, for example, anaerobic pond effluent (Chapter 10), as at Melbourne, Australia (Chapter 9), Ben Slimane, Morocco (Kouraa et al, 2002*) and Daqahla, Egypt (El Sharkawi et al, 1995*). BOD removals above 90 per cent are achieved at short retention times (2–6 days); retention times less than 2 days are not recommended as they are too short to permit the development of a healthy flocculent sludge (even so the activated sludge concentration is only 200–400 mg/l, in contrast to the 2000–6000 mg/l found in conventional systems and oxidation ditches). In common with all activated sludge systems, aerated lagoons are not particularly effective in removing faecal bacteria: reductions are only 90–95 per cent and further treatment may therefore be necessary (Chapters 12, 21 and 22).

Design

The rate of bio-oxidation of wastewater in an aerated lagoon has been found to be approximated well by first-order kinetics – equation 5.7:

$$L_e = \frac{L_i}{1 + k_1\theta}$$

In the case of aerated lagoons, the BOD of the effluent (L_e) is due to two separate fractions: (1) the small amount of the influent waste not oxidized in

Figure 20.1 *An Aerated Lagoon*

the lagoon, and (2) the bacterial cells synthesized during oxidation (see Figure 3.4). These fractions are generally referred to as the 'soluble' and 'insoluble' BOD, respectively. It is convenient (and conceptually more correct) to apply first-order kinetics only to the removal of the soluble fraction:

$$S_e = \frac{L_i}{1 + \kappa\theta}$$

(20.1)

where S_e is the soluble BOD in the effluent (ie the fraction of the influent BOD which escapes oxidation), mg/l; and κ is the first-order rate constant for soluble BOD removal, day^{-1}.

All the influent BOD is assumed to be soluble (ie $S_i = L_i$). The retention time in the lagoon is 2–6 days, with 4 days the most usual value. A typical design value for κ is 2.5 day^{-1} at 20°C; its values at other temperatures can be estimated from the equation (Metcalf and Eddy, Inc, 1991):

$$\kappa_T = 2.5(1.06)^{T-20}$$

(20.2)

The quantity of bacteria synthesized in the lagoon is related to the quantity of soluble BOD removed:

Figure 20.2 *Floating 'Aire-O$_2$ Triton' Aerator-mixer with Two Propellers – One for Mixing and one for Fine Bubble Distribution of the Air Which is Supplied by a Compressor*

$$\frac{dX}{dt} = Y\frac{dS}{dt}$$

(20.3)

where X is the cell concentration in the lagoon, mg/l; and Y is the yield coefficient (dimensionless, and defined by this equation as the mass of cells formed per unit mass of soluble BOD consumed).

Y is typically 0.6–0.7. On a finite time basis, say one retention time, equation 20.3 can be rewritten for the whole lagoon as:

$$\frac{XV}{\theta} = \frac{Y(L_i - S_e)V}{\theta}$$

(20.4)

where V is the lagoon volume, m^3.

The rate of cell synthesis must be balanced by the sum of the rates at which the cells leave the lagoon in the effluent and at which they die in the lagoon. The rate at which the cells leave the lagoon is QX where Q is the flow through the lagoon. The rate at which some of the cells in the lagoon die is proportional to the quantity of cells present; it is usually given as bXV where b is the rate of autolysis in day^{-1} (equation 3.4; typically $b = 0.07$ day^{-1} at 20°C). Thus:

$$\frac{Y(L_i - S_e)V}{\theta} = bXV + QX$$

$$(20.5)$$

Rearranging and writing V/Q as θ:

$$X = \frac{Y(L_i - S_e)}{1 + b\theta}$$

$$(20.6)$$

This quantity of cells X can be converted to an equivalent ultimate BOD by considering the chemical equation for their complete oxidation:

$$C_5 H_7 NO_2 + 5O_2 \rightarrow 5CO_2 + 2H_2O + NH_3$$

Thus 1 g of cells has an ultimate BOD of $(5 \times 32/113) = 1.42$ g. Since $BOD_5/BOD_u \approx 2/3$, 1 g of cells has a BOD_5 of 0.94 g. Therefore the total effluent BOD is given by:

$$L_e = S_e + 0.94X$$

$$(20.7)$$

Oxygen requirement

The quantity of oxygen required for bio-oxidation (R_{O2}, kg/h) is the amount of total (ie soluble + insoluble) ultimate BOD removed:

$$R_{O2} = [1.5(L_i - L_e)Q] \times 10^{-3}/24$$

$$(20.8)$$

Substituting equation 20.7 (rewritten in terms of ultimate BOD):

$$R_{O2} = [1.5(L_i - S_e)Q - 1.42XQ] \times 10^{-3}/24$$

$$(20.9)$$

that is, the oxygen requirement is the ultimate soluble BOD removed less the ultimate BOD due to the cells wasted in the effluent.

Nitrification

Nitrification (the autotrophic bacterial conversion of ammonia to nitrite and then to nitrate – Chapter 3) may occur in aerated lagoons (and almost certainly in oxidation ditches – see later in this chapter) in warm climates. Nitrification requires 3.1 mg O_2 per mg ammonia-N nitrified (Chapter 3); it also requires ~7 mg of alkalinity as $CaCO_3$ per mg ammonia-N nitrified.

The kinetic equations are as follows:

$$\theta_s = 1.6(\mu_T - b)^{-1}$$

$$(20.10)$$

where θ_s is the solids retention time (the 'sludge age') in the aerated lagoon, days – since there is no solids (sludge) recirculation in an aerated lagoon $\theta_s = \theta$, the V/Q hydraulic retention time, days; μ_T is the specific growth rate of the nitrifying bacteria at $T°C$, day^{-1} (given by equation 20.11); and b is their endogenous decay rate, day^{-1} (taken as 0.2 day^{-1}). The coefficient 1.6 in equation 20.10 is the ratio of the peak to average influent ammonia-N loads (in, for example, kg N/day) – that is, it is a factor of safety to allow the nitrifying bacterial population to become accustomed to fluctuations in influent ammonia-N concentrations.

$$\mu_T = 0.8(1.086)^{T-20} \left(\frac{C_e}{K_{s(N)} + C_e} \right) \left(\frac{DO}{K_{s(DO)} + DO} \right)$$

$$(20.11)$$

where C_e is the required effluent ammonia-N concentration, mg/l; $K_{s(N)}$ is the Monod half-saturation constant for ammonia-N (see equations 3.4 and 20.12), mg/l; DO is the in-lagoon dissolved oxygen concentration, mg/l (typically 1–2 mg/l); and $K_{s(DO)}$ is the Monod half-saturation constant for DO, mg/l (typically 0.5 mg/l).

The value of $K_{s(N)}$ varies with temperature, as follows (Horan, 1990):

$$K_{s(N)(T)} = 0.733(1.1246)^{T-20}$$

$$(20.12)$$

A minimum hydraulic retention time (= sludge age in aerated lagoons) of ~3 days is needed at temperatures >20°C to permit nitrification to occur.

The oxygen required for nitrification is given by:

$$R_{O2} = 3.1(C_i - C_e)Q \times 10^{-3}/24$$

$$(20.13)$$

where R_{O2} is the nitrification oxygen requirement, kg/h; and C_i and C_e are the influent and effluent ammonia-N concentrations, respectively, mg/l.

The total oxygen requirement is the sum of the requirements for bio-oxidation (equation 20.8 or 20.9) and for nitrification (equation 20.13).

Aerator performance

The aerators must supply both sufficient oxygen for bio-oxidation and sufficient power to mix the lagoon contents. The power required for mixing

(P_m, W/m³) is ~3 W/m³ for the 'Triton' aerator-mixer shown in Figure 20.2 (Aeration Industries International Inc, 2002*). For conventional surface aerators (of the type common in conventional activated sludge units), P_m is much higher; Horan (1990) gives the equation:

$$P_m = 5 + 0.004X$$

(20.14)

where X is the cell (ie suspended solids) concentration in the lagoon, mg/l. As X is typically in the range 200–400 mg/l, the power required for mixing is ~6 W/m³ for conventional surface aerators (ie around twice that used by modern aerator-mixers).

Usually more power is required for mixing than for oxygen supply for bio-oxidation, but this must be checked as follows: manufacturers certify that their aeration equipment has an 'oxygen transfer rate' of so many kg O_2/kWh under standard test conditions – these are: tap water as the test liquid at 20°C and initially with zero dissolved oxygen concentration. This standard rating has to be corrected for conditions in the aerated lagoon, as follows (Nogaj, 1972):

$$O_L = O_0[\alpha][(1.024)^{T-20}]\left[\frac{\beta C_{s(T,A)} - C_L}{C_{s(20,0)}}\right]$$

(20.15)

where O_L is the oxygen transfer rate in the aerated lagoon, and O_0 is the oxygen transfer rate under standard test conditions.

The first correction term is to allow for the nature of the liquid to be aerated:

α = the ratio of the oxygen transfer rate in the wastewater to that in tap water at the same temperature (typically for domestic wastewaters, a = 0.8).

The second term is an Arrhenius temperature correction term. The third term is a dissolved oxygen correction term which allows for the difference between the DO concentration in the lagoon (typically 1–2 mg/l) and that adopted in the standard rating test (initially zero):

$C_{s(T,A)}$ = O_2 saturation concentration (ie O_2 solubility) in distilled water at temperature T and altitude A. The values of $C_{s(T)}$ at sea level (760 mm Hg) are given in Table 20.1 for T = 15–30°C. The correction for altitude is made by considering the mean air pressure P_A (mm Hg) at that altitude:

Table 20.1 *Solubility of Oxygen in Distilled Water at Sea Level at Various Temperatures*

Temperature (°C)	Solubility (mg/l)
15	10.07
16	9.86
17	9.65
18	9.46
19	9.27
20	9.08
21	8.91
22	8.74
23	8.57
24	8.42
25	8.26
26	8.12
27	7.97
28	7.84
29	7.70
30	7.57

Source: Montgomery et al (1964)

$$C_{s(T,A)} = C_{s(T,0)} (P_A/760)$$

(20.16)

$C_{s(20,0)}$ = O_2 saturation concentration in distilled water at 20°C and at sea level (= 9.08 mg/l),

C_L = DO concentration in the lagoon (1–2 mg/l), and

β = the ratio of the O_2 saturation concentration in the wastewater to that in distilled water (typically for domestic wastewaters, $\beta = 0.95$).

Modern aerators are rated at ~1.5–2 kg O_2/kWh.

Construction

The construction of aerated lagoons is essentially the same as that for waste stabilization ponds (Chapter 13). The major differences are: greater depths (usually 3–5 m), steeper embankment slopes (1 to 1.5–2) and the provision of a high-density liner to prevent scour by the turbulence induced by the aerators.

Effluent treatment

Consider a typical domestic waste with L_i = 300 mg/l. For θ = 4 d and T = 20°C and assuming κ = 2.5 day^{-1}, b = 0.07 day^{-1} and Y = 0.65, equations 20.1, 20.5 and 20.7 give:

$$S_e = \frac{L_i}{1 + \kappa\theta} = \frac{300}{1 + (2.5 \times 4)} = 27 \text{ mg/l}$$

$$X = \frac{Y(L_i - S_e)}{1 + b\theta} = \frac{0.65(300 - 27)}{1 + (0.07 \times 4)} = 140 \text{ mg/l}$$

$$L_e = S_e + 0.94X = 27 + (0.94 \times 140) = 160 \text{ mg/l}$$

Thus the BOD of the lagoon effluent is 160 mg/l, but >80 per cent of this is due to the bacterial cells present. If these cells (or most of them) are removed from the effluent prior to discharge, the effluent BOD will be considerably reduced. There are two ways to do this: (1) discharge into a series of maturation ponds, or (2) discharge into a sedimentation pond.

Discharge into maturation ponds

If the final effluent is to be re-used in agriculture or aquaculture (Chapters 21 and 22), then discharge into a series of maturation ponds is the favoured option in order to achieve the required microbiological quality. The maturation ponds are designed as described in Chapter 12, with the assumption either that the *E coli* count is reduced in the aerated lagoon by 90 per cent, or – in the case of restricted irrigation – that there is no helminth egg reduction in the aerated lagoon.

As the aerated lagoon effluent is high in suspended solids (~200–400 mg/l), provision has to be made in the first maturation pond for the settlement and subsequent digestion of these solids. This is simply done by increasing the depth in this pond to 2 m. Regular desludging will be required (see Chapter 14).

Discharge into a sedimentation pond

This is the preferred option when the final effluent is discharged into a surface water. The sedimentation pond should be designed according to the following requirements (Metcalf and Eddy, Inc, 1991):

- the hydraulic retention time must be sufficient to allow the settleable solids to settle,
- sufficient volume must be provided for sludge storage,
- algal growth must be minimized, and
- odours must be controlled.

Hydraulic retention time. Two considerations are relevant here: first, the minimum retention time for solids sedimentation is 6 h; and second, to minimize algal growth, the maximum retention time is 2 days. Generally a retention time of 1 day is used.

Odour control. To control any odours emanating from the anaerobic digestion of the settled solids, there must be a minimum liquid depth of 1 m above the sludge layer at its maximum depth (ie just before the pond is desludged). Often a depth of 1.5 m is used.

On the basis of the above two considerations, the liquid volume and surface area of the sedimentation pond can be calculated, as follows:

1   Volume (V, m^3):

$$V = Q\theta$$

(20.17)

2   Surface area (A, m^2)

$$A = Q\theta/D_L$$

(20.18)

where Q is the inflow, m^3/day; θ is the hydraulic retention time, typically 1 day; and D_L is the liquid depth required for odour control, typically 1.5 m.

Sludge storage. The calculation of the volume required for the storage of digested sludge is done in the following three steps:

1 Calculate the total mass of suspended solids added per year:

$$M = 365Q(SS_i - SS_e) \times 10^{-3}$$

(20.19)

where M is the total mass of suspended solids added, kg/year; Q is the inflow, m^3/day; SS_i and SS_e are the influent and required effluent suspended and solids concentrations, respectively, mg/l (= g/m^3); and the factor 10^{-3} converts g to kg.

The value of SS_i in equation 20.19 is computed as follows:

$$SS_i = SS_{RW} + X$$

(20.20)

where SS_{RW} is the suspended solids concentration in the raw wastewater, mg/l; and X is the cell concentration given by equation 20.6 (this assumes that the SS_{RW} are not biodegraded in the lagoon).

2 Calculate the mass of fixed and volatile suspended solids added, MFS and MVS (kg/year), assuming that 70 per cent of the total solids are volatile:

$$M_{FS} = 0.3M$$

(20.21)

$$M_{VS} = 0.7M$$

(20.22)

3 Calculate the volume required for sludge storage:
(i)   assuming that within a period of one year the volatile solids are reduced by 75 per cent, the following equation gives the mass of volatile solids present at the end of year n:

$$(M_{vs})_n = 0.25 n M_{vs}$$

(20.23)

(ii)   thus the mass of total solids present after n years is:

$$(M)_n = n M_{FS} + 0.25 n M_{vs}$$

(20.24)

(iii)   determine the pond depth for sludge storage (DS, m), assuming that the sludge compacts to an average value of 15 per cent solids and that the density of the accumulated sludge is 1060 kg/m³:

$$D_s = [(M)_n / A]/[0.15 \times 1060]$$

(20.25)

Thus the sedimentation pond has a surface area of A m² (equation 20.18) and a total depth of $(D_L + D_S)$. The term n in equations 20.23 and 20.24 is the required desludging frequency – once every n years.

Aerated lagoons or anaerobic ponds?

Often in developing countries when aerated lagoons have been installed (not uncommonly for the 'reason' that they are more 'sophisticated' and therefore 'better' than WSP), the wastewater treatment authority finds that it cannot afford to pay the electricity bill for them, so the aerators are switched off – with the result that the 4-day lagoons quickly convert themselves into 4-day anaerobic ponds and BOD removal remains high, especially at temperatures of ≥20°C (Tables 10.1 and 10.2). (The aerators are generally only switched on again when important or foreign visitors are expected.) The question to be asked, therefore, is: shouldn't anaerobic ponds have been used in the first place? Or, when anaerobic ponds are followed by aerated lagoons: shouldn't anaerobic and secondary facultative ponds have been used?

The answer to the first question is straightforward: if there is no effluent ammonia-N requirement (and so nitrification in an aerated lagoon is not a consideration), an honest comparison between the two technologies (especially when high-rate anaerobic ponds are considered) will always favour anaerobic ponds – particularly when annual electricity costs are properly quantified (and transparently presented) at the project prefeasibility stage (remember that money spent on electricity is money gone forever, but money spent on land is an investment – Chapters 6 and 9). The answer to the second question also requires an honest comparison to be made between the two systems: an aerated lagoon requires less land than a secondary facultative pond [the retention times, especially at temperatures >20°C, may not be too different, but the difference in depth (3–4 m for aerated lagoons vs 1.5 m for facultative ponds) is significant], but it requires a large annual expenditure on electricity. Could this expenditure be used not for electricity, but to finance a loan to buy more land or to convey the wastewater further out of town to an area where land is less expensive?

Design example

Design an aerated lagoon and sedimentation pond system to treat a unit flow of 1000 m^3/day of domestic wastewater which has BOD and SS concentrations of 300 and 400 mg/l, respectively. Effluent requirements are ≤20 mg BOD/l and ≤30 mg SS/l. The design temperature is 20°C.

Solution
(a) Aerated lagoon

Take θ = 4 days, κ = 2.5 day^{-1}, b = 0.07 day^{-1} and Y = 0.65. From equations 20.1, 20.6 and 20.7:

$$S_e = \frac{L_i}{1 + \kappa\theta} = \frac{300}{1 + (2.5 \times 4)} = 27 \text{ mg/l}$$

$$X = \frac{Y\,(L_i - S_e)}{1 + b\theta} = \frac{0.65\,(300 - 27)}{1 + (0.07 \times 4)} = 140 \text{ mg/l}$$

$$L_e = S_e + 0.94X = 27 + (0.94 \times 140) = 160 \text{ mg/l}$$

Lagoon size: assume a depth of 3 m, so the lagoon mid-depth area is given by:

$$A = Q\theta/D = 1000 \; 4/3 = 1340 \text{ m}^2$$

Choose two lagoons in parallel, each 26 m square at mid-depth.

Aeration: estimate the quantity of oxygen required from equation 20.8:

$$R_{O2} = 1.5(L_i - L_e)Q = 1.5(300 - 160)1000 = 210{,}000 \text{ g/day} = 8.8 \text{ kg/h}$$

Assume that the aerators have a standard rating of 1.8 kg O_2/kWh and correct for field conditions from equation 20.15 (assume α = 0.8, β = 0.95, c_L = 1 mg/l and zero altitude):

$$O_L = O_0\alpha(1.024)^{T-20}\left(\frac{\beta C_{s(T,A)} - C_L}{C_{s(20,0)}}\right)$$

$$= 1.8 \times 0.8 \times 1 \times \left(\frac{(0.95 \times 9.08) - 1}{9.08} \right)$$

$$= 1.2 \text{ kg } O_2/\text{kWh}$$

The aerator power required for bio-oxidation = 8.8/1.2 = 7.3 kW.

Choose a 'Triton' aerator-mixer which uses 3 W/m^3 for complete mixing. As the lagoon volume is (1340 x 3) m^3, the power required for mixing is therefore 12 kW. Thus the power requirement for mixing is greater than that for oxygen supply.

(b) Sedimentation ponds

Pond area: take $\theta = 1$ day and $D_L = 1.5$ m. From equation 20.18:

$$A = Q\theta/D_L = 1000 \times 4/1.5 = 2670 \text{ m}^2$$

Sludge storage: from equation 20.20 the concentration of suspended solids entering the sedimentation pond is:

$$SS_i = SS_{RW} + X = 400 + 140 = 540 \text{ mg/l}$$

From equations 20.19, 20.21 and 20.22:

$$M = 365Q(SS_i - SS_e) \times 10^{-3}$$

$$= 365 \times 1000 \ (540 - 30) \times 10^{-3}$$

$$= 186,000 \text{ kg/year}$$

$$M_{FS} = 0.3M = 0.3 \times 186,000 = 56,400 \text{ kg/year}$$

$$M_{VS} = 0.7M = 0.7 \times 186,000 = 131,600 \text{ kg/year}$$

From equations 20.24 and 20.25 and choosing n = 3 years:

$$(M)_n = nM_{FS} + 0.25nM_{VS}$$

$$= (3 \times 56\ 400) + (0.25 \times 3 \times 131,600)$$

$$= 268,000 \text{ kg}$$

$$D_s = [(M)_n/A]/[0.15 \times 1060]$$

$$= (268,000/2670)/(0.15 \times 1060)$$

$$= 0.63 \text{ m}$$

Thus the sedimentation pond area is 2670 m^2 and its total depth is 1.5 + 0.63 = 2.13 m (say, 2.2 m).

OXIDATION DITCHES

Oxidation ditches are a direct modification of conventional activated sludge (Baars, 1962; Barnes et al, 1983; Environmental Protection Agency, 2000b*). Their essential operational features are that they receive raw wastewater (after preliminary treatment) and provide longer retention times: the hydraulic retention time is commonly 0.5–1.5 days and that for the solids 20–30 days. The latter, achieved by recycling >95 per cent of the activated sludge, ensures minimal excess sludge production and a high degree of mineralization in the small amount of excess sludge that is produced. Sludge handling and treatment is almost negligible since the small amounts of waste sludge can be readily dewatered without odour on drying beds. The other major difference is in reactor shape: the oxidation ditch is a long continuous channel, usually oval in plan and 2–3 m deep (Figure 20.3). The ditch liquor is aerated by several aerators (eg 'Triton' aerator-mixers – Figure 20.2), which impart a velocity to the ditch contents of 0.3–0.4 m/s to keep the activated sludge in suspension. The ditch effluent is discharged into a secondary sedimentation tank to permit solids separation and sludge return and to produce a settled effluent with low BOD and SS. Removals consistently >95 per cent are obtained for both BOD and SS.

The concentration of total SS in the ditch is 3000–5000 mg/l. In order to prevent the concentration exceeding this range, the return sludge flow is diverted to the drying beds for a short period each day; this period is best determined by operational experience (a simple field check on the ditch SS concentration is to fill a 1000-ml graduated cylinder to the mark with the ditch liquor; if the solids concentration is 3500–4500 mg/l, the volume of sludge which settles in 30 minutes should be ~200 ml). Alternatively the sludge wastage rate may be estimated by considering the solids retention time.

The oxidation ditch was developed in The Netherlands to provide small communities of 200–15,000 people with wastewater treatment facilities at the same cost per person as conventional activated sludge works serving much larger populations. At present there are few oxidation ditches in developing countries since waste stabilization ponds are usually more favourable, both in terms of costs and faecal bacterial removal, although where there is a reliable electricity supply but insufficient land for ponds they are being increasingly used. As noted in Chapter 9, oxidation ditches were found by Arthur (1983*) to be cheaper than aerated lagoons and biofilters, and also cheaper than waste stabilization ponds when land costs exceeded US$50,000–150,000 per ha.

Design

Oxidation ditch design is purely empirical. The depth is 2–3 m and the volume is dependent on the retention time which in turn is based on the sludge loading

Figure 20.3 *Typical Oxidation Ditch Installation*

factor, γ. This is the mass of BOD applied to the ditch liquor suspended solids per day; it is measured in g BOD per g solids per day (ie day^{-1}). The mass of BOD entering the ditch is L_iQ g/d, where L_i is the influent BOD (mg/l, $= g/m^3$) and Q the flow (m^3/day); the mass of suspended solids in the ditch is SV where S is the ditch liquor suspended solids concentration (mg/l) and V the ditch volume (m^3). Thus the sludge loading factor is given by:

$$\gamma = \frac{L_i Q}{SV}$$

(20.26)

or, since $V/Q = \theta$:

$$\gamma = \frac{L_i}{S\theta}$$

(20.27)

Design values commonly used in Europe are $\gamma = 0.05$ day^{-1} and $S = 4000$ mg/l which give, for a typical domestic waste ($L_i = 300$ mg/l), a retention time of 1.5 day. However, in warm climates much higher loadings, and therefore shorter retention times, are possible (Arceivala and Alagarsamy, 1970): a comparison between the design criteria used in temperate and warm climates is given in Table 20.2.

Aeration
Oxygen is required at a rate of $\sim$1.5 g O_2/g BOD applied. Such a rate of supply includes an allowance for the endogenous respiration of the sludge and maintains aerobic conditions along the entire length of the ditch.

Sludge wastage
To control the rate of solids accumulation in the ditch, a proportion of the ditch solids must be wasted each day. The rate of wastage is governed by the desired solids retention time (SRT): thus, if the desired SRT is θ_s days, then $100/\theta_s$ per cent of the ditch solids must be wasted each day. This can be achieved by diverting $100/\theta_s$ per cent of the flow from the ditch directly to waste. However, it is more usual to waste the sludge from the sludge return line from the secondary sedimentation tank. The percentage $100/\theta_s$ must therefore be corrected for the change in concentration due to sedimentation. Noting that the inflow concentration to the sedimentation tank is the ditch SS concentration S, the quantity of waste sludge to be diverted to the drying beds, expressed as a percentage of the raw wastewater flow Q, is:

Table 20.2 *Design Criteria for Oxidation Ditches in India and Europe*

Parameter	India	Europe
Sludge loading factor (day^{-1})	0.1–0.3	0.05
Aeration requirement (kg O_2/kg BOD applied)	1.5–2.0	2.0
Excess sludge production (g/hd day)	5–10	25–30
Area of sludge drying beds (m²/hd)	0.025	0.35
Overall land requirement (m²/hd)	0.125	1.2

Source: Arceivala and Alagarsamy (1970)

$$\frac{100}{\theta_R} \left(\frac{S}{S_R} \right)$$

where S_R is the the solids concentration in the sludge return line (= underflow concentration from the sedimentation tank).

For example, choosing θ_s = 30 days and S = 4000 mg/l and assuming that S_R = 50,000 mg/l, the sludge wastage rate would be 0.27 per cent. This illustrates the extremely low rate of sludge production in oxidation ditches.

Construction

Since oxidation ditches are likely to be used in developing countries only for large (and probably only very large) flows, they should be constructed with vertical walls of reinforced concrete, and they should be as deep as possible: 3 m wherever feasible, but at least 2 m.

Design example

Design an oxidation ditch scheme to serve a population of 100,000. The effluent flow is 80 l/person day and the BOD contribution is 40 g/person day. The design temperature is 20°C and the ditch site is at sea level.

Solution
(a) Oxidation ditch

- Flow Q = 80 x 100,000 l/day = 8 000 m^3/day
- Influent BOD L_i = 40 x 1000/80 = 500 mg/l

From Table 20.2 choose γ = 0.20 day^{-1} and S = 4000 mg/l. Then from equation 20.26:

$$V = \frac{L_i Q}{S\gamma} = \frac{500 \times 8000}{4000 \times 0.20} = 5000 \text{ m}^3$$

$$\theta = V/Q = 5000/8000 = 0.625 \text{ day} = 15 \text{ h}$$

The oxygen requirement is taken as 1.5 x the BOD load:

$$R_{O2} = (1.5 \times 40 \text{ g/person day}) \times (100,000 \text{ people})$$

$$= 6000 \text{ kg/day} = 250 \text{ kg/h}$$

The aerator rating is now corrected for field conditions using equation 20.15:

$$O_L = O_0 \alpha (1.024)^{T-20} \left(\frac{\beta c_{s(T,A)} - c_L}{c_{s(20,0)}} \right)$$

$$= 1.8 \times 0.8 \times 1 \times \left(\frac{(0.95 \times 9.08) - 1}{9.08} \right)$$

$$= 1.2 \text{ kg } O_2/\text{kWh}$$

The power for the oxygen supply is therefore $250/1.2 = 208$ kW. The power for complete mixing is ($5000 \text{ m}^3 \times 3 \text{ W/m}^3$) – that is 15 kW. Thus the required power is that for oxygen supply.

(b) Sedimentation tank
The area is based on a peak overflow rate of 25 m^3/m^2 day and a retention time of 2 h at peak flow. Since the sludge flow is returned to the ditch (ignoring the small volume wasted), the peak overflow is simply taken as 2 × inflow for a population of 100,000 (Chapter 8). Therefore:

- area of tank   = $(2 \times 8000)/25 = 640 \text{ m}^2$
- depth of tank   = (2×8000) $(2/24)/640 = 2$ m

Choose two oxidation ditches in parallel, each followed by a sedimentation tank 20 m in diameter and 2 m deep.

(c) Drying beds
Assume an area of 0.025 m^2 per person (Table 20.2); thus:

- Drying bed area   = $0.025 \times 100\,000 = 2500 \text{ m}^2$.

21

Wastewater Re-use in Agriculture

WHY RE-USE WASTEWATER?

Water is becoming scarcer and scarcer in developing countries and also in parts of some industrialized countries. In arid and semi-arid areas especially, but in fact everywhere, wastewater is simply too valuable to waste. It contains scarce water and valuable plant nutrients, and crop yields are higher when crops are irrigated with wastewater than with freshwater (Table 21.1). Farmers also save on artificial fertilizers: in Mexico, for example, this saving is around US$135/ha year, which is a significant amount of money for subsistence farmers (Future Harvest, 2001*).

Treated wastewater is used for crop irrigation in many parts of the world. Israel, for example, uses over 65 per cent of its wastewater in this way, and plans to use over 90 per cent by 2010 (Friedler, 2001*); and in the desert areas of the US, such as Arizona and California, there are large wastewater re-use schemes (Asano, 1998). Australia is another good example (Dillon, 2000), and India has been using wastewater for irrigation for nearly 100 years (Shende et al, 1988). Mexico City, the second largest city in the world, uses all its wastewater for irrigation (Duron, 1988).

As water becomes scarce, the competition between urban water demand and agricultural water demand increases. In the not too distant future it will have to be 'water for cities and treated wastewater for agriculture'. This must be recognized and planned for, and this means that wastewater has to be considered as part of a country's water resources; it is in fact a very dependable

Table 21.1 *Crop Yields for Wastewater and Freshwater Irrigation*

Irrigation water	Wheat	Moong beans	Rice	Potato	Cotton
Raw wastewater	3.34	0.90	2.97	23.11	2.56
Settled wastewater	3.45	0.87	2.94	20.78	2.30
Waste stabilization pond effluent	3.45	0.78	2.98	22.31	2.41
Fresh water + NPK	2.70	0.72	2.03	17.16	1.70

Note: Yields in t/ha year
Source: Shende (1985)

water resource (Asano, 2002), especially during droughts (Bruins, 1999). In his analysis of water resource availability, development and use in the Middle East, Beaumont (2000*) found that each cubic metre of water used by industry and the service sector generates at least 200 times more wealth than when used by agriculture, and he concludes that *'as water shortages increase, many countries will be best served by the reallocation of irrigation water to meet the growing water needs of the urban regions'*. Irrigation water will still, of course, be needed, and treated urban wastewater will become one of the principal irrigation water sources near cities in developing countries: this is happening now, but it will have to happen much more in the near future.

Guidelines for assessing the environmental impacts of proposed wastewater re-use schemes are given (within the context of US and Californian environmental law, but applicable in principle elsewhere) by Kontos and Asano (1996*). An extremely useful document for government departments planning wastewater use is the 'Queensland Water Recycling Strategy' (Environmental Protection Agency, 2001*); Queensland is a tropical state of Australia whose population is expected to increase by 40 per cent in the next 20 years, so placing great pressures on existing water resources.

Of course, if treated (or even untreated) wastewater is discharged into a river, it is eventually re-used downstream for irrigation and/or urban supply. This is termed 'indirect re-use', but here we are concerned with 'direct re-use' – that is, the use of treated wastewater for crop irrigation, or for aquaculture (Chapter 22), without prior discharge to river.

Wastewater re-use in Islamic countries

In 1978 the Leading Council of Islamic Scholars of Saudi Arabia issued a 'fatwa' (an authoritative religious ruling) on wastewater re-use. Prior to this it was unclear whether treated wastewaters were Islamically 'pure' and there had been a consequent reluctance to use treated wastewater for crop production and landscape and urban green space irrigation (Abderrahman, 2001). As noted by Farooq and Ansari (1983) there are three ways in which 'impure' water may be transformed into 'pure' water:

1 self-purification of the water (eg removal of the impurities by sedimentation),
2 addition of pure water in sufficient quantity to dilute the impurities, and
3 removal of the impurities by the passage of time or physical effects (eg sunlight and wind).

The first and third of these transformations are essentially similar to those achieved by modern wastewater treatment processes, especially waste stabilization ponds.

PUBLIC HEALTH PROTECTION

Crop irrigation with untreated wastewater, though often practised (and generally liked by farmers as it is so 'rich' in nutrients and organics), cannot be recommended as it causes too much disease in those who work in the raw-wastewater-irrigated fields and in those who consume the raw-wastewater-irrigated crops, especially salad crops and vegetables eaten uncooked. The health risks are simply too high when raw domestic wastewater is used to irrigate crops. (Irrigation with untreated wastewater is discussed in more detail in the final section of this chapter.)

Actual and potential health risks

For an *actual* health risk to be caused by crop irrigation with wastewater, all of the following four steps must occur:

1   an infective dose of an excreted pathogen reaches the field (or the pathogen multiplies in the field to form an infective dose);
2   the infective dose reaches a human host;
3   the host becomes infected; and
4   the infection causes disease (or further transmission).

If only the first three of these occur and not the fourth, then the risk is only a *potential* risk and not an actual risk. (These four steps also apply to aquacultural re-use (Chapter 22), with the substitution of 'aquaculture pond' for 'field'.)

Finally, but very importantly, the use of treated wastewater for crop irrigation (or for aquaculture pond fertilization) is only of public health *importance* if it causes a risk that is higher than that to which people are already exposed – that is, if it results in an excess incidence or prevalence of disease, or an *excess* intensity of infection, above what may be termed the 'background' level.

Restricted and unrestricted irrigation

Restricted irrigation refers to the irrigation of all crops *except* salad crops and vegetables which may be eaten uncooked. Unrestricted irrigation includes the irrigation of salad crops and vegetables eaten uncooked. This distinction is important as the groups of people exposed are different: for restricted irrigation it is necessary to protect the health of the fieldworkers, especially children working or playing in wastewater-irrigated fields, and of neighbouring communities (who may be at risk from wastewater aerosols from spray or sprinkler irrigation systems); and for unrestricted irrigation the health of the crop consumers must also be protected.

The epidemiological evidence

Shuval's appraisal

Professor Hillel Shuval and his colleagues at the Hebrew University of Jerusalem undertook an extensive review of the available credible epidemiological evidence for actual health risks resulting, and not resulting, from crop irrigation with wastewater (Shuval et al, 1986*). Their main conclusions were:

- irrigation with raw wastewater causes an excess prevalence of *Ascaris* and hookworm infection, and an excess intensity of these infections, both in those who work in raw-wastewater-irrigated fields (Figures 21.1 and 21.2) and in those who consume raw-wastewater-irrigated crops eaten uncooked (Figure 21.3);
- irrigation with treated wastewater does not cause any excess prevalence of *Ascaris* infection among crop consumers (Figure 21.4); and
- irrigation with raw wastewater also causes excreted bacterial disease in those who consume raw-wastewater-irrigated crops eaten uncooked – the evidence for this is mainly the outbreak of cholera in Jerusalem in 1970 when raw-wastewater-irrigated lettuce was on sale; when this was removed from the market, the epidemic ceased (Fattal et al, 1986).

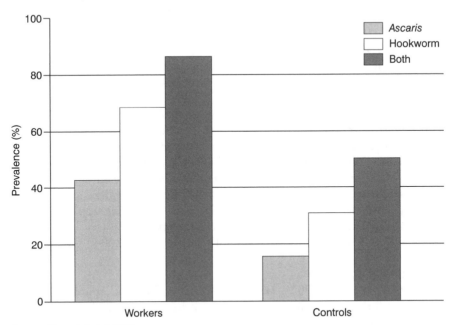

Source: Shuval et al (1986*).

Figure 21.1 *Excess Prevalence of* Ascaris *and Hookworm Infections in 'Sewage Farm' Workers in India Compared with a Control Group (a 'sewage farm' practises raw wastewater irrigation)*

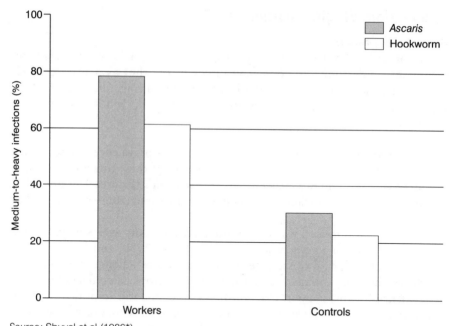

Source: Shuval et al (1986*).

Figure 21.2 *Excess Intensity of* Ascaris *and Hookworm Infections in Sewage Farm Workers in India Compared with a Control Group*

The 1989 WHO guidelines

In 1989 the World Health Organization published guidelines for the microbiological quality of treated wastewaters used for crop irrigation (and also for aquaculture – Chapter 22) (World Health Organization, 1989*). Based principally on the conclusions of the above epidemiological review by Shuval et al (1986*), these guidelines were: for restricted irrigation, ≤1 human intestinal nematode eggs/l; and for unrestricted irrigation, the same egg guideline level and ≤1000 *E coli*/100 ml. They require some modification to take into account: (a) the extensive new epidemiological research, principally that by Dr Ursula Blumenthal at the London School of Hygiene and Tropical Medicine and her colleagues in Mexico, and (b) recent applications of quantitative microbial risk analysis to wastewater re-use (see later in this chapter). (Revised guidelines will be published by WHO, 2004* – see below.)

Blumenthal's appraisal

Blumenthal et al (2000*) reviewed all the credible epidemiological, experimental and risk analysis evidence published since Shuval et al (1986*). Their main conclusions, together with those from more recent studies (Blumenthal et al, 2001; Blumenthal and Peasey, 2002), were:

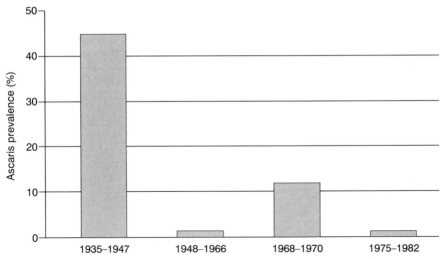

Note: Farmers on the outskirts of Eastern Jerusalem used raw wastewater for crop irrigation, including salad crop irrigation. Prior to the creation of the State of Israel in 1948, these crops were on sale in Western Jerusalem and *Ascaris* prevalence was high. Following partition of the city in 1948 these crops were no longer on sale in Western Jerusalem and *Ascaris* prevalence declined dramatically. When the city was reunited in 1966 the crops were again available and *Ascaris* prevalence rose once more. Following the outbreak of cholera in the city in 1970, the irrigation of crops with raw wastewater was banned and *Ascaris* levels dropped again.
Source: Shuval et al (1986*).

Figure 21.3 Ascaris *Prevalence among Residents of Western Jerusalem, 1935–1982*

(a) Restricted irrigation
- E coli *guideline*: epidemiological studies in Israel, Mexico and the US showed that faecal coliform levels of $10^6/100$ ml of treated wastewater were associated with excess viral infection (but not disease), but not at faecal coliform levels of $\leq 10^4/100$ ml – thus suggesting that $\leq 10^5$ E coli/100 ml would be an appropriate guideline value.
- *Nematode egg guideline*: studies in Mexico also showed that an egg level of 1 per litre of treated wastewater was insufficiently protective for children under the age of 15 years – thus indicating that a stricter guideline of ≤ 0.1 egg per litre was more appropriate when children under 15 are exposed, through either working or playing in wastewater-irrigated fields.

(b) Unrestricted irrigation
- E coli *guideline*: epidemiological studies in Mexico showed that when the faecal coliform level in treated wastewater was $3 \times 10^4/100$ ml, there was an excess risk of disease of 6×10^{-3} per person per year, but quantitative microbial risk analysis (see later in this chapter) shows that when the E coli level is 1000/100 ml, the risk of infection is $\sim 10^{-4}$ per person per year – that is $< 10^{-3}$ per person per year, which is the WHO tolerable risk of infection from drinking fully treated drinking water.

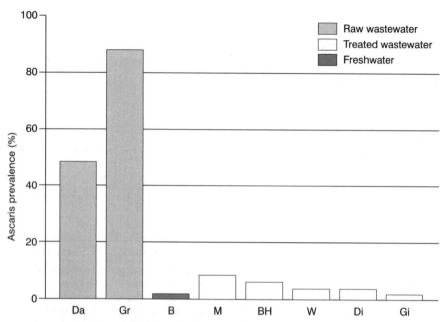

Note: In Darmstadt (Da), and especially its suburb Griesheim (Gr), raw wastewater was used for crop irrigation and *Ascaris* prevalence was very high. In Berlin (B), where treated wastewater was used for irrigation, *Ascaris* prevalence was no higher than in other cities which used freshwater for irrigation (Marburg, M; Bad Homburg, BH; Wiesbaden, W; Dillenburg, Di; and Giesen, Gi). Treatment in Berlin was conventional treatment with both primary and secondary sedimentation which removed almost all the *Ascaris* eggs.
Source: Shuval et al (1986*).

Figure 21.4 Ascaris *Prevalence among Residents of Selected German Cities Immediately After the Second World War*

- *Nematode egg guideline*: studies in Mexico suggested that the egg level should be reduced to ≤0.1 per litre, as for restricted irrigation, in order to protect children under 15 when (as expected) their fieldworker-parents bring home 'unrestricted' produce direct from the fields or when such produce is bought in local shops (but not in shops in neighbouring towns or cities).

Experimental wastewater-irrigation of salad crops

(a) Helminth eggs
Stott et al (1994*) report on two separate sets of experiments, in one of which lettuces were irrigated with waste stabilization pond effluents containing various levels of human intestinal nematode eggs per litre (*Ascaris*, *Trichuris* and *Necator*); and in the other lettuces were irrigated with freshwater containing various numbers of eggs of the chicken roundworm, *Ascaridia galli*, and the lettuces were then fed to immunosuppressed chicks which were

monitored for *Ascaridia* infection (these chicken–*Ascaridia* experiments were done as a model for human–*Ascaris* infection).

The first set of experiments was conducted in northeast Brazil. Lettuces were spray-irrigated with raw wastewater (160–200 eggs/l) and the effluents from an anaerobic pond (14–18 eggs/l), a primary facultative pond (0.2–0.4 egg/l) and a tertiary maturation pond (0 egg/l). After five weeks irrigation the lettuces irrigated with raw wastewater and the anaerobic pond effluent had counts of 30–60 eggs/plant and 0.6 egg/plant, respectively, but those irrigated with the two effluents having <1 egg/l had no eggs on their leaves.

In the second set of experiments conducted in glasshouses in West Yorkshire, England, lettuces were spray-irrigated with treated wastewater seeded with ≤1, 10 and 50 unembryonated viable *A galli* eggs/l. After five weeks irrigation the mean egg counts per individual lettuce plant were 0.04, 0.24 and 0.64, respectively, but 54–78 per cent of the eggs were inviable. When lettuces with these levels of egg contamination were fed to immunosuppressed chicks, at a rate of one lettuce plant per chick per week for six weeks, none developed *Ascaridia* infection. Thus the risk to consumers of salad crops contaminated with very low numbers of nematode eggs at, or shortly after, harvest is likely to be minimal.

(b) Faecal bacteria

In a series of experiments over three consecutive years in southern Portugal, radishes and lettuces were drip- and furrow-irrigated with waste stabilization pond effluent (Bastos and Mara, 1995*). To simulate unfavourable conditions, the use of these 'clean' irrigation techniques was counterbalanced by the choice of salad crops grown (one is a root crop and the other grows close to the soil). The pond effluent quality was $2–5 \times 10^3$ *E coli* per 100 ml – that is, a little higher than the WHO guideline for unrestricted irrigation and this provided the basis for field-testing the guideline. At harvest, *E coli* levels on the crops were $\sim 10^3$ and $\sim 10^4$ per 100 g (fresh weight) for radishes and lettuces, respectively (ie within the range of acceptability for ready-to-eat foods – see Gilbert et al, 2000* and below). Salmonella numbers were very low in the pond effluents and rarely detected on either crop. These results thus provide support for the WHO guideline level of ≤1000 *E coli* per 100 ml for unrestricted irrigation.

Protozoan pathogens

Melloul et al (2002*) found that children aged 2–14 living in El Azzouzia, the raw-wastewater-irrigation area of Marrakech, Morocco had a higher prevalence of giardiasis and amoebiasis than children of the same ages living in a neighbouring area where freshwater was used for irrigation: 67 per cent (*Giardia intestinalis*, 39 per cent; *Entamoeba histolytica*, 28 per cent), compared with 26 per cent (*Giardia*, 20 per cent; *E hystoytlica*, 6 per cent). Younger children (2–8) and boys (2–14) had higher prevalences than older children (9–14) and girls (2–14); and children in El Azzouzia whose fathers were farm workers had higher prevalences than those whose fathers were not. There was also a higher incidence of *Salmonella* infections in the children from El Azzouzia than in those from the other area (21 per cent, compared with 1.1 per cent). This study is the first to provide good evidence for the transmission of protozoan infections where raw wastewater is used for crop irrigation, and it reinforces recommendations that only treated wastewater should be used for irrigation.

The new WHO guidelines

The World Health Organization's new guidelines for the microbiological quality of wastewaters used for crop irrigation will be published in 2004 (World Health Organization, 2004*). It is expected that the new recommendations will be that:

1   only *treated* wastewater be used for crop irrigation;
2   for restricted irrigation, treated wastewaters contain $\leq 10^5$ *E coli* per 100 ml, and ≤ 1 human intestinal nematode egg per litre or, if children under 15 years are exposed, ≤ 0.1 egg/l; and
3   for unrestricted irrigation, treated wastewaters contain ≤ 1000 *E Coli* per 100 ml, and ≤ 1 human intestinal nematode egg per litre or, if local children under 15 years are exposed, ≤ 0.1 egg/l.

1000 *E coli* per 100 ml

The guideline value of ≤ 1000 *E coli* per 100 ml created more than a little controversy when it was originally introduced in 1989 (see Shelef, 1991). It has to be asked, therefore, if 1000 *E coli* per 100 ml is sufficiently protective of consumers' health.

This is an important question to ask because:

• The State of California (1978*) requires ≤ 2.2 total coliforms per 100 ml for unrestricted irrigation;
• The World Health Organization (1973) required ≤ 100 *E coli* per 100 ml in 80 per cent of samples for unrestricted irrigation; and
• The US Environmental Protection Agency and the US Agency for International Development require zero *E coli* per 100 ml for unrestricted irrigation (and this is a recommendation not only for the US, but for developing countries as well) (Environmental Protection Agency, 1992 – these guidelines are currently under revision).

So is 1000 *E coli* per 100 ml acceptable? The answer to this question is *Yes*, because (Mara, 1995):

• In the US, river water can be used for unrestricted irrigation if it contains ≤ 1000 *E coli* per 100 ml (Environmental Protection Agency, 1973).
• In the European Union bathing (ie whole body immersion) is permitted if recreational waters contain ≤ 2000 *E coli* per 100 ml (Council of the European Communities, 1976 – this Directive is currently being revised).

- The International Commission on Microbiological Specifications for Foods (1974) allows foods eaten uncooked to contain up to 100,000 *E coli* per 100 g fresh weight, although preferably <1000.
- In the European Union, foods are permitted to contain high *E coli* and coliform numbers, for example, shellfish eaten raw (such as oysters) can contain up to 230 *E coli* per 100 g live weight, and dairy products are allowed to have high total coliform numbers: milk, 500/100 ml; butter, 1000/100 g; ice cream, 10,000/100 g; and soft cheese, 10,000,000/100 g; and 'hard cheese made from raw milk' can contain up to 10,000,000 *E coli*/100 g (Council of the European Communities, 1991b, 1992).
- In the United Kingdom ready-to-eat foods (sandwiches, salads, pizzas, desserts, etc) can contain up to 10,000 *E coli*/100 g (Gilbert et al, 2000*).
- Table 12.2 shows that when faecal coliform numbers are reduced in a series of waste stabilization ponds to 7000/100 ml, there are no salmonellae and no campylobacters, and only very low numbers of rotaviruses and other enteroviruses.
- Vaz da Costa Vargas and Mara (1988) found that local lettuce on sale in a market in Portugal contained around 1,000,000 faecal coliforms per 100 g, and the faecal coliform numbers on lettuce irrigated with conventionally treated wastewater containing 6×10^6 faecal coliforms per 100 ml fell to around 2×10^4 per 100 ml (ie better than the above ICMSF requirement) five days after irrigation ceased.
- Quantitative microbial risk analysis (discussed at the end of this chapter) shows that the health risks associated with irrigation with treated wastewater containing 1000 *E coli* per 100 ml are lower than the tolerable risk of infection of 10^{-3} per person per year from drinking fully treated drinking water (World Health Organization, 2003*).

So the WHO guideline level of no more than 1000 *E coli* per 100 ml is perfectly satisfactory. It has been accepted legally in France, for example (Conseil Supérieur d'Hygiène Publique, 1991; see also Faby et al, 1999*).

Water engineers, who are used to the requirement of zero *E coli* per 100 ml of treated drinking water, may instinctively think that 1000 *E coli* per 100 ml of irrigation water is simply too high. Yet as shown above, foods in industrialized countries are allowed to have higher numbers of coliforms and *E coli*. It is always worthwhile determining *E coli* numbers in or on foods, especially those eaten uncooked, which are on sale in local markets – water engineers (and indeed the local people) will be very surprised at the high levels commonly found.

Options for public health protection

The best option for public health protection is to treat wastewaters to the WHO guideline values given above, and this is most appropriately done in waste stabilization ponds (Chapters 9–12), wastewater storage and treatment reservoirs (Chapter 16), or other treatment processes (Chapters 17–20)

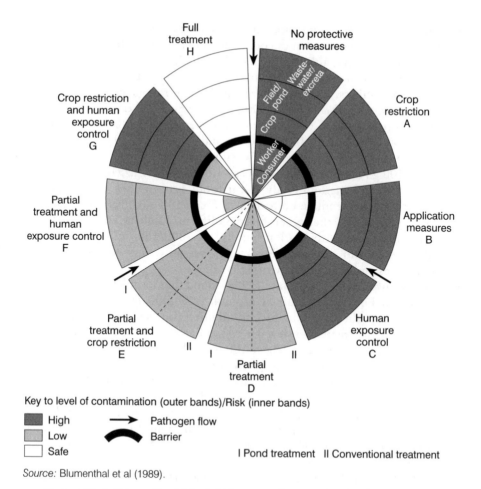

Figure 21.5 *Generalized Model Showing the Levels of Relative Risk to Human Health Associated with Different Combinations of Control Methods for the Use of Wastewater in Agriculture and Aquaculture*

supplemented with maturation ponds (Chapter 12). However, when 'full' treatment to the WHO guideline values is not possible for some reason (usually financial), then there are still ways in which public health can be protected. These are:

- partial treatment,
- crop restriction,
- the method of wastewater irrigation, and
- human exposure control.

These can be combined in various ways to protect the fieldworkers and/or the crop consumers, as shown in Figure 21.5.

Partial treatment and crop restriction

These two go together as partial treatment here means treatment to achieve ≤ 1 or ≤ 0.1 egg/l and $\leq 10^5$ *E coli*/100 ml – that is, for restricted irrigation. In fact this will often be the preferred level of treatment and re-use purpose as partial treatment obviously costs less than full treatment (ie to ≤ 1000 *E coli*/100 ml) (see the design example in Chapter 12). However, this must be agreed with the local farmers who have to undertake not to use the partially treated wastewater to irrigate salad crops and vegetables eaten uncooked (ie for unrestricted irrigation). Farmer participation in the whole wastewater re-use project cycle – planning, design, implementation and management – is essential for the success of re-use projects (see van Vuren, 1998). Engineers (and planners) clearly need to talk to farmers.

Method of wastewater application

The most common methods of wastewater application in developing countries are flood irrigation and furrow irrigation. Another method is 'localized' irrigation, a term which includes drip irrigation (also called trickle irrigation) and 'bubbler' irrigation. Drip irrigation is extremely economical with irrigation water: the wastewater is applied in plastic pipes fitted with emitter buttons from which the wastewater is intermittently discharged to wet only the root zone of the plants (Figure 21.6), so evaporative losses from the soil surface are minimized. It is a relatively expensive technology and can normally be justified only when irrigation water, including treated wastewater, is very scarce and therefore has a very high value. However, low-cost drip irrigation systems are being developed, at a cost of around one quarter of conventional systems, especially for small-scale farmers in developing countries (Polak et al, 1997*; see also Intermediate Technology Consultants, 2003*).

Drip irrigation with treated wastewater has the advantage over the other methods of wastewater application in that the World Health Organization (1989*, 2004*) does not specify any microbiological quality requirements for the treated wastewater when applied to the field in this way. There is a problem, however, with emitter clogging. This is commonly caused by soil algae (which are attracted to the emitter by the nutrients in the wastewater effluent), rather than the algae in waste stabilization pond effluents. Commercially available emitters vary in their clogging potential, and a careful choice of emitter has to be made when irrigating with treated wastewater (Taylor et al, 1995*).

Bubbler irrigation is especially useful for the wastewater irrigation of trees, such as fruit trees and nut trees. Instead of emitters, short vertical pipes are used; the height of these pipes decreases along the length of the distribution pipe to compensate for frictional head losses, so that each tree receives the same amount of treated wastewater (Hillel, 1987*).

Human exposure control

Fieldworkers (and their employers) need to be aware of the health risks associated with treated wastewater re-use. In particular, they should wear

Figure 21.6 *Drip Irrigation of Cotton with Maturation Pond Effluent at Nicosia, Cyprus*

rubber boots to protect themselves from hookworm infection, and they should have hand-washing facilities available to them as they leave the field. This is very important, although few employers provide either boots or hand-washing facilities, and few fieldworkers will wear boots (since it is easier to work barefoot in wet soils). However, they should be encouraged to do so, as a healthy workforce is a productive workforce.

Consumers can protect themselves by using hygienic food preparation practices: by cooking wastewater-irrigated vegetables and rigorously washing wastewater-irrigated crops eaten uncooked (salad crops, fruits and certain vegetables). Fruit and vegetable growers should also decontaminate their produce; advice is given by the World Health Organization (Beuchat, 1998*).

CROP HEALTH

Irrigation with wastewater can, at least potentially, damage crops. Compliance with the Food and Agriculture Organization's recommendations for the quality of *waters* used for irrigation (Ayers and Westcot, 1989*; see also Westcot, 1997*) will effectively eliminate such risks. For domestic wastewaters the most relevant FAO recommendations are for the following five parameters, and these need to be regularly checked during the irrigation season:

- electrical conductivity
- sodium absorption ratio
- boron concentration
- total nitrogen concentration
- pH.

Electrical conductivity

This is used as a measure of the dissolved salts concentration, which represents the 'salinity hazard'. Wastewaters contain more salts than drinking waters as we consume table salt (sodium chloride) far in excess of our physiological requirements. For safe irrigation (Figure 21.7) the electrical conductivity should be less than 75 mS/m at 20°C (the unit of conductivity is millisiemens per metre, though it is often expressed as decisiemens per cm, but this is not an SI preferred unit; it is necessary to specify the temperature of measurement as conductivity varies greatly with temperature).

Irrigation with wastewater that is too saline causes interference with the capacity of a plant's roots to absorb water and nutrients, and therefore reduces crop yields. Nevertheless, saline wastewaters can be used for irrigation even though the crop yield may be reduced (it is better to produce some crops than none), and certain crops commonly irrigated with treated wastewaters (for example, cotton) are tolerant of medium-to-high levels of salinity. For further details, the FAO review by Rhoades et al (1992*) should be consulted.

Sodium absorption ratio

This is used as a measure of the 'sodium hazard' of an irrigation water. The SAR, which is dimensionless, is defined as:

$$SAR = \frac{[Na^+]}{[0.5([Ca^+] + [Mg^{2+}])]^{0.5}}$$

(21.1)

where $[Ca^+]$, $[Mg^{2+}]$ and $[Na^+]$ are the concentrations of calcium, magnesium and sodium ions in the irrigation water, expressed in milliequivalents per litre. Concentrations of these ions in mg/l are converted to meq/l by multiplying by 0.050, 0.082 and 0.044 for calcium, magnesium and sodium, respectively.

For safe irrigation, the SAR should be less than 18 (Figure 21.7). Irrigation with waters with higher SAR values causes 'sodium saturation' of the soil: calcium and magnesium atoms in the clay minerals which make up the soil are displaced by sodium ions in the irrigation water, especially treated wastewater with its higher sodium levels than the local drinking water. Eventually the soil becomes saturated with sodium, and a sodium-saturated soil is difficult to work (when dry it forms hard unmanageable clods), its internal drainage is seriously affected, and the crops have difficulty in absorbing nutrients and water.

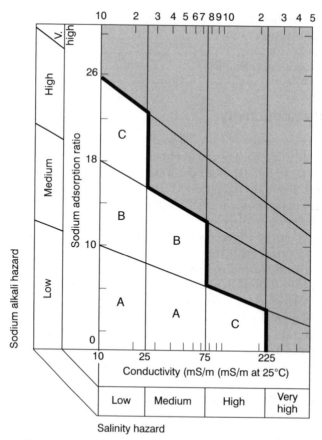

Note: Waters in regions A and B are acceptable for almost all irrigation purposes; those in regions C should be avoided wherever possible; and those in the shaded area should not be used at all.
Source: Adapted from United States Department of Agriculture (1954).

Figure 21.7 *Classification of Irrigation Waters Based on Conductivity and Sodium Absorption Ratio*

Boron

This element is present in wastewater from perborates in domestic detergents. Most crops are tolerant of 2 mg B/l, but citrus fruit trees and deciduous nut trees can only tolerate ~0.5 mg B/l (Table 21.2).

Total nitrogen

Too much nitrogen can reduce crop yields or cause crop damage. There may be a luxuriant growth of the non-useful parts of the crop (eg large green leaves on maize plants), or certain crops (eg lettuce) can suffer from 'leaf burn' –that is the edges of their leaves turn brown. Most crops can tolerate 30 mg total N/l, but some only 5 mg total N/l. Crop tolerances to total nitrogen are given in the FAO guidelines.

Table 21.2 *Recommended Maximum Concentrations of Boron in Irrigation Waters According to Crop Tolerance*

Boron concentration (mg B/l)	Crops
<0.5	Lemon, blackberry
0.50–0.75	Avocado, grapefruit, orange, apricot, peach, cherry, plum, fig, grape, walnut, pecan, cowpea, onion
0.75–1	Garlic, sweet potato, wheat, barley, sunflower, beans, strawberry, peanut
1–2	Sweet pepper, pea, carrot, radish, potato, cucumber
2–4	Lettuce, cabbage, celery, turnip, oats, maize, squash
>4	Sorghum, tomato, alfalfa, parsley, beetroot, sugar beet, cotton

Source: Ayers and Westcot (1989*)

pH

The permissible pH range for irrigation waters is 6.5–8.4, which does not present a problem for treated domestic wastewaters.

Industrial effluents

If municipal wastewaters with a high proportion of industrial effluents are to be re-used in agriculture, then a more detailed physicochemical analysis is necessary as crop health is affected by many more parameters (eg heavy metals – Table 21.3). The FAO guidelines should be consulted for further details (Ayres and Westcot, 1989*; Westcot, 1997*). However, heavy metal accumulation in crops irrigated with domestic wastewater in India has been found to be lower than permissible levels, despite the wastewater having been used for irrigation at the same site for ~30 years (Yadav et al, 2002*).

TREATMENT OPTIONS FOR RE-USE

Waste stabilization ponds (Chapters 9–12) and wastewater storage and treatment reservoirs (Chapter 16) are two excellent treatment options prior to wastewater re-use in agriculture. They can easily achieve the required microbiological quality and, when treating domestic wastewater, also achieve the required physicochemical qualities (Table 21.4). In the soil, the pond algae act as 'slow release' fertilizers and so contribute to increased crop yields and soil organic matter, thus improving the water-holding capacity of the soil.

Other treatment processes usually require additional treatment to achieve the required microbiological quality in, for example, maturation ponds

Table 21.3 *Recommended Maximum Metal Concentrations in Irrigation Waters*

Metal	Maximum concentration (mg/l)
Aluminium	5
Arsenic	0.1[a]
Beryllium	0.1
Cadmium	0.01
Cobalt	0.05
Chromium	0.1
Copper	0.2
Fluoride	1
Iron	5
Lead	5
Lithium	2[b]
Manganese	0.2
Molybdenum	0.01
Nickel	0.2
Selenium	0.1
Vanadium	0.02
Zinc	2

Notes:
[a] Toxic to rice at 0.05 mg/l
[b] Toxic to citrus fruits at 0.075 mg/l
Source: Ayers and Westcot (1989*)

(Chapter 12). There are other disinfection techniques, but these are not recommended as:

- in the case of ultra-violet disinfection, the high-intensity ultra-violet lamps are expensive imported items;
- in the case of chemical disinfection, the chemicals are expensive (eg ozone) or needed in high doses (eg up to 20 mg chlorine/l), and even then they will not be effective in reducing the numbers of helminth eggs and protozoan cysts;
- faecal bacterial regrowth may occur: a few resistant bacteria may survive to multiply in an environment that is much less competitive as most of the other faecal and non-faecal bacterial will have been killed; and
- environmentally harmful compounds can be produced, for example chlorinated organics, many of which are carcinogenic and/or teratogenic.

QUANTITATIVE MICROBIAL RISK ANALYSIS

Quantitative microbial risk analysis (QMRA) permits health risks – here risks from consuming wastewater-irrigated crops – to be calculated. The reference level of tolerable risk is that adopted by the World Health Organization for a

Table 21.4 *Physicochemical Quality of Three Waste Stabilization Pond Effluents in Israel*

Parameter	Pond A	Pond B	Pond C
Chloride (C1$^-$)	532	104	408
Bicarbonate (HCO$_3^-$)	176	320	677
Sulphate (SO$_3^{2-}$)	44	20	15
Boron (B)	Nil	0.1	0.3
Phosphorus (P)	1.6	Nil	9
Sodium (Na)	194	62	215
Calcium (Ca)	59	32	73
Magnesium (Mg)	292	47	122
SAR	3.4	1.6	3.9
pH	7.0	7.1	6.9

Note: Concentrations in mg/l, except SAR and pH
Source: Watson (1962)

person becoming ill with an excreta-related gastrointestinal infection (ie any of those in Categories I and II, Chapter 2) as a result of drinking fully treated drinking water. This tolerable risk is 10^{-3} per person per year, which means that an individual has a 1 in 1000 chance of becoming ill, or one person in a community of 1000 may become ill, from drinking fully treated drinking water over a 12-month period (World Health Organization, 2003*).

Of course, carefully obtained epidemiological evidence is best to assess the extent of actual health risks resulting from treated wastewater re-use. However, if the calculated risks from consuming wastewater-irrigated crops are less than 10^{-3} per person per year, we can safely assume that the risks are acceptable. If they are greater than 10^{-3} per person per year, then we might consider them too high. However, Haas (1996) has argued that even 10^{-3} is too low. It is certainly very low when compared with global diarrhoeal disease statistics: in developing countries the *actual* incidence of diarrhoeal disease (rather than infection) is ~1.3 per person per year, and in 'established market economy' countries it is ~0.2 per person per year (Murray and Lopez, 1996b; see also Wheeler et al, 1999*); in other words, in developing countries everybody has diarrhoea at least once a year, and even in industrialized countries individuals are at the high annual diarrhoeal disease risk of ~1 in 5.

Only an outline introduction to QMRA is given here. Comprehensive details are given by Haas et al (1999) and in Fewtrell and Bartram (2001*). A general introduction to risk perception is given in Slovic (2000).

Dose-response models

There are two dose-response models currently used: the exponential model and the β-Poisson model. Both are used to calculate first the risk of infection which results from ingesting a single dose d of a microbial pathogen, and then the annual risk resulting from multiple exposures to the dose d. Which model is used depends on the type of microbial pathogen: the exponential model is used for the protozoa *Cryptosporidium parvum* and *Giardia intestinalis* (also called *G lamblia*), and the β-Poisson model is used for the excreted viral and bacterial pathogens.

Exponential model

The basic equation for the exponential dose-response model is:

$$P_I(d) = 1 - \exp(-rd)$$

(21.2)

where $P_I(d)$ is the probability of an individual, or the probable proportion of a community, becoming infected after ingesting a singe dose of d excreted protozoan pathogens; and r is a dimensionless 'pathogen infectivity' constant. The value of r is 0.0042 for *Cryptosporidium* and 0.0199 for *Giardia* (Rose et al, 1991; Haas et al, 1999). When rd is small, equation 21.2 becomes:

$$P_I(d) = rd$$

(21.3)

Equation 21.2 can be rearranged to calculate the maximum dose corresponding to any given level of risk:

$$D = -r^{-1}\ln[1 - P_I(d)]$$

(21.4)

When $P_I(d) = 0.5$ (ie 50 per cent of the community is infected), d becomes N_{50}, the median infectious dose. From equation 21.4:

$$N_{50} = -r^{-1}\ln(0.5) = 0.69/r$$

(21.5)

β-Poisson model

The basic equation for the β-Poisson dose-response model is:

$$P_I(d) = 1 - [1 + (d/N_{50})(2^{1/\alpha} - 1)]^{-\alpha}$$

(21.6)

where α is a dimensionless pathogen infectivity constant. Values of N_{50} and α for selected excreted viral and bacterial pathogens are given in Table 21.5.

Equation 21.6 can be rewritten as:

$$d = \{[1 - P_I(d)]^{-1/\alpha} - 1\}\{N_{50}/(2^{1/\alpha} - 1)\}$$

(21.7)

Equations 21.2–21.7 are for a single exposure to the pathogen dose d.

Table 21.5 *Values of N_{50} and α for Selected Excreted Viral and Bacterial Pathogens*

Pathogen	N_{50}	α
Rotavirus	6.17	0.253
Campylobacter	896	0.145
Vibrio cholerae	243	0.25
Shigella	1120	0.21
Salmonella	23,600	0.313

Source: Haas et al (1999)

Multiple exposures

People regularly drink drinking water or eat wastewater-irrigated crops, so it is necessary to be able to calculate the annual risk of infection resulting from multiple, rather than single, exposures to the dose *d*.

The annual risk of infection per person from *n* exposures per year to a pathogen dose *d* is denoted by $P_{I(A)}(d)$, which is given by:

$$P_{I(A)}(d) = 1 - [1 - P_I(d)]^n$$

(21.8)

where $P_I(d)$ on the right-hand side of the equation is, as before, the risk of infection from a single exposure to the pathogen dose *d*; and *n* is the number of days in a year when a person is exposed to this single dose *d*. For drinking water *n* is 365 as people drink water every day; for wastewater-irrigated crops *n* could be 365 if the crops were eaten every day, but it could obviously be less, for example, 365/2 if the crops were eaten every second day.

The terms on the right-hand side of equation 21.8 are explained as follows:

- $[1 - P_I(d)]$ is the risk of *not* becoming infected from a single exposure to the dose *d*;
- $[1 - P_I(d)]^n$ is the risk of *not* becoming infected from *n* exposures to the dose *d*; and
- $1 - [1 - P_I(d)]^n$ is therefore the risk of *becoming* infected from *n* exposures to the dose *d*.

Infection and disease

Only a proportion of infected individuals will develop the disease:

$$P_D(d) = \gamma P_I(d)$$

(21.9)

where $P_D(d)$ is the probability of disease in an individual exposed to a single dose *d*; and γ is a constant with a value between 0 and 1.

Worked example

Shuval et al (1997*) used QMRA to calculate the risks associated with the consumption of salad crops irrigated with (a) untreated wastewater, (b) wastewater treated to the WHO guideline level of ≤1000 *E coli* per 100 ml, and (c) wastewater treated to the recommendation of the US Environmental Protection Agency and the US Agency for International Development of zero *E coli* per 100 ml (Environmental Protection Agency, 1992). They assumed that a person eats 100 g of wastewater-irrigated lettuce every second day; there is one virus per 10^5 *E coli*; and a 3-log pathogen die-off occurs between harvest and consumption. Laboratory tests indicated that the mean volume of wastewater remaining on 100 g of lettuce after irrigation was 10.8 ml.

Untreated wastewater

Untreated wastewater is taken to contain 10^7 *E coli* per 100 ml – that is, 10^5 per ml and therefore 10.8×10^5 *E coli* per 10.8 ml. This results in a count of $10.8 \times 10^5 \times 10^{-5}$ (ie 10.8) viruses per 100 g of lettuce at harvest, which is reduced by the 3-log die-off to 1.08×10^{-2} virus per 100 g lettuce at consumption. This is the single dose *d* to which an individual is exposed every second day – that is on 365/2 days per year.

For rotavirus infection equations 21.6 and 21.8, with N_{50} = 6.2 and α = 0.253, yield:

$$P_I(d) = 1 - [1 + (1.08 \times 10^{-2}/6.2) \ (2^{1/0.253} - 1)]^{-0.253}$$

$$= 6.3 \times 10^{-3}$$

$$P_{I(A)}(d) = 1 - [1 - (6.3 \times 10^{-3})]^{365/2}$$

$$= 0.68$$

This is much higher than WHO's tolerable risk of infection of 10^{-3} per person per year (but lower than the actual incidence of diarrhoeal disease in developing countries, which is ~1.3 per person per year).

Wastewater with 1000 *E coli* per 100 ml

The *E coli* and virus counts are now lower by a factor of 10^4 – that is, 100 g of lettuce contains 1.08×10^{-6} virus. The equations yield:

$$P_I(d) = 6.3 \times 10^{-7}$$

$$P_{I(A)}(d) = 1.2 \times 10^{-4}$$

that is *less* than the tolerable risk of infection of 10^{-3} per person per year.

Wastewater with 1 *E coli* per 100ml

Using an *E coli* count of 1/100 ml (rather than 0/100 ml), the resulting virus count per 100 g of lettuce is a thousand-fold less than in the second example – that is, 1.08×10^{-9}. The equations yield:

$$P_I(d) = 6.3 \times 10^{-10}$$

$$P_{I(A)}(d) = 1.2 \times 10^{-7}$$

that is excessively safe when compared with the tolerable risk of infection of 10^{-3} per person per year.

Shuval et al (1997*) calculated the additional costs of treating the wastewater to one *E coli* per 100 ml, rather than to 1000 *E coli* per 100 ml, and then the cost of each case of disease avoided: for rotavirus disease this was US$3.5 millions and for hepatitis A US$35 millions! Clearly such costs can never be justified, and the money would obviously be better spent on primary health care facilities (even hospitals).

The above worked example, assumes a constant *E coli*–virus ratio and a constant die-off between harvest and consumption, rather than a range of values for each parameter and multi-trial Monte Carlo simulations. Nevertheless it produces reasonably good order-of-magnitude estimates of risk. QMRA studies in the US, which included Monte Carlo simulations, have shown that the risks of viral infection were 10^{-3}–10^{-5} per person per year for consuming salad crops irrigated with a conventional (activated sludge) effluent; effluent disinfection (in this case with chlorine) reduced the risks to 10^{-7}–10^{-9} per person per year (Tanaka et al, 1998). Sleigh and Mara (2003b*) detail a 'freeware' computer program for Monte Carlo QMRA.

IRRIGATION WITH UNTREATED WASTEWATER

As noted earlier in this chapter, crop irrigation with untreated wastewater is common (see also Feenstra et al, 2000*; Ensink et al, 2002*; van der Hoek et al, 2002*; and, more generally, International Water Management Institute, 2003*). It is, in fact, more common than irrigation with treated wastewater as most wastewater in developing countries is not treated (Chapter 1) and many farmers only have untreated wastewater with which to irrigate their crops. The epidemiological evidence presented earlier in this chapter clearly shows that the resulting health risks are very high, and this is confirmed by the QMRA study of Shuval et al (1997*) referred to above. However, irrigation with untreated wastewater will not, of course, cease – at least not in the short to medium term. What, then, can be done to lessen these very high health risks?

This question was addressed in The Hyderabad Declaration on Wastewater Use in Agriculture of 14 November 2002 (Resource Centre on Urban Agriculture and Forestry, 2002*; see also Drechsel et al, 2002*). The Declaration notes that '*without proper management, wastewater use possesses* *serious risks to human health and the environment*', and recommends that, until treatment becomes feasible, guidelines should be developed '*for untreated wastewater use that safeguard livelihoods, public health and the environment*', together with the '*application of appropriate irrigation, agricultural, post-harvest and public health practices that limit risks to farming communities, vendors and consumers*'. Guidelines for the microbiological quality of treated wastewaters used for crop irrigation cannot, of course, be relaxed, and this means that the very high health risks resulting from irrigation with untreated wastewater have to be managed, at least to some degree, by other means (Figure 21.5; see also van der Hoek et al, 2002*). These include crop restriction (ie only restricted irrigation), human exposure control (footwear to avoid hookworm infection, and hand-washing to reduce bacterial, viral and Ascaris infections), keeping very young children away from the raw-wastewater-irrigated fields, and regular anti-helminthic chemotherapy (ie regular 'deworming') for fieldworkers and any exposed children.

Wastewater treatment should be gradually phased in, for example, primary treatment (in, for example, short-retention-time anaerobic ponds) should be implemented first as it is so very effective in reducing nematode egg counts (Chapter 11) and thus the health risks posed by these nematodes, and this is clearly much better than no treatment at all. Of course, municipal authorities may be reluctant or unable to invest in even primary treatment, but anaerobic ponds can fairly easily be excavated by farmers on a small part of their land (or they can group themselves into a cooperative for this purpose). The heath risks from irrigation with untreated wastewater *can* be managed, at least to some extent, but the farmers need to understand the risks, how their practices (eg not wearing anything on their feet, poor personal hygiene) aggravate these risks, and how relatively simple things can be done to reduce them. Diarrhoeal disease (due to all transmission routes, not just raw-wastewater irrigation) is likely to be high in poor farming communities, so interventions to improve water supplies, sanitation and hygiene will be required, in addition to specific improvements in irrigation practices, before any real health improvements become apparent.

22

Wastewater Re-use in Aquaculture

WHAT IS AQUACULTURE?

Aquaculture means 'water farming', just as agriculture means 'field farming', and so it encompasses fish culture and growing aquatic vegetables. The fish most frequently grown in aquaculture ponds are carp and tilapia. Local species should be grown – in India, for example, Indian major carp are mainly grown, such as catla (*Catla catla*), mrigal (*Cirrhina mrigala*) and rohu (*Labeo rohita*). Kolkata (formerly Calcutta) provides the world's largest example of wastewater-fed fisheries (Jana, 1998*; Nandeesha, 2002*): around 3500 ha of fishponds are fertilized with 550,000 m^3/day of untreated wastewater (Figure 22.1), and fish production (Indian major carp, with some tilapia and silver carp) is ~20 tonnes/day, equivalent to ~18 per cent of the city's demand for fish. The average fish yield is 4 t/ha year, although the better managed ponds produce 7–8 t/ha year. Some 17,000 local people work on the fishponds (Edwards, 2001*), and the fish sell for around US$1/kg – it is a highly profitable business.

In China and Indonesia where wastewater-fed (or excreta-fertilized) aquaculture has been practised for many hundreds of years, several carp species are often grown in the same pond (a practice known as 'polyculture'), with each species occupying a different ecological niche. The fish grown include bighead carp (*Aristichthys nobilis*), silver carp (*Hypophthalamichthys molitrix*), grass carp (*Ctenopharyngodon idellus*), and common carp (*Cyprinus carpio*).

Figure 22.1 *Some of the Kolkata East Wastewater-fed Fishponds*

Figure 22.2 *Harvesting Indian Major Carp from the Kolkata East Wastewater-fed Fishponds*

Tilapia are widely cultured throughout the developing world – they are even called 'aquatic chickens' as they are so easy to produce and they provide high-quality animal protein at an affordable price in many countries (Coward and Little, 2001*). The most commonly cultured species are Nile tilapia (*Oreochromis niloticus*) and Mozambican tilapia (*O mossambicus*). An improved strain of *O niloticus* has been developed through selective breeding by the World Fish Center – the so-called GIFT (genetically improved farmed tilapia) strain (Pullin et al, 1991; ICLARM, 2000). This grows ~60 per cent faster than other strains and can be harvested three times a year rather than twice. As yet there has been almost no work on growing the GIFT strain in wastewater-fed fishponds; clearly, given the popularity of tilapia as a high-protein food, this is an area of research urgently needed. Some initial work has been done in Ho Chi Minh City, Vietnam: polluted urban canal water, which is essentially septic tank effluents and untreated industrial wastewaters, is batch-fed into a shallow pond and left for seven days, when GIFT brood fish are introduced; the resulting young fish are raised to fingerling size after five weeks; they are then harvested and sold to local fish farmers for ~US$4/kg. A 1000 m^2 pond produces ~200 kg of fingerlings every 6–8 weeks. The fish farmers then raise the fingerlings intensively in freshwater ponds, using industrialized fish food, to marketable size (~250–350 g) within four months (Minh, 2002).

In Asia particularly, a wide range of aquatic vegetables is grown (not just watercress as in most industrialized countries), for example, water spinach (*Ipomoea aquatica*), water chestnut (*Eleocharis dulcis* and *E tuberosa*), water bamboo (*Zigania* spp), water calthrop (*Trapa* spp) and lotus (*Nelumbo nucifera*).

Extensive reviews of wastewater-fed aquaculture are given by Edwards and Pullin (1990) and Edwards (1992*, 1999*). Yan et al (1998*) note that wastewater-fed aquaculture complies with the fundamental Chinese philosophical principles of 'holism, harmony, self-resiliency, regeneration and circulation', and that its objectives are the conversion of wastes into usable resources (ie food), environmental protection (pollution being avoided by waste utilization), and sustainable development.

Hoan (1996) gives interesting data for Hanoi: in the Thanh Tri district of the city, the main wastewater-re-use area, a polyculture of tilapia, silver carp and two Indian major carp (mrigal and rohu) grown in wastewater-fed ponds yields ~5.6 t/ha year, compared with ~4.1 t/ha year from non-wastewater-fed ponds – a ~36 per cent increase due to the use of wastewater. There is a much greater profit (ie fish sales less all operating costs) from wastewater-fed ponds: US$1000/ha/year, compared with US$300 from non-wastewater-fed ponds – a 230 per cent increase, due in part to the higher fish yield but also because expensive fish food does not have to be purchased.

There has been a large research effort in Lima, Peru on growing tilapia in wastewater-fed ponds, including in the final maturation ponds at San Juan WSP site. Yields of fish grown in these maturation ponds (without supplementary feeding) are ~4.5 tonnes/ha per harvest, with two harvests per year (Cavallini, 1996*; Nava, 2001).

WASTEWATER-FED AQUACULTURE

As noted above, treated wastewater can be profitably used to fertilize fishponds and aquatic vegetable ponds. As with crop irrigation with treated wastewater (Chapter 21), the treated wastewater used for aquaculture must be of a minimum microbiological quality to ensure that the products of aquaculture (fish, aquatic vegetables) are safe and that there is no excess risk of infection to the aquaculture pond workers.

Microbiological quality guidelines

Human nematode infections (which are important in the case of wastewater re-use in agriculture) are not important in aquacultural re-use. Rather, it is the human trematode infections that are of major concern; these are the Category V water-based helminthic infections (Chapter 2), and the most important of these are:

- the human schistosomes or blood flukes, principally *Schistosoma mansoni*, *S haematobium* and *S japonicum*,
- the Oriental liver fluke, *Clonorichis sinensis*, and
- the giant intestinal fluke, *Fasciolopis buski*.

All these trematodes have an aquatic snail as their primary intermediate host. The schistosomes do not have a secondary host, but *Clonorchis* has fish (usually members of the carp family) and *Fasciolpsis* has aquatic vegetables as secondary hosts. Thus, in endemic areas, the schistosomes present a risk to the aquaculture pond workers, and the other two to the consumers of the aquaculture products. Cancer of the bile duct ('cholangiocarcinoma') is a not uncommon outcome of chronic clonorchiasis (Chapter 2; see also Wiwanitkit, 2003*) and this disease usually has a high prevalence whenever the local people eat uncooked fish grown in wastewater-fed fishponds.

Because these trematodes undergo massive asexual multiplication in aquatic snails (Chapter 2), the World Health Organization (1989*) microbiological quality guideline for aquaculture is:

> zero viable human trematode eggs per litre of treated wastewater.

The consumers also need protection against Category II bacterial diseases (Chapter 2), and the WHO guideline for this is:

> ≤1000 *E coli* per 100 ml of aquaculture pond water.

If the *E coli* count is above this guideline level, then there is a risk that bacterial pathogens will be present, not only on the skin of the fish, but also in their flesh and internal organs (Buras et al, 1987*; Pal, 1991). However, Cavallini (1996*), who investigated Nile tilapia grown in fishponds fed with waste stabilization pond effluents at the San Juan WSP site in Lima, Peru, found that pathogen-free fish were obtained when the fishpond waters contained up to 10^4 *E coli* per 100 ml – so there is a margin of safety in the WHO guideline (see also World Health Organization, 1995, 1999*). Hepher et al (1986) found that *E coli* die-off was higher when fish (tilapia) were present than when they were absent. [**Note added in proof:** The 2004 revised WHO bacterial guideline for *E coli* numbers in wastewater-fed fish ponds will be $\leq 10^4/100$ ml, rather than $\leq 1000/100$ ml as in the 1989 guidelines – a relaxation of an order of magnitude (see WHO, 2004*). In practice (and as shown in the Design Example on p260) this will make little or no difference to waste-water-fed fishponds designed on the basis of a total N loading of 4 kg/ha day.]

Buras et al (1987*) proposed that the sanitary quality of fish grown in wastewater-fed ponds should be assessed by the bacterial count per gram of fish muscle (ie flesh). For numbers of both total aerobic bacteria (ie the 'standard plate count' on nutrient agar at 35–37°C) and *E coli* the quality is interpreted as follows:

- 0–10 per g: Very good
- 11–30 per g: Medium
- 31–50 per g: Poor
- >50 per g: Unacceptable

WASTEWATER-FED FISHPOND DESIGN

The design procedure given here for wastewater-fed fishponds is based on the concept of *minimal* wastewater treatment for *maximal* production of microbiologically safe fish (Mara et al, 1993; Mara, 1997*). The design steps are as follows:

1   Design an anaerobic pond and a secondary facultative pond, as detailed in Chapters 10 and 11.
2   Use equation 12.12 to determine the total nitrogen concentration in the facultative pond effluent (C_e, mg N/1).
3   Design the wastewater-fed fishpond, which receives the facultative pond effluent, on the basis of a surface loading of total nitrogen (λ_s^{TN}) of 4 kg/ha day. (Too little nitrogen results in a low algal biomass in the fishpond and consequently small fish yields. Too much nitrogen gives rise to high concentrations of algae, with the resultant high risk of severe dissolved oxygen depletion at night and consequent fish kills. A loading of ~4 kg total N/ha day is optimal.)

The fishpond area (A_{fp}, m²) is given by the following version of equation 11.1:

$$A_{fp} = 10 C_e Q / \lambda_s^{TN}$$

$$(22.1)$$

Use equation 11.7 to calculate the retention time in the fishpond (θ_{fp}, days), with a fishpond depth of 1 m.

4   Use the following version of equation 12.3 to calculate the number of *E coli* per 100 ml of fishpond water (N_{fp}):

$$N_{fp} = N_i/(1 + k_T\theta_a)\,(1 + k_T\theta_f)\,(1 + k_T\theta_{fp})$$

(22.2)

N_{fp} should be $\leq$1000 per 100 ml. If it is not, increase θ_{fp} until it is (or consider having a maturation pond ahead of the fishpond).

5   Use equation 12.14 or equation 12.15 to determine the concentration of NH_3-N first in the facultative pond effluent (assume that the conversion of organic nitrogen in the anaerobic pond to ammonia produces an ammonia concentration in the effluent of the anaerobic pond – that is, in the influent to the facultative pond – equal to 75 per cent of the total nitrogen concentration in the raw wastewater), and then in the fishpond.

The ammonia concentration is the total concentration of NH_3 and NH_4^+ (ie 'free and saline' ammonia). In order to protect the fish from free ammonia (NH_3) toxicity, the concentration of NH_3 should be <0.5 mg N/1. The percentage (p) of free ammonia in aqueous solutions depends on temperature (T, K) and pH, as follows (Emerson et al, 1975; see also Erickson, 1985):

$$p = 100[10^{(pK_a-ph)} + 1]$$

(22.3)

where pK_a is given by:

$$pK_a = 0.09018 + (2729.92/T)$$

(22.4)

where T is the absolute temperature in degrees Kelvin (K = °C + 273).

Equations 22.3 and 22.4 (or Table 22.1 which is derived from them) should be used to determine the free ammonia concentration in the fishpond, assuming a pH of 7.0 (the pH range in wastewater-fed fishponds is usually 6.5–7.5).

Fish yields

Good fishpond management can be achieved by having small ponds, generally $\leq$1 ha, that can be stocked with fingerlings at the rate of 3/m^2, fertilized with facultative pond effluent and then harvested 3 months after stocking. During this time the fingerlings will have grown from ~20 g to ~200 g. Partially draining the pond will ensure that almost all the fish can be harvested. This

Table 22.1 *Percentage of Free Ammonia (NH₃) in Aqueous Ammonia* (NH_3) *in Aqueous Ammonia* (NH_3+NH_4) *Solutions at 10–25 °C and pH 7.0–8.5*

Temperature (°C)	Percentage of free ammonia in aqueous ammonia solutions at pH			
	7.0	7.5	8.0	8.5
10	0.186	0.586	1.83	5.56
11	0.201	0.633	1.97	5.99
12	0.217	0.684	2.13	6.44
13	0.235	0.738	2.30	6.92
14	0.253	0.796	2.48	7.43
15	0.273	0.859	2.67	7.97
16	0.294	0.295	2.87	8.54
17	0.317	0.996	3.08	9.14
18	0.342	1.07	3.31	9.78
19	0.368	1.15	3.56	10.50
20	0.396	1.24	3.82	11.20
21	0.425	1.33	4.10	11.90
22	0.457	1.43	4.39	12.70
23	0.491	1.54	4.70	13.50
24	0.527	1.65	5.03	14.40
25	0.566	1.77	5.38	15.30

Source: Emerson et al (1975)

cycle can be done two or three times per year. Allowing for a 30 per cent fish loss due to mortality, poaching and consumption by fish-eating birds, the annual yield is:

$$(3 \times 200 \text{ g fish per m}^2) (10^{-6} \text{ tonnes/g}) (10^4 \text{ m}^2/\text{ha}) \times (2\text{–}3 \text{ harvests per year}) \times$$
$$(0.7, \text{ to allow for the 30 per cent loss})$$

$$= 8\text{–}12 \text{ tonnes of fish per hectare per year.}$$

INTEGRATED AGRICULTURAL–AQUACULTURAL RE-USE

If there is a high local demand for fish, then it is often sensible to use treated wastewater in both agriculture and aquaculture (Food and Agriculture Organization, 2001). In practice this means first use the treated wastewater to grow fish and/or aquatic vegetables, and then use the effluent from the aquaculture ponds for crop irrigation. In Kolkata, for example, the fishpond effluent is used to cultivate rice; alternatively, fish can be grown in rice paddies (see Berg, 2002*). In the Zhujiang delta area in southern China crops such as sugar cane and mulberry bushes are grown on the fishpond embankments, and rice paddies are fertilized with fishpond effluents, in this centuries-old model of intensive integrated agriculture and aquaculture (Ruddle and Zhong, 1988).

DESIGN EXAMPLE

Design a wastewater-fed fishpond system to receive the effluent from the secondary facultative pond designed in Chapter 11. Take the total nitrogen and ammonia concentrations in the raw wastewater as 50 mg N/l and 30 mg N/l, respectively.

Solution

The anaerobic pond has an area of 3340 m² and a retention time of 1 day (Chapter 10), and the secondary facultative pond has an area of 26,500 m² and a retention time of 4 days (Chapter 12).

Fishpond area

Assuming no total nitrogen removal in the anaerobic pond and a pH of 7.5 in the facultative pond, the total nitrogen concentration in the effluent from the facultative pond is determined from equation 12.12:

$$C_e = C_i \exp\{-[\,0.0064(1.039)^{T-20}][\theta_f + 60.6(pH - 6.6)]\}$$

$$= 50 \exp\{-[0.0064(1.039)^{25-20}][4 + 60.6(7.5 - 6.6)]\}$$

$$= 32 \text{ mg total N/l.}$$

Using equation 22.1 the fishpond area is:

$$A_{fp} = 10C_e Q/\lambda_s^{TN}$$

$$= 10 \times 32 \times 10{,}000/4$$

$$= 800{,}000 \text{ m}^2 \ (80 \text{ ha})$$

Using equation 22.2, determine the number of E coli per 100 ml of fishpond water:

$$N_{fp} = N_i/(1 + k_T\theta_a)(1 + k_T\theta_f)(1 + k_T\theta_{fp})$$

The retention time in the fishpond is given by equation 11.7:

$$\theta_{fp} = 2A_{fp}D_{fp}/(2Q - 0.001eA_{fp})$$

With $D_{fp} = 1$ m and $e = 5$ mm/day:

$$\theta_{fp} = (2 \times 800{,}000 \times 1)/[(2 \times 10{,}000) - (0.001 \times 5 \times 800{,}000)]$$

$$= 100 \text{ days.}$$

E coli numbers

$$k_{B(T)} = 2.6\ (1.19)^{T-20}$$

$$= 6.2\ d^{-1}\ \text{for}\ T = 25°C$$

$$Nfp = 5 \times 10^7/[1 + (6.2 \times 1)][1 + (6.2 \times 4)][1 + (6.2 \times 100)]$$

$$= 430\ \text{per}\ 100\ \text{ml (satisfactory as} <1000)$$

Free ammonia

As $T = 25°C$, use equation 12.15 to determine the concentration of total ammonia in the facultative pond effluent:

$$C = C_i/\{1 + [5.035 \times 10^{-3}(A/Q)][\exp(1.540 \times (pH - 6.6))]\}$$

With $C_i = 0.75 \times 50 = 37.5$ mg/l and pH = 7.0:

$$C = 37.5/\{1 + [5.035 \times 10^{-3}(26\ 500/10,000)][\exp(1.540 \times (7.0 - 6.6))]\}$$

$$= 36.6\ \text{mg/l}$$

Note: this value is higher than the total N concentration determined above for the facultative pond effluent. This is an inherent problem with two empirical equations derived from different data sets. However, it is a conservative error since the free ammonia concentration is slightly overestimated.

The percentage of free ammonia is given by equations 22.3 and 22.4:

$$pK_a = 0.09018 + (2729.92/T)$$

$$= 0.09018 + [2729.92/(25 + 273)]$$

$$= 9.25$$

$$p = 100[10^{(pK_a-pH)} + 1]^{-1}$$

$$= 0.566\ \text{per cent}$$

Thus the concentration of free ammonia in the fishpond is 0.00566 x 36.6 = 0.21 mg N/l (satisfactory as <0.5 mg N/l).

Pond areas

- Anaerobic pond   3340 m²
- Facultative pond   26,500 m²
- Fishpond   800,000 m²
- Total   829,840 m²

Thus only 3.6 per cent of the total area is used for wastewater treatment.

References

Journal articles which are available on the Internet are marked (*) at the end of the reference, and the journal URLs are given at the end of this list.

Abderrahman, W A (2001) 'Water Demand Management in Saudi Arabia' in Faruqui, N I, Biswas, A K and Bino, M J (eds) *Water Management in Islam*, pp68–78, United Nations University Press, Tokyo

Abis, K and Mara, D D (2003) 'Research on Waste Stabilization Ponds in the United Kingdom – I. Initial Results from Pilot-scale Facultative Ponds', *Water Science and Technology*, vol 48, no 2, pp1–8 (*)

ABLB and CTGREF (1979) *Lagunage Naturel et Lagunage Aéré: Procédés d'Epuration des Petits Collectivités*, Agence de Bassin Loire–Bretagne and Centre Technique du Génie Rural, des Eaux et des Fôrets, Orléans

Adams, S M (2002) *Biological Indicators of Aquatic Ecosystem Health*, American Fisheries Society, Alpharetta, GA

Aeration Industries International, Inc (2002) *Aire-O_2 Triton Aerator/Mixer*, available at http://www.aiero2.com/triton.htm

Afsah, S, Laplante, B and Wheeler, D (1996) *Controlling Industrial Pollution: A New Paradigm*, Policy Research Working Paper no 1672, The World Bank, Washington, DC; available at http://www.worldbank.org/nipr/work_paper/1672/wp1672.pdf

Agency for International Development (1982) *Constructing Stabilization Ponds*, Water for the World Technical Note no SAN 2.C.5, Agency for International Development, Washington, DC; available at http://www.lifewater.org/wfw/san2/san2c5.pdf

Agunwamba, J C (2001) 'Analysis of Socioeconomic and Environmental Impacts of Waste Stabilization Pond and Unrestricted Wastewater Irrigation: Interface with maintenance', *Environmental Management*, vol 27, no 3, pp463–476 (*)

Agunwamba, J C (2002) 'Optimal Design for Dispersion Experiments', *Water Research*, vol 36, no 18, pp4570–4582 (*)

Akrivos, J, Mamais, D, Katsara, K and Andreakis, A (2000) 'Agricultural Utilization of Lime Treated Sewage Sludge', *Water Science and Technology*, vol 42, no 9, pp203–210 (*)

Al-Salem, A A and Lumbers, J P (1987) 'An Initial Evaluation of Al Samra Waste Stabilization Ponds (Jordan)', *Water Science and Technology*, vol 19, no 12, pp33–37

Albertson, O E (1995) 'Is $CBOD_5$ Test Viable for Raw and Settled Wastewater?', *Journal of Environmental Engineering, American Society of Civil Engineers*, vol 121, no 7, pp515–520 (*)

Amahmid, O, Asmama, S and Bouhoum, K (2002) 'Urban Wastewater Treatment in Stabilization Ponds: Occurrence and removal of pathogens', *Urban Water*, vol 4, no 3, pp255–262 (*)

American Public Health Association (1998) *Standard Methods for the Examination of Water and Wastewater*, 20th ed, American Public Health Association, Washington, DC; additional methods available at http//www.techstreet.com/stan_methgate.tmpl

Arceivala, S J (1981) *Wastewater Treatment and Disposal: Engineering and Ecology in Pollution Control*, Marcel Dekker, New York

Arceivala, S J and Alagarsamy, S R (1970) 'Design and Construction of Oxidation Ditches under Indian Conditions' in Sastry, C A (ed) *Low Cost Waste Treatment*, pp172–184, Central Public Health Engineering Research Institute, Nagpur

Archer, H E and Mara, D D (2003) 'Waste Stabilization Pond Developments in New Zealand', *Water Science and Technology*, vol 48, no 2, pp9–16 (*)

Arridge, H, Oragui, J I, Pearson, H W, Mara D D and Silva, S A (1995) '*Vibrio cholerae* O1 and Salmonellae Removal Compared with the Die-off of Faecal Indicator Bacteria in Waste Stabilization Ponds in Northeast Brazil', *Water Science and Technology*, vol 31, no 12, pp249–256 (*)

Arthur, J P (1983) *Notes on the Design and Operation of Waste Stabilization Ponds in Warm Climates of Developing Countries*, Technical Paper no 7, The World Bank, Washington, DC; available at: http://www-wds.worldbank.org/servlet/ WDS_IBank_Servlet?pcont=details&eid=000178830_98101904165457

Asano, T (1998) *Wastewater Reclamation and Reuse*, Technomic Publishing Co, Lancaster, PA

Asano, T (2002) 'Water from Wastewater – the Dependable Water Resource', *Water Science and Technology*, vol 45, no 8, pp23–33 (*)

Ayaz, S Ç and Akça, L (2001) 'Treatment of Wastewater by Natural Systems', *Environment International*, vol 26, no 3, pp189–195 (*)

Ayers, R S and Westcot, D W (1989) *Water Quality for Agriculture*, Irrigation and Drainage Paper no 29, rev 1, Food and Agriculture Organization, Rome; available at http://www.fao.org/docrep/003/T0234E/T0234E00.htm

Ayres, R M and Mara, D D (1996) *Analysis of Wastewater for Use in Agriculture: A Laboratory Manual of Parasitological and Bacteriological Techniques*, World Health Organization, Geneva; available at http://www.leeds.ac.uk/civil/ceri/water/tphe/ publicat/reuse/parasitanal.pdf

Ayres, R M, Alabaster, G P, Mara, D D and Lee, D L (1992) 'A Design Equation for Human Intestinal Nematode Egg Removal in Waste Stabilization Ponds', *Water Research*, vol 26, no 6, pp863–865 (*)

Baars, J K (1962) 'The Use of Oxidation Ditches for the Treatment of Sewage from Small Communities', *Bulletin of the World Health Organization*, vol 26, no 4, pp465–474

Baird, R B and Smith, R K (2002) *Third Century of Biochemical Oxygen Demand*, Water Environment Federation, Alexandria, VA

Baker, J M and Graves, QB (1968) 'Recent Approach to Trickling Filter Design', *Journal of the Sanitary Engineering Division, American Society of Civil Engineering*, vol 94, no SA1, pp65–84

Barbagallo, S, Cirelli, G L, Consoli, S and Somma, F (2003) 'Wastewater Quality Improvement through Storage: A case study in Sicily', *Water Science and Technology*, vol 47, no 7–8, pp169–176 (*)

Barnes, D, Forster, C F and Johnstone, D W M (1983) *Oxidation Ditches in Wastewater Treatment*, Pitman Books Ltd, London

Bastos, R K X and Mara, D D (1995) 'The Bacterial Quality of Salad Crops Drip- and Furrow-irrigated with Saste stabilization Pond Effluents: An evaluation of the WHO guidelines', *Water Science and Technology*, vol 31, no 12, pp425–430

Beach, M (2001) 'Water, Pollution and Public Health in China, *The Lancet*, vol 358, 1 September, p735 (*)

Beaumont, P (2000) 'The Quest for Water Efficiency – Restructuring of Water Use in the Middle East', *Water, Air and Soil Pollution*, vol 123, no 1–4, pp551–564 (*)

Ben Aim, R M and Semmens, M J (2003) 'Membrane Bioreactors for Wastewater Treatment and Reuse: A success story', *Waster Science and Technology*, vol 47, no 1, pp1–5 (*)

Berg, H (2002) 'Rice Monoculture and Integrated Rice–Fish Farming in the Mekong Delta, Vietnam: Economic and ecological considerations', *Ecological Economics*, vol 41, no 1, pp95–107 (*)

Berkman, D S, Lescano, A G, Gilman, R H, Lopez, S L and Black, M M (2002) 'Effects of Stunting, Diarrhoeal Disease, and Parasitic Infection during Infancy on Cognition in Late Childhood: A follow-up study', *The Lancet*, vol 359, no 9306, pp564–571 (*)

Bern, C, Hernandez, B, Lopez, M B and others (2000) 'Epidemiologic Studies of *Cyclospora cayetanensis* in Guatemala', *Emerging Infectious Diseases*, vol 6, no 6, pp766–774 (*)

Bernhard, C and Kirchgessner, N (1987) 'A Civil Engineer's Point of View on Watertightness and Clogging of Waste Stabilization Ponds', *Water Science and Technology*, vol 19, no 12, pp365–367

Bernhard, C and Degoutte, G (1990) *Le Génie Civil des Bassins de Lagunage Naturel*, Report no FNDAE/7, Centre National du Machinisme Agricole, du Génie Rural, des Eaux et des Fôrets, Anthony

Beuchat, L R (1998) *Surface Decontamination of Fruits and Vegetables Eaten Raw*, Report no WHO/FSF/FOS/98.2, World Health Organization, Geneva; available at http://www.who.int/fsf/Documents/Surface_decon.pdf

Bewicke, D and Potter, B A (1984) *Chlorella: The Emerald Food*, Ronin Publishing, Berkeley, CA

Bitton, G (2002) *Encyclopedia of Environmental Microbiology* (6 vols), John Wiley & Sons Inc, New York, NY

Blumenthal, U J and Peasey, A (2002) *Critical Review of Epidemiological Evidence of the Health Effects of Wastewater and Excreta Use in Agriculture*, London School of Hygiene and Tropical Medicine, London

Blumenthal, U J, Strauss, M, Mara, D D and Cairncross, S (1989) 'Generalised Model of the Effect of Different Control Measures in Reducing Health Risks from Waste Reuse', *Water Science and Technology*, vol 21, Brighton, pp567–577

Blumenthal, U J, Mara, D D, Peasey, A, Ruiz-Palacios, G and Stott, R (2000) 'Guidelines for the Microbiological Quality of Treated Wastewater Used in Agriculture: Recommendations for revising the WHO guidelines', *Bulletin of the World Health Organization*, vol 78, no 9, pp1104–1116 (*)

Blumenthal, U J, Cifuentes, E, Bennett, S, Quigley, M and Ruiz-Palacios, G (2001) 'The Risk of Enteric Infections Associated with Wastewater Reuse: The effect of season and degree of storage', *Transactions of the Royal Society of Tropical Medicine and Hygiene*, vol 95, no 2, pp131–137

Borsuk, M E and Stow, C A (2000) 'Bayesian Parameter Estimation in a Mixed-order Model of BOD Decay' *Water Research*, vol 34, no 6, pp1830–1836 (*)

Brainerd, E and Siegler, M V (2003) *The Economic Effects of the 1918 Influenza Epidemic*, Discussion paper no DP3791, Centre for Economic Policy Research, London; available at http://www.cepr.org.uk/pubs/dps/DP3791.asp

Broome, J M, Morris, P M and Nathambwe, J G (2003) 'Hybrid Treatment Systems – Anaerobic Ponds and Trickling Filters in Zimbabwe', *Water Science and Technology*, vol 48, no 2, pp349–356 (*)

Bruins, H J (1999) 'Drought Mitigation Policies: Wastewater Use, Energy and Food Provision in Urban and Peri-urban Africa' in Grossman, D, van den Berg, L M and

Ajaegbu, H I (eds) *Urban and Peri-Urban Agriculture in Africa*, pp257–266, Ashgate Publishing, Aldershot and Brookfield, VT

Bucksteeg, K (1987) 'German Experiences with Sewage Treatment Ponds', *Water Science and Technology*, vol 19, no 12, pp17–23

Buras, N, Duek, L, Niv, S, Hepher, B and Sandbank, E (1987) 'Microbiological Aspects of Fish Grown in Treated Wastewater', *Water Research*, vol 21, no 1, pp1–10 (*)

Burridge, S (2000) *Operational Experiences of Filter Fly Control within Southern Water*, MSc dissertation, Centre for Environmental Health Engineering, University of Surrey, Guildford

Butler, D and Graham, N J D (1995) 'Modelling Dry Weather Wastewater Flow in Sewer Networks', *Journal of Environmental Engineering, American Society of Civil Engineers*, vol 121, no 2, pp161–173 (*)

Campos, H M and von Sperling, M (1996) 'Estimation of Domestic Wastewater Characteristics in a Developing Country Based on Socio-economic Variables', *Water Science and Technology*, vol 34, no 3–4, pp71–79 (*)

Caribbean Environment Programme (2002) *Convention for the Protection and Development of the Marine Environment of the Wider Caribbean Region (and its three Protocols)*, Caribbean Environment Programme, Kingston; available at http://www.cep.unep.org

Catunda, P F C (1994) 'Post-treatment of UASB Effluent' in van Haandel, A C and Lettinga, G *Anaerobic Sewage Treatment: A Practical Guide for Regions with a Hot Climate*, pp162–199, John Wiley & Sons, Chichester

Catunda, P F C and van Haandel, A (1996) 'Improved Performance and Increased Applicability of Waste Stabilization Ponds by Pretreatment in a UASB Reactor', *Water Science and Technology*, vol 33, no 7, pp147–156 (*)

Cavalcanti, P F F, Medeiros, E J S, Silva, J K M and van Haandel, A (1999) 'Excess Sludge Discharge Frequency for UASB Reactors', *Water Science and Technology*, vol 40, no 8, pp211–220 (*)

Cavallini, J M (1996) *Aquaculture Using Treated Effluents from the San Juan Stabilization Ponds, Lima, Peru: Executive Summary*, 2nd ed, Report no OPS/CEPIS/PUB/96.21, CEPIS, Lima; available at http://www.cepis.org.pe/bvsaar/i/fulltext/aquaqulture/aquaqulture.pdf

Ceballos, B S O, Soares, N E, Moraes, M R, Catão, R M R and Konig, A (2003) 'Microbiological Aspects of an Urban River Used for Unrestricted Irrigation in the Semi-arid Region of North-east Brazil', *Water Science and Technology*, vol 47, no 3, pp51–57 (*)

Cemagref and Agences de l'Eau (1997) *Le Lagunage Naturel: Les Leçons Tirées de 15 Ans de Pratique en France*, Centre National du Machinisme Agricole, du Génie Rural, des Eaux et des Fôrets, Lyon

Central Pollution Control Board (1996) *Pollution Control Acts, Rules and Notifications Issued Thereunder*, 4th ed, Pollution Control Series no PCL/2/1992, vol 1, Central Pollution Control Board, New Delhi

Chan, M-S (1997) 'The Global Burden of Intestinal Nematode Infections – Fifty Years on', *Parasitology Today*, vol 13, no 11, pp438–443 (*)

Chang, I-S, le Clech, P, Jefferson, B and Judd, S (2002) 'Membrane Fouling in Membrane Bioreactors for Wastewater Treatment', *Journal of Environmental Engineering, American Society of Civil Engineers*, vol 128, no 11, pp1018–1029 (*)

Chart, H (1998) 'Toxigenic *Escherichia coli*', *Journal of Applied Microbiology*, vol 84, no S1, pp77S–86S (*)

Chaudhry, R, Premlatha, M M, Mohanty, S, Dhawan, B, Singh, K K and Dey, A B (2002) 'Emerging Leptospirosis, North India', *Emerging Infectious Diseases*, vol 8, no 12, pp1526–1527 (*)

Chin, J (2000) *Control of Communicable Diseases Manual*, 17th ed, American Public Health Association, Washington, DC

Chromagar (2002) *CHROMagar E Coli*, available at http://www.chromagar.com/products/ecoli.html

Clay, S, Hodgkinson, A, Upton, J and Green, M (1996) 'Developing Acceptable Sewage Screening Practices', *Water Science and Technology*, vol 33, no 12, pp229–234 (*)

Coker, A O, Isokpehi, R D, Thomas, B N, Amisu, K O and Obi, C L (2002) 'Human Campylobacteriosis in Developing Countries', *Emerging Infectious Diseases*, vol 8, no 3, pp237–243 (*)

Conseil Supérieur d'Hygiène Publique (1991) *Recommandations Sanitaires concernant l'Utilisation après Epuration des Eaux Residuaires Urbaines pour l'Irrigation des Cultures et des Espaces Verts*, Ministère de la Santé, Paris

Cook, G and Zumla, A I (2002) *Manson's Tropical Diseases*, 21st ed, Saunders/Elsevier Science, London

Corea, E J H (2001) *Appropriate Disposal of Sewage in Urban and Suburban Sri Lanka*, PhD thesis, University of Leeds, Leeds; available at http://www.leeds.ac.uk/civil/ceri/water/tphe/publicat/theses/corea/corea.html

Council of the European Communities (1976) 'Council Directive of 8 December 1975 Concerning the Quality of Bathing Water (76/160/EEC)', *Official Journal of the European Communities*, no L31, pp 1–7 (5 February); available at http://europa.eu.int/eur-lex/en/consleg/pdf/1976/en_1976L0160_do_001.pdf

Council of the European Communities (1979) 'Council Directive of 30 October 1979 on the Quality Required of Shellfish Waters (79/923/EEC)', *Official Journal of the European Communities*, no L281 pp 47–52 (10 November); available at http://europa.eu.int/eur-lex/en/consleg/pdf/1979/en_1979L0923_do_001.pdf

Council of the European Communities (1991a) 'Council Directive 91/271/EEC of 21 May 1991 Concerning Urban Waste Water Treatment', *Official Journal of the European Communities*, no L135, pp 40–52 (30 May); available at http://www.europa.eu.int/eur-lex/en/consleg/pdf/1991/en_1991L0271_do_001.pdf

Council of the European Communities (1991b) 'Council Directive of 15 July 1991 Laying Down the Health Conditions for the Production and Placing on the Market of Live Bivalve Molluscs (91/492/EEC)', *Official Journal of the European Communities*, no L268, pp1–14 (24 September)

Council of the European Communities (1992) 'Council Directive 92/46/EEC of 16 June 1992 Laying Down the Health Rules for the Production and Placing on the Market of Raw Milk, Heat-treated Milk and Milk-based Products', *Official Journal of the European Communities*, no L268, pp 1–32 (14 September)

Coward, K and Little, D C (2001) 'Culture of the "Aquatic Chicken": Present concerns and future prospects', *Biologist*, vol 48, no 1, pp12–16; available at http://www.iob.org/editorial_display.asp?edname=728.htm&cont_id=24

Craggs, R J, Davies-Colley, R J, Tanner, C C and Sukias, J P (2003) 'Advanced Pond System: Performance with high rate ponds of different depths and areas', *Water Science and Technology*, vol 48, no 2, pp259–268 (*)

Curtis, T P (1990) *Mechanisms of Removal of Faecal Coliforms from Waste Stabilization Ponds*, PhD thesis, University of Leeds, Leeds

Curtis, T P, Mara, D D and Silva, S A (1992a) 'Influence of pH, Oxygen and Humic Substances on Ability of Sunlight to Damage Faecal Coliforms in Waste Stabilization

Pond Water', *Applied and Environmental Microbiology*, vol 58, no 4, pp1335–1343 (* – abstract only)

Curtis, T P, Mara, D D, and Silva, S A (1992b) 'The Effect of Sunlight on Faecal Coliforms in Ponds: Implications for research and design', *Water Science and Technology*, vol 26, no 7–8, pp1729–1738

Curtis, T P, Mara, D D, Dixo, N G H and Silva, S A (1994) 'Light Penetration in Waste Stabilization Ponds', *Water Research*, vol 28, no 5, pp1031–1038

D'Arcy, B J, Todd, R B and Wither, A W (1999) 'Industrial Effluent Control and Waste Minimization: Case studies by UK regulators', *Water Science and Technology*, vol 39, no 10–11, pp281–287 (*)

Davies-Colley, R J, Donnison, A M and Speed, D J (2000) 'Towards a Mechanistic Understanding of Pond Disinfection', *Water Science and Technology*, vol 42, no 10–11, pp149–158 (*)

Dean, C and Horan, N J (1995) *Applications of UASB Technology in Mauritius*, Tropical Public Health Engineering Research Monograph no 7, University of Leeds, Leeds; abstract available at http://www.leeds.ac.uk/civil/ceri/water/tphe/publicat/monog/monog.html

DeGarie, C J, Crapper, T, Howe, B M, Burke, B F and McCarthy, P J (2000) 'Floating Geomembrane Covers for Odour Control and Biogas Collection and Utilization in Municipal Lagoons', *Water Science and Technology*, vol 42, no 10–11, pp291–298

Department of Energy (1993) *Alternative Wastewater Treatment: Advanced Integrated Pond Systems*, Office of Energy Efficiency and Renewable Energy, Department of Energy, Washington, DC

Department of the Environment and Department of Health (1990) Cryptosporidium *in Water Supplies: Report of the Group of Experts*, HMSO, London

De Pauw, N, Van Damme, D and Van der Veken, D (1999) *European Biotic Index Manual for Secondary Schools*, Universiteit Gent, Ghent

DHI Software (2002) *MIKE 11*, available at http://www.dhisoftware.com/mike11/Description/What_is_MIKE_11.htm

Dillon, P (2000) 'Water Reuse in Australia: Current status, projections and research' in Dillon, P J (ed) *Water Recycling Australia*, pp99–104, CSIRO Land & Water and Australian Water Association, Atarmon, NSW

Dobbins, W E (1964) 'BOD and Oxygen Relationships in Streams', *Journal of the Sanitary Engineering Division, American Society of Civil Engineers*, vol 90, no SA3, pp53–78

Dolan, R J (1995) 'Good Science and Compliance Decisions', *Water Environment Research*, vol 67, no 2, p252

Döller, P C, Dietrich, K, Fillipp, N and others (2002) 'Cyclosporiasis Outbreak in Germany Associated with the Consumption of Salad', *Emerging Infectious Diseases*, vol 8, no 9, pp783–788 (*)

Drakides, C and Trotouin, T (1991) *Etude Normative du Lagunage Naturel: Commentaires et Illustrations d'une Technique d'Epuration en Languedoc-Rousillon,* Verseau, Montpellier

Drechsel, P, Blumenthal, U J and Keraita, B (2002) 'Balancing Health and Livelihoods: Adjusting wastewater irrigation guidelines for resource-poor countries', *Urban Agriculture Magazine*, no 8, pp7–9 (*)

Dudgeon, D (2002) 'An Inventory of Riverine Biodiversity in Monsoonal Asia: Present status and conservation challenges', *Water Science and Technology*, vol 45, no 11, pp11–19 (*)

Duron, N S (1988) 'Mexican Experience in Using Sewage Effluent for Large Scale Irrigation' in Pescod, M B and Arar, A (eds) *Treatment and Use of Sewage Effluent for Irrigation*, pp249–257, Butterworths, London

Edberg, S C, Rice, E W, Karlin, R J and Allen, M J (2000) '*Escherichia coli*: The Best Biological Drinking Water Indicator for Public Health Protection', *Journal of Applied Microbiology*, supplement to vol 88, pp106S–116S (*)

Edwards, P (1992) *Reuse of Human Wastes in Aquaculture*, Water and Sanitation Report no 2, The World Bank, Washington, DC; available at http://www-wds.worldbank.org/servlet/WDS_Ibank_Servlet?pcont=details&eid=000009265_39 610030757

Edwards, P (1999) *Wastewater-fed Aquaculture: State of the Art*, Food and Agriculture Organization, Rome; available at http//www.fao.org/ag/ags/agsm/sada.asia/docs/doc/edwards1.doc

Edwards, P (2001) 'Public Health Issues of Wastewater-fed Aquaculture', *Urban Agriculture Magazine*, vol 1, no 3, pp20–22 (*)

Edwards, P and Pullin, R S V (1990) *Wastewater-fed Aquaculture*, Environmental Sanitation Information Center, Asian Institute of Technology, Bangkok

El-Gohary, F A and Nasr, F A (1999) 'Cost Effective Pre-treatment of Wastewater' *Water Science and Technology*, vol 39, no 5, pp97–103 (*)

El Sharkawi, F, El Sebaie, O, Hossam, A and Abdel Kerim, G (1995) 'Evaluation of Daqhala Wastewater Treatment Plant: Aerated lagoon and pond system', *Water Science and Technology*, vol 32, no 11, pp111–119 (*)

Emerson, K, Russo, R C, Lund, R E and Thurston, R T (1975) 'Aqueous Ammonia Equilibrium Calculations: Effect of pH and temperature', *Journal of the Fisheries Research Board of Canada*, vol 32, no 12, pp2379–2383

Englehardt, J D (1997) 'Bayesian Benefit–Risk Analysis for Sustainable Process Design' *Journal of Environmental Engineering, American Society of Civil Engineers*, vol 123, no 1, pp71–79 (*)

Engstrand, L (2001) '*Helicobacter* in Water and Waterborne Routes of Transmission', *Journal of Applied Microbiology*, vol 90, no S6, pp80S–84S (*)

Ensink, J H J, van der Hoek, W, Matsuno, Y, Munir, S and Aslam, M R (2002) *Use of Untreated Wastewater in Peri-Urban Agriculture in Pakistan: Risks and Opportunities*, Research Report no 64, International Water Management Institute, Colombo; available at http://www.iwmi.cgiar.org/pubs/pub064/Report64.pdf

Environment Agency (2002) *The Microbiology of Drinking Water (2002) – Methods for the Examination of Water and Associated Materials*, Standing Committee of Analysts, Environment Agency, Nottingham; available at http://www.dwi.gov.uk/regs/pdf/micro.htm

Environment Protection Agency (2002) *Wastewater Lagoon Construction*, Environment Protection Agency of South Australia, Adelaide, SA; available at http://www.environment.sa.gov.au/epa/pdfs/guide_lagoon.pdf

Environmental Protection Agency (1973) *Water Quality Criteria 1972*, Report no EPA-R3-73-003, Environmental Protection Agency, Washington, DC

Environmental Protection Agency (1977) *Upgrading Lagoons*, Report no EPA-625/4-73-001B, Environmental Protection Agency, Cincinnati, OH

Environmental Protection Agency (1983) *Design Manual: Municipal Wastewater Stabilization Ponds*, Report no EPA-625/1-83-015, Environmental Protection Agency, Cincinnati, OH

Environmental Protection Agency (1992) *Guidelines for Water Reuse*, Report EPA/625/R–92/004, Environmental Protection Agency, Washington, DC

Environmental Protection Agency (1993) *Constructed Wetlands for Wastewater Treatment and Wildlife Habitat: 17 Case Studies*, Report no 832-R-93-005, Office of Wastewater Management, Environmental Protection Agency, Washington DC; available at http://www.epa.gov/owow/wetlands/construc/content.html

Environmental Protection Agency (2000a) *Chemical Precipitation*, Wastewater Technology Fact Sheet, Environmental Protection Agency, Washington, DC; available at http://www.epa.gov/owm/mtb/chemical_precipitation.pdf

Environmental Protection Agency (2000b) *Oxidation Ditches*, Wastewater Technology Fact Sheet, Environmental Protection Agency, Washington, DC; available at http://www.epa.gov/owm/mtb/oxidation_ditch.pdf

Environmental Protection Agency (2001) *Queensland Water Recycling Strategy*, Environmental Protection Agency of Queensland, Brisbane, QLD; available at http://www.env.qld.gov.au/environment/environment/suswater/final_qwrs_strategy.pdf

Environmental Protection Agency (2002) *Rock Media Polishing Filter for Lagoons*, Wastewater Technology Fact Sheet, Environmental Protection Agency, Washington, DC; available at http://www.epa.gov/owm/mtb/polfilla.pdf

Erikson, R J (1985) 'An Evaluation of Mathematical Models for the Effects of pH and Temperature on Ammonia Toxicity to Aquatic Organisms', *Water Research,* vol 19, no 8, pp1047–1058

Esen, I I and Al-Shayji, Y (1999) 'Estimation of Dispersion Number in Waste Stabilization Ponds', *Water Science and Technology*, vol 40, no 7, pp41–46 (*)

Faby, J A, Brissaud, F and Bontoux, J (1999) 'Wastewater Reuse in France: Water quality standards and wastewater treatment technologies', *Water Science and Technology*, vol 40, no 4–5, pp37–42 (*)

Farooq, S and Ansari, Z I (1983) 'Water Use in Muslim Countries – An Islamic Perspective', *Environmental Management*, vol 7, no 2, pp119–123

Fattal, B, Yekutiel, P and Shuval, H I (1986) 'Cholera Outbreak in Jerusalem 1970 Revisited: The case for transmission by wastewater irrigated vegetables' in Goldsmith, J R (ed) *Environmental Epidemiology*, pp49–59, CRC Press, Boca Raton, FL

Favorov, M O and Margolis, H S (1999) 'Hepatitis E virus Infection: An enterically transmitted cause of hepatitis' in Scheld, W M, Craig, W A and Hughes, J M (eds) *Emerging Infections 3*, pp1–16, ASM Press, Washington, DC

Feachem, R, Bradley, D, Garelick, H and Mara, D D (1983) *Sanitation and Disease: Health Aspects of Excreta and Wastewater Management*, John Wiley & Sons, Chichester; available at http://www.leeds.ac.uk/civil/ceri/water/tphe/publicat/watsan/sandis/sandis.html

Feenstra, S, Hussain, R and van der Hoek, W (2000) *Health Risks of Irrigation with Untreated Urban Wastewater in the Southern Punjab, Pakistan*, Report no 107, Institute of Public Health and International Water Management Institute, Lahore; available at http://www.iwmi.cgiar.org/health/wastew/R-107.pdf

Feitelson, E and Chenowith, J (2002) 'Water Poverty: Towards a meaningful indicator', *Water Policy*, vol 4, no 3, pp263–281 (*)

Fewtrell, L and Bartram, J (2001) *Water Quality: Guidelines, Standards and Health*, IWA Publishing, London; available at http://www.who.int/water_sanitation_health/Documents/IWA/iwabooktoc.htm

Field, J and Sierra, R (2002) *Anaerobic Granular Sludge Bed Technology*, available at http://www.uasb.org

Food and Agriculture Organization (2001) *Integrated Agriculture–Aquaculture*, Fisheries Technical Paper no 407, Food and Agriculture Organization, Rome

Foresti, E (2002) 'Anaerobic Treatment of Domestic Sewage: Established technologies and perspectives', *Water Science and Technology*, vol 45, no 10, pp181–186 (*)

Franci, R (1999) *Gerenciamento do Lodo de Lagoas de Estabilização não Mecanizadas*, Associação Brasileira de Engenharia Sanitária e Ambiental, Rio de Janeiro

Frederick-van Genderen, G (1995) *The Performance of Full-scale Waste Stabilization Ponds Treating Saline Wastewater*, PhD thesis, University of Surrey, Guildford

Frenck, R W and Clemens, J (2003) '*Helicobacter* in the Developing World', *Microbes and Infection*, vol 5, no 8, pp705–713 (*)

Friedler, E (2001) 'Water Reuse – An Integral Part of Water Resources Management: Israel as a case study', *Water Policy*, vol 3, no 1, pp29–39 (*)

Friedler, E, Juanicó, M and Shelef, G (2003) 'Simulation Model of Wastewater Stabilization Reservoirs', *Ecological Engineering*, vol 20, no 2, pp121–145 (*)

Future Harvest (2001) 'Wastewater Irrigation: Economic necessity or threat to health and environment,' available at http://www.futureharvest.org/earth/wastewater.shtml

Gambrill, M P (1990) *Physicochemical Treatment of Tropical Wastewater*, PhD thesis, University of Leeds, Leeds

Gameson, A L and Wheatland, A B (1958) 'The Ultimate Oxygen Demand and Course of Oxidation of Sewage Effluents', *Journal and Proceedings of the Institute of Sewage Purification*, no 2, pp106–119

Gawasiri, C M (2003) *Modern Design of Waste Stabilization Ponds in Warm Climates: Comparison with Traditional Design Methods*, MSc(Eng) dissertation, School of Civil Engineering, University of Leeds, Leeds

Gelda, R K, Auer, M T, Effler, SW, Chapra, S C and Storey, M (1996) 'Determination of Reaeration Coefficients: Whole-lake Approach', *Journal of Environmental Engineering, American Society of Civil Engineers*, vol 122, no 4, pp269–275 (*)

Gijzen, H J (2002) 'Anaerobic Digestion for Sustainable Development: A natural approach' *Water Science and Technology*, vol 45, no 10, pp321–328 (*)

Gilbert, R J, de Louvois, J and Donovan, T (2000) 'Guidelines for the Microbiological Quality of Some Ready-to-eat Foods Sampled at the Point of Sale', *Communicable Disease and Public Health*, vol 3, no 3, pp163–167 (*)

Girgin, S, Kazanci, N and Dügel, M (2003) 'Ordination and Classification of Macroinvertebrates and Environmental Data of a Stream in Turkey', *Water Science and Technology*, vol 47, no 7–8, pp133–139 (*)

Gloyna, E F and Espino, E (1969) 'Sulfide Production in Waste Stabilization Ponds' *Journal of the Sanitary Engineering Division, American Society of Civil Engineers*, vol 95, no SA3, pp607–628

Gotaas, J B (1956) *Composting: Sanitary Disposal and Reclamation of Organic Wastes*, World Health Organization, Geneva

Grace, R A (1978) *Marine Outfall Systems: Planning, Design, and Construction*, Prentice-Hall Inc, Englewood Cliff, NJ

Greenwood-Smith, S L (2002) 'The Use of Rapid Environmental Assessment Techniques to Monitor the Health of Australian Rivers', *Water Science and Technology*, vol 45, no 11, pp155–160 (*)

Grimason, A M, Smith, H V, Thitai, W N, Smith, P G, Jackson, M H and Girdwood, R W A (1993) 'Occurrence and Removal of *Cryptosporidium* spp oocysts and *Giardia* spp Cysts in Kenyan Waste Stabilization Ponds', *Water Science and Technology*, vol 27, no 3–4, pp97–104

Gu, R and Stefan, H G (1995) 'Stratification Dynamics in Wastewater Stabilization Ponds', *Water Research*, vol 29, no 8, pp1909–1923 (*)

Gunnerson, C G (1988) *Wastewater Management for Coastal Cities: The Ocean Disposal Option*, Technical Paper no 77, The World Bank, Washington, DC;

available at http://www-wds.worldbank.org/servlet/WDS_Ibank_Servlet?pcont= details&eid=000178830_9811904165665

Gupta, R S (2000) 'The Natural Evolutionary Relationships among Prokaryotes', *Critical Reviews in Microbiology*, vol 26, no 2, pp111–131 (*)

Haas, C N (1996) 'Viewpoint: Acceptable health risk', *Journal of the American Water Works Association*, vol 88, no 12, p8

Haas, C N, Rose, J B and Gerba, C P (1999) *Quantitative Microbial Risk Analysis*, John Wiley & Sons, New York

Haberl, R (1999) 'Constructed Wetlands: A chance to solve wastewater problems in developing countries', *Water Science and Technology*, vol 40, no 3, pp11–17 (*)

Hadden, R D M and Gregson, N A (2001) 'Guillain-Barré Syndrome and *Campylobacter jejuni* Infection', *Journal of Applied Microbiology*, vol 90, no S6, pp145S–154S (*)

Hall, D O and Rao, K K (1999) *Photosynthesis*, 6th ed, Cambridge University Press, Cambridge

Harleman, D R F and Murcott, S (1999) 'The Role of Physical-chemical Wastewater Treatment in the Mega-cities of the Developing World', *Water Science and Technology*, vol 40, no 4–5, pp75–80 (*)

Hepher, B, Sandbank, E, Shroeder, G L and others (1986), 'Wastewater Reclamation (global) Israel' in Zandstra, I (ed) *Reclamation of Nutrients, Water and Energy from Wastes: A Review of Selected IDRC-supported Research*, pp49–72, Report no IDRC-MR124e, International Development Research Centre, Ottawa

Heritage, J, Evans, E G V and Killington, R A (1996) *Introductory Microbiology*, Studies in Biology Series, Cambridge University Press, Cambridge

Heritage, J, Evans, E G V and Killington, R A (1999) *Microbiology in Action*, Studies in Biology Series, Cambridge University Press, Cambridge

Hillel, D (1987) *The Efficient Use of Water in Irrigation: Principles and Practices for Improving Irrigation in Arid and Semiarid Regions*, Technical Paper no 64, The World Bank, Washington, DC; available at http://www-wds.worldbank.org/servlet/ WDS_IBank_Servlet?pcont=details&eid=000178830_98101904165352

Ho, A Y, Lopez, A S, Eberhart, M G and others (2002) 'Outbreak of Cyclosporiasis Associated with Imported Raspberries, Philadelphia, Pennsylvania, 2000', *Emerging Infectious Diseases*, vol 8, no 8, pp783–788 (*)

Hoan, V Q (1996) *Wastewater Reuse through Aquaculture in Hanoi: Status and Practices*, MSc dissertation, Asian Institute of Technology, Bangkok

Horan, N J (1990) *Biological Wastewater Treatment Systems: Theory and Operation*, John Wiley & Sons, Chichester

Huang, J, Renau Jr, R B and Hagedorn, C (2000) 'Nitrogen Removal in Constructed Wetlands Employed to Treat Domestic Wastewater', *Water Research*, vol 34, no 9, pp2582–2588 (*)

Hunt, C E (2003) *Thirsty Planet: Strategies for Sustainable Water Management*, Zed Books, London

Hunter, P R (2003) 'Drinking Water and Diarrhoeal Disease due to *Escherichia coli*', *Journal of Water and Health*, vol 1, no 2, pp65–72 (*)

Hurse, T J and Connor, M A (1999) 'Nitrogen Removal from Wastewater Treatment Lagoons', *Water Science and Technology*, vol 39, no 6, pp191–198 (*)

Hurst, C J, Crawford, R L, Knudsen, G R, McInerney, M J and Stenzenbach, L D (2001) *Manual of Environmental Microbiology*, 2nd ed, American Society for Microbiology Press, Washington, DC

ICLARM (2000) 'Improving the Productivity of Tilapia Farming in Asia', *ICLARM Impacts*, vol 1, no 2, pp3–6

Institution of Civil Engineers (1989) *Long Sea Outfalls*, Thomas Telford, London

Institution of Water and Environmental Management (1988) *Biological Filtration*, Institution of Water and Environmental Management, London

Institution of Water and Environmental Management (1992) *Preliminary Processes*, 3rd ed, Institution of Water and Environmental Management, London.

Intermediate Technology Consultants (2003) *Low Cost Micro Irrigation Technologies for the Poor*, Intermediate Technology Consultants, Rugby; available at http://itcltd.com/docs/amit%20final%20report%20-%20final.pdf

International Agency for Research on Cancer (1994) *IARC Monographs on the Evaluation of Carcinogenic Risks to Humans _ vol 61: Schistosomes, Liver Flukes and* Helicobacter pylori, International Agency for Research on Cancer, Lyon

International Commission on Microbiological Specifications for Foods (1974) *Microorganisms in Food: 2 – Sampling for Microbiological Analysis: Principles and Scientific Applications*, University of Toronto Press, Toronto

International Water Management Institute (2003) 'Reuse of Wastewater in Agriculture', available at http://www.iwmi.cgiar.org/health/wastew/index.htm

Iqbal, S (1999) *Duckweed Aquaculture: Potentials, Possibilities and Limitations for Combined Wastewater Treatment and Animal Feed Production in Developing Countries,* Report no 6/99, Sandec, Dübendorf; available at http://www.sandec.ch/files/duckweed.pdf

IWA Specialist Group (2000) *Constructed Wetlands for Pollution Control: Processes, Performance, Design and Operation*, IWA Publishing, London

IWA Task Group (2001) *River Water Quality Model No. 1*, IWA Publishing, London

Jana, B B (1998) 'Sewage-fed Aquaculture: The Calcutta model', *Ecological Engineering*, vol 11, no1, pp73–85 (*)

Jasuja, M (2002) *Water Supply & Sanitation Coverage in UNEP Regional Seas: Need for Regional Wastewater Emissions Targets?* United Nations Environment Programme, The Hague; available at http://www.gpa.unep.org/documents/RS%20Sanitation%20&%20WET%20draft%20 report.pdf

Jiménez, B, Barrios, J A and Andreoli, C (2002) 'Biosolids Management in Developing Countries: Experiences in Mexico and Brazil', *Water21*, August, pp56–58

Jiménez-Cisneros, B E, Maya-Rendón, C and Salgado-Velázquez, G (2001) 'The Elimination of Helminth Ova, Faecal Coliforms, *Salmonella*, and Protozoan Cysts by Various Physicochemical Processes in Wastewater and Sludge', *Water Science and Technology*, vol 43, no 12, pp179–182 (*)

Johnson, M and Mara, D D (2002) 'Research on Waste Stabilization Ponds in the United Kingdom – II. Initial Results from Pilot-scale Maturation Ponds, Reedbed Channel and Rock Filters', in *Pond Technology for the New Millennium*, pp11–18, New Zealand Water and Wastes Association, Auckland

Johnstone, D J and Horan, N J (1994) 'Standards, Costs and Benefits: An international perspective', *Journal of the Institution of Water and Environmental Management*, vol 8, no 5, pp 450–458

Johnstone, D J and Horan, N J (1996) 'Institutional Developments, Standards and River Quality: A UK history and some lessons for industrializing countries', *Water Science and Technology*, vol 33, no 3, pp 211–222 (*)

Johnstone, D W M and Norton, M R (2000) 'Development of Standards and Their Economic Achievement and Regulation in the 21st Century' in Horan, N J and Haig, M (eds) *Wastewater Treatment: Standards and Technologies to Meet the Challenges of the 21st Century*, Proceedings of the CIWEM and AquaEnviro Technology Transfer Joint Millennium Conference, vol 1, pp45–52, Terence Dalton Publishers, London

Jones, K (2001) 'Campylobacters in Water, Sewage and the Environment', *Journal of Applied Microbiology*, vol 90, no S6, pp68S–79S (*)

Jones & Attwood Ltd (2002) 'Jeta Grit Removal Systems' available at http://www.jones-attwood.com/jeta.pdf; 'Filtech Screens', available at http://www.jones-attwood.com/filtech.pdf; 'Wash-flow', available at http://www.jones-attwood.com/washflow.pdf

Juanicó, M (1996) 'The Performance of Batch Stabilization Reservoirs for Wastewater Treatment, Storage and Reuse in Israel', *Water Science and Technology*, vol 33, no 10/11, pp149–159 (*)

Juanicó, M and Shelef, G (1991) 'The Performance of Stabilization Reservoirs as a Function of Design and Operation Parameters', *Water Science and Technology*, vol 23, no 7–8, pp1509–1516

Juanicó, M and Shelef, G (1994) 'Design Operation and Performance of Stabilization Reservoirs for Wastewater Irrigation in Israel', *Water Research*, vol 28, no 1, pp175–186

Juanicó, M and Dor, I (1999) *Hypertrophic Reservoirs for Wastewater Storage and Reuse: Ecology, Performance, and Engineering Design*, Springer Verlag, Heidelberg

Juanicó M, Weinberg, H and Soto, N (2000) 'Process Design of Waste Stabilization Ponds at High Altitude in Bolivia', *Water Science and Technology*, vol 42, no 10–11, pp307–313 (*)

Juwarkar, A S, Oke, B, Juwarkar, A and Patnaik, S M (1995) 'Domestic Wastewater Treatment through Constructed Wetlands in India', *Water Science and Technology*, vol 32, no 3, pp291–294 (*)

Kalbermatten, J M, Julius, D S, Gunnerson, C and Mara, D D (1982) *Appropriate Sanitation Alternatives: A Planning and Design Manual* (Chapter 4: Economic Analysis), Johns Hopkins University Press, Baltimore, MD; available at http://www-wds.worldbank.org/servlet/WDS_Ibank_Servlet?pcont=details&eid=000178830_98 101911364168

Kayombo, S, Mbwette, T S A, Mayo, A W, Katima, J H Y and Jørgensen, S E (2002) 'Diurnal Cycles of Variation of Physical-chemical Parameters in Waste Stabilization Ponds', *Ecological Engineering*, vol 18, no 3, pp287–291 (*)

Kayombo, S, Mbwette, T S A, Mayo, A W, Katima, J H Y and Jørgensen, S E (2003) 'Effects of Substrate Concentrations on the Growth of Heterotrophic Bacteria and Algae in Secondary Facultative Ponds', *Water Research*, vol 37, no 12, pp2937–2943 (*)

Kirk, J T O (1994) *Light and Photosynthesis in Aquatic Ecosystems*, 2nd ed, Cambridge University Press, Cambridge

Kivaisi, A K (2001) 'The Potential for Constructed Wetlands for Wastewater Treatment and Reuse in Developing Countries: A review', *Ecological Engineering*, vol 16, no 4, pp545–560 (*)

Klock, J W (1971) 'Survival of Coliform Bacteria in Wastewater Treatment Lagoons', *Journal of the Water Pollution Control Federation*, vol 43, no 10, pp2071–2083

Koch, A L (2003) 'Development of the Sacculus Marked Emergence of the Bacteria', *American Society for Microbiology News*, vol 69, no 5, pp229–233

Kontos, N and Asano, T (1996) 'Environmental Assessment for Wastewater Reclamation and Reuse Projects', *Water Science and Technology*, vol 33, no 10–11, pp473–486 (*)

Kouraa, A, Fethi, F, Fahde, A, Lahlou, A and Ouazzani, N (2002) 'Reuse of Urban Wastewater treated by a Combined Stabilization Pond System in Benslimane (Morocco)', *Urban Water*, vol 4, no 4, pp373–378 (*)

Lai, P C C and Lam, P K S (1997) 'Major Pathways for Nitrogen Removal in Wastewater Stabilization Ponds', *Water, Air and Soil Pollution*, vol 94, no 1–2, pp125–136 (*)

The Lancet (2002) 'The Economics of HIV in Africa', *The Lancet*, vol 360, no 9326, p1 (*)

Lawty, R, Ashworth, J de B and Mara, D D (1996) 'Waste Stabilization Pond Decommissioning: A painful but necessary decision', *Water Science and Technology*, vol 33, no 7, pp107–115 (*)

Leclerc, H, Mossel, D A A, Edberg, S C and Struijk, C B (2001) 'Advances in the Bacteriology of the Coliform Group: Their suitability as markers of microbial water safety', *Annual Review of Microbiology*, vol 55, pp201–234 (*)

Lens, P, Zeeman, G and Lettinga, G (2001) *Decentralized Sanitation and Reuse*, IWA Publishing, London; available at http://www.iwaponline.com/wio/2002/04/default001.htm

Levenspiel, O (1998) *Chemical Reaction Engineering*, 3rd ed, John Wiley & Sons, New York

Ligman, K, Hutzler, N and Boyle, W C (1974) 'Household Wastewater Characterization', *Journal of the Environmental Engineering Division, American Society of Civil Engineers*, vol 100, no EE1, pp 201–213

Liran, A, Juanicó, M and Shelef, G (1994) 'Coliform Removal in a Stabilization Reservoir for Wastewater Irrigation in Israel', *Water Research*, vol 28, no 6, pp1305–1314

Lloyd, B J, Vorkas, C A and Guganesharajah, R K (2003) 'Reducing Hydraulic Short-circuiting in Maturation Ponds to Maximize Pathogen Removal Using Channels and Wind Breaks', *Water Science and Technology*, vol 48, no 2, pp153–162 (*)

Madhou, M (2002) *Development of Water Quality Indexing Systems for Riverine Ecosystems of Mauritius*, MPhil thesis, University of Mauritius, Réduit

Malan, W M (1964) *A Guide to the Use of Septic Tank Systems in South Africa*, CSIR Report no 219, National Institute for Water Research, Pretoria

Mantilla M G, Moeller Ch G, Flores B R and Pozo R F (2002) 'The Performance of Waste Stabilization Ponds in Mexico', in *Pond Technology for the New Millennium*, pp69–73, New Zealand Water and Wastes Association, Auckland

Mara, D D (1976) *Sewage Treatment in Hot Climates*, John Wiley & Sons, Chichester

Mara, D D (1987) 'Waste Stabilization Ponds: Problems and controversies' *Water Quality International*, no 1, pp20–22

Mara, D D (1995) 'Faecal Coliforms – Everywhere (but not a cell to drink)', *Water Quality International*, no 3, pp29–30

Mara, D D (1996) 'Waste Stabilization Ponds: Effluent quality requirements and implications for process design', *Water Science and Technology*, vol 33, no 7, pp23–31 (*)

Mara, D D (1997) *Design Manual for Waste Stabilization Ponds in India*, Lagoon Technology International, Leeds; available at http://www.leeds.ac.uk/civil/ceri/water/tphe/publicat/pdm/indiaall.pdf

Mara, D D (2003) *Design Manual for Waste Stabilization Ponds in the United Kingdom*, School of Civil Engineering, University of Leeds, Leeds; available at http://www.leeds.ac.uk/civil/ceri/water/ukponds/pdmuk/pdmuk.html

Mara, D D and Alabaster, G (1995) 'An Environmental Classification of Housing-Related Diseases in Developing Countries', *Journal of Tropical Medicine and Hygiene*, vol 98, pp41–51

Mara, D D and Clapham, D (1997) 'Water-related Carcinomas: Environmental classification', *Journal of Environmental Engineering, American Society of Civil Engineers*, vol 123, no 5, pp416–422 (*)

Mara, D D and Horan, N J (2003) *Handbook of Water and Wastewater Microbiology*, Academic Press, London

Mara, D D and Pearson, H W (1987) *Waste Stabilization Ponds: Design Manual for Mediterranean Europe*, World Health Organization Regional Office for Europe, Copenhagen

Mara D D and Pearson, H W (1992) 'Sequential Batch-fed Effluent Storage Reservoirs: A new concept of wastewater treatment prior to unrestricted crop irrigation', *Water Science and Technology*, vol 26, no 7–8, pp1459–1464

Mara, D D and Pearson, H W (1998) *Design Manual for Waste Stabilization Ponds in Mediterranean Countries*, Lagoon Technology International, Leeds; available at http://www.leeds.ac.uk/civil/ceri/water/tphe/publicat/pdm/medall.pdf

Mara, D D and Pearson, H W (1999) 'A Hybrid Waste Stabilization Pond and Wastewater Storage and Treatment Reservoir System for Wastewater Reuse for both Restricted and Unrestricted Irrigation', *Water Research*, vol 33, no 2, pp591–594 (*)

Mara, D D, Edwards, P, Clark, D and Mills, S M (1993) 'A Rational Approach to the Design of Wastewater-fed Fishponds', *Water Research*, vol 27, no 12, pp1797–1799

Mara, D D, Sleigh, A and Tayler, K (2001a) *PC-based Simplified Sewer Design*, School of Civil Engineering, University of Leeds, Leeds; available at http://www.efm.leeds.ac.uk/CIVE/Sewerage

Mara, D D, Pearson, H W, Oragui, J I, Arridge, A and Silva, S A (2001b) *Development of a New Approach to Waste Stabilization Pond Design*, Tropical Public Health Engineering Research Monograph no 12, School of Civil Engineering, University of Leeds, Leeds; available at http://www.leeds.ac.uk/civil/ceri/water/tphe/publicat/monog/mono5.pdf

Marais, G v R (1966) 'New Factors in the Design, Operation and Performance of Waste Stabilization Ponds', *Bulletin of the World Health Organization*, vol 34, no 5, pp737–763

Marais, G v R (1970), 'Dynamic Behaviour of Oxidation Ponds' in McKinney, R E (ed) *Proceedings of the Second International Symposium for Waste Treatment Lagoons*, pp15–46, University of Kansas, Lawrence, KS

Marais, G v R (1974) 'Faecal Bacterial Kinetics in Waste Stabilization Ponds' *Journal of the Environmental Engineering Division, American Society of Civil Engineers*, vol 100, no EE1, pp119–139

Marais, G v R and Shaw, V A (1961) 'A Rational Theory for the Design of Sewage Stabilization Ponds in Central and South Africa', *Transactions of the South African Institution of Civil Engineers*, vol 3, pp205–227

Marais, G v R and van Haandel, A C (1996) 'Design of Grit Channels by Parshall Flumes', *Water Science and Technology*, vol 33, no 7, pp195–210 (*)

Mariño, M and Boland, J (1999) *An Integrated Approach to Wastewater Treatment: Deciding Where, When and How Much to Invest*, Directions in Developments Series, The World Bank, Washington, DC; available at http://www-wds.worldbank.org/servlet/WDS_IBank_Servlet?pcont=details&eid=000009265_39610030757

Martin, D (2002) *The River Ecosystem Classification System*, Environment Agency, Bristol: available at http://www.environment-agency.gov.uk/commondata/103599/river_e1.doc

Mayo, A W (1995) 'Modeling Coliform Mortality in Waste Stabilization Ponds', *Journal of Environmental Engineering, American Society of Civil Engineers*, vol 121, no 2, pp140–152 (*)

McGarry, M G and Pescod, M B (1970) 'Stabilization Pond Design Criteria for Tropical Asia' in McKinney, R E (ed) *Proceedings of the Second International Symposium for Waste Treatment Lagoons*, pp114–132, University of Kansas, Lawrence, KS

Meadows, B S (1973) 'Effluent Standards in Kenya', in Mara, D D and Fraser, J I (eds) *Proceedings of a Seminar on Sewage Treatment*, pp2.1–2.14, University of Nairobi, Nairobi

Meiring, P G, Drews, R J, van Eck, H and Stander, G J (1968) *A Guide to the Use of Ponds Systems in South Africa for the Purification of Raw and Partially Treated Sewage*, CSIR Special Report no WAT 34, National Institute for Water Research, Pretoria

Melbourne Water (2002) 'Western treatment plant', available at http://www.melbourne water.com.au/content/environment/sewerage_system/western_treatment_plant.asp

Melching, C S and Flores, H E (1999) 'Reaeration Equations Derived from U.S. Geological Survey Database', *Journal of Environmental Engineering, American Society of Civil Engineers*, vol 125, no 5, pp407–414 (*)

Melloul, A, Amahmid, O, Hassani, L and Bonhoum, K (2002) 'Health Effect of Human Wastes Use in El Azzouria (The wastewater spreading area of Marrakesh city, Morocco)', *International Journal of Environmental Health Research*, vol 12, no 1, pp17–23 (*)

Mendonça, S R (2000) *Sistemas de Lagunas de Estabilización: Cómo Utilizar Aguas Residuales en Sistemas de Regadío*, McGraw-Hill Interamericana, Santa Fé de Bogotá

Metcalf and Eddy, Inc (1986) *Wastewater Engineering: Collection and Pumping of Wastewater*, McGraw-Hill, New York

Metcalf and Eddy, Inc (1991) *Wastewater Engineering Treatment, Disposal, and Reuse*, 3rd ed, McGraw-Hill, New York (Note: 4th ed, *Wastewater Engineering: Treatment and Reuse*, 2003)

Middlebrooks, E J (1988) 'Review of Rock Filters for the Upgrade of Lagoon Effluents', *Journal of the Water Pollution Control Federation*, vol 60, no 9, pp1657–1662

Middlebrooks, E J (1995) 'Upgrading Pond Effluents: An overview', *Water Science and Technology*, vol 31, no 12, pp353–368 (*)

Middlebrooks, E J, Middlebrooks, C H, Reynolds, J H and others (1982) *Wastewater Stabilization Lagoon Design, Performance and Upgrading*, Macmillan Publishing, New York

Miller, H I and Conko, G (2001) 'The Perils of Precaution', *Policy Review*, no 107, pp25–39 (*)

Mills, S W, Alabaster, G P, Mara, D D, Pearson, H W And Thitai, W N (1992) 'Efficiency of Faecal Bacterial Removal in Waste Stabilization Ponds in Kenya', *Water Science and Technology*, vol 26, no 7–8, pp1739–1748

Minh, Phan Van (2002) personal communication, Ho Chi Minh City, Vietnam

Ministry of Urban Development (1993) *Manual on Sewerage and Sewage Treatment*, 2nd ed, Government of India Press, New Delhi

Moe, C L, Sobsey, M D, Samsa, G P and Mesolo, V (1991) 'Bacterial Indicators of Risk of Diarrhoeal Disease from Drinking-water in the Philippines', *Bulletin of the World Health Organization*, vol 69, no 3, pp305–317

Montgomery, H A C, Thom, N S and Cockburn, A (1964) 'Determination of Dissolved Oxygen by the Winkler Method and the Solubility of Oxygen in Pure Water and Sea Water', *Journal of Applied Chemistry*, vol 14, no 7, pp280–296

Moshe, M, Betzer, N and Kott, Y (1972) 'Effect of Industrial Wastes on Oxidation Pond Performance', *Water Research*, vol 5, no 10, pp1165–1171

Muller, R (2001) *Worms and Human Disease*, 2nd ed, CABI Publishing, Wallingford; available at http://www.cabi-publishing.org/Bookshop/ReadingRoom/0851995160.asp

Murray, C J L and Lopez, A D (1996a) *The Global Burden of Disease*, Global Burden of Disease and Injury Series vol 1, Harvard School of Public Health, Boston, MA

Murray, C J L and Lopez, A D (1996b) *Global Health Statistics*, Global Burden of Disease and Injury Series vol 2, Harvard School of Public Health, Boston, MA

Nandeesha, M C (2002) 'Sewage-fed Aquaculture Systems of Kolkata: A century-old innovation of farmers', *Aquaculture Asia*, vol 7, no 2, pp28–32; available at http://www.streaminitiative.org/NACA-Publications/AA-April-June/SewerageFedAquacultureSystemsOfKolkata.pdf

Nataro, J P and Kaper, J B (1998) 'Diarrheagenic *Escherichia coli*', *Clinical Microbiology Reviews*, vol 11, no1, pp142–201 (*)

National Research Council (1946) 'Sewage Treatment at Military Installations', *Sewage Works Journal*, vol 18, no 5, pp787–1028

National Research Council (1993) *Managing Wastewater in Coastal Urban Areas*, The National Academies Press, Washington, DC; available at http://www.nap.edu/books/0309048265/html/index/html

National River Conservation Directorate (2003) *Technology*, Ministry of Environment and Forests, New Delhi; available at http://envfor.nic.in/nrcd/tech.html

National Rivers Authority (1994) *Discharge Consents and Compliance: The NRA's Approach to Control of Discharges to Water*, Water Quality Series no 17, National Rivers Authority, Bristol

Nava, H (2001) 'Wastewater Reclamation and Reuse for Aquaculture in Perú', *Journal of Soil and Water Conservation*, vol 56, no 2, pp81–87

Neder, K D, Carneiro, G A, Queiroz, T R and de Sousa, M A (2002) 'Selection of Natural Treatment for Algae Removal from Stabilization Pond Effluents in Brasília, Using Multicriteria Methods', *Water Science and Technology*, vol 46, no 4–5, pp347–354 (*)

Nelson, K L (2002) 'Development of a Mechanistic Model of Sludge Accumulation in Primary Wastewater Stabilization Ponds', in *Pond Technology for the New Millennium*, pp551–560, New Zealand Water and Wastes Association, Auckland

Neville-Jones, P J D and Chitty, A D (1996) *Sea Outfalls – Construction, Inspection and Repair*, CIRIA Report no 159, Construction Industry Research and Information Association, London

Nishimura, S and Yoda, M (1997) 'Removal of Hydrogen Sulfide from an Anaerobic Biogas Using a Bio-scrubber', *Water Science and Technology*, vol 36, no 6–7, pp349–356 (*)

Nogaj, R J (1972) 'Selecting Wastewater Aeration Equipment', *Chemical Engineering*, vol 79, no 4, pp95–102

Oragui, J I, Curtis, T P, Silva, S A and Mara, D D (1987) 'The Removal of Excreted Bacteria and Viruses in Deep Waste Stabilization Ponds in Northeast Brazil', *Water Science and Technology*, vol 19, Rio, pp569–573

Oragui, J I, Arridge, H, Mara D D, Pearson, H W and Silva, S A (1993) '*Vibrio cholerae* O1 (El Tor) Removal in Waste Stabilization Ponds in Northeast Brazil', *Water Research*, vol 27, no 4, pp727–728

Oragui, J I, Arridge, H, Mara, D D, Pearson, H W and Silva, S A (1995) 'Rotavirus Removal in Experimental Waste Stabilization Ponds with Different Geometries and Configurations', *Water Science and Technology*, vol 31, no 12, pp285–290 (*)

Oswald, W J (1975) *Waste Pond Fundamentals*, unpublished document, The World Bank, Washington, DC

Oswald, W J (1976) 'Experiences with New Pond Designs in California' in Gloyna, E F, Malina, J F and Davis E M (eds) *Ponds as a Wastewater Treatment Alternative*, pp257–272, University of Texas Press, Austin, TX

Oswald, W J (1988a) 'The Role of Microalgae in Liquid Waste Treatment and Reclamation' in Lembi, C E and Waaland, J R (eds) *Algae and Human Affairs*, pp255–281, Cambridge University Press, Cambridge

Oswald, W J (1988b) 'Micro-algae and Wastewater Treatment' in Borowitzka, M A and Borowitzka, L J (eds) *Micro-algal Biotechnology*, pp305–328, Cambridge University Press, Cambridge

Oswald, W J (1991) 'Introduction to Advanced Integrated Wastewater Ponding systems', *Water Science and Technology*, vol 24, no 5, pp1–7

Oswald, W J (1995) 'Ponds in the Twenty-first Century', *Water Science and Technology*, vol 31, no 12, pp1–7

P & L Systems (2002) *Insect Control Equipment*, available at: http://www.pandlsystems.com

Paing, J (2001) *Bilan du Carbone et du Soufre dans le Lagunage Anaérobie: Contrôle de l'Emission d'H$_2$S pour la Réduction des Nuisances Olfactives*, PhD thesis, Université Montpellier I, Montpellier

Pal, D (1991) *Studies on the Interaction of some Common Sewage-borne Bacteria with the Defence System of Mrigal* (Cirrhinus mrigala) *in the East Calcutta Sewage-fed Fishponds, India*, PhD thesis, University of Calcutta, Kolkata

Palmhive Technical Textiles (2002) 'Nuisance Fly Netting', available at: http://www.palmhive.co.uk/pages/prod_geo_hor_env.htm

Pan American Health Organization (2000) *Informe Regional sobre la Región de las Américas: Agua Potable y Saneamiento – Estado Actual y Perspectivas.*, Pan American Health Organization, Washington, DC

Pano, A and Middlebrooks, E J (1982) 'Ammonia Nitrogen Removal in Facultative Waste Stabilization Ponds' *Journal of the Water Pollution Control Federation*, vol 54, no 4, pp344–351

Parashar, U D, Hummelman, E G, Bresee, J S, Miller, M A and Glass, R I (2003) 'Global Illness and Death by Rotavirus Disease in Children', *Emerging Infectious Diseases*, vol 9, no 5, pp565–572 (*)

Parhad, N M and Rao, N V (1974) 'Effect of pH on Survival of *E coli*', *Journal of the Water Pollution Control Federation*, vol 46, no 5, pp980–986

Patterson, K L, Porter, J W, Ritchie, K B and others (2002) 'The Etiology of White Pox, a Lethal Disease of the Carribean Elkhorn Coral, *Acropora palmata*', *Proceedings of the National Academy of Science*, vol 99, no 13, pp8725–8730 (*)

Pearce, D W and Warford, J J (1993) *World Without End: Economics, Environment and Sustainable Development*, Oxford University Press, New York

Pearson, H W (1987) 'Estimation of Chlorophyll *a* as a Measure of Algal Biomass in Waste Stabilization Ponds', in *Seminario Regional de Investigación sobre Lagunas de Establización*, pp158–170, CEPIS, Lima; method available on-line in Annex II of Mara and Pearson (1998)

Pearson, H W, Mara, D D, Thompson, W and Maber, S P (1987a) 'Studies on High Altitude Waste Stabilization Ponds in Peru', *Water Science and Technology*, vol 19, no 12, pp349–353

Pearson, H W, Mara, D D, Mills S W and Smallman, D J (1987b) 'Factors Determining Algal Populations in Waste Stabilization Ponds and the Influence of Algae on Pond Performance', *Water Science and Technology*, vol 19, no 12, pp131–140

Pearson, H W, Mara, D D, Mills, S W and Smallman, D J (1987c) 'Physiochemical Parameters Influencing Faecal Bacterial Survival in Waste Stabilization Ponds', *Water Science and Technology*, vol 19, no 12, pp145–152

Pearson, H W, Mara, D D, Konig, A, de Olivera, R, Silva, S A, Mills, S and Smallman, D J (1987d) 'Water Column Sampling as a Rapid and Efficient Method of Determining Effluent Quality and the Performance of Waste Stabilization Ponds, *Water Science and Technology*, vol 19, no 12, pp109–113

Pearson, H W, Mara, D D and Bartone, C R (1987e) 'Guidelines for the Minimum Evaluation of the Performance of Full-scale Waste Stabilization Ponds', *Water Research*, vol 21, no 9, pp1067–1075

Pearson, H W, Mara, D D and Arridge, H (1995) 'The Influence of Pond Geometry and Configuration on Facultative and Maturation Pond Performance and Efficiency', *Water Science and Technology*, vol 19, no 12, pp129–139 (*)

Pearson, H W, Avery, S T, Mills, S W, Njaggah, P and Odiambo, P (1996a) 'Performance of the Phase II Dandora Waste Stabilization Ponds – the Largest in Africa: The case for anaerobic ponds, *Water Science and Technology*, vol 33, no 7, pp91–98 (*)

Pearson, H W, Mara D D, Arridge, H, Cawley, L R and Silva, S A (1996b) 'The Performance of an Innovative Tropical Experimental Waste Stabilization System Operating at High Organic Loadings', *Water Science and Technology*, vol 33, no 7, pp63–73 (*)

Pearson, H W, Mara D D, Oragui, J I, Cawley, L R and Silva, S A (1996c) 'Pathogen Removal Dynamics in Experimental Deep Effluent Storage Reservoirs', *Water Science and Technology*, vol 33, no 7, pp251–260 (*)

Peña Varón, M R (2002) *Advanced Primary Treatment of Domestic Wastewater in Tropical Countries: Development of the High-rate Anaerobic Pond*, PhD thesis, University of Leeds, Leeds; available at http://www.leeds.ac.uk/civil/ceri/water/tphe/publicat/theses/penavaron/penavaron.html

Peña Varón, M R, Rodrigues, J, Mara, D D and Spulveda, M (2000) 'UASBs or Anaerobic Ponds in Warm Climates? A preliminary answer from Colombia', *Water Science and Technology*, vol 42, no 10/11, pp59–65 (*)

Peña Varón M R, Mara, D D and Piguet, J M (2002) 'Improvement of Mixing Patterns in Pilot-scale Anaerobic Ponds Treating Domestic Sewage', *Water Science and Technology*, vol 48, no 2, pp235–242 (*)

Penrose, H (2001) *Werribee Farm: A History, 1892–2000*, Melbourne Water, Melbourne; available at http://www.melbournewater.com.au/content/environment/sewerage_system/western_treatment_plant.asp

Persson, J (2000) 'The Hydraulic Performance of Ponds of Various Layouts', *Urban Water*, vol 2, pp243–250 (*)

Pesce, S F and Wunderlin, D A (2000) 'Use of Water Quality Indices to Verify the Impact of Cordoba City (Argentina) on Suquía River', *Water Research*, vol 34, no 11, pp2915–2926 (*)

Pfeffer, J T (1970) 'Anaerobic Lagoons: Theoretical consideration' in McKinney, R E (ed) *Proceedings of the Second International Symposium for Waste Treatment Lagoons*, pp310–320, University of Kansas, Lawrence, KS

Phelps, E B (1944) *Stream Sanitation*, John Wiley & Sons, New York

Polak, P, Nanes, B and Adhikari, D (1997) 'A Low Cost Drip Irrigation System for Small Farmers in Developing Countries', *Journal of the American Water Resources Association*, vol 33, no 1, pp119–124 (*); see also http://www.ideorg.org/html/gallery/lodrip.html

Postel, S (1997) *The Last Oasis: Facing Water Scarcity*, Worldwatch Institute, Washington, DC

Prüss, A, Kay, D, Fewtrell, L and Bartram, J (2002) 'Estimating the Burden of Disease from Water, Sanitation and Hygiene at a Global Level', *Environmental Health Perspectives*, vol 110, no 5, pp537–542 (*)

Pullin, R S V, Eknath, A E, Gjedrem, T, Macaranas, J M and Abella, T A (1991) 'The Genetic Improvement of Farmed Tilapias (GIFT) Project: The story so far', *Naga*, vol 14, no 2, pp3–6

Rao, T D and Viraraghavan, T (1985) 'Treatment of Distillery Wastewater (spent-wash) – Indian Experience' in Bell, J M (ed) *Proceedings of the 40th Industrial Waste Conference Purdue University*, pp53–57, Ann Arbor Science, Stoneham, MA

Reed, S C (1985) 'Nitrogen Removal in Wastewater Stabilization Ponds', *Journal of the Water Pollution Control Federation*, vol 57, no 1, pp39–45

Reed, S C and Brown, D (1995) 'Subsurface-flow Wetlands: A Performance Evaluation', *Water Environment Research*, vol 67, no 2, pp244_248

Reed, S C, Middlebrooks, E J and Crites, R W (1988) *Natural Systems for Waste Management and Treatment*, McGraw-Hill Book Co, New York

Regmi, T P, Thompson, A L and Sievers, D M (2003) 'Comparative Studies of Vegetated and Non-vegetated Submerged-flow Wetlands Treating Primary Lagoon Effluent', *Transactions of the American Society of Agricultural Engineers*, vol 46, no 1, pp17–27

Relman, D A (1998) '*Cyclospora*: Whence and Where to?' in Scheld, W M, Craig, W A and Hughes, J M (eds) *Emerging Infections 2*, pp185–194, ASM Press, Washington, DC

Resource Centre on Urban Agriculture and Forestry (2002) 'The Hyderabad Declaration', *Urban Agriculture Magazine*, no 8, p4 (*)

Rhoades, J D, Kandiah, A and Mashali, A M (1992) *The Use of Saline Waters for Crop Production*, Irrigation and Drainage Paper no 48, Food and Agriculture Organization, Rome; available at http://www.fao.org/docrep/T0667E/T0667E00.htm

Ringuelet, R (1983) 'Un bel example d'épuration des eaux domestiques poussé jusqu'à la décomtamination fécale avec méthodes naturelles douces et rustiques: le bassin versant de l'étang de Salces-Leucate', *Techniques et Sciences Municipales: Eau*, vol 4, pp187–201

Rose, J B, Haas, C N and Regli, S (1991) 'Risk Assessment and Control of Waterborne Giardiasis', *American Journal of Public Health*, vol 81, no 6, pp709–713

Ruddle, K and Zhong, G (1988) *Integrated Agriculture-Aquaculture in South China: The Dike-pond System of the Zhujiang Delta*, Cambridge University Press, Cambridge

Saidam, M Y, Ramadan, S A and Butler, D (1995) 'Upgrading Waste Stabilization Pond Effluent by Rock Filters', *Water Science and Technology*, vol 31, no 12, pp369–378 (*)

Sala, L, Mujeriego, R, Serra, M and Asano, T (2002) 'Reuse and Conservation: Spain sets the example', *Water21*, August, pp18–20

Satcher, D (1995) 'Emerging Infections: Getting ahead of the curve', *Emerging Infectious Diseases*, vol 1, no 1, pp1–6 (*)

Sawyer, C N, McCarty, P L and Parkin, G F (2002) *Chemistry for Environmental Engineering and Science*, 4th ed, McGraw-Hill, New York

Schulz, H N (2002) '*Thiomargarita namibiensis*: Giant microbe holding its breath', *American Society for Microbiology News*, vol 68, no 3, pp122–127

Shanahan, P and others (2001) 'River Water Quality Model no 1 (RWQM1) – 1: Modelling approach; 2: Biochemical process equations; 3: Biochemical submodel selection; and 4, 5: Case studies 1 and 2, *Water Science and Technology*, vol 45, no 5, pp1–60 (a series of five papers) (*)

Sharma, S (2002) 'Wouldn't you like a nice anaerobic sludge blanket?', *Clean Ganga Newsletter*, April; available at http://www.cleanganga.com/articles/april/april3.php

Shelef, G (1991) 'Wastewater Reclamation and Water Resources Management', *Water Science and Technology*, vol 24, no 9, pp251–265

Shelef, G and Azov, Y (2000) 'Meeting Stringent Environmental and Reuse Requirements with an Integrated Pond System for the Twenty-first Century', *Water Science and Technology*, vol 42, no 10, pp299–305 (*)

Shende, B, Chakrabarti, C, Rai, R P, Nashikkar, V J, Kshirsagar, D G, Deshbhratar, P B and Juwarkar, A S (1988) 'Status of Wastewater Treatment and Agricultural Reuse with Special Reference to Indian Experience and Research and Development Needs' in Pescod, M B and Arar, A (eds) *Treatment and Use of Sewage Effluent for Irrigation*, pp185–209, Butterworths, London

Shilton, A N (2001) *Studies into the Hydraulics of Waste Stabilization Ponds*, PhD thesis, Massey University, Palmerston North; available at http://www.leeds.ac.uk/civil/ceri/water/tphe/publicat/theses/shilton/shilton.html

Shilton, A N and Harrison, J (2003a) 'Development of Guidelines for Improved Hydraulic Design of Waste Stabilization Ponds', *Water Science and Technology*, vol 48, no 2, pp173–180 (*)

Shilton, A N and Harrison, J (2003b) *Guidelines for the Hydraulic Design of Waste Stabilization Ponds*, Massey University, Palmerston North; available at http://www.leeds.ac.uk/civil/ceri/water/tphe/publicat/pdm/pdm.html

Shuval, H I, Adin, A, Fattal, B, Rawitz, E and Yekutiel, P (1986) *Wastewater Irrigation in Developing Countries: Health Effects and Technical Solutions*, Technical Paper no 51, The World Bank, Washington, DC; available at http://www-wds.worldbank.org/servlet/WDS_IBank_Servlet?pcont=details&eid=000178830_98101904164938

Shuval, H, Lampert, Y and Fattal, B (1997) 'Development of a Risk Assessment Approach for Evaluating Wastewater Reuse Standards for Agriculture, *Water Science and Technology*, vol 35, no 11–12, pp15–20 (*)

Silva, S A (1982) *On the Treatment of Domestic Sewage in Waste Stabilization Ponds in Northeast Brazil*, PhD thesis, University of Dundee, Dundee

Silva, S A, de Oliveira, R, Soares, J, Mara, D D and Pearson, H W (1995) 'Nitrogen removal in pond systems with different configurations and geometries' *Water Science and Technology*, vol 31, no 12, pp321–330 (*)

Skerry, G P and Parker, C D (1979) 'Development of an Improved Quantitative Relationship between Bacterial Die-off, Design and Operational Factors for Anaerobic–Aerobic and Maturation Type Lagoon System', *Progress in Water Technology*, vol 11, no 4–5, pp427–443

Skillicorn, P, Spira, W and Journey, W (1993) *Duckweed Aquaculture: A New Aquatic Farming System for Developing Countries*, The World Bank, Washington, DC; available at http://www-wds.worldbank.org/servlet/WDS_IBank_Servlet?pcont=details&eid=000009265_3970128103342

Slanetz, L W, Bartley, C H, Metcalf, T G and Nesman, R (1970) 'Survival of Enteric Bacteria and Virus in Municipal Sewage Lagoons' in McKinney, R E (ed) *Proceedings of the Second International Symposium for Waste Treatment Lagoons*, pp132–141, University of Kansas, Lawrence, KS

Sleigh, P A and Mara, D D (2003a) *Monte Carlo Program for Facultative Pond Design*, available at http://www.efm.leeds.ac.uk/CIVE/Mcarlo/index.html

Sleigh, P A and Mara, D D (2003b) *Monte Carlo Program for Estimating Disease Risks in Wastewater Reuse*, available at http://www.efm.leeds.ac.uk/CIVE/Mcarlo/index.html

Slovic, P (2000) *The Perception of Risk*, Earthscan Publications, London

Smith, T (1895) 'Notes on *Bacillus coli communis* and Related Forms, Together with Some Suggestions Concerning the Bacteriological Examination of Water', *American Journal of the Medical Sciences*, vol 110, no 3, pp283–302

Sotelo, J (2003) 'Neurocysticercosis', *British Medical Journal*, vol 326, no 7388, pp511–512 (*)

Stalzer, W and von der Emde, W (1972) 'Division of Wastewater Flow', *Water Research*, vol 6, pp 371–373

State of California (1978) *Wastewater Reclamation Criteria*, California Administrative Code, Title 22, Division A, Environmental Health, Department of Health Services, Berkeley, CA; available at: http://www.dhs.ca.gov/ps/ddwem/publications/waterrecycling/purplebookupdate6-01.pdf (this is the June 2001 update)

Stephenson, T, Judd, S, Jefferson, B and Brindle, K (2000) *Membrane Bioreactors for Wastewater Treatment*, IWA Publishing, London

Stockholm International Water Institute (2002) 'The 2002 Stockholm Statement: Urgent Action Needed for Water Security – Recommendations from the Stockholm Water Symposia, 1998_2002', *Water Science and Technology*, vol 47, no 6–7, pp5–7

Stott, R, Ayres, R M, Lee, D and Mara, D D (1994) *An Experimental Evaluation of Potential Risks to Human Health from Parasitic Nematodes in Wastewaters Treated in Waste Stabilization Ponds and Used for Crop Irrigation*, Tropical Public Health Engineering Research Monograph no 6, University of Leeds, Leeds; abstract available at http://www.leeds.ac.uk/civil/ceri/water/tphe/publicat/monog/monog.html

Stott, R, Jenkins, T, Bahgat, M and Shalaby, I (1999) 'Capacity of Constructed Wetlands to Remove Parasite Eggs from Wastewaters in Egypt', *Water Science and Technology*, vol 40, no 3, pp117–123 (*)

Stott, R, May, E, Matsushita, E and Warren, A (2001) 'Protozoan Predation as a Mechanism for the Removal of *Cryptosporidium* oocysts from Wastewaters in Constructed Wetlands', *Water Science and Technology*, vol 44, no 11–12, pp191–198 (*)

Stott, R, May, E, Ramirez, E and Warren, A (2003) 'Predation of Cryptosporidium oocysts by Protozoa and Rotifers: Implications for water quality and public health', *Water Science and Technology*, vol 47, no 3, pp77–83 (*)

Streeter, H W and Phelps, E B (1925) *A Study of the Pollution and Natural Purification of the Ohio River*, Public Health Bulletin no 146, US Public Health Service, Washington, DC

Sundaravadivel, M and Vigneswaran, S (2001) 'Constructed Wetlands for Wastewater Treatment', *Critical Reviews in Environmental Science and Technology*, vol 31, no 4, pp351–409 (*)

Surampalli, R Y, Banjeri, S K, Pycha, C J and Lopez, E R (1995) 'Phosphorus Removal in Ponds', *Water Science and Technology*, vol 31, no 12, pp331–339 (*)

Sunset Solar Systems (2002) *Little River Pond Mills*, available at http://www.pondmill.com

Surrey Advertiser (1998) 'Sewage Farm Flies "making our life hell"', available at: http://www.surreyad.co.uk/news/22-5-98/news1150.html

Swanson, G R and Williamson, K J (1980) 'Upgrading Lagoon Effluents with Rock Filters', *Journal of the Environmental Engineering Division, American Society of Civil Engineers*, vol 106, no EE6, pp1111–1129

Tanaka, H, Asano, T, Schroeder, E D and Tchobanoglous, G (1998) 'Estimating the Safety of Wastewater Reclamation and Reuse using Enteric Virus Monitoring Data', *Water Environment Research*, vol 70, no 1, pp39–51

Tanner, C C (2001) 'Plants as Ecosystem Engineers in Subsurface-flow Treatment Wetlands', *Water Science and Technology*, vol 44, no 11–12, pp9–17 (*)

Talling, J F (2001) 'Environmental Controls on the Functioning of Shallow Tropical Lakes', *Hydrobiologia*, vol 458, no 1–3, pp1–8 (*)

Taylor, H D, Bastos, R K X, Pearson, H W and Mara, D D (1995) 'Drip Irrigation with Waste Stabilization Pond Effluents: Solving the Problem of Emitter Fouling', *Water Science and Technology*, vol 31, no 12, pp417–424 (*)

Taylor, H D, Gambrill, M P, Mara, D D (1994a) *Lime Treatment of Municipal Wastewater*, Tropical Public Health Engineering Research Monograph no 3, University of Leeds, Leeds; abstract available at http://www.leeds.ac.uk/civil/ceri/water/tphe/publicat/monog/monog.html

Taylor, H D, Gambrill, M P, Mara, D D and Silva, S A (1994b) 'Upgrading a Low-cost Physicochemical Wastewater Treatment Plant to Solve Operational Problems, *Water Science and Technology*, vol 29, no 12, pp247–254 (*)

Tebbutt, T H Y (1998) *Principles of Water Quality Control*, 5th ed, Butterworth-Heinemann, Oxford

Thirumurthi, D (1969) 'Design Principles of Waste Stabilization Ponds', *Journal of the Sanitary Engineering Division, American Society of Civil Engineers*, vol 95, no SA2, pp311–329

Tilche, A and Orhon, D (2002) 'Appropriate Basis of Effluent Standards for Industrial Wastewaters', *Water Science and Technology*, vol 45, no 12, pp1–11 (*)

Tool, H R (1967) 'Manometric Measurement of the Biochemical Oxygen Demand', *Water and Sewage Works*, vol 114, no 6, pp211–218

Toumi, A, Nejmeddine, A and El Hamouri, B (2000) 'Heavy Metal Removal in Waste Stabilization Ponds and High Rate Ponds', *Water Science and Technology*, vol 42, no 10–11, pp17–21 (*)

Townsend, C B (1937) 'The Elimination of the Detritus Pump', *Journal and Proceedings of the Institute of Sewage Purification*, no 2, pp58–87

Tsagarakis, K P, Mara, D D and Angelakis, A N (2003) 'Application of Cost Criteria for Selection of Municipal Wastewater Treatment Systems', *Water, Air and Soil Pollution*, vol 142, no 1–4, pp187–210 (*)

UK Legislation (1994) *The Surface Waters (River Ecosystem) (Classification) Regulations 1994*, Statutory Instrument 1994 no 1057; available at http://www.legislation.hmso.gov.uk/si/si1994/UKsi_19941057_en_1.htm

United Nations Environment Programme (2002) *Global Environment Outlook 3*, Earthscan, London; available at http://www.grida.no/geo/geo3/english/pdf.htm

United Nations Environment Programme (2003) *Regional Seas Conventions and Protocols*, available at http://www.unep.ch/seas/main/hconlist.html

United States Department of Agriculture (1954) *Diagnosis and Improvement of Saline and Alkali Soils*, Agriculture Handbook no 60, United States Department of Agriculture, Washington, DC

University of Leicester (2002) *The Gram Stain*, Department of Microbiology and Immunology, University of Leicester, Leicester; available at http://www-micro.msb.le.ac.uk/video/Gram.html

Van Damme, D (2001) 'Biological Assessment of Water Quality: Simple methods and guidelines', *Waterlines*, vol 20, no 1, pp2–5 (*)

Van der Hoek, W, Hassan M U, Ensink, J H J, Feenstra, S and others (2002) *Urban Wastewater: A Valuable Resource for Agriculture – A Case Study from Haroonabad,*

Pakistan, Research Report no 63, International Water Management Institute, Colombo; available at http://www.iwmi.cgiar.org/pubs/pub063/Report63.pdf

van der Roest, H F, Lawrence, D P and van Bentem, A G N (2002) *Membrane Bioreactors for Municipal Wastewater Treatment*, IWA Publishing, London

van Haandel, A C and Lettinga, G (1994) *Anaerobic Sewage Treatment: A Practical Guide for Regions with a Hot Climate*, John Wiley & Sons, Chichester

van Vuren, G (1998) *Farmers' Participation in Water Management*, A A Balkema, Rotterdam and Brookfield, VT

Vaz da Costa Vargas, S and Mara, D D (1998) 'The Bacterial Quality of Lettuce and Alfalfa Spray-irrigated with Trickling Effluent', in *Proceedings of Water Reuse Symposium IV: Implementing Water Reuse*, pp739–801, AWWA Research Foundation, Denver, CO

Viner, A B and Smith, I R (1973) 'Geographical, Historical and Physical Aspects of Lake George', *Proceedings of the Royal Society of London, Series B*, vol 184, no 1076, pp235–270

Viraraghagan, T, Ruiu, C and Waite, D (2002) 'Wind-powered Lagoon Aerator: A Performance Analysis', *Fresenius Environmental Bulletin*, vol 11, no 7, pp384–389

von Sperling, M (1996a) 'Comparison Among the most Frequently Used Systems for Wastewater Treatment in Developing Countries', *Water Science and Technology*, vol 33, no3, pp59–72 (*)

von Sperling, M (1996b) 'Design of Facultative Ponds Based on Uncertainty Analysis', *Water Science and Technology*, vol 33, no 7, pp41–47 (*)

von Sperling, M (1999) 'Performance Evaluation and Mathematical Modeling of Coliform Die-off in Tropical and Subtropical Waste Stabilization Ponds', *Water Research*, vol 33, no 6, pp1435–1448 (*)

von Sperling, M (2002) 'Relationship between First-order Decay Coefficients in Ponds, for Plug Flow, CSTR and Dispersed Flow Regimes', *Water Science and Technology*, vol 45, no1, pp17–24 (*)

von Sperling, M (2003) 'Influence of the Dispersion Number on the Estimation of Coliform Removal in Ponds', *Water Science and Technology*, vol 48, no 2, pp181–188 (*)

von Sperling, M and Chernicharo, C A L (2002a) 'Urban Wastewater Treatment Technologies and the Implementation of Discharge Standards in Developing Countries', *Urban Water*, vol 4, no 1, pp105–114 (*)

von Sperling, M, Chernicharo, C A L, Soares A M E and Zerbini, A M (2002b) 'Coliform and Helminth Eggs Removal in a Combined UASB Reactor – Baffled Pond System in Brazil: Performance evaluation and mathematical modelling' *Water Science and Technology*, vol 45, no 10, pp237–242 (*)

Vorkas, C A and Lloyd, B J (2000) 'A Comparative Assessment of Bacteriophages as Tracers and Models for Virus Removal in Waste Stabilization Ponds', *Water Science and Technology*, vol 42, no 10–11, pp127–138 (*)

Wamukwamba, C K and Share, W (2001) 'Sewage Waste Management in the City of Lusaka' in Scott, R (ed) *People and Systems for Water Sanitation and Health*, pp211–212, WEDC, University of Loughborough, Loughborough; available at http://www.lboro.ac.uk/wedc/papers/27/7%20-%20Sanitation/14%20-%20Wamukwamba.pdf

Water Environment Federation (1994a) *Pretreatment of Industrial Wastes*, Manual of Practice FD-3, Water Environment Federation, Alexandria, VA

Water Environment Federation (1994b) *Preliminary Treatment for Wastewater Facilities*, Manual of Practice no OM-2, Water Environment Federation, Alexandria, VA

Water Environment Federation (2001) *Wastewater Biology: The Microlife*, 2nd ed, Water Environment Federation, Alexandria, VA

Water Pollution Control Laboratory (1968) *Water Pollution Research 1967*, HMSO, London

Water Pollution Research Board (1973) *Water Pollution Research 1972*, HMSO, London

Water Research Centre (1990) *Design Guide for Marine Treatment Schemes*, 4 vols, Report no UM 1009, Water Research Centre, Swindon

Water Research Centre (1995) *Treatment of Sewage Discharges to Tidal Waters*, Report no TT 004, Water Research Centre, Swindon

Watercare Services Ltd (2002) 'Mangere Lagoon Restored', *Mangere Matters*, September, Watercare Services Ltd, Auckland; available at http://www.watercare.co.nz/assets/Publications/mangere_matters/MMSept02.pdf

Watson, J L A (1962) 'Oxidation Ponds and Use of Effluent in Israel', *Proceedings of the Institution of Civil Engineers*, vol 22, pp21–40

Wehner, J F and Wilhelm, R H (1956) 'Boundary Conditions of Flow Reactor', *Chemical Engineering Science*, vol 6, no 2, pp 89–93 (*)

Welch, E B (1992) *Ecological Effects of Wastewater: Applied Limnology and Pollutant Effects*, 2nd ed, Chapman & Hall, London

Westcot, D W (1997) *Quality Control of Wastewater for Irrigated Crop Production*, Water Reports no 10, Food and Agriculture Organization, Rome; available at http://www.fao.org/docrep/W5367E/W5367E00.htm

Wheeler, D (2000) *Greening Industry: New Roles for Communities, Markets and Governments*, Oxford University Press, New York; available at http://www.worldbank.org/research/greening/TableofContentsnew.html

Wheeler, J G, Sethi, D, Cowden, J M, Wall, P G, Rodrigues, L C, Tomkins, D S, Hudson, M J and Roderick, P J (1999) 'Study of Infectious Intestinal Disease in England: Rates in the community, presenting to general practice, and reported to national surveillance', *British Medical Journal*, vol 318, pp1046–1050 (*)

Wickers, G E, Goodin, J R and Field, D V (1985) *Plants for Arid Lands*, Unwin Hyman, London

Williams, J, Bahgat, M, May, E, Ford, M, Loveridge, R and Butler, J (1995) *Microbial Treatment Processes in Gravel Bed Hydroponic Constructed Wetlands*, Research Monograph in Wastewater Treatment and Reuse in Developing Countries no 3, University of Portsmouth, Portsmouth

Wiwanitkit, V (2003) 'Clinical Findings Among 62 Thais with Cholangiocarcinoma', *Tropical Medicine and International Health*, vol 8, no 3, pp228–230 (*)

Woese, C R, Kandler, O and Wheelis, M L (1990) 'Towards a Natural System of Organisms: Proposal for the domains of Archaea, Bacteria and Eucarya', *Proceedings of the National Academy of Science*, vol 87, no 12, pp4576–4579 (*)

World Bank (1996) *Handbook on Economic Analysis of Investment Operations*, The World Bank, Washington, DC; available at http://www.wds.worldbank.org/servlet/WDSContentServer/WDSP/IB/2000/08/14/000094946_00072905315620/Rendered/PDF/multi_page.pdf

World Bank (2002) *New Ideas in Pollution Regulation*, available at http://www.worldbank.org/nipr/index.htm

World Commission on Environment and Development (1987) *Our Common Future*, Oxford University Press, New York

World Health Organization (1973) *Reuse of Effluents: Methods of Wastewater Treatment and Health Safeguards*, Technical Report Series no 517, World Health Organization, Geneva

World Health Organization (1989) *Health Guidelines for the Use of Wastewater in Agriculture and Aquaculture*, Technical Report Series no 778, World Health Organization, Geneva; available at http://whqlibdoc.who.int/trs/WHO_TRS_778.pdf

World Health Organization (1993) *Guidelines for Drinking Water Quality: Volume 1 – Recommendations*, World Health Organization, Geneva

World Health Organization (1995) *Control of Foodborne Trematode Infections*, Technical Report Series no 849, World Health Organization, Geneva

World Health Organization (1999) *Food and Safety Issues Associated with Produce from Aquaculture*, Technical Report Series no 883, World Health Organization, Geneva; available at http://www.who.int/fsf/Documents/trs883.pdf

World Health Organization (2002) 'Children bear the heaviest burden of environmental disease', available at http://www.who.int/peh/ceh/articles/burden.htm

World Health Organization (2003) *Guidelines for Drinking Water Quality*, 3rd ed, World Health Organization, Geneva; available via http://www.who.int/water_sanitation_health/index.html

World Health Organization (2004) *Health Guidelines for the Use of Wastewater in Agriculture*, World Health Organization, Geneva; to be available via http://www.who.int/water_sanitation_health/index.html

Wright, J F, Sutcliffe, D W and Furse, M T (2000) *Assessing the Biological Quality of Fresh Waters: RIVPACS and Other Techniques*, Freshwater Biological Association, Ambleside

Xu, P, Brissaud, F and Fazio, A (2002) 'Non-steady-state Modelling of Faecal Coliform Removal in Deep Tertiary Ponds', *Water Research*, vol 36, no 12, pp3074–3082 (*)

Yadav, R K, Goyal, B, Sharma, R K, Dubey, S K and Minhas, P S (2002) 'Post-irrigation Impact of Domestic Sewage Effluent on Composition of Soils, Crops and Ground Water – a Case Study', *Environment International*, vol 28, no 6, pp481–486 (*)

Yan, J, Rusong, W and Wang, M (1998) 'The Fundamental Principles and Ecotechniques of Wastewater Aquaculture', *Ecological Engineering*, vol 10, no 2, pp191–208 (*)

Yan, J, Wang, R and Wang, M (2001) 'The Fundamental Principles and Ecotechniques of Wastewater Aquaculture', *Ecological Engineering*, vol 10, no 2, pp191–208 (*)

Yanez, F (1993) *Lagunas de Estabilización: Teoría, Diseño, Evaluación y Mantenimiento*, Ministerio de Salud Pública, Quito

Yu, H, Tay, J-H and Wilson, F (1997) 'A Sustainable Municipal Wastewater Treatment Process for Tropical and Subtropical Regions in Developing Countries', *Water Science and Technology*, vol 35, no 9, pp191–198 (*)

Zimmo, O R (2003) *Nitrogen Transformations and Removal Mechanisms in Algal and Duckweed Waste Stabilization Ponds*, PhD thesis, International Institute for Infrastructural, Hydraulic and Environmental Engineering, Delft

Journal URLs

The following journals are available at Science Direct (http://www.sciencedirect.com):
Chemical Engineering Science
Critical Reviews in Environmental Science and Technology
Critical Reviews in Microbiology
Ecological Economics
Ecological Engineering
Environment International

Microbes and Infection
Parasitology Today
Urban Water
Water Policy
Water Research
The URLs of other journals are:
Annual Review of Microbiology: http://micro.annualreviews.org
Applied and Environmental Microbiology: http://aem.asm.org
British Medical Journal: http://www.bmj.com
Bulletin of the World Health Organization: http://www.who.int/bulletin/index.htm
Clinical Microbiology Reviews: http://cmr.asm.org
Communicable Disease and Public Health: http://www.phls.org.uk/publications/ CDPHind.htm
Emerging Infectious Diseases: www.cdc.gov/ncidod/EID/index.htm
Environmental Health Perspectives: http://ehp.niehs.nih.gov
Environmental Management: http://link.springer.de/link/service/journals/00267/ index.htm
International Journal of Environmental Health Research: http://www.tandf.co.uk/ journals/titles/09603123.html
Journal of the American Water Resources Association: http://www.awra.org/jawra
Journal of Applied Microbiology: http://www.blackwellpublishing.co./journals/jam/
Journal of Environmental Engineering, American Society of Civil Engineers: http://ojps.aip.org/eeo/?jsessionid=276651042280284906
Journal of Water and Health: http://www.iwaponline.com/jwh/toc.htm
The Lancet: http://www.thelancet.com
Policy Review: http://www.policyreview.org
Proceedings of the National Academy of Sciences: http://www.pnas.org
Tropical Medicine and International Health: http://blackwellpublishing.com/ journals/tmi/
Urban Agriculture Magazine: http://www.ruaf.org/newslgeneng.html
Water, Air and Soil Pollution: http://www.kluweronline.com/issn/0049-6979/current
Waterlines: http://isacco.ingentaselect.com/vl=79944246/cl=22/nw=1/catchword/ itpub/ 02628104/contp1-1.htm
Water Science and Technology: http://www.iwaponline.com/wst/toc.htm
Water Supply: http://www.iwaponline.com/ws.toc.htm

IWA waste stabilization pond conference proceedings

The International Water Association has organized six conferences on waste stabilization ponds, the proceedings of which are published in *Water Science and Technology* (*WST*). All are available on-line, except those of the first international conference:

First international conference (Lisbon, 1987): *WST*, 1987, vol 19, no 12
Second international conference (Berkeley, 1993): *WST*, 1995, vol 31, no 12
Third international conference (João Pessoa, 1995): *WST*, 1996, vol 33, no 7
Fourth international conference (Marrakech, 1999): *WST*, 2000, vol 42, no 10–11
First Latin American regional conference (Cali, 2000): *WST*, 2002, vol 45, no 1
Fifth international conference (Auckland, 2002): *WST*, 2003, vol 48, no 2
Sixth international conference (Avignon, 2004): *WST*, 2005 (in press)

Details of further conferences in this series will be available at http://www. iwahq.org.uk (click on 'Events').

IWA wastewater re-use conferences

The IWA has organized six conferences on wastewater reclamation, recycling and reuse, the proceedings of which are published in *Water Science and Technology* (*WST*) or *Water Supply* (*WS*). They are all available on-line, except those of the first conference:
    First international conference (Costa Brava, 1991): *WST*, 1991, vol 24, no 9
    Second international conference (Iraklio, 1995): *WST*, 1996, vol 33, no 10–11
    First Mediterranean regional conference (Milan, 1998): *WST*, 1999, vol 40, no 4–5
    Third international conference (Paris, 2000): *WST*, 2001, vol 43, no 10
    Second Mediterranean regional conference (Iraklio, 2002): *WS*, 2003, vol 3, no 4
    Fourth international conference (Mexico City, 2003): *WST*, 2004 (in press)
Details of further conferences in this series will be available at http://www.iwahq.org.uk (click on 'Events').

Sanitation Connection

Sanitation Connection is a directory of publications on low-cost sanitation in developing countries, including appropriate wastewater treatment and wastewater reuse in agriculture and aquaculture, which are available on the Internet. Its URL is http://www.sanicon.net/home.php3; click on the topic required and then on 'publications'; each publication has its own page with a link to the on-line document. Topic coordinators do their best to keep the list of publications up-to-date, so it is a very useful resource.

Index

acceptable risk, 247
activated sludge, 71
actual health risks, 232
advanced pond systems, 102–104
aerated lagoons, 71, 101, 213–225
aerators
  field performance, 217–219
  floating, 215
agricultural re-use, 42–43, 230–252
agricultural–aquacultural re-use,
  integrated, 259–260
Al Samra ponds, 95–96, 171
algae, 37, 114–116,
algal biomass, 125–130
algal productivity, 125–126
algal–bacterial mutualism, 86
ammonia, 52, 149–150, 198
  toxicity, 130, 258
amoebiasis, 9
anabolism, 28–29
anaerobic digestion, 31–33
anaerobic ponds, 85, 105–113, 147,
  222–223
  by-pass pipework 169–170
  cover, 169–170
  depth, 108
  design, 108–109
  desludging, 176–179
  E coli removal, 147
  high-rate, 110–111
  in series, 110–112
  sludge accumulation, 109–110
Ancylostoma duodenale, 14
aquacultural re-use, 42–43, 253–262
aquatic vegetables, 256
Archaea, 21–35
Arrhenius constant, 59–60
Aruba protocol, 53–54
ascariasis, 9
Ascaridia galli, 236–237

Ascaris lumbricoides, 10, 11, 14, 140,
  233–236
autolysis, 28–29
Avogadro's number, 127

Bacteria, 21–35
bacterial growth
  curve, 26–27
  growth kinetics, 26–29
bacteriochlorophylls, 132
bacteriophages, 24
Bancroftian filariasis, 9
BATNEEC, 54
beta-Poisson dose-response model,
  248–249
biochemical oxygen demand – see BOD
biofilters, 71, 207–212
biotic index, 38–40
BOD (biochemical oxygen demand),
  3–4, 49–51, 85, 87–88
  5-day, 57–58
  curves, 57
  filtered, 51, 121
  removal kinetics, 56–68
  surface loading, 114, 118–120, 128
  ultimate, 57–58, 66–67
  volumetric loading, 108–109
boron, 244
bubbler irrigation, 241

Campylobacter, 13,
campylobacteriosis, 9
cancer, 16
carp, 253
  Indian major, 253
Cartagena convention, 53
catabolism, 28–29
CATNAP, 54
chemical oxygen demand – see COD
Chlamydomonas, 105, 114, 129, 130

Chlorella, 114, 129, 130
Chlorobiaceae, 130–132
chlorophyll *a*, 125, 129
cholera, 9
clonorchiasis, 9
Clonorchis sinensis, 16, 43, 256
COD (chemical oxygen demand), 3
coliform bacteria, 33–34
column sampler, 186
complete mixing, 58–60, 86–88
composite exponential, 64–65
conductivity, 243
constant velocity grit channels, 81–83
constructed wetlands, 71, 100–101,
   194–199
continuous culture, 27
Cromatiaceae, 130–132
crop restriction, 241
crop yields, 230
cryptosporidiosis, 9
Cryptosporidium parvum, 12, 140–141
Culex quinquefasciatus, 9
Cyclospora cayentanensis, 10

Dandora ponds, 95
data storage and analysis, 186–187
decentralized treatment, 70–71
denitrification, 31
dispersed flow, 60–62
dispersion number, 61–62
dissolved oxygen
   diurnal variation in ponds, 115
   sag curve, 44–47
domains of life, 21–22
dose–response models, 247–249
drip irrigation, 241

E coli, 9, 13, 34–35, 42–43, 52,
   237–239, 256
   enteropathogenic, 13
   removal equations, 125, 141–148
effluent discharge
   coastal waters, 52–54
   inland waters, 43–47
effluent quality, 41–55, 94, 121–122,
effluent standards, 48–54
effluent take-off levels, 168
electrical conductivity, 243
embankment
   protection, 160–162

slope, 159
emerging infectious diseases, 16
Entamoeba histolytica, 12, 237
enterobiasis, 9
Escherichia coli – see *E coli*
Euglena, 114, 129, 130
Eukarya, 21–22
excreta-related diseases, 8–19
   cancers, 17–18
   environmental classification, 8–17
   global burden, 18–19
excreted load, 10
exponential dose–response model, 248

facultative ponds, 85–86, 114–135
   algae, 116
   BOD removal, 120–121
   depth, 120
   design, 118–125
   E coli removal
   function, 115
   mixing, 115–117
   stratification, 115–117
faecal coliforms – see *E coli*
faecal indicator bacteria, 33–35
faeces, 1
faeco-oral diseases, 9, 12–14
fasciolopsiasis, 9
Fasciolopsis buski, 16, 43, 256
filariasis, 9, 16
first-order kinetics, 56–64,
fish yields, 258–259
fishponds, 257–259
flow measurement, 84
flow regimes, 60–62
fly control, 176, 211
freeboard, 165
freshwater biology, 38–40
future projections, 77

geohelminthiases, 9, 14, 19
geotechnical aspects, 158–162
Giardia intestinalis, 12, 140–141, 237
Giardia lamblia – see *Giardia intestinalis*
giardiasis, 9
Gram stain, 24
grit
   disposal, 84
   removal, 81–84
   separators, 84

gross areal oxygen production, 126
growth curve, 26–27
growth kinetics, 26–29

health risks
  actual, 232
  potential, 232
Helicobacter pylori, 16
helminth eggs, 42–43, 198, 233–237
  removal equation, 124
helminths, 37
Henry's law, 106
hepatitis, 9
high-rate algal ponds, 102–103
hookworms, 9, 140
human exposure control, 241–242
humus removal, 212
hybrid pond-reservoir system, 190
hydraulic flow regimes, 60–62
hydraulic loading rate, 152
hydrogen sulphide, 106–107
hymenolepiasis, 9

incidence, 12
industrial wastewaters, 75, 112, 245
infection, 12
infectivity, 10
infiltration, 75
inlet structures, 166–168
insect-vector diseases, 9, 16
intestinal nematode eggs – see helminth
  eggs
irradiance, 127
irrigation
  localized (bubbler), 241
  localized (drip), 241
  restricted, 232
  unrestricted, 232
  untreated wastewater, 233–235,
    251–252

land prices, 72
latency, 10
Leptospira interrogans, 16
leptospirosis, 9
light intensity, 126–128, 140
light-and-dark-bottle test, 125–126
lime-assisted sedimentation, 71–72
lining of ponds, 162
localized irrigation, 241

location of ponds, 158
logarithmic growth, 26

macrophyte ponds, 101–102
Mangere ponds, 98–100
Marais' theorem, 88
maturation ponds, 85–86, 136–157, 220
  bacterial removal, 138–140
  BOD removal, 1481–49
  depth, 136
  design, 141–151
  E coli removal, 141–148
  function, 136
  helminth egg removal, 140–141
  pathogen removal mechanisms,
    137–141
  viral removal, 137–138
  von Sperling's equations
McGarry and Pescod equation, 118–119
membrane bioreactors, 72
microbiology, 20–35
micro-invertebrates, 38–40
micro-organisms, 20–22
mid-depth area, 164–165
minimal water quality index
Monod equation, 28
multiple exposures, 249
multiplication, 10
mutualism, 86

Necator americanus, 14
nematode eggs – see helminth eggs
nitrification, 30–31, 151
nomenclature, 21
norovirus, 9, 22
nutrient removal, 149–151, 216–217

odour, 106–107
Oreochromis, 255
outlet structures, 166–169
oxidation ditches, 71, 225–229
oxypause, 114

Pano and Middlebrooks equations,
  149–150
partial treatment, 241
peak wastewater flow, 76
permeability, coefficient of, 162
persistence, 11
pH, 25, 107, 114, 139, 245

phase separators, 204–205
phosphorus removal in ponds, 151
photo-inhibition, 128
photon flux density, 127
photosynthesis, 37, 125–126
photosynthetic bacteria, 130–132
photosynthetic bacteria, 31
photosynthetically active radiation, 127
physicochemical river water quality, 48
Planck's constant, 127
plug flow, 60, 86–88
pond effluent polishing, 151–152
pond geometry, 163–164
potential health risks, 232
preliminary treatment, 78–84
prevalence, 12
Proctor test, 159
protozoa, 35–36, 237–238
protozoan cysts, 140–141
purple ponds, 130–132
Pyrobotrys, 114

QMRA, 11, 246–251
quantitative microbial risk analysis – see
    QMRA

Reed's equation, 149
restricted irrigation, 232
retarded exponential, 65–66
re-use – see wastewater re-use
risks
    actual, 232
    potential, 232
risk analysis – see QMRA
rock filters, 151–152
rodent-vector diseases, 9, 17
rotavirus, 9, 22

Salmonella, 13,
salmonellosis, 9
Scenedesmus, 129, 130
Schistosoma, 16, 43, 256
schistosomiasis, 9, 10
screening, 78–80
scum guard, 167–168
sedimentation pond, 220–222
Shigella, 13
shigellosis, 9
sludge accumulation, 109–110
sludge drying beds, 110, 204

sludge layer, 118
sodium adsorption ratio, 243
specific growth rate, 26
Streeter–Phelps equation, 45–47
strongyloidiasis, 9
sullage, 1
sulphates, 106–107
sulphides, 106–107
toxicity, 128–129
susceptibility, 12
suspended solids, 5, 94, 196
sustainability, 69–70

Taenia saginata, 14
Taenia solium, 14
taeniasis, 9, 14
temperature, 25, 59–60, 109, 139
design, 109
theoretical oxygen demand, 2–3
tilapia, 255,
tolerable risk, 247
total nitrogen, 244,
    removal in ponds, 149
treatment objectives, 41–42
tree of life, 22–23
treebelt, 171
trematode eggs, 43, 256
trichuriasis, 9
Trichuris trichiura, 14, 140
typhoid, 9

UASBs, 71, 101
ultimate BOD, 57–58
uncertainty, 121–124
unrestricted irrigation, 232
upflow anaerobic sludge blanket reactors
    – see UASBs
urine, 1

Vibrio cholerae, 13, 25, 85, 107
viruses, 22–24, 137–138

waste stabilization ponds, 71, 85–187
    advantages, 89–92
    disadvantages, 93–94
    evaluation, 183–186
    functions, 85–86
    high altitude, 100
    large systems, 95–100
    layout, 86–87

monitoring, 182–183
operation and maintenance, 175–181
physical design, 158–174
rehabilitation, 180
staffing levels, 179
start-up, 175
types, 85–86
upgrading, 173–174
usage, 94–100
wastewater
  application, 241
  collection, 5
  flows, 74–76
  loads, 77
wastewater re-use, 42–43, 230–262
  guidelines, 42–43
  Islamic countries, 231

wastewater storage and treatment
  reservoirs, 71, 188–193
wastewater strength, 4–5
wastewater treatment
  investment, 5–6
  options, 69–73
water-based helminthiasies, 14
Wehner–Wilhelm equation, 61
Werribee ponds, 96–98
white towel test, 176–177
WHO guidelines – see wastewater re-use
  guidelines
wind aerators, 132
wind mixing, 115–117

yersiniosis, 9